The Conservation of
European Cities

The Conservation of European Cities

edited by
Donald Appleyard

The MIT Press
Cambridge, Massachusetts, and
London, England

Unless noted otherwise, material in chapters 1–22 was published
originally in *Urban Conservation in Europe and America: Planning, Conflict, and Participation in the Inner City* (Rome, Italy: Commission for
Educational and Cultural Exchange between Italy and the United
States of America, 1975).

This book was set in Baskerville by dnh typesetting, inc., and
printed and bound by Halliday Lithograph Corporation in the
United States of America.

Library of Congress Cataloging in Publication Data
Main entry under title:

The Conservation of European Cities.

    Based on a conference held at the American Academy in Rome,
June 1975.
    Enl. version of the conference proceedings published in 1977
under title: Urban conservation in Europe and America.
    Bibliography: p.
    Includes index.
    1.   Urban renewal—Europe—Congresses. I. Appleyard,
Donald. II. Urban conservation in Europe and America.
HT178.E8C66 1979   309.2′62′094   79-12778
ISBN 0-262-01057-7

To my European family, friends, and memories

Contents

Acknowledgments

The genesis of this book was an invited conference held at the American Academy in Rome in June 1975, which brought together about thirty urban planners, architects, architectural historians, and social scientists from 12 countries (Belgium, Denmark, France, Greece, Italy, the Netherlands, Portugal, Sweden, Turkey, the United Kingdom, Yugoslavia), and visiting Fulbright scholars from the United States. The conference was promoted and sponsored by the Binational Commissions administering the Fulbright-Hayes Program in thirteen European countries and in Israel, as one of their cooperative multilateral projects. Each Commission provided funds for the participation of experts (national or American) coming from its own country. The issues to be discussed concerned the future of the inner city, and participants were asked to present specific case studies of their experience with conflicts and citizen participation in inner city planning and conservation. The conference proceedings were published in June in 1977 in a limited edition, entitled *Urban Conservation in Europe and America*, by the Commission for Educational and Cultural Exchange between Italy and the United States (Appleyard, 1977). The American Academy in Rome and the Istituto di Urbanismo at the University of Rome were cosponsors, and the Cultural Office of the American Embassy in Rome supported its publication.

This book, though substantially changed (eight new essays joining fourteen of the original) is still rather like a revised edition. For that reason many people have, through the first publication, contributed significantly to this volume. First I would like to thank before all others, Cipriana Scelba, Director of the Fulbright Commission in Italy, who proposed the conference, who convened the organizational meetings, invited the participants through her colleagues on the other European Commissions, arranged accommodation, and carried through numerous other essential tasks to make this event happen.

Special thanks are due to the other members of the conference steering committee, Henry Millon, Professor of Architecture at M.I.T., then Director of the American Academy in Rome, who hosted the meeting in the Villa Aurelia, and Gabriele Scimemi, Director of the Istituto di

Urbanismo at the University of Rome, who provided contacts throughout Europe that were essential in finding some of the most interesting participants. Most of all I wish to thank Dr. Lisa Ronchi who coordinated the difficult editorial production of the first book, which has been the foundation of this work. Her sheer persistence brought it into being, and her essay on Rome, published here, contributed a fascinating personal insight to the subject being studied.

Richard T. Arndt, Chairman of the Commission for Educational and Cultural Exchange between Italy and the United States, provided essential support for the foundation volume. Responsibility for reporting, recording, typing, and editing were in the capable hands of a number of people: Robert Jensen, Harvey Bryan, Cristina Young, Maria Luisa Letizia, Andrew Tesoro, Stephen Heiken, Ellis Goldberg, and Evie Roberts. Some of the ideas in this introduction emerged from seminars and discussions with U.C. Berkeley students, especially Jay Claiborne.

The Urban Institute of the University of Rome, the American Academy in Rome, and the Institute of Urban and Regional Development at the University of California, Berkeley, each provided welcome support in producing the manuscript.

The editing of this book has been fulfilling in many ways. As an ex-European who moved from Britain to the United States twenty years ago, I found it deeply satisfying to renew acquaintances with old colleagues and familiar cities and to look back over the changes that have taken place in European planning and architecture since World War II. Through Guggenheim and Fulbright fellowships, I was able to travel to many of the cities that are mentioned in this volume. The opportunity given by these essays to look behind the picturesque facades and discover the perceptions and attitudes of their inhabitants has been an intellectual revelation and delight that I hope the reader will share. May you look at these cities in a different way on your next visit.

The Conservation of
European Cities

Introduction   Donald Appleyard

Historic Warsaw constructed
after World War II

The Houses of Parliament in
London dwarfed by new office
buildings

Stockholm's teahouse amid the elms, scene of tense demonstrations when representatives of the transit authority came to cut the trees down because they interfered with the new subway route

The skyline of historic Buda with the cranes for the new Hilton

The skyline of Jerusalem from the western approach with the Hilton already installed

"The last old building," from Erik Ortvad's *Sight Seeing 2000* p. 23 Zurich: Flamberg Verlag AG, 1971)

Bijlmermeer, outside Amsterdam, a new town for 100,000 inhabitants. Photo courtesy of the City of Amsterdam.

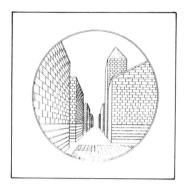 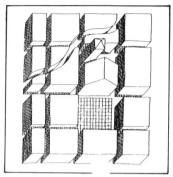

 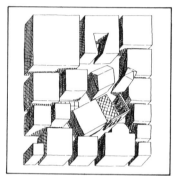

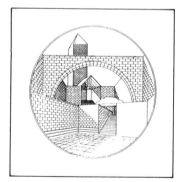 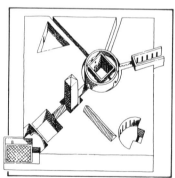

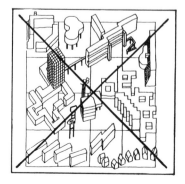

Illustration from *Rational Architecture: The Reconstruction of the European City* by Leon Krier and others showing three models of conceiving urban space: first, blocks which result from the street pattern; second, streets and squares which result from the position of the blocks; and third, the streets and squares as "precise spatial types" with the block as a result. Rejected is the fourth alternative, common until now in modern architecture, "objects that do not form a describable space."

"A spatial continuity that is functionally complex and visually simple rearticulates the contemporary system of disintegrated functions (zoning). At the heart of a strict relationship between the typology of buildings and the morphology of urban spaces, is a redefinition of the dialectic between public edifices (monuments) and the urban tissue."
Courtesy Editions des Archives d'Architecture Moderne, Brussels, 1978.

Aerial view of Port Grimaud, the instant fishing village on the French Riviera designed by François Spoerry, Courtesy François Spoerry, architect, Mulhouse, France. and *Landscape Architecture Quarterly*

The centers of many cities rank among our most valued built environments, since they are the oldest, sometimes reaching back thousands of years. At the same time, they are most likely to be the scenes of intense conflict between new and old, between different functions and population groups. Historically, they have been the sites of protest, the proving ground for revolutionary movements. Today, contemporary urban struggles are still fought out over such historic terrain.

The centers of American cities have been more or less spurned in the quest for extended urban growth, or they have been the focus for renewal programs that ignored their heritage and existing populations. The conservation movement in America has until now been primarily concerned with saving the natural environment. But the spirit of conservation is now entering the cities. The activism of the 1960s and 1970s has moved into the neighborhoods. Their conservation is the new rallying cry. It is also a sign of renewed middle-class interest in the central city. For the first time since World War II, 1973 saw the values and rents of central city housing begin to rise more rapidly than suburban values (Conservation Foundation, 1977). The issue of neighborhood conservation and revitalization is now high on the national agenda.

In Europe this process has been going on for a much longer time. There, urban conservation has always been of greater public concern than natural conservation. European cities have a much richer urban heritage, while there has been relatively less suburbanization and central city abandonment, so the demographic patterns of European cities have taken a somewhat different form from those in the United States. Now, however, there are signs of convergence as American suburbanization slows down. A study of the European experience should therefore be timely and illuminating.

The essays in this volume have been selected to bring out some of the principal themes and conflicts of urban conservation in Europe. Beginning in part I with examples of controversies over *development and redevelopment*, which have in

most cases been the precursors of conservation attitudes and policies, the book moves on to essays which describe *conservation* efforts and their problems. The essays cover both studies in the conservation of some historically significant areas, such as the historic quarter of Plaka in Athens or Diocletian's Palace in Split, and the conservation of more humble neighborhoods.

Historic and *neighborhood* conservation are closely related. Despite the greater cultural attention to, and tourist pressures on, historic areas, ordinary people still live in them, and so the movements to conserve historic and local neighborhoods have supported each other. Although it is commonly thought that the historic conservation movement has spread its interests beyond the monuments to the surrounding neighborhoods, an alternate theory argues that the conservation movement in Britain did not really get underway until middle-income groups began to realize that older neighborhoods were indeed quite habitable and possessed qualities not to be found in the new suburbs and new towns.

Within these major themes the essays place varying emphasis on *physical* and *social* conservation, though they all try to integrate the two. The physical conservationists are usually architects, architectural historians, physical planners, or archaeologists, but they may also be journalists like Fergusson who represent a growing middle-class public, young and middle-aged, increasingly disaffected by new development and the destruction of the old city.

Those concerned with social conservation either come from the social sciences or are socially committed architects, planners, and social workers, some of whom represent the various resident associations, citizen action groups, and political activists who are organized on behalf of disadvantaged social groups in European society. The differences in emphasis are not always conscious or obvious. One detects a physical orientation in the omission of social information, as in the chapter on Utrecht, just as one detects a social orientation when physical description is omitted, as in François d'Arcy's chapter. Nevertheless, the majority of chapters here try to achieve the difficult *integration* of social and physical conservation.

Another difference relates to the role of planning in different European countries. In some ways northern and southern Europe are as far apart in planning style as each is from the United States. Northern Europe has a relatively long history of planning legislation which, supported by a large planning bureaucracy, has brought fairly effective physical planning to its cities. Southern Europe has had a more diverse experience. Turkey and Yugoslavia have witnessed authoritarian governments of the right and left, while in Italy, although there is planning legislation, cities have weak taxing powers, planning is more overtly linked to political parties, the planning bureaucracy has less credibility, and obedience to planning laws is generally low. In Rome it is claimed that several hundred thousand contraventions of the building laws have been perpetrated in the last thirty years. All this explains, for instance, the very different tone of Ceccarelli's and Shankland's papers. However, in recent years, the apolitical, bureaucratic style of northern European planning has been increasingly brought into question as it has become identified with unwanted development or when its bureaucratic nature has frustrated public participation. Planners as well as developers have threatened the old cities.

The reader should be aware that this book contains a mixture of "inside" and "outside" papers. The "inside" papers, such as those on Split, Amsterdam, Elsinore, and Utrecht, are written by planners and others whose agencies are directly responsible for urban planning. Of necessity these chapters tend to be technical and to avoid controversy or criticism. It is sometimes difficult to tell what is really going on. On the other hand, "outside" papers by local planners and others outside the establishment, such as those on Venice, Plaka, Bath, Brussels, Grenoble, and Stockholm, are much more critical and give a more rounded picture of events in those cities, although they too provide only a certain view. The established planners in those cities could perhaps make a better case for their activities than is stated here.

At a deeper level, these papers differ in their ideological approach to planning. We can discern four ideological styles, present in varying mixes within each chapter. The first is *economic*. The style of planning which gives primacy to economic growth and development is paid scant attention in most of these papers, except for that on Utrecht. Indeed, the market view of the city is seen by many as one of the chief problems of European cities. The contributors from Venice and Lambeth, with their concerns about employment, also worry about the economic aspect, but theirs is more a social concern. The second and much more prevalent is the *conservationist* style of planning, one which gives primacy to the quality, care, and meaning of the physical heritage of European cities. The paper on Bath epitomizes the strong public support for this view, while the studies in several historic quarters are examples of professional viewpoints. This architectural and environmental orientation has been one of the traditional foundations of European planning.

The third emphasis evident in this volume is the *political* view of planning. It has two distinct substyles, both radical. The *formal* style, heavily influenced by Marxism, comprises a conceptual view of the role of planning in political struggles and is exemplified or implied in the chapters on Venice, Bologna, and Grenoble and the ARAU paper on Brussels. Interestingly, it is not evident in the Yugoslav paper, which holds an empirical, conservationist view. The other, more pragmatic, is the *participatory action* style described most fully in the Miller and Ahlgren and McKean papers but also in the ARAU paper. Finally, an emerging ideology on the European scene is the *empirical* approach, which uses social and attitudinal surveys to discover what people want. Most papers evidence some blend of approaches. D'Arcy's paper, for instance, sets a piece of empirical research in a political framework. ARAU has a strong formal ideology but suppresses it to concentrate on citizen action over conservationist issues. The papers on London and Bolton, Elsinore and Plaka attend to conservationist values using empirical methods.

The principal themes of this book will be the role that physical conservation plays in the lives of those who inhabit cities, the functional, social, and cultural significance of this environment to the different populations who live in the inner city, and the ways in which their needs and values can be satisfied and supported. The physical environment will also be seen as political territory, part of an often unconscious power struggle between different populations, professionals, and decision makers. What we shall give only small attention to will be the economics of conservation, the housing market, employment problems of the inner city, and the provision of public services to low-income groups. Where actual costs are given, the author should note the date of writing and adjust for current exchange rates.

Most of the essays are about *neighborhoods*, since conservation, to a marked degree, cares for the detailed and small-scale qualities of cities, their people, the maintenance or rehabilitation of houses, public buildings, street character, small industry, local open spaces, trees, and back yards. Only a few of the essays, particularly Shankland's on London, Ceccarelli's on Venice, and Bandarin's on Bologna, make more than passing reference to the role of conservation at the metropolitan scale, though this is becoming an increasingly important issue. The danger in dealing only with individual neighborhoods is that each case study may be interpreted as representative of all neighborhood processes in a single city or even a country. Some of the neighborhoods described are in decay, others are in advanced stages of revitalization. Neighborhoods of each type may well be found in every city described. The examples should therefore be examined more as samples of neighborhood conservation types than as necessarily representative.

The principal message from these papers is that although Europeans are now aware of the devastating impact that development, tourism, and redevelopment can have on historic cities and old neighborhoods, their conservation efforts are fraught with conflicts. We shall find that conservationists differ among themselves about what conservation means: that policies and acts of conservation can unexpectedly defeat their original intentions; that physical conservation provides no assurance of social conservation, the maintenance of the existing population; that the administrative structure of planning, created in a period when

planning was synonymous with development, is ill-suited to the small-scale, community-oriented needs of conservation; that social conservation may result in physical deterioration, and so on.

Conservation itself, like so many planning concepts, is often a mirage, an illusion that it is possible to retrieve the past or conserve the present by contemporary action. In fact, everything we touch, even the conceptual act of designating a neighborhood for conservation, changes our view of it and subtly modernizes it. The process is most evident in the effects of tourism. As MacCannell says in his book, *The Tourist* (1976), "the final victory of modernity . . . is not the disappearance of the non-modern world, but its artificial preservation and reconstruction in modern society."

This introduction attempts to structure the various facets of the conservation issue by first sketching the recent history of European cities and then describing the viewpoints of and conflicts between a number of groups, those with a development orientation, the tourists, the conservationists, the social action movements. An analysis of the resulting crisis in modern planning and architecture is followed by a review of the main case studies in the book, with reference to the issues of decaying neighborhoods, pioneering and gentrification, and efforts to achieve integrated social and physical conservation. The new kinds of planning and education that are needed for successful conservation are followed by some implications for conservation planning in the United States.

The Postwar Years

It is possible to identify *four* phases in the planning of European cities since World War II. The first years, roughly the 1940s and early 1950s, were devoted to the reconstruction of bombed cities, the provision of mass housing for the homeless, and the working out of ambitious plans for the physical development of metropolitan areas. Resources were limited and mostly under public control. By the 1960s, however, many European countries had taken off on an economic boom. Massive private developments, office and commercial complexes accompanied by substantial public infrastructure commitments, especially in highways, marked an American-style change in many European cities. The third phase was one of growing opposition to both public and private development from conservationists and citizen action groups, supported by large sections of the public. This stage was followed quickly by the fourth, the economic recession, energy crisis, and high rates of inflation that mark the European scene in the mid-1970s. This last phase, which has helped the conservation cause by slowing down development, has perhaps given the conservationists a false sense of their powers, while those with social concerns are suffering from the squeeze on social programs. There are signs that economic priorities may once again threaten the conservation of inner neighborhoods, if and when development gets underway again.

The effects of these phases on the historic city of Venice are tellingly outld by Paolo Ceccarelli in a paper that views the nonplanning of Venice within a national, even international, political framework, a sad tale of conflict, intrigue, political games, and inaction played under the spotlights of UNESCO and world opinion.

The brutal destruction of old city centers during World War II left people first in a state of shock and grief at the loss of a world that could never quite be returned. For "modern" planners and architects, however, whose ideologies had grown from the Charter of Athens and the annual meetings of the Congrès International d'Architecture Moderne (CIAM), existing cities were cramped, dirty, congested, and oppressive, and the bombed sites were symbols of opportunity—an opportunity to throw off the shackles of the past. Young architects in those years were ready to tear down most of old London. The Victorian city was too ubiquitous and dominant to be loved. Our designs for new cities were beautiful, inventive, and free. In them the sun shone, the skies were blue, helicopters flew "quietly" overhead, cars traveled freely on uncongested streets, housing was clean, light, spacious, and new. The inhabitants would obviously be happy. None of this had yet been built, nothing existed to smear the image. The era of the "heroic" city building had begun.

The centers of Rotterdam, Coventry, the City of London, and Hamburg, all laid waste by bombing, were planned anew to retain the shells of a few surviving monuments but substantially to forget the past. This was a period when planners in Brussels, which came through the war unharmed, became ashamed of the dinginess of their city in contrast to Rotterdam's rebirth (see Strauven, this volume). Most of the really historic cities—Rome, Paris, Amsterdam, Venice—had in fact survived the war. Warsaw, a city totally destroyed, stood almost alone in its serious effort to rebuild the old city center in its original form. At the time, western European planners saw this as a strange nostalgic act. They had not experienced to such a degree the threat to national identity that had overwhelmed the Poles. Nevertheless, in many cities, new buildings, such as those near the Ponte Vecchio in Florence, or Coventry Cathedral in England, were consciously designed in relation to their historic surroundings though modern in detail.

The 1950s were marked by massive public housing developments, some on the bombed sites of inner cities, many in the growing suburbs and new towns. It was not until the 1960s that Europe experienced the unprecedented economic development that spurred the construction of office buildings, shopping and commercial centers, and transportation facilities, initiating a new era of demolition. Conscious efforts were made in London to decentralize offices, policies that were successful in suburban centers such as Croydon. But decentralization failed to materialize on the massive scale typical of America. Automobile ownership was less widespread and urban freeway systems had not been constructed. The center cities therefore continued to thrive as seats of government, administration, corporate headquarters and their accompanying special industries, and retail and service facilities. The result was necessarily the razing of older buildings and sites to make way for newer and usually larger buildings.

Some cities, such as Paris, constructed large new centers like La Défense in an effort to cluster new development and avoid scattered destruction. The plan for Rome's new Centro Direzzionale to the east of the historic center was envisioned along the same lines, but never materialized because of Italy's less authoritarian planning structure. London's development was more scattered, with a few larger complexes like Victoria Street, the South Bank, and Notting Hill Gate, which nevertheless dominated the city. In Brussels, witnessing rapid growth as the "Capital of Europe," chunks of the old inner city were torn down for new development.

Development Means Destruction

The planning of the enormous Hoog Catharijne commercial project in Utrecht (see chapter 2) epitomizes the whole set of hopes and attitudes that were and are held by those who believe that large-scale redevelopment of old cities is justified. The Hoog Catharijne was originally planned by the city of Utrecht in an area next to the historic center of the city, around the railroad station. The intent was to "keep the old city open for traffic" by providing "a new nervous system and a larger and better heart." This replacement was accompanied by the pious, but less than ingenuous admonition that "all new elements . . . had to make a perfect match with the characteristic, historical features of Utrecht." At the same time the area selected for replacement was devalued by the use of "modernistic" language. In the familiar phrases of urban renewal planners, the existing area was "not of particular interest," being a nineteenth century neighborhood, with businesses, a barracks, and some "out-of-date buildings." The plan lay dormant until a large construction company proposed to develop such a center on the 24 hectares of land around the railway station. The massive new complex, "unique in the Netherlands," contains department stores, a Holiday Inn, a new railway station, an industries fair building, and parking for 5000 cars. As J.P. Barendsen admits, the complex looks ("naturally"!) like "a large concrete colossus."

To counter the qualms of the conservationists, two lavish brochures produced by the developers enlisted the support of an architectural critic. Miletus, San Marco, Regent Street in London, and Haussmann's Paris were not immodestly cited as predecessors to this triumph of urban design, while the crc referred to the area replaced as "scruffy, full of lorries, a neighborhood best forgotten." Again, this psychological downgrading of the old city was a necessary prelude to justification of the new. Though he disliked the disruption of the city skyline by the office building that now competes with Old Dom, the expert went on to argue that each era had always constructed its own monuments with little respect for previous surroundings. He would adapt over time. Others might not wish to.

From an economic viewpoint we see the close intermeshing and interdependence of the city government, which retains ownership of the land and finances the infrastructure, including parking garages, with private development. There is even the strong possibility that the city has assisted in the demise of the historic shopping center through its new competition, though precautions were taken not to duplicate historic center shops in the Hoog Catharijne.

There is an omission in this presentation. We hear nothing of what happened to the population and firms that previously occupied the 24 developed hectares. How many were there? and what happened to them?

Mr. Barendsen tells us that the city is not so enthusiastic or chauvinistic as it once was about the scheme even though, unlike in American renewal projects, it has maintained ownership of the land. Efforts have been made to prevent business moving from the old city to the new complex, and the old city has been pedestrianized to keep its commerce viable. But opposition to the scheme has grown, opposition that in Mr. Barendsen's words, has given "romanticized attention to anything that is small scale and . . . old, with an aversion to anything that resembles concrete and commerce." The Hoog Catharijne is only a sample of what has taken place all over Europe.

Public and semipublic institutions, especially hospitals and universities, have also expanded to take over surrounding neighborhoods, a phenomenon which has been called "institutional creep." University College, London, is changing the face of Georgian Bloomsbury, reducing the number of cheap residential hotels; while in Bath, a technical college, police station, and post office disrupt the integrity of the old city. The University in Venice took over housing badly needed by lower-income groups. The result was an embarassing squatter invasion.

New transportation facilities have torn into European cities to a markedly lesser degree than the earlier railways, or the urban freeways in the United States. Nevertheless, stretches of freeway have been planned through or very close to the older centers. At one time in the 1960s, though it is scarcely believable today, there were plans for an elevated freeway along the northern edge of the city of Venice. Paris now has a freeway along the right bank of the Seine through the heart of the city. Liverpool and Bristol have sizable stretches of motorway encircling their centers. But the massive London motorway system was aborted after a widespread "Homes before Cars" campaign fought it during a local government election and the newly elected Council vetoed it. In Zurich, too, an attempt to build a freeway alongside the river was brought to a standstill.

Subway systems are generally less destructive than surface or elevated freeways, yet in some cases they too have threatened valued places. One day in the early 1970s a team of men arrived in one of Stockholm's central parks to cut down a group of elms whose roots were interfering with the alignment of a new subway route. The elms surrounded a well-known and beloved teahouse. The men were met by a crowd of irate Stockholm citizens. The transit engineers claimed that no alternative route was possible, but after months of impasse they found another path. In Amsterdam, the new metro, designed as a "cut and cover" system because of the difficulty of tunneling with a high water table, has entailed the clearance of structures over the alignment. One route passes through the old Neumarket historic quarter. After the original populations were evicted, young radicals occupied the areas affected and opposed the project. Rome's transit system creeps along secretly through the city's precious archaeological heritage, an action bemoaned with dramatic intensity in Fellini's *Roma*.

While the freeway may have been slowed, the amount of traffic continued inexorably to increase and now saturates the old street systems of European cities. The impacts are innumerable. Traffic blocks the streets; it invades the quietest of residential neighborhoods, bringing with it danger, noise, vibration, fumes and dust; it takes what little open space there is for light, air and recreation. The cars have to be parked somewhere, so they now cover the ground level of most neighborhoods like a metallic flood; the most striking visual change in these cities outside the major development projects. The streets and piazzas that the tourists love to photograph are crammed with Renaults, Fiats, Volkswagens, and Fords, let alone motor scooters, mopeds, vans of all sizes and shapes, and other forms of motorized transport. All of these have contributed dramatically to the sense of congestion that pervades European cities today.

The grime from industrial and domestic air pollution that used to cover Britain's cities has been rolled back through air pollution controls, conversion from domestic coal fires, and extensive cleaning of facades. But the outdoor sculpture of Venice is suffering from an advanced state of "marble cancer" caused mostly by air pollution from the petrochemical plants of Marghera.

Tourism: The Stifling Embrace

John Evelyn would be astounded at the levels that mass tourism has now reached and the effects it has had on the objects of its attraction. Traveling and learning about other peoples and places is a healthy and civilizing activity. World tolerance might increase if people knew each other better. Indeed, Dean MacCannell argues that tourism is one of the central and unifying activities of modern culture: "The empirical and ideological expansion of modern society [is] linked in diverse ways to modern mass leisure, especially to international tourism and sight-seeing." (MacCannell, 1976, p. 3). Tourism for many is an attempt to reestablish cultural roots, for others a search for frontiers and new horizons. MacCannell claims it is even more than this: "Modern man has been condemned to look elsewhere, everywhere, for his authenticity, to see if he can catch a glimpse of it reflected in the simplicity, poverty, chastity, or purity of others" (MacCannell, 1976, p. 41).

Yet tourism is also a rather frivolous activity. As an escape from everyday life, it demands more entertainment and relaxation than education. And, since contacts are fleeting and limited, tourist perceptions and attitudes are often superficial and romantic, colored by nostalgia.

Tourists do not leave a city untouched by their presence. A classic instance of the observer affecting the observed, the tourist, through his demands, subtly and sometimes drastically changes the character of a place. Residents in most cities want tourists for economic reasons and will change their cities and lives to serve them. A tourist-oriented veneer begins to cover the old city like a film. The change occurs in several ways.

First, the tourists are attracted to the "set pieces," those famous places that are "sacralized" (MacCannell, 1976) in tourist literature and that dominate the postcards. The "sacralization" of tourist attractions creates for tourists a moral imperative to visit them. It is absolutely necessary for most tourists to take their own photographs or to be photographed in front of these places. Thus, "The vast majority of tourists are still satisfied to be taken to their destination and thence to a limited range of places selected by tour operators" (Hall, 1974, p. 392). Such places are then built up as romantic scenery to satisfy the tourists' desires and expectations. Most of this happened long ago in European cities. Beggars and markets, though still found in Eastern cities like old Delhi (TCPO, 1975), have long been cleared away. Events, concerts, *son et lumière* displays have further set them off from the rest of the city. Funds are provided for their restoration while the neighborhoods around may be neglected or destroyed.

Such pieces in essence become tourist territory. The Piazza di Spagna in Rome, though it seems Italian to American tourists, is seen as American turf, lost to the local residents. In a city like Venice, whose artistic heritage is perceived internationally to be in "crisis," foreign countries or corporations are now in fact responsible for restoration of many set pieces. The French are looking after Sansovino's Library, the British more modestly take care of the small Loggia.

Congestion now surrounds many of these famous historic places. The Greater London Council has estimated that on occasions tourist buses have brought 8000 people to see the changing of the guard in Whitehall on a Sunday morning. Parking for buses and cars crowds the streets and piazzas of many European cities, making conditions unpleasant for the residents, who cannot travel around so easily and who are subject to noise, air pollution, and intrusive strangers. The capacity of streets in many old cities is just not enough to cope with this problem.

Tourists need hotels. The typical tourist would like to stay in modern comfort, close to the center, with a view of the historic city from the bedroom window, perhaps a swimming pool, and easy parking. The result is predictable. New hotels have sprung up right in or near historic centers. The skylines of Jerusalem, Athens, and Istanbul are each dominated by Hilton Hotels. A new Hilton, astonishingly, is under construction right in the historic quarter of Buda next to the cathedral in Communist Budapest. The gigantic Russia Hotel dominates Red Square in Moscow. There can be no more devastating symbols of tourism's power. In Bath too, the famous Pulteney Bridge is now neighbored by a modern hotel atop a convenient parking garage, replacing an old street of Georgian buildings. To gain a view for themselves, hotels destroy the view for everyone else. Like tourists they fail to *see* the destruction they wreak on the cities that give them sustenance.

Tourists like to shop and be entertained in the evenings. Souvenir stands, boutiques, antique shops, and other stores therefore cluster around the hotels and set pieces. Nightclubs and entertainment as well as cultural activities are supported by their presence. In some cities these facilities replace local service stores. In the old Plaka quarter of Athens the bars, nightclubs, and late evening entertainment, while bringing in business, create unpleasantly noisy and congested conditions for the residents.

Increases in hotel accommodation and services for tourism can take away needed housing from residents. A 1971 discussion paper entitled "Tourism and Hotels in London," prepared for the Greater London Council cautioned, "If we are not careful, London will indeed have

200,000 more hotel beds by 1980, but 100,000 fewer houses than we want."

Tourism does, of course, affect the economic and employment base of cities. For smaller cities it can be overwhelming. Venice is an extreme example of a tourist-dominated city. For years, Ceccarelli tells us, the destiny of the city was seen to be focused entirely on tourism. Hotels expanded, the international jet set acquired apartments, and the artisan population, even those in the tourist-oriented glass and lace industries, became severely depleted. Fishing has declined; even gondoliers are disappearing. Most Venetians work in tourist services or leave for the industrial city of Mestre on the mainland. The traditional economic base of Venice has been "dismantled." The "life" seen by the tourist is carried on by dummy craftsmen, a spectacle staged for the eager observer. While tourism subtly kills the traditional "life" it came to see, it has an insatiable thirst for that life. The loss of local community back at home leads tourists to search for it elsewhere. Museums are not enough. Local crafts and activities are hungrily sought out and photographed. Since change in the traditional life is inevitable, historic cities will inevitably be dragged into the manufacture of "staged authenticity," a phenomenon that I shall discuss later.

Residents are ambivalent toward tourism. Surveys in York, England, showed that about 80 percent of the population felt tourism was beneficial because it improved public transport, provided good theaters, and helped preserve old buildings (Hall, 1974). Tourists are now said to account for 20 percent of public transport revenues in London. There is a strong tendency among the educated, however, to view tourism as a kind of cultural prostitution or at least a reduction in value. Schoonbrodt fears that the Marol in Brussels will be "reduced to a touristic curiosity." This "rhetoric of moral superiority," MacCannell argues, is a species of one-upmanship:

The tourist critique of tourism is based on a desire to go beyond the other "mere" tourists to a more profound appreciation of society and culture, and it is by no means limited to intellectual statements. All tourists desire this deeper involvement with society and culture to some degree; it is a basic component of their motivation to travel. (MacCannell, 1976, p. 10)

A superior attitude toward the mass tourist is common among professionals, yet what right have we to deny them what we wish to do ourselves? Reader be reminded that your involvement in the cities presented in this volume is most likely to be a touristic one.

Tourism, nevertheless, can be a fickle asset subject to international crises, recessions, and energy shortages. It does not provide the regular kinds of jobs that people need; and the economic gains from it more and more are drawn away into international tourist chains.

Yet tourism is not likely to stop. Some argue that through management of information and guides, tourism should be consciously spread away from the few points of concentration that destroy the surroundings of the set pieces. Such a spread of interest might assist in saving the *architettura minore* of Italian cities and what is left of Bath. The growth of educated independent tourists who wish to search for the authentic in the back streets and distant places may encourage such a movement, though there is always the fear that they (we) may simply be precursors of further destruction.

The Growing Opposition

As Europe moved through the 1950s and 1960s, as more modern buildings and whole cities were built, and as the old cities were torn down or eaten away, many cities approached a "tipping point," where the old was becoming more rare than the new. The unpredicted negative effects of the automobile began to mount. The Buchanan Report, *Traffic in Towns,* was published in 1963. By the early 1970s, professionals had begun to lose their ideological hold over public values and differ among themselves. Opposition to development has come from two main quarters, the first from those concerned with the *physical* conservation of the older city and its replacement by disliked modern buildings and transport systems, the second from those involved in *social* issues, especially the displacement of social groups. Sometimes the two combine; at other times they operate separately and in recent years have been found on different sides of the issues.

The Conservation Movement

Adam Fergusson's blistering indictment of the modern "sack of Bath" documents, in the strongest terms, the feelings and viewpoints of those who protest the modernization of old cities. In Bath, the monuments have been preserved. "The set pieces—Royal Crescent, the Circus Milsom Street, the Pump Room, and so on—stand glorious and glistening . . . for tourists to come and see in their thousands every year." But their context is in danger of destruction, "like mountains without foothills, Old Masters without frames."

The British classify historic buildings in three grades (I, II, III). It is the Grades II and III buildings that have been susceptible to destruction. Meanwhile new housing, hotels, department stores, a technical college, police station, and post office have been planned and constructed. A major tunnel under the city center was projected. Fergusson allocates blame for Bath's state of affairs at the door of the "unimaginative" and "timid" city Council, and to the Chief Architect and various members of the Royal Fine Arts Commission, a prestigious national body that is meant to protect the country's architectural heritage and set its aesthetic standards. With so many public and professional figures brought to task, the private developers are almost exempt from liability.

Groups in other cities have also protested the destruction of valued buildings and places, not always with much success. The destruction of Les Halles in Paris was opposed, without effect, while the American Embassy in London had earlier replaced a fine Georgian terrace in Grosvenor Square with hardly a public murmur. More protests have been directed against the design of the new buildings than destruction of the old, but these have usually not gathered momentum until after the new has been built, a less than effective time to protest. Ordinances often fail to keep new

buildings in harmony with the old. Even though all new buildings must be in Bath stone or reconstituted Bath stone, the traditional material actually contributes to Bath's uglification when clothing, for example, a bus station, a tower block, a motor showroom, a public lavatory, or a multideck car park. Jerusalem has a similar ordinance and similar problems (Kutcher, 1973). It is more the scale and overall design of buildings that have effect. "Discord," "squat nastiness," "ersatz," "soullessness," "packing-case constructions," "hencoops," "biscuit tins," are among the expressions used by Fergusson to describe these new buildings. In Brussels the critics from the Atelier de Recherche et d'Action Urbaine (ARAU) have used equally scathing expressions—"denuded," "monoculture," "gloomy glossy towers," "social storage systems"—to describe their own city's feats of modern architecture.

In Paris, the controversy over Les Halles became a national issue. After the market had departed, an enormous mixed-use commercial complex was proposed for the site, with a large cultural center on the neighboring Plateau Beaubourg, symbolizing the achievements of the Pompidou administration. The surrounding areas of slumlike housing at densities of 300 persons per hectare were to be rehabilitated at reduced densities, obviously for a higher-income population. In the summer of 1971, amid sharp protests, the cast-iron buildings were torn down (Evenson, 1973). But before the huge new complex had started construction, Giscard d'Estaing came to power. One of his first symbolic acts was to halt its development. The earlier designs were left high and dry, and now plans are to top the underground complex with an urban open space. Meanwhile, completion of the futuristic scaffolding and pipes that are the exterior of the Centre Pompidou has apparently been greeted with enthusiasm by Parisians and foreigners alike. Perhaps its social success and complexity of detail allow it to fit better the existing texture of the city than the typical, bland products of *l'architecture moderne*.

Strong objections have been made to the intrusion of new buildings on the skylines of many older cities. The towers of La Défense looming behind the Arc de Triomphe and the black tower of the Montparnasse hovering behind the Place de la Concorde have been sharply condemned by Parisians (Evenson, 1973). As in Bath, prestigious professionals have been attacked. A student publication from the Université de Vincennes bitterly denounced the French Commission of Monuments and Sites for turning a blind eye to these intrusions. ARAU makes similar fun of Brussels's "translucent building."

Neglect of the past has in some countries been part of a conscious effort to become westernized. Cansever's brief review of Istanbul's history tells of such a case. Whereas the Ottomans adapted their Roman-Byzantine monuments to Ottoman use without extensive destruction, westernization, "which meant Paris," brought Haussmannesque boulevards, "western cubist buildings," and careless, even deliberate, destruction of historic buildings and areas. While the monuments have been saved, the surrounding artisans' quarters, some in wooden houses, have been destroyed or are in seriously dilapidated condition. A study by Dr. Nezih Eldem, an architectural professor at the Technical University of Istanbul, proposes that the wooden houses be converted for students' quarters, removing incompatible uses, but this would raise problems for the present inhabitants.

Popular disaffection with modern buildings has been fueled by the huge chunks of public housing that now surround most European cities. The early "humanistic" postwar housing, pioneered by the Scandinavians, with its textures, colors, balconies, and decoration, has been replaced by a more hard-nosed modern style, mostly in concrete, supported by the dominance of prefabrication techniques and emphasis on speed and quantity. Stockholm's latest new towns or Amsterdam's Biljmermeer are not much less monotonous than the latest blocks to be found in Moscow.

As a consequence of these "outrages," urban conservation groups have flourished all over Europe. Conservation in Britain, for instance, unlike the American variety, had urban origins.

This contrast illustrates the elaborate context in which the British amenity movement operates: nothing is untouched; and conservation, which implies the cherishing of what exists, can only be understood against a background of historical, scientific, aesthetic, cultural and social concerns, all of which overlap. Wilderness has had far less emphasis in Britain than in younger emptier countries. (Civic Trust, 1976, p. 17)

The same can be said of other European countries. By 1976 some 1250 local amenity societies were registered with Britain's Civic Trust, the umbrella organization for urban conservation (Civic Trust, 1976). These groups are not concerned only with historic conservation. *Amenity*, a word that has had a long currency in British planning, covers a range of environmental qualities analogous to *aesthetics* and *livability* in the American vocabulary (Smith, 1974). Other organizations, such as the Town and Country Planning Association, have been more professional in nature but influential over a wider range of planning issues, while the Conservation Society and Friends of the Earth are newer organizations more concerned with general environmental matters. In Italy the educated conservationists have gathered around Italia Nostra and ANCSA (the National Association for Artistic Historic Centers) and the two National Institutes of Urbanism and Architecture: INU and IN/ARCH (Rossi Doria, 1976).

Many urban conservationists in Britain are professionals brought up on the townscape ideologies of *The Architectural Review*, but most appear to be educated middle-class citizens who dislike the starkness and arrogance of modern buildings and prefer the quietness and picturesque qualities of old towns. Leading this public are figures like the poet John Betjeman in Britain and the filmmaker Jacques Tati in France, whose merciless parodies of modern architecture hit the world in the mid 1960s. Lesser known but equally devastating are the cartoons of the Danish ex-architect Erik Ortvad in his *Sight Seeing 2000* (1971).

The Social Protest
While conservationists protest the loss of an urban heritage, others have attacked the dislocation of social groups due to redevelopment. It is true that European redevelopment in the 1950s was undertaken in order to build public

housing for lower-income populations, and much more public housing is still built there than in the U.S. But many of the public housing urban renewal programs left razed and vacant sites unbuilt upon for several years, while certain population groups, often young singles and couples, found it very difficult to find housing accommodation. And in the 1960s and early 1970s the private redevelopment of European cities began to displace working-class residents in ways similar to those of American projects.

Nicole Brasseur's account of the huge Manhattan project in Brussels will sound familiar to American readers. Large office and commercial buildings with their service motorways are replacing a number of old neighborhoods in the central area of the city. Fifty-three hectares, "the greatest reconstruction area up till now [1972] in the whole of Europe," are planned for redevelopment in the northern quarter around the North Station. Some thirty "skyscrapers," housing for 12,000, and parking for 16,000 cars are projected. The area in 1972 was occupied by about 10,000 working-class inhabitants, most of whom rented and many of whom were foreign immigrants. Adequate relocation housing had not been provided, and many would like to stay in the quarter if social and other services were improved. The recession has temporarily, perhaps permanently, halted redevelopment, with several of the new office buildings and a large wasteland left vacant.

In Brussels an active and innovative protest group emerged in 1970. The group is called ARAU (the Atelier de Recherche et d'Action Urbaine) and is led by young architects and planners. Its history, principles, and modes of action are described by Francis Strauven and René Schoonbrodt. The group's concerns integrate the social and physical. They argue that the city has long been the site of struggles for territory that in Brussels have so far been won by the international corporations and the affluent, acting through traditional planning powers. The city and national government have in fact accommodated themselves mostly to the needs of these groups, an American style of planning that is apparently more characteristic of Belgian tradition than of many other European countries. The ideological basis of Schoonbrodt's paper is clearly the class struggle, yet the ARAU group, he tells us, has confined itself to matters of counterplanning and design, leaving to others fights over issues such as land speculation. They feel that by sticking closely to the "loss of urban life" issues they have been more effective. Their five years of struggle in numerous controversies in which they have searched for creative alternatives to establishment plans endows these papers with remarkable authority. They show that resistance to unwanted development can be carried out with bravado, wit, and imagination. The group is now associated with many community groups in the city and with other environmental groups. They have an ongoing public tour for visitors called "Alternative Brussels" which takes visitors to the sites of urban battles, a political version of Goodey's town trails (see chapter 22).

Grass roots groups have been flourishing all over Europe since the confrontations of the late 1960s, many inspired by American models. These groups, mostly led by young activists, often professionals or students, have been concerned primarily with social conservation, the maintenance of existing populations, but also with the same problems of disamenity that the physical conservationists attack: dilapidation, heavy traffic, noise, air pollution, and the need for better sanitation and services. Peter Hain, in his *Community Politics* (1977), gave three structural reasons for the emergence of community action groups in Britain. First, the "facelessness of the new industrialism, coupled with the break-up of traditional community life, left in its wake a sense of social rootlessness" and led to an effort to restore community identity and solidarity; second, the rise of the welfare state created an extensive and complex network of social services that nevertheless failed to benefit many groups who needed active help in understanding the system and making demands; and third, the impact of physical development threatened the housing of lower income groups. A fourth reason, in Britain, was disillusionment of young radicals with party politics. Indeed, the desire for community identity was felt most strongly by the young, middle-class activists, while the lower-income families they defended were often apathetic. Although many of these groups have moved from confrontation to negotiation in recent years, in what some see as a corresponding loss in effectiveness, the movements have endured and are now serviced by such excellent journals as Britain's *Community Action* and Italy's *Città Classe*. Charles McKean's chapter will describe some of the more recent constructive efforts by such groups to improve the environment of Britain's inner cities.

A Crisis for Modernity

Why is it that, after fifty years of modern architecture, urban development, and planning, there is now a turning away toward the past, not only on the part of the public but on the part of the professions? The reasons are manifold and differ among various social groups.

Some argue that it is a reaction against the discomforts of the modern city, its densities, traffic congestion, smog, overload. This may be true for the middle and upper classes. In the modern city, air pollution, noise, traffic, litter, garbage, long commutes, and energy breakdowns cannot be avoided by any group. But for the lower classes the modern city is a considerably superior environment to that of the nineteenth-century city, with its disease, filth, industrial pollution, poor lighting, and lack of home comforts.

Another reason is the rapidity of change that has been difficult for people to absorb. Change no longer conveys a sense of freedom when it takes place too fast and out of one's control. Change, then, represents a loss more than a gain. Our personal and cultural identities are threatened. The past, after all, is evidence that a society has existed. Wipe it away and a culture begins to feel, like a man without a memory, shallow and superficial. The anxieties created are not unlike the grief experienced after the personal loss of family or friend. Continuity is broken, and without continuity, Marris tells us, "we cannot interpret what events mean to us, nor explore new kinds of experience with confidence" (Marris, 1975). We turn, therefore, to the past as a repository for our sentiments and values, to escape the difficulties of the present. Such conservatism is fundamental to our survival.

This almost magical power of the past does not lie only in the intrinsic beauty of what is being preserved, survivals of an age when towns were made by artisans, but above all in the identity they confer. This sense of continuity seems today more important than ever, as national groups and ethnic minorities battle for identity and survival in an age of multi-national economic groupings, uniform machine-made products, and supra-national political settlements. . . .

To any generation, an identifiable past offers a line of communication with others: between the living, the dead, and those still to be born. It provides a reference to previous experience; an illustration of how man went about creating a civilized environment; a reservoir and perpetual source of historical delight; a culture to be accepted, altered, rejected, re-interpreted or rediscovered. (Shankland, 1975, pp. 25–26)

One of the dilemmas of modern life is that physical comfort, cheaper products, and security are in fact bought at the cost of depersonalization.

The old city exemplifies the human scale, individuality, care and craftmanship, richness and diversity that are lacking in the modern plastic, machine-made city with its repetitive components and large-scale projects.

Towns which have developed in stages over the years . . . constitute a unique open museum of diverse architectural forms. Even if the styles of the buildings are the same, they are not assembled on the same street in the same sequence: they both embody the skill of their individual designers and makers, and the decisions and the idiosyncracies of successive town authorities. (Shankland, 1975, p. 25)

This is not a superficial richness but a richness and depth of meaning, activity, and social distinction. It reaches into the economic and social structure of the city.

Immense damage—environmentally—has already been done: it has brought a shift from a fine-grain to a coarse-grain environment. This is very obvious in the surface texture—the change from small-scale buildings with much less to beguile the eye. The coarse, crude, slab-like character of post-war buildings slaps you in the face in every British city, from pavement to skyline. It is also apparent in the economic and social pattern of the city. All these small-scale business enterprises which provided the enormous variety of service trades and occupations, which are one of the reasons people congregate in cities . . . disappear because the high rents of new buildings cannot be sustained by the turnover of small businesses depending on low overheads. No umbrella repairers, picture-frame makers, pastry cooks, or ballet-shoe makers. No voluntary organizations, small publishers or chiropodists. Only large-scale, highly capitalized, high turn-over and big-profit entrepreneurs need apply. (Ward, 1976, p. 9)

Underlying these attitudes, and perhaps their deeper reason, is the rebellion of the young and educated against the large-scale corporate and public power of which most new development is a manifestation. The members of ARAU are particularly clear on this point. Modern architecture and town planning, for them, have been co-opted by capitalism and its servants in local and national governments.

While modern architecture in its revolutionary origin as a universal language wanted to be a prefiguration of a socialist society, it was soon roped in by reaction, and turned into its own opposite, only to degenerate finally into a streamlined prefiguration of an air-conditioned consumer society, an antiurban kind of architecture, the production of which already supposes the end of democracy. (Strauven, this volume)

The young rebel against the new, the symbols of large-scale corporations, and powerful government agencies who have taken over the forms of modernism for their own purposes. Just as the early modern planners and architects rebelled against the nineteenth-century city and historic revivalism, this generation reacts to *their* antihistoricism by resurrecting the past. The meaning of *modern* has totally changed. The old represents history and meaning, the acceptance of years of use by many people; the new is shallow, belonging only to the few who create and finance it. Not surprisingly, the majority will favor the old, especially if it becomes the threatened underdog.

While the new structures and changes in our cities are viewed as political acts, the symbolism of the older monuments and quarters has undergone subtle but significant

changes since they were built. As their origin recedes into history they become politically *desymbolized;* that is, they are not so clearly preserved as symbols of their originators, creators, or users, but rather as cultural symbols of a common heritage. Whereas originally they belonged to one social group, often a hated and powerful one, now they are treasured as belonging to all. Love increases with time, since meaning mellows. Only such a transformation can explain, for instance, why many ex-colonial countries, thirty years after decolonization, have begun to repair and restore the formerly hated symbols of colonialism, the buildings of the colonial administration and former homes of the slaveowners, or why the Soviets have painstakingly restored the czarist palaces. Not all groups can yet face such restoration.

A lawyer in Manchester (New Hampshire), asked when that town would stop destroying the buildings of the Amoskeag mill complex, replied, "Not as long as anybody's alive who ever had to work in them" (Greiff, 1971, p. 30).

Perceptions of historic monuments and quarters are therefore dominated by only the vaguest of interpretations. They are vehicles for the imagination, suggestive starting points for reminiscing about history. Inevitably, *idealization* of the past becomes a common component of these recollections, a phenomenon described with subtle insights by Raymond Williams in a study of British attitudes toward the countryside (Williams, 1973). Visions of a Golden Age are projected onto the remains, a projection that powerfully influences the selection and kinds of transformation that are planned when restoration takes place.

. . . The physical city of the past not only reflected the community, but the whole city belonged to its inhabitants, and as such constituted a public resource, used and managed in its entirety. The presence of different social classes integrated in one urban fabric, often even in the same building, was evidence and guarantee of undifferentiated use and consumption. It was never a city of class differences, hierarchically subdivided as modern cities are. (Cervellati, 1978, p. 5)

This utopian view of the medieval city, expressed by the Chief Architect of the modern-day Commune of Bologna, is, however idealized, what provides conservation planners with their social inspiration. The transfer of value from the new to the old will differ in intensity depending on the rapidity of physical and social change, the extent of destruction, and the amount of history that survives. Apparently the less history we have the more we hunger for it. Hence the lengths to which California will go to uncover and preserve even early-twentieth-century buildings. The faster the rate of change, the more recent the past that is valued (Lowenthal, 1975).

This rebirth of the past has its healthy and its neurotic aspects. To value one's heritage, to save it and care for it, is an important part of a society's self-identity, awareness, and maturity. If it becomes a necessity, a world to cling to as an escape from current responsibilities, then it is less laudable. Nostalgia, David Lowenthal (1975) tells us, was originally labeled a disease, a homesickness experienced by soldiers on distant campaigns. However, it is no easy diagnosis to label certain attitudes "merely" nostalgic and others healthy. Too often the accusations of nostalgia come from those whose identity is bound up more with the new than the old.

All this has created a more serious crisis for the European architect than his American counterpart faces, since there is more to destroy, a higher and more widespread standard of historic achievement against which to be judged. There is also the vulnerability of possessing greater power. There are about two-thirds as many architects in Britain as there are in the United States, and they are responsible for the design of a wider range of buildings, particularly in the housing field.

For the first time the modern architect has found himself to be unpopular, his work rejected by the working classes, who dislike his impersonal utopian housing projects, and by his intellectual peers in other fields, who have turned to the past. After occupying the role of societal leader, the avant-garde, he finds that the rug has been pulled from under his feet. He is still trying to understand what happened.

Architects have always talked in terms of crisis. Now we have a real one. The profession has reacted in bewildered disarray. Some, usually those connected with large commercial projects, have continued trying to design modern buildings, oblivious to public disaffection. Others hope it is only the large ones that people don't like. In a recent retrospective exhibit at London's Architectural Association, the leading firms carefully omitted displaying their high-rise projects. Still others have withdrawn into extremism and fantasy. High technology and space-age futurism are countered by brutalistic primitivism.

But many have begun to search for security and meaning in different periods of the past. This search for meaning has propelled the study of semiology to the forefront of architectural thinking. But apart from a few interesting personal interpretations this movement has been characterized mostly by obscure language and uninteresting abstractions. Those who actually study existing cities and buildings have been engaged in more fruitful explorations, though it is fascinating in how many ways the old city can be used to support and justify contemporary ideologies. For the old city is not, as some would have it, a scientific fact, which can justify future actions; it is simply history which can offer us only some of our future options. We are living in different times.

The Architectural Review for years idealized indigenous functional architecture and the townscape of indigenous towns and villages, concentrating on usable details and picturesque photographic images. Though derided as superficial and cosmetic in its concerns, its influence has continued to spread in the sphere of urban design and is closely in tune with the British conservation movement. I shall say more of this ideology in the next section.

Another group of historicists is emerging in continental Europe. This Marxist group of architects has drawn on a different past. In an elegant book entitled *The Reconstruction of the European City* (1978) published by Maurice Culot's Editions des Archives d'Architecture Moderne in Brussels, contributors call for a return to the typological elements of the traditional city, the street, the square, the avenue, the arcade, the park, and so on. This structuralist style of thinking does not involve much analysis beyond classification, but it does inspire urban designs that look like eighteenth- and nineteenth-century cities. Some even go so far as to praise the Stalinist architecture of Stalinalle in East Berlin and Spanish architecture during the Franco period for their "conservative" nature. This seems to be an extremist reaction to the individualism and fragmentation of modern architecture. But it is true that one of the few surveys coming out of the U.S.S.R. has indicated that Leningrad residents prefer the Stalin period buildings (lining boulevards and grouped around courtyards) to the CIAM-style modern high-rise suburbs.

The political implication is that a return to the eighteenth- or nineteenth-century city will re-establish an "urban culture" and hopefully reintegrate the fast dispersing working class. Garden cities, according to one writer, were just another capitalist device to pacify and diffuse the explosive potential of the old working-class districts. The resulting designs of Krier and Rossi look to an outsider as authoritarian and impersonal as La Ville Radieuse. On the other hand the call for multifunctional *quartiers* and the more site-specific infill projects of ARAU do draw life from the existing city. Lacking in the structuralist analysis, however, seems to be any great concern with the relationship between the physical form of the city, everyday life, and the actual inhabitants, who are rarely mentioned except as a political force. The *process* of design appears to be closed and formalistic, though the forms are intriguing and the drawings beautiful. But how will the public react to these monuments of a new ideology?

What the public likes, of course, can cover a wide range of environments. One thing seems clear. At this time, they prefer the forms of the past to the present. The fact that Port Grimaud, the instant pastiche of a Mediterranean village for the affluent, is the third most popular tourist attraction in France, tells us something. Ordinary people like the cute, the picturesque, the decorated, combined with modern comforts and their own yacht.

All this reassessment of the forms of postmodern architecture provides no assurance yet that the public will get better cities. The architectural profession is dominated by theorists and the professal media. The primacy of local people and conditions are too easily forgotten in this peer-dominated world. The sensitivity of buildings and schemes to local contexts and clients is simply incommunicable through the current media. It will take aggressive citizens and responsive professionals to shake designers out of this abstract, placeless world. Seeking inspiration in the past, in the *genius loci*, in the particular needs and values of ordinary people, creative and responsive designers may forge acceptable and life-enhancing new environments. But much of this will depend on learning how to listen to people outside the professions, to understand what they want, how they see, and indeed to collaborate with them in the creation of more human architecture and cities. The European architects for the most part do not seem yet to have broken out of their own cocoon.

Historic Conservationists

The year 1975 was nominated European Architectural Heritage Year by the Council of Europe. This year of conferences and intense conservation activity marked a culmination of over fifteen years of meetings by architectural historians, urban conservators, archaeologists, architects, and planners who were dedicated to preserving Europe's patrimony.

European conferences on historic conservation sponsored by the Council of Europe began in the mid-1960s. By then it seemed apparent to many that "This prestigious heritage was in peril. Never before had the fatal consequences of senseless urban development in the historic localities of Europe become so apparent." (Council of Europe, 1975, p. 22). From an initial concern with individual monuments the movement has broadened its domain of interest to the preservation of whole areas of historic cities. A campaign was launched in July 1973 at a conference in Zurich attended by 300 delegates from 28 European countries, including several from eastern Europe. For the year 1975 (EAHY), some 50 projects were identified to exemplify the achievement and problems of historic conservation in cities all over western Europe. Conferences were held in Edinburgh, Bologna, and the small town of Krems in Austria.

The intensity with which certain countries are pursuing historic conservation can be illustrated by a report from the Netherlands (Council of Europe, 1975). Some 40,000 monuments are now protected in that country, with an annual expenditure (in 1974) of 160 million florins for restoration. The 1961 Monuments Act designates not only houses, churches, farms, mills, town halls, and castles, but also village views, areas of old buildings, canals, and associated greenery. All monuments protected are more than fifty years old. The Dutch government is now registering buildings up to 1924.

The activity of conservationists is formalized in most countries. In western Europe conservation specialists work in planning departments or as consultants. In eastern Europe they work in separate conservation agencies (see Marasovic, this volume). Conservators in Poland, for instance, have sizable departments, separate from city architects' offices, and responsible for historic areas. The conflicts between conservation and development are therefore institutionalized, each with an advocate. The development agencies are the more powerful, but the conservators have exclusive power over their historic areas.

The historic conservation movement, from its origins in the nineteenth century, has passed through a number of phases and is still very much a field of controversy. The questions revolve around how to deal with the past, what to preserve, how much, and in what ways.

The original motive of historic conservation was patriotism. The preservation of a country's monuments, its religious, regal, aristocratic, and military complexes reinforced its sense of identity. Such monuments were almost always buildings used by the powerful, and it is these which still attract the tourists. These are the places that Mac-Cannell argues are "sacralized" by society. One cannot visit Rome without going to St. Peter's and the Roman Forum, or London without paying homage to the Tower, Buckingham Palace, and Westminster Abbey. Neither can governments ignore them. They allocate considerable sums of money to their care, often for political as well as touristic

reasons. Thus, King Vittorio Emmanuele tore down medieval dwellings housing some 30,000 people to uncover parts of the Roman Forum as well as to set off his new monument to Italian unity. Iran is now busily restoring and in some cases completing mosques which have not until this time been finished.

Early conservation measures imposed restrictions on the architecture, appearance, and use of historic buildings. With no tax concessions or subsidies to cover maintenance it proved a burden for their owners. This kind of *passive* conservation entombed the historic city, turning it into a deteriorating museum, a policy now being abandoned in favor of *active* conservation. The French, for instance, now consider dropping the old term "safeguarded" areas in favor of "revitalized" or "rehabilitated" ones.

Many conservationists now espouse concepts such as "active conservation," "revitalization," and "reanimation." Such positions acknowledge the need for the social and economic life of historic centers to survive. The policy of active conservation has its problems, however. That neutral-sounding term can lead to wholesale commercial takeover of historic places, leaving very little of the authentic past. In Diocletian's Palace at Split, nearly all styles of conservation have been tried out,

From neo-classical concepts of purification, which fortunately remained only in the conceptual stage here, to romantic restorations and so-called scientific preservation, first in the passive sense and finally, for the present, in the active sense. (Marasovic, this volume)

As the field of conservation became professionalized, works of aesthetic merit as well as places of historic significance became codified. Many began to view their work as a science, using new tools and techniques to detect the relics of different eras in the quest for authenticity. Careful and exhaustive surveys are now made to establish detailed typologies of different styles and building types (see Marasovic, this volume). For many, the sole aim is to seek knowledge. The destiny of the studied places is often irrelevant, since the findings are recorded in photographs and in books. Other "purists" seek to restore such buildings in exactly their original shape if the evidence is available, treating free interpretation, replication, or artistic license as unwarranted fakery.

Other conservationists have extended their concerns from buildings and monuments to the conservation of whole quarters. As Fergusson affirms, wiping away the settings to historic monuments undermines their meaning. Besides, these old quarters have aesthetic and social meanings in their own right. Journals like *Architectural Review* have long argued the value and delight of "townscape." Townscapists worry less about the individual buildings or interiors than the texture of floorscape, vistas, sequences, landmarks, street furniture, signs, lamps, and so on; the "experience" of the place. (Cullen, 1961; Worskett, 1969; de Wolfe, 1963). Their work has been extremely influential in the conservation of British cities. By emphasizing outdoor perspectives and photography and developing notation systems for recording the character of the townscape experience, they have developed a set of techniques that both lend value to the picturesque and provide a means of recreating it. It is surface conservation and therefore scorned by the purists, but though it is a less rigorous view of buildings than that of the architectural historians, it may be a perception closer to that of the urban resident and certainly the tourist. It also allows more flexibility in adapting uses. The danger is that picturesque, genteel, but essentially similar veneers will be coated over all historic cities and quarters, until they have no depth or difference.

There is no doubt that successful conservation tends to produce a rather unreal atmosphere. Buildings may be perfectly restored but any feeling of a living city has evaporated, sunk without a trace beneath a pile of tourist trinkets or a blanket of middle-class gentility, expressed not by the so-called vulgarity of the neon lights but by the pallid pink glow from the carriage lamp. At a superficial level we should rid ourselves of the view that conservation means tidiness and come to accept that a little more natural vulgarity helps. (Worskett, 1977, p. 19)

We can then distinguish between *surface* and *deep* conservation whether passive or active. Surface conservation attends to the external appearance and character of historical areas. In the center of Rome, passive conservation has controlled the appearance of buildings without active programs of external upgrading. The old city with its peeling paint and sun-washed facades looks authentically old. But the interiors have been modernized (see Ronchi, this volume). In Warsaw the old center was reconstructed in exact historical form while the interiors were altered. In Norwich, England, the Civic Trust, following townscape principles, sponsored the repainting of facades and sign controls in an attempt to restore the earlier townscape.

Deep conservation attempts to restore a historic environment in a rigorous, complete, and accurate form, inside as well as outside. While many historic buildings have been so preserved, the efforts of cities like Bologna have been to integrate deep restoration with active reuse (see Bandarin, this volume). In Bologna, this scientific study of urban morphology has achieved exorcist proportions. Highly detailed surveys of building history and typological classifications have been undertaken with the sustained enthusiasm of archaeologists or ecologists. This digging to the roots seems to be in part an environmental reaction to the corruption of Italian capitalism and the instability of the state, and in part a rejection of the picturesque values that tourism and townscapers have projected on Italian towns (de Wolfe, 1963). However, while the uncovering of historical form may be authentic, the conversion to livable occupancy unavoidably coats those roots with a veneer of modernity. Conservation too often conserves the form but modernizes the surface. The old becomes new. A common mode of avoiding this, which has become one of the conservation styles, is to strip away the surface materials and expose the brick, concrete, or wood structures (see Raban, this volume).

Another issue that brings historic conservationists and sometimes cultural groups or nations into conflict is the question of what to preserve. There are now many conflicts concerning the salvage of different eras. These *era conflicts*, between, say, whether to preserve medieval remains or dig for Roman relics beneath them, create serious dilemmas. Murals have been identified as belonging to the wrong era merely to justify their preservation. In Athens, archaeologists wish to excavate under the nineteenth-century working-class quarter of Plaka to uncover the ancient Greek city. In Jerusalem, the scene of such bitter conflicts that Israel was voted out of UNESCO, new dwellings have been built over the historic foundations on reinforced concrete piers located according to directions from archaeologists. The archaeologists will thus be able to continue their work beneath the new city, while, strangely, the new buildings atop this framework are built in stone to replicate the style of medieval dwellings. But the more serious problems in Jerusalem have been between the excavations of the Arabs and the Israelis, each group accusing the other of destroying their past. Whereas many of these conflicts are between historians of different eras, they can therefore blow up to public and even international proportions when patriotism and cultural identity are involved. In other cases, as in Istanbul, cultures willingly give up their heritage in order to "westernize" (see Cansever, this volume).

Almost a separate movement has gathered around the issues of protecting cities and neighborhoods from auto traffic and trucks. The Buchanan Report (1963) first conceptualized the conflicts between access and environment, and began a movement to create "environmental areas" in cities, where the environment for living would dominate access for traffic (see Smith, this volume). This movement has spread in Europe, making its most dramatic achievements in the increasing pedestrianization of historic centers, such as Munich, Norwich, Besançon, Uppsala, and parts of Rome and Florence. This movement's existence was symbolized by the Better Towns with Less Traffic conference, held by the Organization for Economic Cooperation and Development in Paris, April 1975 (OECD, 1975). At this conference the several ideas for controlling traffic in cities were proposed and discussed. While the mainstream of this movement involves the management of transport systems, there are several effects on the quality and conservation of neighborhoods. One of the more interesting examples of this interrelation is the *woonerven* (residential yards) of Delft, Holland, where the street environment is designed as pedestrian territory in which the car is allowed if it conforms to the rules. (Appleyard et al., 1979). This movement has still to be brought into a closer relationship with the conservation movement.

The most persistent controversy in historic conservation is over the quest for "authenticity," between deep and surface conservation. Consider the consequences of this desire within the paradigm of tourism. Following Erving Goffman's studies of front and back environmental regions,

A back region, closed to audiences and outsiders, allows concealment of props and activities that might discredit the performance out front. In other words, sustaining a firm sense of social reality requires some *mystification*. (MacCannell, 1976, p. 93)

MacCannell describes the importance, to tourists, of penetrating the authentic back regions of cities, where the people are "real" and act naturally. Tourists are forever wanting to get off the beaten track to "go with the natives." In response, those who manage tourist settings and cater to tourists now engage in "staged authenticity," allowing the tourist to penetrate or feel he has penetrated into the "real" back regions. MacCannell in fact identifies six stages on the continuum between "front" and "back." First there is the classic front region, totally dedicated to display, including all the props. Second is the touristic front region (decorated, say, with fishing nets or pots to look like an authentic back region); third, a front region totally organized to look like a back region (in other words, a simulation); fourth, a back region that is organized to be open to outsiders; fifth, a back region that is cleaned up or altered so that tourists can catch an occasional glimpse; and finally the authentic back region, closed off to the public. Historic conservation, although searching for the ultimate level of authenticity—the place as it actually was—nearly always has to be a compromise, cleaning up the authentic back regions for habitation or tourist display. Also, while a policy of deep conservation may be pursued in a physical sense, the social conservation of the existing inhabitants is often ignored, or Ceccarelli's "dummy craftsmen" are subsidized to enact the authentic life that has long gone, or a few token stores

Types of conservation

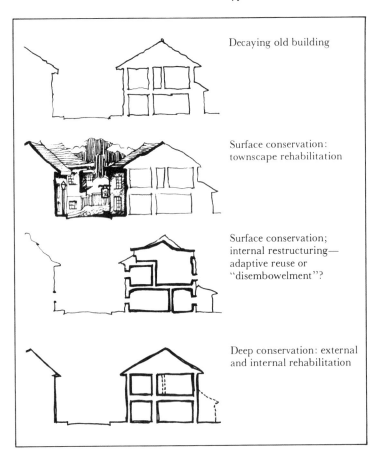

Decaying old building

Surface conservation: townscape rehabilitation

Surface conservation; internal restructuring— adaptive reuse or "disembowelment"?

Deep conservation: external and internal rehabilitation

Phases of "staged authenticity"

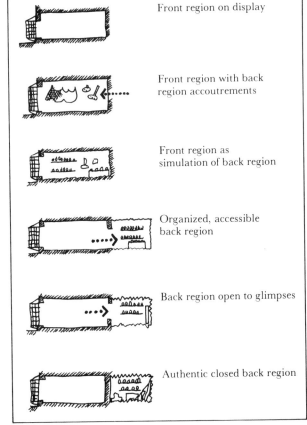

Front region on display

Front region with back region accoutrements

Front region as simulation of back region

Organized, accessible back region

Back region open to glimpses

Authentic closed back region

survive by converting to a tourist market. But this I shall address at a later time.

Criticisms of conservation in the name of authenticity take several forms. Conservationists, of course, are usually more critical of falsity than are tourists. Many Italian architects and planners are critical of the surface conservation that has taken place in Rome, where, although the ancient center appears to retain its historic integrity, many, many buildings have been internally reconstructed, i.e., adapted to new uses (see Ronchi, this volume). Although the center of Rome to the casual observer remains that same melange of ancient, medieval, Renaissance, and nineteenth-century buildings, it has in reality been "disemboweled." It has also, they say, risen half a story, through construction of surreptitious penthouse additions. Only a trained eye or long-time resident can detect the new window frames, nameplates, and roof tiling set into or behind the ancient, still peeling, facades. Here, history is curiously turned inside out. The exterior, usually a frontal display, is authentic; the back regions are false. Penetration leads not to deeper truths but to disappointment.

For those interested in preserving the townscape, this transformation does not make much difference. In fact, such adaptive reuse to keep the old center occupied could be seen as a benefit. Unfortunately, the changes in Rome have been accompanied by a population change that replaces the working-class residents with the rich. Such "gentrification," Italian-style, is bitterly attacked by Italian architects and planners, though many unwittingly spearhead it by living in such quarters themselves.

Another critique of much conservation is that it tries to "fix" a past that was produced by a flow of events, an inherently impossible task. A city, it is said, should not be turned into a museum, though individual buildings can be. In the former Summer Palace of the Russian czars at Petrovarts, the dining table is laid ready for the czar's meal, a setting admired by thousands of working people who visit the palace daily. This cannot so easily happen to cities, but it is possible. In Venice little change has occurred in living conditions for centuries. Now the population is leaving.

Much of the city is vacant. The exteriors have been preserved for the tourist, increasingly empty scenery.

A further criticism attacks the selective nature of much conservation. It records only upper-class history, and a cleaned-up version at that. The mills that created Bath's wealth have gone, and now the artisans' quarters are being "reduced to rubble." In Williamsburg, a classic example of a selectively embalmed past, only certain pieces are retained.

What Williamsburg represents is upper-class WASP history. The streets are clean; the slave cabins and outhouses have been suppressed. It is history without depth and without continuity. The clock has stopped and the past has been enshrined behind glass. . . . having put history in its niche, one can admire it and forget it. There is no spillover of history or art as a living presence able to enrich our lives. (Greiff, 1971, p. 7)

The educated complain of the kitsch in many historic places: the souvenir shops with cheap plastic replicas of the monuments, sugary colored postcards, garish china, glass, ashtrays, and other trivia. But the new conservation selects history in its own way. Authenticity is striven for through the exposure of structure and materials. By simplifying the decoration to white plaster, by introducing larger windows and clean lines, modern architects have recreated historic buildings in keeping with their own preferred imagery. The past has been remade into the modern. However elegantly this is done—in many Italian restorations, especially museums like the Uffizi and Milan's Castello Sforza, it is carried through impeccably—these places belie the wish for authenticity. We desire, in fact, a selective and modern kind of history, not the place as it actually was, but a clean modern version of it.

An accompanying problem has been the commercialization of history, a more frequent occurrence in the United States so far, but beginning in Europe. A recent criticism of Boston's new Faneuil Hall Market, restored by one of the city's better-known architects, illuminates the problem.

The preservation idiom is already a cliché as empty of imagination as the skyscraper curtain-wall was in the Sixties. "Ye Olde" design is the new kitsch of advanced capitalism, self-conscious for all its charm and boring for all its originality. Even the best use of cliché cannot give it the life that mass culture has drained from it already.

Something happened to the rootedness of the old buildings when they were scrubbed and arranged and organized. Thompson [the architect] did not purify them in the Williamsburg style, but he changed their relationship to the world around them, related them instead to a timeless, airless, placeless standard that exists outside any specific context. (Kopkind, 1977, p. 22)

All that conservation seeks, the richness and depth of the past, can become homogenized through restoration. After all, architects are part of a worldwide homogeneous culture supported by their international journals. The success of Ghirardelli Square in San Francisco has spawned a number of other restored historic-commercial centers, such as the Cannery, Gaslight Square in St. Louis, and Seattle's Pioneer Square in the United States. These places are delightful, intimate in scale, and, at first appearance, rich and diverse, all those attributes that new development lacks. But as more of them appear they exhibit the same middle-class veneer of boutiques, exposed bricks, ferns, tasteful signs, and exotic imports. In Europe, too, boutiques and other services, are spreading over formerly working-class historic centers. A San Francisco planner remarked recently with enthusiasm that Diocletian's Palace would become a Yugoslav version of Ghirardelli Square.

Admitting that as soon as we touch history it can no longer be authentic, how can we satisfy our search for "truth?" There are still many ways suggested by Mac-Cannell's typology. Some places we *do not touch*. This in fact is impossible to achieve, since the modern world inevitably touches everything, but the effort to hold off may help save some authentic historic and traditional places and populations. They will have to be subsidized in many cases to pursue their traditional lives, and basic amenities will need to be provided. This kind of conservation may no longer be possible in the more famous historic quarters which have already been transformed, but it can be achieved in other neighborhoods, such as those in Bologna, which are not yet the object of large-scale tourism. Here, the objectives of historic and social conservation may coincide.

In popular historic places, maintenance of the existing population with its traditional economic and social structure is probably impossible. Here, the authentic physical past, front and back regions, can be retained untouched, though the people will engage in modern pursuits. One of the most poignant examples is the untouched cell in what is left of the gruesome Nazi prison in Warsaw. The peeled paint, primitive furniture, battered walls, and other traces of time and human presence engrave themselves on the mind of a visitor. Places which are not overly tidied and sanitized, where the decisions and actions of the original occupants are still in evidence, can achieve an authenticity even if surrounded by a framed setting. Fragments of the past left in their original shape, if large enough to counter the dominance of modern settings, can serve as reminders (Lynch, 1974). The millstones in the walls of the underpass at Vallingby, old street pavements, furniture, foundations, facades, interiors, trees, many more things can survive demolition than are presently allowed. *Staged settings*, out in the streets if possible, with the original sounds, smells, actors, and events using the various techniques of social realism and cinema verité are likely to flourish and spread as the new antiquarians become more inventive. *Son et lumière* is only a beginning. The urban studies center in Chester, England, has a nearly full-scale medieval street, and the York Folk Museum has several streets, with shops full of nineteenth-century wares that can be touched and smelled. But they have no actors or events to compare with California's Renaissance Fayres. These simulations can intensify aspects of the historical experience by turning it into a theatrical production and thus perhaps siphon off some of the pressures on the real historic places, a policy similar to that suggested by M. H. Krieger in his "What's Wrong with Plastic Trees?" (Krieger, 1973). In Ireland tourists can now spend "medieval weekends" in old country houses, complete with wine, wassail, and medieval garments. In Hawaii's Polynesian Village, students from the islands give instruction in the skills and dances of their native villages in reconstructed settings.

Localizing History

There is a relationship between the salvage of a great relic of antiquity, far away, and the saving of only locally known notable features of one's own home city. (Preface to *The Conservation of Cities* [UNESCO, 1976])

It is common for conservation experts to believe that they, more than anyone else, know what should be preserved. It has been said of some conservators that they see historic quarters almost as their personal landscapes, just as the early archaeologists strode about their "digs" and as some planning directors view their cities. These conservation experts decide which style or epoch to preserve and in many cases redesign new old buildings (Lynch, 1975). In some cases, even in eastern Europe, inhabitants resist this domination. To them the local and personal history of the place as well as their present needs is more meaningful than official history.

Interest in the conservation of neighborhoods and the emergence of neighborhood groups and organizations may indeed be fertile soil in which the motives behind tourism can be satisfied on neighborhood turf, bringing tourism home. This is one of the drives behind the Town Trails program in Britain, described in the chapter by Brian Goodey. The *Bulletin for Environmental Education (BEE)*, under the guidance of Colin Ward and Tony Fyson, has been involved for a number of years in communicating ways in which people, especially children in schools, can learn about their local cities. The Town Trail movement has caught on in Britain, and as of 1975, 250 trails already existed. These trails are more modest in scale than America's tourist or scenic trails, but more ambitious in their intent. They are almost always pedestrian in nature and are often designed by teachers and children in the schools or enthusiastic local geographers, planners, or anyone else. As much benefit seems to be gained from designing them and making the brochures as there is from walking them. Participants are often asked to draw their own image maps and to make notes for intergroup communication. The walks are not only historic. Many are issue-based, taking people to urban problems, while others are designed to reveal how the city functions, as well as its origins. Their intention is to expand people's awareness of their own city, at all levels. As one participant put it, "The last few days have been an eye-opener for me. I had no idea what went on behind these factory walls . . . I was handed brochures and found that the furniture they made was for our school." (Goodey, this volume).

Most neighborhood conservation today is home-oriented, private rehabilitation. Neighborhoods are coalescing around outside threats, but knowledge of and care for the neighborhood or local community as a historical environment is much more rare. For one thing, many of the enthusiasts for conservation are newcomers to these neighborhoods with little idea of their history. The call for the conservation of local and recent history (Lynch, 1972) will not receive much response unless some self-reflexive programs like those for town trails first encourage awareness of it. Here is an opportunity for neighborhoods and communities to discover the history of their own settings, a history they can actively uncover, care for, and, if necessary, forget. It could be much more satisfying than the remote history of important but distant places.

Decaying Neighborhoods

The historic city has been, until now, either guarded by the antiquarians or exploited by commerce. It is time that ordinary citizens took part. The questions remain, whose history are we to conserve? and what about the present inhabitants? The conservation search must acknowledge the pluralism of history and the current city. The social conflicts that have emerged in the centers of European cities have alerted leaders of the conservation movement to present social realities.

People in positions of responsibility . . ., conservationists and planners alike, today acknowledge that it would be futile to try to safeguard an architectural heritage through action affecting only its physical aspects. A conservation policy must fit in with economic and social objectives.

Thus stated Professor Alfred Schmid in a keynote speech to the 1975 Council of Europe Congress on the European Architectural Heritage. What does this mean?

While European cities have not experienced the degree of deterioration evident in most American central cities, many of the working-class neighborhoods discussed in this book, in London and Bolton, in Istanbul and Venice, Split and Bologna, Amsterdam and Stockholm, suffer from dilapidation, crowding, lack of elementary sanitation, poor daylight, lack of open space, heavy traffic, noise, fumes, and other disamenities. Physical age is one of the major causes; the departure of the young and active, leaving the old and poor, is another. The remaining populations have no interest in historic conservation; they are plagued by the problems of poverty and poor living conditions. There are other reasons, too.

Charles McKean, in his book *Fight Blight,* lists the causes of blight in British cities. Delay in implementation of local authorities' plans is a major reason. In neighborhoods designated as Comprehensive Development Areas, the length of time it takes councils to acquire all the buildings and demolish them has been as long as fifteen years, during which time the area becomes "derelict, vandalized and dangerous." The routes of new motorways, arterials, and roadwidenings have also been plagued by blight through governmental acquisition. These are similar to American situations, even though public housing rather than middle- and upper-income housing may ultimately be built. Many programs of acquisition have outstripped councils' ability to rebuild. A recent study found that 75 percent of vacant land in inner city areas is publicly owned. Authorities are under little pressure to do anything about it. Many are waiting unrealistically for developers to come along. Other areas are left out of current programs. Public bodies such as railways, the military, the utility companies, and port authorities are all careless with their land. Changing social patterns render certain building types obsolete, and they deteriorate, without sufficient financing to maintain them. Churches are a good example. Zoning has forced small industries from residential areas and housing from commercial areas, often leaving the empty shells. Traffic has made some buildings unlivable.

All this has contributed to a general image of Britain's inner cities that is dominated by shabbiness, dereliction, dilapidation, and blight. This in itself worsens the situation.

In this deteriorating climate, outside planners and conservationists, who depend on appearance, too easily misperceive the concerns of the residents. Conservationists see the need for salvaging the physical heritage, the elegant but decaying facades, the wastelands, and the scruffy backyards, while the residents are concerned about jobs, sanitation, traffic, and safe places for children. Cities, in some cases, see the population itself as a detriment to the area, particularly new, poor, and foreign migrants.

In Grenoble, known as one of the more progressive French cities, it happens to be young Algerian men who come to France for a few years, and then return to Algeria. Their neighborhood, vividly described by d'Arcy, has traditionally been the entry point into the city but has always been viewed by conservative citizens as a "cancer" to be cleaned away. It is well known as the site of illegal activities of various kinds, and the Algerians are seen as the predominant group. A deeper study of the social ecology reveals a much more heterogeneous population than the visible Algerians. Stable Italian and Portuguese families also live there, but seldom come out of their houses. D'Arcy describes this street as a finely balanced community performing an important function for various groups in the city. But unlike other, quieter, populations, who can often be ignored in the interests of conservation, the group here is a visible, provocative, intractable "problem" for Grenoble's middle-class residents.

The difficulties of dealing with these neighborhoods are as formidable as those in the United States, though European governments allocate more money to public housing. The old solutions of tearing them down and replacing them with new apartments is increasingly in question, yet the new efforts to rehabilitate and conserve neighborhood character have their own problems.

Pioneering and Gentrification

Another "solution" to the difficulties of financing historic and physical conservation is to allow or encourage the private market to rehabilitate the housing. It usually means a middle- or upper-class invasion of lower-class neighborhoods. The British label this process by the deceptively quaint expression, "gentrification." It is a common phenomenon in European cities and is beginning to spread in the United States.

Gentrification has not yet been studied systematically. Most commonly it is a private process involving a chain of "gentrifiers." Those who spearhead invasions of lower-income districts are in fact more like "pioneers" than gentry. They are often students, artists, and design professionals looking for cheap accommodation and interested in living in mixed neighborhoods. They seem to experience the sense of adventure associated with camping in the wilderness. They are often single people or couples without children. In the Trastevere, the Jordaan, Chelsea, and Islington, Telegraph Hill and Greenwich Village, the process has inexorably transformed the character of historic quarters. It occurs in many eastern European cities, too.

Ironically many of the complaints about gentrification come mostly from the pioneers. Jane Jacob's book *The Death and Life of Great American Cities* described the same richness of life in Greenwich Village that used to attract artists to the Trastevere in Rome. The pioneer migrants are usually welcome and only marginally affect the social life in such an area. However, they usually do not wish to live under the same conditions as the inhabitants and therefore improve their dwellings. As more are attracted, the neighborhood becomes socially mixed, still retaining much of its original character, but it becomes "chic" and relatively safe even for more conventional young professionals, executives, secretaries, and the like. By this time, real-estate speculators are actively buying, converting, and selling. The pioneers resent the destruction of character caused by the gentrifiers, sometimes even more than the original working-class population. The area loses its "life" and "integrity." The old bars or wine shops fold. Boutiques, art galleries, specialty shops, and high-priced restaurants take their place. Everyone mourns the passing of working-class culture, especially

those (we?) who initiate its demise. The physical process of change in all its surreptitious manifestations is described vividly in Lisa Ronchi's personal experience of living in Rome and her sequences of neighborhood photographs (this volume). In the next chapter, the social process and what it means to a community is recounted with telling satire by Jonathan Raban in an extract from his fascinating book, *Soft City*. Here are the "young pioneers," living in elegant austerity, trying to penetrate the in-group humor of the working-class remnants, a story of unwanted patronage that is taking place even today in many American cities. Some pictures of the Jordaan illustrate the contrasts between the environments of the pioneers and the old working class.

Why does gentrification occur? Why do the affluent wish to return to or now stay in the central city? In the words of François d'Arcy:

Why is it that now, at least, part of the upper classes are not able to create their space anymore and are going back to spaces created by their ancestors? In other terms, what we define as rehabilitating is to try to reimpose old values on what a city is, on those buildings, those areas, which have been completely left to all the people and which have been uninteresting for the upper classes for a certain period of time. But we must also consider that if we of the upper class go back to these areas and again try [to impose] our values in how we say they should be used, then the people who are occupying the space have to move out. What is the reason why the upper class is no longer able to create its own space? Is it a lack of imagination about what the space should be or is it . . . that what we suffer is not so much that we don't like the space that we've created but the segregation [in the suburbs] into which we are forced in the attempt to go back to the central spaces in the city? Are we looking for aesthetic values or for a kind of . . . community which would include all the groups of a society so that we won't live in a segregated society?. . . The economic rules of the occupation of space which prevail, at least in western society, no longer allow the coexistence of different income groups in the same space.

Traditionally the affluent have led the expansion of the city, creating new neighborhoods for themselves and leaving their former residences to the next group down the social ladder. An area like Islington in London was built as a middle-income speculative development in the 1860s, with pleasant Georgian terraces and squares. By the early 1900s these groups were moving north to the new suburbs, and by the 1930s and after World War II the houses had been subdivided into working-class apartments. Not until the 1960s was the area "discovered" by the middle-class professionals who were finding Chelsea, Kensington, and Hampstead too expensive and were searching for new inner locations. Housing originally built for the middle classes has more spacious accommodations than new housing. This cycle has been called "re-gentrification" by one British cabinet Minister. The reasons for the return of the middle class must be several. First, it is usually the young unmarried or just-marrieds who constitute the primary groups wanting to live in the inner city. Then there are those with families who can afford private schools and second homes in the country. These groups reject the suburbs, with their emphasis on conventional family life and values, for the inner city world of change, fashion, diversity, and the stimulating social life of parties, meetings, celebrations, the outdoor cafes and coffeehouses. The flavor added by the presence of "colorful" working-class groups is not only exciting; it assuages some of the middle-class guilt by creating an appearance of heterogeneous living, of "slumming it" with the poor, though much of it is actually played out in the romantic and patronizing vein that Tom Wolfe calls "radical chic."

While private gentrification is difficult to control, many planning actions can encourage it. Historic and neighborhood conservation programs are among these. Though less visible, provocative, and brutal than urban redevelopment projects, they can have the same effects. Many physical planners turn a blind eye to the issues of social conservation or naïvely hope that rehabilitation will not lead to removal. Others actively collaborate with authorities to clean out undesirables in the name of economic survival or development of the center city. In these cases people cannot be blamed for seeing conservation as simply a more subtle way for the affluent to take over working- and lower-class territory.

Such concerns were expressed in tentative terms by one of the participants at the 1975 Rome workshop:

Planners have a very bad name in certain local areas . . . because of redevelopment that is synonymous with removal. I fear that somehow . . . we are taking a similar position, when we claim that the middle class is in a better position to maintain historical buildings than the previous lower income group. It is probably true that they can pay the rents and probably create a tax base that is better than the previous group, but I'm trying to look at this whole problem about the image of planning and the image of planners in the city, especially in certain parts of the city, in the lower income areas . . . how planning has been moving now more with the power structure and the economic structure in the city. I mean, in many ways, they're technicians. Is this going to be continued and [will] preservation and conservation be a new enemy to the community, I mean the lower income community who live in that area? Will it be synonymous with removal? . . . We can use all very subtle historical terms and we can support operas and cinemas and all those cultural things that the nineteenth century city was known for. The argument now is going to be very deeply embedded in an ideological mystification. . . . Before I think it was more brutal, at least for the people who lived in the area, . . . and now I see a very subtle soft approach. . . .

But even for socially conscious planners, conservation creates a recurring dilemma, for as soon as environmental conditions are improved, a neighborhood almost inevitably becomes attractive to a higher social group. In the next section I shall discuss some of the efforts to counteract this tendency and to understand the complexity of inner city rehabilitation. The extent of gentrification appears to vary considerably among European cities. In southern Europe, at least in Italy, more of the affluent have always lived in the center than in Britain, where the single house has always been more popular. In Rome and Bologna it appears that the working classes have a precarious foothold in the center city. In London, on the other hand, gentrification dominates only in certain areas (see Shankland, Willmott, and Jordan, this volume).

Toward Integrated Conservation?

The case studies presented here, from Plaka in Athens to London, England, provide a range of experiences, positive and negative, technical and political, from different European cities. Each essay deals in varying degrees with *physical conservation,* the preservation or restoration of the urban fabric for aesthetic or historical and touristic reasons; or the improvement of the physical fabric in order to make a neighborhood sufficiently livable for modern standards; and, *social conservation,* the maintenance in that neighborhood of the existing population. These goals are frequently in conflict, and cities tend to emphasize one or two rather than all three, though paying them all lip service. Indeed, it is difficult in many instances to detect what actual living conditions are like unless social surveys are reported. It is also difficult to tell the nature of the existing population, let alone predict its survival possibilities after conservation programs are carried through. Further, the pressures on planners to be optimistic when reporting their country's work at international meetings are extremely powerful, even though the Rome conference actively tried to encourage critical viewpoints. These papers do not, then, answer all the questions one would like to ask about each city, but they do provide clues.

Starting with Plaka in the context of capitalist Greece, and Split in Communist Yugoslavia, we are offered two essays by architectural historians who clearly have some social concerns. Both neighborhoods lie atop or amid ancient ruins. In Plaka, below the Acropolis in Athens, a neighborhood of mostly nineteenth-century or older buildings is sandwiched between the pressures of the archaeologists, who wish to uncover a substratum of ancient Greek remains that lie beneath the quarter, and the tourists, who flock to the district for evening entertainment in its restaurants and nightclubs. Both threatening groups are probably American! The existing population, part middle-class and part working-class, suffers from noise, traffic, and other unpleasant living conditions. It is not clear, however, if objections come from both classes. It could be that the middle-class residents object to the envi-

ronmental nuisances, while the working-class community earns its living from the entertainment.

Inventories were made of buildings and uses, and population questionnaires were distributed. A majority of the residents belong to the middle- and upper-income groups, though it is not clear whether these are newly arrived "gentry" or of long residential standing. The population nevertheless is considerably mixed. About half would prefer to keep the old facades while modernizing the interiors. Complaints about environmental conditions relate as already mentioned to the nuisance created by the entertainment facilities and their accompanying traffic.

The physical conservation problems of Plaka are those of era conflict. The dilemma is whether to conserve the existing surface buildings or to dig below the surface to explore the ruins. Dionysis Zivas is against the archaeologists. In his essay he proposes to designate the entire area as a historic quarter, creating an institution that would grant owners long-term loans at low-interest rates to introduce modern comforts, restore the old, or reconstruct compatible new buildings. Unwilling owners would have to sell or have their property expropriated. Other policies would restrict traffic in the area, build some parking garages, and control the visual intrusiveness of entertainment signs. The primary concerns of this report are for the aesthetic preservation of existing buildings and improved livability for the residents, as against the desires of the archaeologists. No distinction is made of attitudinal differences among the mixed population; neither are measures to control rent increases proposed. The probability is that the lower-income population will not be able to remain in the quarter.

Diocletian's Palace in Split is a small city in itself—a building that is a city. While some 3000 working-class people still live in the former place of splendor (under damp and dilapidated housing conditions), and many of the larger storage areas off the main pedestrian routes are now unused, the current plan foresees turning ground floors into public use, for tourist offices, educational and cultural institutions, catering, etc. Old houses will be modernized, reducing densities; pedestrian traffic will be spread to reduce congestion; parking lots will be constructed around the palace; and the original sewer system will be reactivated, electric wires removed, and new lighting installed to illuminate the monuments. We do not know whether the existing population will be able to stay there after this restoration, but it is known that the planners favor public uses rather than private ones for the palace itself. The report by Marasovic has official backing. It is technical in nature and describes the various archaeological, building condition, and demographic surveys that give a clear picture of the situation, lacking only a social survey of resident attitudes toward living in the palace. The difficulties of sorting out which of the different eras to preserve are not discussed, although this must be a problem. The poor living conditions are described in terms of dilapidation. It is not clear whether neighborhood living conditions are tolerable, though the palace is already a pedestrian precinct. Neither do we know whether the low-income population would prefer to stay or leave. The plans in any case are to reduce densities and to convert the ground floors to business, public, and tourist uses in a program of active revitalization. The presence of three agencies responsible for Split's planning, a conservation agency, a housing, and a planning agency, suggests a simple and straightforward decision-making process. There is no hint of conflicts between these agencies, but in other eastern European countries such conflicts are well known. Jiri Hruza, the Deputy Chief Architect for Prague, made this point at a 1970 conference in Split, speaking, presumably, of Czech experience:

According to general opinion, a permanent struggle exists between the preservationists and historians on the one side and the city planners and architects on the other side. City politicians are appearing as arbiters, influenced mainly by the possibilities of the city budget and short term demands. The preservationist is sometimes the little-bit too eccentric defender of the historical and cultural heritage. On the contrary the city planner is often the one-sided practical man, who is able to sacrifice immense historical values in favor of his dreams or in favor of some trivial and questionable necessity of everyday life.

It should be remembered that most European planners, and especially those from eastern Europe, are from the modern architectural tradition.

We find, in Plaka and Split, quite different priorities. In the former, comfort of the existing population receives priority over the archaeological remains and the tourist. However, the remains, unlike those in Split, are below the ground and difficult to reach. In Split planners appear more concerned with historic preservation and conversion to public uses that would encourage tourism. Conditions will be improved for some of the existing population, but densities will be reduced. It would be interesting to explore further whether these differences are due to the political systems of the two communities or the different physical conditions.

The situation of Venice, reported by Paolo Ceccarelli, is perhaps the gloomiest in the book. Venice is a city which draws out the strongest feelings from us all. Its ethereal setting in the placid lagoon, the pastel pinks, reds, and yellows of its ornamented palaces and ordinary houses reflecting in the waters of its canals filled with plying watercraft; its crowded *calli* and bridges, its *campi* with their magnificent parochial churches, surrounding shops and bars, and (now closed) wells, a seemingly perfect expression of its social life; the mysteries of San Marco, the glowing hues of Giorgone, Titian, Tintoretto and Carpaccio, concerts on San Giorgio or in the Fenice, the boat trips out to isolated Torcello with its hovering Madonna, the glassblowers on Burano, and the succulent Venetian cuisine, all these still make it a unique city.

It was evidently decaying, and tourism was clearly its principal activity, but when, in early November 1966. the *acqua alta* (high water) rose over two meters above its normal peak and stayed that way, the disaster suddenly alerted the world to what had been creeping on gradually for many years.

. . . the scene looked like a gigantic funeral. Skeletons of boats blocked the calli (streets). Great black smears of fuel oil besmirched walls and pavements. Mattresses, chairs, tables, and garbage were scattered everywhere; dead pigeons, rats, and cats floated in the canals. Debris choked every basement, every ground floor. Almost every store in the city had been devastated, as had hundreds of artisans' workshops. Thousands of library books had been destroyed. Furniture had been ruined in flooded houses, public documents in lawyers' offices. Sixteen thousand ground floor residents had been deprived of all their possessions and damage estimates ranged as high as $64 million. The injury done to statues, paintings, frescoes, palaces and churches was all but incalculable. (Davis, 1973, p. 126)

The news that Venice is sinking has become embedded in the international mind. It is a vivid image. The disaster triggered an international aid program under the aegis of UNESCO and the Italian government, and the full dimensions of the Venetian "crisis" are now more clearly known than ever before. The problems are multiple.

The flooding was indeed caused partly by the sinking of the city, itself due to the tapping of artesian wells by industry and the city itself, which extracted supporting ground water. But the ecology of the lagoon has also been altered by extensive fill of the *barene*, the tidal flats, and the dredging of a deep water channel to Marghera, which have accentuated dramatically the tidal action. Also, over six thousand tankers navigate the Venetian lagoon annually. These, with the *motoscafi* and other fast-moving watercraft, are eating away at building foundations. Dampness is rising to affect paintings and murals, and air pollution from Marghera's petrochemical plants, from domestic heating furnaces and guano from the city's 50,000 pigeons have affected some 35 percent of the city's external sculpture with marble "cancer" or other forms of disintegration. At times now, *acqua bassa*, low water, is as much a problem as *acqua alta*, since it fails to take the sewage away and exposes lower walls, creating unhealthy conditions. The *acqua bassa* also withdraws horizontal support from building foundations, further weakening them.

But the crisis finally brought international attention to Venice, and in the long run its physical structure may be saved. National and international organizations and corporations have flocked to assist the city in distress. The national government, through a special law, allocated near-ly $500 million to the city in 1972, almost none of which has been spent. The inflatable dam may be built across the Malamocco entrance to the lagoon, the air pollution controlled, sewage systems constructed, paintings, sculpture, palaces, and monuments restored. But while all of this may occur, housing is likely to be rehabilitated only for those who can afford it.

Ceccarelli's paper, which spends little time on the physical problems of Venice, brings up forcefully the question of *social conservation*, the preservation of a social life that has existed for centuries, the opportunity for working Venetians to stay on their island. Today, that social life is disintegrating. While Venetians move out—the population fell from 192,000 people in 1951 to fewer than 100,000 in 1971 and in 1976 was estimated at 80,000—the lower-income migrants come in from Friuli and other regions. Housing lies vacant; the dialects that distinguished one quarter of the city from another are merged; even the Venetian dialect is contaminated. The population could become as transient as the tourists, temporary visitors in an alien shell.

The most difficult problem is the state of the city's housing. A special survey conducted under UNESCO auspices ascertained that of approximately 40,000 dwellings, between 17,000 and 19,000 needed repair. Two-thirds of the ground floor flats are unsuitable for habitation. One-third of all apartments surveyed were under 60 square meters in floor area. 48 percent had no heating or inadequate heating, 19 percent had less than 2 hours of sunlight in 24 hours, while 45 percent had only 2 to 4 hours. Nearly one-half of the houses showed signs of damp (Rinaldi, 1976). This catalogue of decay was accompanied by a questionnaire survey which confirmed that 33 percent of Venetians, mostly manual workers, wished to move out of their houses, even though 87 percent wished to remain on the island of Venice. There are other difficulties of life in Venice. Private cars must be parked in the huge and expensive parking garages in the Piazzale Roma. To travel, say, to the hospital is a slow and difficult journey along the canals.

The conclusion is that the Venetian population is being forced to move, reluctantly, out of the city, because of poor housing. Indeed considerable numbers now commute to work in Venice from suburban Mestre. The outward-moving population are, as usual, the younger generation leaving the old and the poor to live with the rich, in the decaying historical center.

Ceccarelli is concerned with living conditions and social conservation. He is not worried about the monuments. They will be taken care of. Indeed, the latest news indicates that the closing of the wells has halted the sinking foundations. The population's future is more in doubt. After the 1975 local elections, a swing to the left broke the impasse in the local city council, though conflicts with the more conservative regional government remained. Even so, for those concerned primarily with social conservation, rehabilitation of the dilapidated housing will be extremely difficult. There are no vacant building sites as in Bologna, so that people cannot be accommodated locally while their houses are repaired. And there is little trust of any government among the Venetians. Also, the large numbers of small ownerships require a complex system of allocations and rent controls that even an efficient bureaucracy would find difficult to manage equitably. It is likely that the housing program will proceed no more quickly than that of Bologna, if it gets going.

While Venice is in deep trouble, Bologna has established an enviable reputation for sensitive physical *and* social conservation. The principal features of this program are described in the chapter by Francesco Bandarin. Bologna has many advantages over Venice. A relatively homogeneous community, it has had a stable Communist city government for many years, and it has not had the kind of tourist or private development pressures experienced by Venice and Rome.

The moderate Communist government has prided itself on efficiency and clean government and has been innovative in a number of planning fields. On the one hand it has conducted extremely careful and rigorous studies of historic building types, designating them for different levels of restoration, and more importantly it has seriously worked at maintaining and even bringing back the working-class population that was moving out to the new suburban hous-

ing estates. This has been a relatively recent change in policy from suburban to inner city investment, one that seeks to retain a working-class constituency in the inner city. The city commune originally proposed a program for expropriating property in the inner city, rehabilitating it with public funds and treating it as public housing. The program aroused intense opposition from homeowners, many of whom were single homeowners or small businessmen, part of the party's constituency. The commune converted the program to one of subsidy and concentrated on a long-term covenant to protect tenants from rent increases or eviction. Grants or loans are provided to building owners. The covenant stipulates that no speculators be involved, and the permanence of actual inhabitants is guaranteed. Rents are to be related to income and will be within the range of public housing rents, that is, about 12 percent of income. The commune has also built new housing in the historic center, following the typology of the original medieval houses, on World War II bombed sites, places that a city like Venice lacks. Low-income residents are then moved into these houses while their own dwellings are rehabilitated. This "rolling" program involves considerable citizen participation and, given its sensitivity to the historic ambience and needs of the residents, is very slow and costly. Only about 300 dwellings have so far been rehabilitated.

The program must therefore be considered more a model of how this kind of work can be carried out than a large-scale program. Its reputation rests on the quality of the work so far done, the thoughtfulness of its methods, and its superb publicity. But the city has set a standard that other Italian cities such as Milan, Bergamo, Pesaro, Brescia, and Ancona are now striving to emulate. Bologna has other innovative programs, such as its free (during rush hour) transit system, social service programs, and vacations for the elderly, that also aid inner city inhabitants.

Can the Bologna experience be exported to Venice? At a 1975 UNESCO meeting in Venice at the time that the new Socialist-Communist coalition had just taken over the Venetian government, opinions varied. One of Bologna's planners remarked that just as Bologna exports salami around the world, so it will export conservation planning.

Indeed, its publicity has that export clearly in mind. Yet a prominent Communist educator from Venice at the same conference announced that Bologna's experience had no relevance for Venice. Who knows? Rivalry between cities over who can develop the most sensitive conservation programs is not, after all, an unhealthy trend. The paradox is that a political party committed historically to revolution should so completely embrace conservation. The Communists become the true conservatives, while capitalism tears the old city apart, disrupting its social and physical structure. Such a stance has presented a reassuring image to the Italian middle classes, so long as it is Communism in kid gloves. In the words of Bologna's slogan, "Conservation is Revolution."

Danish conservation and "slum clearance" legislation, similar to British conservation area laws, allows the government and municipality to subsidize landlords who improve their property, if designated by the city as of architectural or historical interest. In return rents must stay at the same level.

Elsinore, a charming country town, has been chosen as one of the first cities in Denmark in which to test the effects of this legislation. A rather simple survey of buildings to be preserved was made throughout the city, after which the city proposed certain priority areas for conservation. Much, however, will depend on private initiative, since there is little public subsidy.

The interesting dimension to the Elsinore study is its detailed social survey. Although it does not tell exactly who lives in the inner city, since it is not a random sample, we gather that the inner city inhabitants are rather older, of higher status, and less family-oriented than the suburban control groups. Fascinating is their contrast in attitudes. Those who live in the center are more satisfied with their housing than suburbanites by 54 percent to 36 percent, despite its poorer quality. Yet they have more detailed complaints about it. Apparently, despite the nuisance, they prefer the atmosphere of living in the center and probably the better access. There is a certain self-selection, the sub-urban population being somewhat less attracted to the old houses and more to modern housing than the center sample. Inner city residents complain about the noise, traffic, and taverns and are in favor of rearranging backyards for gardens and play space, but not for parking. Their most common desire is for home ownership. One-third of those in the center would like to move, but mostly to other places within the center. The inner city residents are treated as a homogeneous group, which is almost certainly not the case. Differences in status as well as ownership will lead to different demands.

In the end, fears that the rehabilitation program will increase rents are widespread. Suggestions are made that the municipality acquire housing and sell or rent to lower-income groups at the same rents as public housing, a program similar to that proposed for Bologna that would require extensive subsidies. So far, a small amount of housing has been rehabilitated.

The Jordaan neighborhood in the heart of Amsterdam, built between the seventeenth and nineteenth centuries (about one-quarter of the buildings are designated public monuments), contains a mixed middle- and working-class population of over 20,000 at densities of about 215 dwellings per hectare. Nearly one-half of the buildings are "dilapidated." Earlier plans called for extensive "improvements," including "traffic corridors, parking garages, open space, and space for low cost housing." These were turned down by citizen opposition because they "would have left little of the historic character of the neighborhood." The intent was to reduce the population from 20,000 to 12,000, a plan that a local newspaper called a "threat," presumably to families with children.

The present plans, reported here by Hans Davidson from the city's Planning Section are much more modest, but even they are problematic. The zoning plan "dictates" a ratio of 50 percent 3-room, 25 percent larger-than-3-room, and 25 percent 2-room apartments. This means increasing space for apartments and reducing businesses, especially those that cause traffic problems. Other plans call for the cleaning out of courtyards, parking restrictions, plans for more open space, selective public acquisition of sites for new developments, private rehabilitation, and traffic controls. The report complains that small-lot ownership is frustrating the planning, but this may be what is preserving the character of the neighborhood. The planners apparently would like to make larger-scale changes.

All these appear to be sensitive proposals, yet one gathers that they are still meeting with community resistance. There is a citizen participation program, but the report tells little about the types of citizens living in the area or whether the proposals come from the citizens or the planners; whether gentrification is taking place, or what exactly the conflicts are. A later visit, summarized in a postscript, clarified some of these questions.

While conditions in central Amsterdam have deteriorated, the population (820,400 in 1971) is declining at the rate of 10,000 a year. Those who stay tend to be "the elderly, single people, small, newly-formed families, and those with low incomes." The city proposes a program of reconstruction, conservation, and renewal that will require government subsidy for as much as 80 or 90 percent of its funds. This money does not yet appear available in the Jordaan.

In the Stockholm case, reported, not by the planning agency, but by an outside observer, Thomas Miller, we obtain a more rounded sense of that particular social and political situation. The Birka district, less than a mile from the center of Stockholm, was built in the nineteenth century to a uniform height of five or six stories, lining the streets and packing the centers of blocks. As in Amsterdam the population has diminished from 18,000 in 1920, mostly working-class families in one- and two-room flats, to its present 6,000, 72 percent of whom are professionals and white collar workers. As late as the early 1960's it was thought by planners and architects "to be self-evident that Birka should be razed and replaced by new housing." By 1970, however, Stockholm's population stopped increasing. New residential areas have "huge" vacancy rates, though there are few vacancies in the inner city. Investors are now turn-

ing their attention to the inner city, while officials are worried about a diminishing tax base because of the aging inner city population. The city now wants to "balance" the population by enlarging apartments for families. Rehabilitation would be carried out by private speculation. Herein lies the conflict, for though one-third of the residents would like their apartments improved, they could not afford the rent increases of larger apartments. They banded together; a newssheet, nine block communities, and a public meeting at which 1300 showed up resulted in a petition demanding guarantees that tenants should have the right to move back into the buildings and of maintenance of reasonable rents, tenant "influence" over planning, and an attack on the "25-50-25" guidelines. In a fascinating discussion of the effects of the consultations, originally initiated by the municipality, Miller shows how they served as a catalyst to mobilize the tenants into a previously nonexistent community that has now exerted powerful pressures on the municipality, even changing rehabilitation policies in another part of the city. The landlords, on the other hand, did not participate in the discussions since they had "nothing to gain." They therefore seem to have lost.

Britain is the European country most accessible to Americans because of a common language. Planning in Britain has a long and well-known history. Conservation has been an important part of it. The Town and Country Planning Association grew out of the Garden Cities Association, which was founded in 1899. The Council for the Preservation of Rural England was formed in 1926, the Georgian Group in 1937, and the Victorian Society in 1958. There was no national urban conservation organization, however, until the formation of the Central Council of Civic Societies, which was largely superseded by the Civic Trust, formed in 1957. At the same time hundreds of local amenity societies had sprouted in different communities by 1974. These amenity groups began actively to combat urban development in the late sixties, and the Civic Trust was largely responsible for the legislation regarding Conservation Areas (CAs) described by David Smith in his paper.

Smith actually describes two parallel pieces of British legislation, one devoted to the establishment of conservation areas, the other focusing on more general environmental improvement, public health, and rehabilitation. These are described in greater detail in his book on *Amenity and Urban Planning* (1974), from which this paper is extracted.

The General Improvement Area (GIA) program came at a time when the government's new housing program was going too slowly, and when reaction to wholesale redevelopment projects was setting in. The program provided subsidies both to individual home owners and to local authorities, who have been involved in redesign of street patterns, landscaping, etc., as well as house improvement. The Conservation Area program, concentrating on areas of historical or architectural importance, also provides state grants.

The experience of the GIA and CA programs has differed between London and the southeast and the rest of the country. In London, where housing is scarce, grants were given extensively to home owners and therefore gave a strong push to speculation and gentrification. Although rents were controlled, landlords managed to "winkle" tenants out of flats through bribery or neglect. In other British cities housing demand is weaker and there were fewer applicants for funding. As Smith points out, therefore, the context of the housing market powerfully influences what happens in residential neighborhoods.

The British legislation was originally couched in physical terms with an inadequate discussion of its social consequences. Grants were made available to anyone who applied. Many of the more blatant effects of gentrification are now being dampened through more careful review of cases, and a new program of Housing Action Areas has been initiated.

Smith's description of the GIA in Bolton, Lancashire, brings attention to a relatively successful program, with 84 percent of respondents noting a positive impact. Many of these nineteenth-century brick houses, probably identical to those described in Orwell's *Road to Wigan Pier* and Roberts's *Classic Slum*, needed intensive internal rehabilitation, including inside sanitation. Another feature of the scheme was the traffic management program which converted streets into pedestrian areas and the back alleys into parking areas. The success of the scheme has been such that 60 percent of the residents prefer this neighborhood to new housing, and several young families have moved in. In an area without pressure from the middle-income market, subsidized conservation and rehabilitation has apparently helped the existing income groups remain, although older residents may have been displaced by the young.

The Shankland, Willmott, and Jordan paper addresses a broader set of issues than most papers in this volume, since it covers not only physical and social conservation, but matters of employment and social services. It is a study of a large London district called Stockwell, just south of the Thames, which contains about 50,000 people. This is one of three studies commissioned by the Department of the Environment (the others were in Birmingham and Liverpool) to analyze in depth the problems of inner-city neighborhoods in order to enlighten national policies toward them. The team consisted of the planning consultants, Shankland Cox and Partners, one of Britain's leading planning firms, and the Institute of Community Studies, represented by sociologist, Peter Willmott.

Stockwell, unlike the other neighborhoods in this volume, is a patchwork of nineteenth-century terrace housing, some around squares and circuses, the rest in terraces, pre–World War II five-story public housing, and postwar projects containing mixtures of slab and point blocks as well as high-density low-rise schemes. By 1976 there were 17 major housing estates in Stockwell; nearly half of all households were council tenants; and some two thirds of the land was in public ownership.

The nineteenth-century squares have largely been "gentrified;" the planners call these areas the "oases." They are occupied by senior civil servants, an MP, senior educators, lawyers and other professionals. However, in Stockwell it appears that this gentrification has occurred only on a small scale, though its visibility, "the repointed brickwork, the Habitat-painted front doors and French-blue house numbers" has given an exaggerated impression. While one-third of the population is professional or white collar, another one-third are skilled manual workers and the rest are semiskilled or unskilled. The most important trend is seen as the decline in skilled workers, the reasons being lack of jobs due to the departure of industry from inner London, and their preference for the suburbs or new towns. At the lower end of the income scale one-fifth of the population are "colored," mostly West Indian. The trend is for the population to become "bipolarized," the rich and poor wishing to live in the neighborhood while the skilled workers depart.

Surveys found two kinds of livability problems, the first environmental, relating to poor maintenance and dilapidation, unattractive appearance, and lack of open space, the second social, referring to the incoming migrants, vandalism, and crime. One of the surveys carried out in connection with this project found a high correlation between "child densities" and "discontentment." Poverty and the lack of jobs for low-skilled people are seen as among the most severe problems in Stockwell.

From this detailed understanding of Stockwell, a number of proposals are made that in some cases differ quite strongly with current governmental policies and with the kinds of policy we see being advocated in Italian cities. "Gentrification" is sees as a minor problem, since quantitatively it is small in scale and helps to upgrade the physical quality of parts of the area.

Contrary to a commonly expressed view, many working class residents seem to welcome the process. Mrs. Simey . . . said: "There are these young people moving into the older houses around here and doing them up. We like to see it. We prefer the old houses to these modern estates. We like to see them get painted up. It cheers you up to see them." She was speaking as a tenant. Mr. Roberts, a West Indian . . . put an owner-occupier's view: "If richer people move in you obviously stand to gain by it, because the value of your house goes up." (Shankland et al., 1977, p. 34)

The main problems are with jobs, housing, and services. Here, both social conservation and dispersal policies are advocated. Those who want to move, between one-quarter and one-third, should be assisted to seek housing in the outer suburbs. This would reduce densities and match people better with jobs, providing more opportunities for those staying to obtain employment.

These policies relate to the whole history of London's planning. Its basic tenets since the Abercrombie postwar plans have been to reduce densities in inner London and decant population to the new towns in order to reduce congestion and improve living conditions. "Nonconforming" industries and traffic-generating office buildings have also been encouraged to disperse. These policies have been so successful that London's population has now declined by over one million people since the war. But in the last few years there has been growing uneasiness over the consequences of these plans. No one quite realized that it would be the young and skilled who would depart from the city, leaving the old and unskilled behind. Parts of the inner city have begun to look dilapidated, though the process has not gone so far as in the inner areas of northeastern American cities. The most striking symbol of industrial departure is the vast area of Docklands, east of the Tower Bridge, which has been a derelict wasteland since the containerized port facilities have moved farther out.

In 1977, the Secretary for the Environment announced that future government investments would be shifted away from the new towns, back to the inner cities. There is also talk of relaxing on "nonconforming" industries and office construction in central London, so that the city can compete with other European cities for corporate headquarters. Over the horizon there may be looming another development era.

Meanwhile, Shankland and his associates embrace pieces of both policies. They still espouse dispersal despite the governmental shift away from it, but they also encourage physical and social conservation. There is no talk of large new housing projects, which are currently under attack from all quarters. They are interested in encouraging or keeping small scale industries, improving the skills of residents, providing welfare services, and making the management of the housing estates more responsive.

In physical terms, the policies advocate rehabilitation of existing housing and humanization of housing estates. The decline of private rental housing is expected to continue, since restrictions through rent controls and the like actively discourage landlords from renting, so further socialization of the terrace housing is foreseen.

One of the main conclusions of the Shankland report is that a new kind of planning will be needed for inner London:

Town planning needs to shift its emphasis towards encouraging and managing the kinds of small-scale change likely to be most relevant, the detailed planning of small sites and of such local environmental schemes. In other words there needs to be a new and more sensitive style of working geared to the management of small scale urban change. (Shankland et al., 1977, p. 46)

Charles McKean, in his book, *Fight Blight,* a "practical guide," documents the various ways in which ordinary citizens can improve their inner-city environments. The chapter extracted here describes some of the groups active on the British scene. They range from the local amenity societies supported by publications of the Civic Trust, to resident action groups who sponsor publications like *Community Action* and *Undercurrents.* The book describes the various ways in which the blight and dereliction that characterize British cities can be combated by action projects, from low-cost temporary improvements to more permanent ways in which people can control their own neighborhoods.

There are four possible kinds of local action:

1. Brightening up a blighted area that is not about to be immediately redeveloped so that it at least makes the locality tolerable to live in.
2. Devising short-term uses for blighted areas that will not take too much money or time, and can be discontinued when development occurs.
3. Because so much blight is caused by Council inaction, inability, or delay, local people and groups should consider doing some of the Council's work themselves.

4. The longer term view of (3) is that local groups could look forward to taking over permanently some of the Council work in their own area.

McKean cites numerous examples of citizen action in his book; modest schemes to plant flowers and trees, lay out communal gardens on leftover public spaces or housing estates, and expand allotments (Victory Gardens); the Kentish Town Fun Art Farm (an urban farm with stables and a riding school, as well as cows, pigs, goats, hens, and rabbits); alternative technology experiments; cleanup, paint-up campaigns; street murals; community festivals; adventure playgrounds; wall construction; the temporary use and reuse of buildings; exhibitions; and the encouragement of small craft industries like the Clerkenwell Workshops. Voluntary labor has helped restore remarkable numbers of old industrial sites in Britain, notably the network of old canals with their locks that thread through and between the old industrial cities, and are now used intensively for recreational purposes. Architects and students have also been involved in several build-it-yourself housing, school, and play projects.

McKean's chapter is pragmatic and technical. Unlike ARAU or Britain's *Community Action* magazine, he displays no bitterness toward the establishment. He advocates working with any established council, while noting the difficulties of making a transition from independent citizen action to cooperation with, or co-option by, the establishment. He also points out other difficulties of citizen action, the rivalries between groups who believe that only they know the answers and the large size of local governments, a particular problem with London's super-boroughs. The variety of successes recounted makes this an optimistic paper, though Europeans committed to larger-scale political change would probably see these actions as superficial, trivial, and naive.

Brian Goodey's chapter has already been discussed. It addresses the long-term issues of our relationship to the existing city and the ways in which children and others might be educated to a better appreciation of local environments and history.

The final chapter, the European Charter of the Architectural Heritage, adopted by the Committee of Ministers of the Council of Europe at the Amsterdam Conference on September 26, 1975, represents the official European policy on historic conservation. This statement, together with the more lengthy Amsterdam Declaration, published in the beautifully illustrated book of the conference, *A Future for Our Past*, affirms the significance of historic conservation in Europe today and acknowledges the necessity of integrating physical and social conservation. The language is optimistic and idealistic. The architectural heritage provides an environment "indispensable for a balanced and complete life," an essential part of the "memory of the human race." Not only is this heritage seen as of irreplaceable spiritual, cultural, social, and economic value, but, because old towns and villages "favored social integration," the structure of historic centers is considered to be "conducive to social balance." Such an idealization of the past may lead to an ideal future, but this at present is more a hope than a reality. Finally, the Committee makes a strong statement in favor of integrated conservation "in a spirit of social justice," which must be one of the "first considerations in all urban and regional planning." The statement concludes that such conservation needs more legal, administrative, financial, and technical support.

And thus historic conservation has come of age. As a major declaration of European policies toward the environment of cities it perhaps marks the final burial of the Charter of Athens, promulgated by the young modern architects of CIAM in the 1920s. This declaration is conservative and is endorsed by the establishment, whereas the Charter of Athens was written by a group of rebels and never directly endorsed by any government, though its thinking infiltrated housing and planning policies throughout Europe. The Amsterdam Declaration provides official recognition that conservation is to be the principal theme of architecture and planning over the coming years. It proposes a moral setting within which architects and planners must work, not only in a few historic quarters, but in every context.

The Politics of Conservation

These different planning experiences demonstrate the increasing social and political centrality of conservation in Europe today. Conservation is being used to further the aims of very different groups, from aesthetes to revolutionaries, capitalists to communists, from city governments to neighborhood groups, middle classes, and working classes.

Clearly the situations in large and small cities differ in magnitude and quality, but common trends can be detected. The populations of most inner cities have dropped dramatically since before the war. London and Venice have been the most salient examples but the same processes have gone on in Amsterdam, Stockholm, and Bologna. This exodus of middle- and working-class populations has been as much a part of conscious planning policy as one of individual decisions. From its origins in the Garden City Movement, a powerful theme in northern European planning has been that of centralization, reducing the densities and poor living conditions of the inner city by building the new towns and residential housing estates that now surround most European cities.

But decentralization was more modest than that in American cities. Without urban freeway networks, commerce was reluctant to move out. In consequence, it remained eager to occupy, redevelop, and expand on central city sites. At the same time large areas of the inner city maintained themselves as prestige neighborhoods. It has been the tradition of European middle and upper classes to live in central city apartments, and this tendency continued. In fact, it has become stronger. A larger population of young single people and childless couples, as well as later marriages and higher divorce rates, have increased the numbers of people without children who find the inner city the most attractive place to live. The middle-class neighborhoods are expanding in the gentrification process.

A new group has also begun to migrate into European central cities. These are the poorer migrants from ex-colonies like the West Indies, Pakistan, Africa, and the East Indies, and from southern Europe and the Middle East. They comprise substantial numbers of the population.

Their presence has given rise to reactions similar to those encountered by minorities in American cities. Crime, vandalism, poverty are now talked of in reference to many British cities, although this is not common in the other European countries.

This complex set of movements and conflicts can be interpreted in several ways. Looking at decaying buildings, the population figures, and the dispersal of jobs, many perceive a "decline" in the inner city. Others, observing new commercial development and gentrification, see the inner city as the arena for a territorial power struggle, in which the affluent take over from the poor, using the planning establishment for their ends. Each employs hyperbole.

The realities lie somewhere in between, depending on the particular city. Local governments, commerce, developers, tourists, conservationists, social activists, the rich, the middle classes, the working and the poor, vie for space or migrate to greener pastures. Commerce wants modernization, prestige buildings, efficiency, and good regional access; demographically, the young upper- and middle-class unmarrieds and childless like to live where the action is; cities want their tax bases sustained; tourism demands "clean" historical places and comfortable hotels. The underproletariat, the quiet occupants of historic central neighborhoods, after sometimes centuries of neglect, find the spotlight of attention turned on their homes. In a very few cases they resist; sometimes others resist on their behalf. Mostly they move away. In the politics of conservation, the question is not so much the conservation of the physical heritage but that of whose environment will be conserved, whose neighborhoods, and which populations. In this struggle, the conflicts are many:

1. Physical and historic conservation are threatened by private and public development, expanding institutions, office buildings, commercial complexes, and transport systems. This situation results from occupation of historic areas by the poor, who have no resources to maintain them. Between the Scylla of development and the Charybdis of deterioration, the conservationists look to public funds, which are limited, or to the sometimes tempting assistance of tourism or gentrification.

2. Social conservation of working-class and poorer quarters is threatened by nearly all land-use changes (unless the facilities are for the use of residents), by gentrification, and frequently by physical conservation and environmental improvement programs that price the environment out of the reach of its inhabitants.

Alliances between different groups depend on the issues and the situation:

1. In many cases city councils and public development corporations have actively promoted private or public development at the cost of the older areas of cities and poorer population groups. Venice and Bath are two obvious examples. Public agencies do not, therefore, necessarily look after the public interest.
2. Commerical interests, real estate developers, and landlords, although mostly in competition with each other, form coalitions and close ranks when threatened by actions that might limit economic growth and profit.
3. Conservationists and citizen action groups, while pursuing different goals, sometimes combine with each other against public or private development, though many of these alliances are precarious.

The principal political issues are whether physical conservation is of benefit only to the affluent, and whether social conservation, that is, the maintenance of the existing population, should always be the priority. The unfortunate fact is that most of the plans presented in this volume, sensitive though they are to the needs and desires of existing residents, will make the areas they cover more attractive to middle- and upper-income populations. This is a continuing dilemma for planners and cities. Yet these studies do offer a number of strategies for grappling with the problems of both physical and social conservation. Most of them are dependent on mixes of public subsidy and private investment. The predominant concern is to prevent the costs from being passed on to tenants through rent raises, which lead to their being priced out of the neighborhood. In Bologna the simpler but more drastic method of expropriation was abandoned when it was found that many of the landowners were small businesses and homeowners, part of the leftist constituency. Complex contracts are now being worked out to try to guarantee the stability of the inner neighborhoods.

Legislation controlling rents is the most common device used by cities to allow poorer populations to remain in their neighborhoods. Rent controls are mentioned in papers from the United Kingdom, Sweden, Denmark, and Italy. But blocking rents discourages landlords from maintaining property and therefore leads to deterioration in the long run.

In Stockholm and Amsterdam, quotas are being proposed to maintain a mix of family sizes, but this does not ensure a continuing income mix. Where there is a middle-class desire to live in a neighborhood, the pressures may become inexorable, if the housing market is still in operation. In an eastern European city like Budapest, where there is no market to support rehabilitation, the dilapidated inner-city neighborhoods are under no pressure, while the higher-status public housing lies around the urban periphery (Szelenyi, 1974). In western European cities all the controls may only result in a holding action, *if* neighborhoods are desirable for middle-income groups. In Rome this appears to be the problem; in Stockholm the pressures seem very light.

Within each city, the size, rate of economic and population growth, the state of the employment situation and the housing market, the extent of home ownership, the demands of tourism, and the uniqueness of the physical environment and its history, will all affect the role that inner city neighborhoods play and the pressures upon them.

Neither is gentrification all bad. Private rehabilitation to save the housing stock and the presence of middle-income and affluent groups to support the tax base help a city's economy. A British Socialist Minister has declared that some gentrification is necessary. The question is, how much?

One of the main issues debated at the Rome seminar was how much these populations really want to stay where they are, an almost unthinkable question among some socially concerned planners because residents are so frequently forced out of their homes without choice, through rising rents, acquisition, bribes, or public action. Yet a 1977 survey of London's residents (Wilcox and Richards, 1977) found that 52 percent wanted to move out, compared with only 28 percent in other cities. This willingness to seek the suburbs was evident in Stockwell and in Venice, but in the latter case residents wished to leave not because of the inner-city location so much as because of dilapidated housing. These desires have been converted into action by the thousands who have already left the inner city. However, if they move because of the "push" of poor housing conditions or redevelopment, they do not act from free choice.

David Smith, speaking at the Rome conference, was skeptical of decentralization policies:

You can argue in general terms that regional planning is a good thing, follows market trends and is inevitable but it doesn't exclude the fact that at the local level, there have been some very brutal displacements of tenants and there has had to be considerable public intervention to protect these people irrespective of the fact that the general market trends suggest that they should move anyway . . . individual families have suffered, they've not been in a position to organize themselves once they've been shifted five miles away and someone else, five miles in another direction.

Miller from Stockholm and others argue also that many low-income jobs remain in the central city.

I think we've got to recognize in European and American cities both, that the job opportunities still exist in the center for the low income population. Let's look at the center city, not necessarily all executives and administrative office people. There are a lot of other people who are in the services, which is the biggest industry now for low-income people, the service industries which are concentrated in the centers. I don't think the old fashioned formulation that industrial jobs and low-income workers somehow are all correlated and all move together physically or that as a general planning goal is really a valid one anymore.

The answers are not simple. Probably most inner-city working-class families feel ambivalent about whether they want to move or not depending on where the jobs are, the condition of their housing, the chances of rehabilitation, whether they can afford to stay where they are, and the nature of the suburban alternatives. As inner-city densities decline, physical conservation and rehabilitation programs get underway and previously unhealthy, overcrowded, and unattractive environments are improved. If the middle classes find them attractive, so may the lower-income groups, especially if there are jobs available. Policies will have to evolve with an understanding of these variables, weighing social needs with regional transportation and work patterns. Each neighborhood may have a different set of problems. The need for careful attitudinal surveys which can distinguish the needs, attitudes, and proposed behavior of different groups will be of critical importance.

Citizen action groups have flourished in the field of urban conservation. The issues are usually small in scale, immediate, and specific. There are strong similarities with the grass roots groups that have emerged on the American scene since the 1960s, with some important differences. In Europe, such groups more frequently seem to pit themselves against the planning and housing authorities rather than private developers, since the planning bureaucracy is much more in control of environmental decisions. Indeed, Manuel Castells, a Marxist sociologist who has been studying urban social movements in Paris, argues that the primary class struggle has moved from the point of production to that of consumption and that planning has become the front for the dominant classes to achieve an efficiently functioning productive capacity:

. . . if it is true that the State expresses in the last resort and through all the necessary intermediaries the combined interests of the dominant classes, then town-planning cannot be an instrument of social change, but only one of domination, integration and regulation of conflicts and its effects should be analyzed from a social point of view, not in relation to some imaginary "spatial order." (Castells, 1973, p. 4)

A characteristic of Britain's citizen action movements is their emphasis on a range of urban environmental problems, whereas, in the United States, conservationists have until recently concentrated far more on the natural environment while social action groups have focused more on social services and housing. This may be partly because the British middle classes in large numbers still live in the inner city.

In other European countries, such as Italy and France, citizen action movements are more allied to political ideologies. The ARAU group in Brussels couches its counterplans in the language of the larger struggle for political power, as does Castells. Ceccarelli, in a paper for the Habitat Conference (1976) analyzes how Italian citizen action groups have in many cases been co-opted by political parties of both the center and left. The Catholic parties see citizen participation as a reaffirmation of local values, the family, the street, the neighborhood. They also see it as a way of diverting social conflicts from the national arena to a lower (and safer) level. The left-wing Marxist parties, on the other hand, see citizen participation as a means of decentralizing power from the (center-right) government and accelerating the government's disintegration. Citizen participation, Ceccarelli argues, cannot therefore be seen as an intrinsic positive ideology in itself. Those who benefit from it are not simply those who participate.

Yet citizen action can help change society, a view that McKean would support. Political parties do not have all the answers. Citizen action movements are more important in this sense than the participatory processes being developed by planners, though the two can mutually support each other; and inner-city neighborhoods, as we have already said, are fertile ground for these movements. Their future will be one of the deciding issues in European urban conservation.

And in America?

Planners in Europe and in the United States have always interacted, as professionals and policy makers move between the continents and read each other's books and journals. However, the interaction is often a slow process when each continent is preoccupied with its own problems. Time lags occur, and policies are misapplied. The relevance of British New Towns to the United States or of Los Angeles or New York to European cities is questionable, to say the least. So we should be cautious of drawing analogies in the sphere of urban conservation.

That historic conservation is more developed in Europe is not surprising, given the dimensions of its heritage. Britain in 1975 had some 2500 designated conservation areas, compared with only 200 in the whole of the United States (Tunnard, 1975). European experience in the methodology of historic conservation, not a primary subject of this volume, should be of utility to American conservationists.

Historic conservation in the United States has been more a private than a public commitment. From Williamsburg to the commercialized restorations of Faneuil Hall Market, Sacramento's Old Town, and the subsidized private renewal of Society Hill in Philadelphia, public funds have supported private gain, producing less-than-authentic reconstructions, replacing poorer populations with affluent consumers. The same processes go on in Europe but with more public control, more care, and in some places, more concern for the less affluent residents. These experiences could prove useful to American planners and conservationists.

The institutionalization of conservators by establishing separate departments in eastern European cities could be an interesting model for some American cities. In Britain, some cities, like Chester, Cheltenham, and Greenwich, have conservation officers. Historic conservation has been under the care of planning departments in America, and this seems the appropriate location, for planning departments are more regulatory than development-oriented. But they have many other things to do. To give more visibility to conservation, separate divisions of conservation, a designated conservation director, or a change of name to Planning and Conservation Departments might be beneficial.

It is unlikely that historic conservationists will ever have the power held by those in eastern Europe, but the popular support for historic conservation may continue to grow. The public will be much more involved, and there may be much more private rehabilitation than in Europe.

The spread of the conservation idea to the neighborhoods of American cities now raises problems very similar to those found in European cities. Recently a breathless audience gathered in the De Young Museum to hear how San Francisco's 13,000-odd Victorian houses had been identified and catalogued. While some 6000 of these have already been restored, i.e., made over usually in bright and contemporary colors, another 7000 lie under all kinds of wood, felt, and plaster "fakery." Restored Victorians are beginning to make more on the market than the new apartment buildings that were about to replace them. Elsewhere in the San Francisco Bay Area the hunt is on for these newly valued structures. At the same time neighborhoods are being organized, usually by young middle-class conservationists, to defend themselves against new development and to "down zone" their ordinances to their present built environment.

In California, the movement has not yet run into heavy social opposition, but this has apparently been the case in the North End of Boston (Kopkind, 1977) and in Washington, D.C. An article in a recent issue of *Working Papers* describes the process of gentrification, American-style.

In a kind of reverse blockbusting, speculators comb neighborhoods on foot and by telephone just ahead of the restoration movement, making attractive cash offers to owners. If the owenrs refuse to sell, the more persistent speculators call in building inspectors who order expensive repairs on the old and dilapidated homes. Homes are bought and sold the same month, week, and even day for profits of up to 100 percent and more.

Block by block, private developers in Washington, D.C., are converting decaying homes into elegant town houses. Some see this restoration movement as a godsend, for it promises both to upgrade the city's housing stock and to expand the tax base. But there is another less rosy side to the neighborhood rehabilitation; it has caused rampant speculation in residential property. (Richards and Row, 1977)

An effort by a citizen's group was initially made to tax the "flippers," those who bought and sold property without improvement. Added to this proposal was a requirement for licensing dealers in residential property, registering vacant property, disclosing seller's purchase prices and costs to buyers of residential property, and strengthening "the tenant's right to first refusal under the District's rent control law by providing cash damages to tenants when their landlords failed to honor this right." But the battle lines, as in Bologna, have become complicated.

Stereotyped class and race roles have been confounded on this crux of self-interest. While poor blacks and their white activist allies come before the council demanding action against the speculators, the black entrepreneurs demand just as righteously to know how a black elected body can even consider taking away a piece of the action they have laboriously, and against great odds, won. (Richards and Row, 1977, p. 57)

The black realtors in D.C. neighborhoods are, however, embarrassed to be put in this position. But then, many speculators have also turned out to be selling primarily to blacks at reasonable prices. All groups combine against the D.C. government, which has evicted thousands of residents in low-income neighborhoods. The D.C. council was also reluctant to interfere with the housing market because of the failure of its poorly written rent control law. The result has been a watering down of the opposition and a withdrawal of the tax on rehabilitation, but there is still a tax on excessive speculation. Meanwhile the conflict has forced a political organization out of the rehabilitators.

As in Europe, the precursors of such gentrification are often the very people who later fight it, and they are often "us," middle-class white progressives:

White activists play an inadvertent role in neighborhood turnover. Their VW's and white faces calm the jitters of prospective home-buyers apprehensive of such threatening surroundings, while their counter enterprises create an aura that speculators and realtors can exploit as a lure for affluent people on the search for urban chic. (Richards and Row, 1977, p. 59)

Other efforts have been made in Alexandria to save a black neighborhood for black families by working out agreements among the families not to sell out, but the high prices offered were ultimately irresistable, and gentrification is underway.

The problems of disinvestment and suburban migration still dominate American thinking about the inner city. Classifications on the basis of degrees of decline have been made (Cannon, Lachman, and Bernhard, 1977) and most concerns relate to ways of restoring the confidence of investors in the inner city. Instances of middle-class reinvestment, like that in Washington, are, however, increasingly frequent. An Urban Land Institute survey undertaken in 1975 (Black, 1975) showed that while the actual number of private, nonsubsidized renovations carried out between 1968 and 1975 was relatively small, just over 50,000 (less than 1 percent of new units constructed), it was nevertheless a growing phenonmen. Much of this private renovation, interestingly, was going on in neighborhoods of architectural or historic significance; 65 percent of cities surveyed were experiencing renovation activity in historic areas, with 42 percent indicating activity *only* in historic areas. The groups engaged in renovation were predominantly in the middle- to upper-income range, small households, consisting of singles and young marrieds, with no or few children, working in white-collar or professional and business occupations. Only a minority were blue-collar workers. The study concludes that a number of national and local policies might be served by the shift of middle- and upper-income housing back to the central city: savings in energy costs; capital and resource savings resulting from the utilization of existing facilities in the central cities; avoidance of the environmental problems associated with further suburban growth; assistance for the fiscal problems of central cities; and the preservation of the inner city neighborhoods. Whether such a program would benefit the poor or simply become another subtle form of urban renewal will depend on a number of factors, including the amount of gentrification, the degree of home ownership and housing abandonment in an existing neighborhood. If gentrification is moderate, as in Stockwell, little harm will be done, indeed there may be benefits. If it is overwhelming as in Rome, the lower-income groups will need protection.

If urban conservation and rehabilitation do finally take off in the United States, studies in this volume will suggest caution against overly crude social analyses, lack of active citizen involvement, or overly narrow social or physical approaches to conservation.

The intensive interactions in small European countries between local and national politics and the firmer realization of the political ideologies involved may also shed helpful light on emerging American issues. Actual strategies of socializing housing, rent control, and the drawing up of special covenants to control speculation could be transferable to the American context.

The conflicts brought out in this volume should not obscure the deeper meaning of conservation to *all* groups in society, to capitalist as well as Socialist societies. Evidence of the past tells us about our origins. In a strange way, though most old cities have been built by builders quite alien to modern democracy, their original meanings no longer threaten. They have become idealized, part of a common cultural heritage, that draws us all together in the effort to save them. On this we have some agreement. The difficulties lie in the realm of social conservation. Inner-city neighborhoods are mysterious and heterogeneous place.

References

Appleyard, D. (editor), *Urban Conservation in Europe and America: Planning, Conflict and Participation in the Inner City*, 1975 Conference Proceedings, European Regional Conference of Fulbright Commissions, Rome, 1977.

Appleyard, D., *Livable Streets: Protected Neighborhoods,* University of California Press, Berkeley, Calif., 1979.

The Architectural Review, "Bath: City in Extremis," *Architectural Review,* May 1973.

Black, J. T., "Private-Market Housing Renovation in Central Cities: A ULI Survey," *Urban Land,* vol. 34, no. 10, November 1975.

Buchanan, C., *Traffic in Towns,* Her Majesty's Stationery Office, London, 1963.

Cannon, D. S., M. L. Lachman and A. S. Bernhard, "Identifying Neighborhoods for Preservation and Renewal," *Growth and Change,* vol. 8, January 1977.

Castells, M., *Urban Struggles and Political Power* (translated by B. L. Lord). François Maspero, Paris, 1973.

Ceccarelli, P. (editor), *Città Classe,* Milan.

Ceccarelli, P., "Power and Participation in Cities," *Italian Participation at the Habitat Conference, Vancouver,* Ministry for Foreign Affairs and Ministry for Public Works of the Republic of Italy, in cooperation with IN/ARCH (National Institute of Architecture), Rome, 1976.

Cervellati, Pier Luigi, "Metropolis or Necropolis: Is the Modern City Feasible?" *Urban Design Forum* (Oxford, England), no. 1, February 1978.

Civic Trust, Great Britain, *Heavy Lorries: A Civic Trust Report,* Civic Trust, London, 1974.

Civic Trust, Great Britain, *The Local Amenity Movement,* Civic Trust, London, 1976.

Council of Europe, *A Future for Our Past,* Congress on the European Architectural Heritage, Amsterdam, October 1975.

Cullen, G., *Townscape,* The Architectural Press, London, 1961.

Davis, J. H., *Venice,* Newsweek Book Division, Mondadori, Milan, 1973.

Department of the Environment, Great Britain, *Inner Area Studies: Liverpool, Birmingham, and Lambeth,* Her Majesty's Stationery Office, London, 1977.

De Wolfe, I., *The Italian Townscape,* The Architectural Press, 1963.

Evenson, N., "The Assassination of Les Halles," *The Journal of the Society of Architectural Historians,* vol. 32, December 1973.

Fergusson, A., *The Sack of Bath: A Record and an Indictment,* Compton Russell Ltd., Salisbury, 1973.

Gale, D. E., "The Back-to-the-City Movement . . . Or Is It? A Survey of Recent Homebuyers in the Mount Pleasant Neighborhood of Washington, D.C.," unpublished paper, Department of Urban and Regional Planning, The George Washington University, Washington, D.C., 1977.

Greiff, Constance M., *Lost America: From the Atlantic to the Mississippi,* The Pyne Press, Princeton, New Jersey, 1971.

Hain, P. (editor), *Community Politics,* John Calder, London, 1976.

Hall, J. M., "The Capacity to Absorb Tourists," *Built Environment,* August 1974, p. 392.

Jacobs, Jane, *The Death and Life of Great American Cities,* Random House, New York, 1961.

Kopkind, Andrew, "Kitsch for the Rich: Class Warfare at Quincy Market," *The Real Paper* (Boston), February 19, 1977.

Krieger, M. H., "What's Wrong with Plastic Trees?," *Science,* vol. 79, February 2, 1973, pp. 446–455.

Kutcher, A., *The New Jerusalem,* Thames and Hudson, London, 1973.

Lichfield, Nathaniel, and Partners, *Bath Minimal Physical Changes Study: Final Report,* London, 1976.

Lowenthal, David, "Past Time, Present Place: Landscape and Memory," *The Geographical Review,* vol. 65, January 1975, pp. 1–36.

Lynch, Kevin, *What Time Is This Place?* MIT Press, Cambridge, Mass., 1972.

Lynch, Kevin, "Some Comments on the Polish-American Seminar on Historic Preservation," unpublished paper, 1975.

MacCannell, Dean, *The Tourist,* Schocken Books, New York, 1976.

Marris, Peter, *Loss and Change,* Routledge and Kegan Paul, London, 1974.

Organization for Economic Cooperation and Development, *Better Towns with Less Traffic,* proceedings of conference held in Paris, April 1975.

Ortvad, E., *Sight Seeing 2000,* Flamberg Verlag, Zurich, 1971.

Richards, Carol and Jonathan Rowe, "Restoring a City: Who Pays the Price?" *Working Papers,* winter 1977, pp. 54–61.

Rossi Doria, B., "The Cultural Institutions and Habitat Policies," *Italian Participation at the Habitat Conference, Vancouver,* Rome, 1976.

Shankland, Graeme, "Why Trouble with Historic Towns?" in *The Conservation of Cities,* The UNESCO Press, Paris, 1975.

Shankland, Graeme, P. Willmott, and D. Jordan, *Inner London: Policies For Dispersal and Balance,* Final report of the Lambeth Inner Area Study, Department of the Environment, Her Majesty's Stationery Office, 1977.

Smith, David, *Amenity and Urban Planning,* Crosby Lockwood Staples, London, 1974.

Szelenyi, I., "Urban Sociology and Community Studies in Eastern Europe: Reflections and Comparisons with American Approaches," paper read at American Sociological Association meeting, Montreal, Canada, August 1974.

Town and Country Planning Organization (TCPO), Government of India, Ministry of Works and Housing, *Redevelopment of Shahjahanabad: The Walled City of Delhi,* New Delhi, 1975.

Tunnard, C., "The United States: Federal Funds for Rescue," in *The Conservation of Cities,* The UNESCO Press, Paris, 1975.

UNESCO, *The Conservation of Cities,* The UNESCO Press, Paris, 1975.

Ward, Colin (editor), *Bulletin of Environmental Education (BEE),* Education Unit of the Town and Country Planning Association, London.

Ward, Colin, "The Urban Predicament," *Bulletin of Environmental Education (BEE),* Town and Country Planning Association, London, vol. 59 (March 1976).

Wilcox, D., and D. Richards, *London: The Heartless City,* Thames Television, London, 1977.

Williams, R., *The Country and the City,* Chatto and Windus, London, 1973.

Worskett, R., *The Character of Towns: An Approach to Conservation,* The Architectural Press, London, 1969.

Worskett, R., "Great Britain: Progress in Conservation" in S. Cantacuzino (editor), *Architectural Conservation in Europe,* The Architectural Press, London, 1977.

I   Development Struggles

1

Venice: Urban Renewal, Community Power Structure, and Social Conflict

Paolo Ceccarelli

Cover from *Difesa di Venezia,* edited by Giorgio Bellavitis for Italia Nostra, Centro Culturale Pirelli, Milano (Venice: Alfieri, 1970), for the exhibition "Una Venezia da Salvare" held in 1970. Photos by Giorgio Lotti and Fulvio Roiter, and from photographic archives of the Comune di Venezia.

Plan of Venice showing industrial Marghera and suburban Mestre. From Bellavitis, *Difesa di Venezia,* p. 75.

ZONE RESIDENZIALI IN ESPANSIONE – ATTREZZATURE COLLETTIVE – VERDE ATTREZZATO ED IMPIANTI SPECIALI

CENTRO STORICO SOGGETTO A P.P.

ATTREZZATURE ECONOMICHE VARIE E PORTO COMMERCIALE

PORTO PETROLI

PORTO INDUSTRIALE

ZONE RURALI E CAMPING

IMPIANTI FERROVIARI

STRADE AUTOMOBILISTICHE PRINCIPALI

TERMINAL STRADALI

COLLEGAMENTI ACQUEI

COMUNE DI VENEZIA: P.R.G. 1962

San Marco, showing the *acqua alta,* which also invades the streets, the *campi,* and the ground floors of the houses, while waves break and pull against their foundations. It was the high tides of January 1966 that dramatized and partly distorted the world's view of a crisis that had already been in existence for several years. From *Rapporto su Venezia,* for UNESCO (Milan: Mondadori, 1969). Photo by G. Lotti.

An aerial view of Venice with
Marghera's industrial zone in
the background. Fortunately,
most of the time the wind blows
the other way. From Bellavitis,
Difesa di Venezia, p. 60. Photos
by G. Lotti and F. Roiter.

The heart of Venice, where
between 17,000 and 19,000
of the 40,000 dwellings need
repair, and two-thirds of the
ground-floor flats are unsuitable for habitation. Nearly one-
half the apartments have no or
inadequate heat, one-fifth have
less than two hours of sunlight
a day, and one-half show signs
of damp. From Bellavitis, *Difesa
di Venezia*, p. 62. Photos by G.
Lotti and F. Roiter.

Lack of open space and new facilities led to adaptive reuse in Sansovino's Scuola Grande della Misericordia, with its murals by Veronese, which has been taken over by a sporting club. From Bellavitis, *Difesa di Venezia,* p. 29. Photos by G. Lotti and F. Roiter.

Suburban Mestre is modern, ugly, and inconvenient for those who work in Venice, but the housing is dry and spacious, and cars can be parked outside it. From Bellavitis, *Difesia di Venezia,* p. 63. Photos by G. Lotti and F. Roiter.

One of the few small rehabilitation projects carried out in Venice before 1975. Under the sponsorship of Italia Nostra, small apartments originally housing 32 residents were converted into three dwelling units adequate by modern standards; the damp ground floors were converted into shops (architect Nani Valle). From Bellavitis, *Difesa di Venezia*, p. 106. Photos by G. Lotti and F. Roiter.

A Communist party poster (postcard)

I LAVORATORI
DIFENDERANNO VENEZIA
CONTRO GLI SPECULATORI

The survival of Venice, both as a unique historical and artistic patrimony, and as a living social and economic organism, has been a matter of hot debate and great emotional involvement in recent years.

The foci of discussion have been the goals to accomplish, the optimal strategies to pursue: the different social and economic philosophies to follow for the sake of a redeemed, happy Venice, rather than the more trivial technical and operational problems involved in the implementation of a massive program of rehabilitation (such as the one envisaged for the Venetian islands).

Besides, the Venice issue has been used by politicians looking for power or re-election both at the national and at the local level, by bureaucrats of international organizations, by frustrated intellectuals and aristocrats eager to gain a larger audience for their theories.

Since abstract discussion and political and intellectual gambling are of little help in problem solving, after several years of quarrels and arguing little progress has been made toward a real improvement of socioeconomic and residential conditions. In several respects, problems are now worse than they were five or ten years ago, since more and more people, especially those who constitute the more firm and alive social texture of the local community—young blue-collar workers, skilled craftsmen, small shopkeepers, active entrepreneurs—have left for good, moving to the mainland suburban developments. Moreover the whole machinery of urban renewal and planning is presently stuck. The implementation of the "special act" for Venice is proceeding very slowly and planned operations are badly behind schedule; funds allocated by the government have never been available (they have only been promised); research programs intended as preliminary to any further decision have been stopped; frustration and a sense of impotence have grown among public officials.

At the same time landlords rehabilitate their buildings piecemeal. Through evicting residents or just raising rents, they first vacate houses, then fix up and re-rent them at higher rents. A slow process of gentrification is going on in Venice, while tensions and conflicts are rapidly rising among lower-income groups.

Political parties—from Christian Democrats to Communists—are playing a long term power game: they watch each other carefully, avoiding any bold actions or clear-cut decisions. A gloomier picture would be difficult to imagine.

I do not want to use this opportunity to analyze once more the perils Venice is facing. The purpose of this short paper is instead to discuss some social and political issues rising from the large housing rehabilitation programs planned for the Venetian islands that some initial decisions have already brought into light.

To make one better understand some of the specific features of housing conditions in Venice, some basic information on key problems must be provided. Behind the apparently erratic behavior of the political establishment in approaching the problems of Venice, there is a more disturbing reality. In the past years a bitter fight has developed among the leading political and economic groups in Italy, and control of the key sectors of economic development, of the most important institutions in the society, of the largest cities and wealthiest regions is at stake. The incoming crisis of the present political regime has opened large spaces for political maneuvering, and the power game has been (and is) played with utmost ruthlessness and cynicism. Venice, and the considerable government investments in housing, public works, anti-pollution devices, are an attractive stake in this game, no less—to give some other examples—than the control of some large public corporations, or funds for the Mezzogiorno, or the social welfare and the educational machineries.

I believe that there is nothing shocking in this; the same thing happens every day, everywhere in the world. The point is to take it into account when a specific situation is analyzed, in order to understand why things that in principle ought to go in a certain direction go in actual fact the opposite way.

What is happening in Venice is no idealistic confrontation of romantic utopians: it is part and parcel of the general capitalist process, with its characteristics of careless exploitation, class struggle, and hypocritical cultural covers. A process that, especially in a rapidly changing society like Italy, can be very violent and uncontrolled.

Three basic stages can be identified in the post–Second World War policies for Venice.

The *first stage* corresponds to the more general economic strategy of Italian governments in the fifties and sixties, to concentrate industries in a few areas. In these years the traditional (since the nineteenth century) economic base of Venice was dismantled. Beginning with the end of the war, shipyards, textile shops, light engineering factories progressively shut down on the grounds that they were no longer competitive. Alternative jobs were offered to the Venetian working class in the huge petrochemical complexes on the mainland or in the tertiary sector: tourism, services, public administration. In a few years Venice changed from a crisis-stricken, but still integrated and balanced, socioeconomic system into an unproductive community living on tourists and public administration. Mass emigration to the mainland occurred, the housing market collapsed, and the very center of local political life moved to Mestre, the booming twin city of Venice on the coast.

At this time there was no official recognition of a "Venetian problem," and the decision to specialize Venice as a major pole of touristic supply was widely accepted, in a world where the demand in this sector was growing fast.

But this oversimplified strategy for economic development is indeed one major cause of subsequent Venetian— and Italian—problems. Tourism is a very fragile economic activity, affected as it is by any minor slowdown in the economy. Moreover, it does not induce any relevant betterment in the social structure of a community. In fact, one of the major weaknesses of the economic base of Venice is a too large underproletariat; this problem is in no way solved because tourism heavily relies upon temporary, peripheral jobs. The mammoth industrial estates developed on the mainland have, moreover, originated heavy pollution, and contributed to the lowering of the water table and the sinking of Venice.

The *second stage,* in the second half of the sixties, corresponded to the increasing awareness that previous policies adopted for Venice could not work and that the situation was getting worse. Mass tourism required planning and investments, and was much less profitable than had been assumed. A new demand for nonpermanent housing, such as weekend facilities, "residences," etc., emerged. Higher incomes and the first inflationary wind zoomed real estate investments.

Taking advantage of the high rate at which buildings were vacated and lower-income residents were leaving Venice, a new strategy was worked out. Venice is conceived of as the upper-class residential section of a larger metropolitan system, where the central business district is in Mestre, on the mainland, and the middle class and working class districts are located in the countryside fringes.

The solution was strongly supported by large real estate corporations and local landlords. Real estate values went up, and in a few months vacant buildings became the scarcest commodity on the market.

A key role in this strategy was to be played by some of the large state controlled holdings operating in Italy. IRI, ENI, etc., through their affiliates in the tourism sector, in transportation, in public construction, are expected to make larger investments to transform some residential areas into "tourist centers," to improve technical infrastructure and possibly the mass transit system. In exchange for their real estate and construction profits, they agree to reduce industrial developments on the mainland.

It was during these years that the "Venice problem" was discovered. This sudden awareness of problems that had been there for at least a decade is most easy to sell through the image of a city to be saved mostly through housing improvements, an upgrading of its social structure, the development of quaternary activities—like educational facilities, research centers, convention and exhibition halls.

Nobody cared much for the majority of Venetians, who still stubbornly insisted on working in industries, artisan shops, on the docks, as sailors, as merchants. They were assumed to be a basic item to embellish and enrich the environment, nothing else. The alternative envisaged for them was to become doormen, janitors, cleaning women in the new educational facilities, porters or waiters in the "tourist centers," dummy craftsmen and workers like the ones performing in Williamsburg or Sturbridge, in the United States.

In this climate a "special bill" for Venice was worked out: its key feature was the allocation of one-half billion dollars for housing rehabilitation, public works, antipollution devices. A very large political coalition endorsed it: every group figured out what advantages they might draw from it. The act became operative in 1972.

The *last stage* began with the worsening of the economic and political crisis in 1973, and is still in process.

The rate of unemployment in Venice rose sharply along with increases in prices and rents due to rampaging inflation. There are no answers to this. Tourism was badly affected by the poor economic performances of the wealthiest European countries and the U.S.; at the same time the industries concentrated in Marghera, on the mainland, underwent a process of restructuring and curtailing employment. The coupled effect of the economic crisis and the rise in the cost of living accounted for unprecedented social tensions among the lower-income groups. Besides, the unfavorable economic conjuncture forced the large public holdings to withdraw (temporarily at least) from the Venetian scene. Perspectives for highly profitable, large scale renewal operations meant for an ever expanding, diversified tourist demand were bleak, and large corporations and financial groups diverted their investments to other sectors.

This retreat caused a new major change in local planning strategies. The political coalition that had endorsed the bill for Venice on the assumption that large scale operations in housing rehabilitation, public works, technical and social infrastructure would soon start lost one of its more powerful allies. State controlled corporations should have represented the economic counterpart to the coalition of local landlords—from the very large ones like the Catholic church to the thousands of middle-class investors owning one or two dwellings. They ought to have provided the

political backing to the local government in its fight to expropriate the local gentry and implement massive renewal projects. They should have also provided through their official position of "public" corporations—i.e., the theoretical assumption that they always behave in favor of the public interest—an ethical cover to any questionable decisions about the relocation of people, the clearing of an area, the construction of new buildings.

This more advanced coalition between the more dynamic segments of the Venetian bourgeoisie, the center-left parties, and the new state technocracy collapsed; and the game was again in the hands of the more traditional economic power groups. Given the economic crisis and inflation, property values sky-rocketed, and local authorities were unable to enforce large scale expropriation measures. They preferred to reach agreements with landlords allowing them to rehabilitate their buildings piecemeal, evicting their former tenants and sharply increasing the new rents. It was under these conditions that at the end of 1974 the Communist Party, which had always been a strong opponent in the local government, decided to back the weakened center-left government. This help was essential to start the implementation of some sections of the Special Act, but it was not enough. The political parties that more openly represented local landlords' interests in the local government left the center-left coalition. In the first part of 1975 Venice in fact did not have any government, until a major political shift occurred in the June 15 elections.[1]

This sketchy analysis of the economic and sociopolitical reasons behind the failure of the planned projects for Venice may make it easier to understand some key problems in the implementation of urban renewal policies in this case. I shall touch upon them briefly in the following paragraphs.

1. There exists a very established and solid complex of big landlords, small investors, individual homeowners that is extremely difficult to break and overcome. Their interests are apparently heterogeneous and often in fact contradictory, but as soon as public action affects them, this variegated complex becomes a firm coalition and pressure group. This was the case in Venice, when the original strategy of the late fifties based on the assumption of

unlimited growth and profits shared by all was downgraded to a fight to exploit the few opportunities left by the crisis. It was the case in Bologna, where local authorities were forced to scrap original plans of extended compulsory expropriation and strict rent controls, to work out much less satisfactory (for the lower-income people living in central areas) agreements based on voluntary rehabilitation projects by landlords.

2. In most Italian cities, central areas are still largely inhabited by lower-income families. These residents do not belong to the more dynamic and advanced segments of the proletariat, but are both the remnants of the original social texture of the city—craftsmen, shopkeepers, petty civil servants, retired people, etc.—and the new army of peripheral workers in services and temporary jobs. Immigrants live in central areas only in a few large cities—Turin being the extreme case, more similar in this to American and western European cities than to the majority of Italian urban areas.

Venice, given its unique geographical and historical features, still has a very large section of the traditional underproletariat living close to higher-income groups. This accounts to a large extent for the exceptional flavor of the Venetian street life and for the aliveness of so many sites, but it also reflects the structural fragility of its economy, the very low level of living standards, sharp social contradictions.

Other social groups living in the Venetian islands are well-to-do people, mostly professionals, top civil servants, hotelkeepers and a small fragment of the ancient aristocracy.

The two groups do not interact in any way, and their attitudes toward the future of Venice differ sharply.

Social groups that have actual influence over the political and social life of the city—middle-class, white-collar workers in the mainland industrial estates—do not live in the historical districts of Venice and do not care much about safeguarding the city, or its survival.

3. The pattern of human ecology in Venice very much affects the structure of local politics. Right after the war Venice had a large left-wing majority. The continuous drainage of population from the islands, the formation of large middle-class neighborhoods on the mainland, and the dispersion of the working class in peripheral developments outside the municipal boundaries have thoroughly altered the political composition of the Venetian constituency. For many years now local governments have been based upon very fragile balances of center-left political groups. This explains the need to ally with influential power groups outside Venice to carry out large scale projects, and the life-buoy role played by the Communist Party after this alliance failed.

An example of the relevance of this division of interests is given by one of the issues at stake in the June 1975 elections. The right-wing parties backed a proposal for reapportionment: the "problem area"—the Venetian islands—should have its own local government, leaving Mestre and its middle-class suburbs as an independent municipality. On the opposite side, one of the most meaningful results of the community action groups operating in Venice was to start joint action with groups fighting for better housing conditions and services in the mainland. The grounds for this joint action was the awareness that the rehabilitation of older districts—with the many problems of relocation involved—is just one aspect of a more complex and large scale planning process. Similar situations exist in other Italian cities with a large historical central district, Bologna being one of the very few exceptions because of the political homogeneity of its constituency.

4. Given these structural conditions, it is evident how harmful to the social and economic texture any simplistic policy for the rehabilitation and renewal of central historical districts can be. The Venetian lower-income groups cannot afford any significant change in the rents they pay, and in the past they have always been forced to move when raises have occurred. In order to stay, they often accept extremely bad housing conditions, contributing to the further decay of buildings.

A conservationist approach to the problems of Venice cannot overlook this tragic reality. To say—as it has been said even by concerned planners—that the issue must be solved through massive public housing programs is just a way to bypass the problem verbally. Present public housing standards and costs inevitably result in relatively high rents that the low-income marginal groups living in Venice cannot afford. Some experimental projects started by the National Housing Agency have produced exactly this result, originating in harsh conflicts and complaints.

A very serious problem is also posed by the relocation of residents. In Venice there are families that have been living in the same district for centuries; because of their peripheral position in the labor market, the very fact that they are located in a specific street or square is their major economic asset. The relocation problem—always one of the most serious pitfalls of urban renewal policies—becomes a key issue in the survival of existing Venetian social patterns.

5. This situation has caused very acute social tensions among the weakest economic groups. For years they have been told that policies under study were meant to change their social conditions and improve their income levels. So far, the only results they have seen are increasing unemployment, higher costs of living, and a progressive decay in the quality of services. Moreover, many families have been evicted because of private housing rehabilitation projects or relocated because of experimental renewal programs by public agencies.

Little by little, spontaneous community action groups have formed to deal with specific issues: to fight the eviction of families living in a given block, to occupy vacant houses, to exert pressures over the local government to obtain the enforcement of legal provisions concerning substandard dwellings, etc.

Local authorities and political parties look at these groups with great suspicion. They do not respect the rules of the game, they always raise unpleasant issues; in many respects, they are much more radical and militant than the left-wing parties and the labor unions. Politically, the only support they can get is from students' organizations and from the so-called extra-parliamentary groups.[2]

To better explain the political effectiveness of this grass-roots movement and the characteristics of its action, I shall mention two issues on which it has been successful.

The first is the so called *auto-riduzione* ("self-reduction," or "civil disobedience" in a more Thoreauian interpretation). It consists in a mass protest against higher electricity and telephone bills and transport fares. The protest is based upon the fact that utility companies and transport agencies are state-owned, the point being that the state cannot fight inflation on the one side, and raise the cost of basic services on the other. The issue became very hot in 1975, and the protest movement, started by local grass-roots organizations, gained a tremendous momentum. The unions were forced to back it, and many planned increases in electrical power rates for lower-income consumers had to be withheld by the government. The Venetian community action organizations were very active on this occasion, and thousands of families rallied with them.

A second interesting case for community action has been one in which the university has been involved. A few months ago, the local government donated to the University of Venice some vacant apartment buildings in which to lodge students. The donation was an ambiguous one, because the university is a rather wealthy institution, whereas there is a need for low-rent public housing. As soon as they heard about it, the community action groups occupied the vacant dwellings, and had families living in substandard housing enter. The student union supported this action, accusing the University Board of being one of the major forces behind the process of social disruption in Venice (this is true for universities in general, Venice being no exception). The whole affair became quite embarrassing, and after some compromising an agreement was reached. The occupants stayed, and they signed rent agreements for no more than 10 percent of their family income—a breakthrough solution that creates a very important precedent for future action.

To solve (or, at least, to attempt to solve) these problems, a radically different approach to the rehabilitation problems of Venice ought to be followed.

First of all, all existing vacant dwellings should be expropriated and rehabilitated, in order to provide rapidly a stock of better houses not far from those to be rehabilitated, and in which people now live. Many of these houses probably do not need expansive repairs. They often belong to real estate companies or landlords that keep them vacant merely to better control the housing market.

A large share of the residential housing stock already belongs to public authorities, and this too might be used as a strategic asset in order to prevent and reduce further relocation of lower-income population.

Policies for Venice have so far developed along two major lines: massive housing rehabilitation programs and technical infrastructure projects. These programs are both relevant and urgent; however, they indicate a reductive view of the complexity of the problems existing in Venice. One wonders, for instance, whether the greatest demand is for thoroughly remodeled dwellings (that at the end will be more expensive than they were before) or rather for essential improvements (better sanitary equipment, some window repairs, etc.) and much larger investment in social infrastructure, services, transportation. Venice badly lacks the most elementary public facilities for children, senior citizens, the disabled; sporting grounds and recreational facilities are practically nonexistent; the public transportation system is still very inadequate. Housing is just one item of a much more complex and articulated pattern of spaces and facilities used by a family in everyday life. To put all interests and efforts in its improvement might be simplistic and might result in an unbearable increase in costs. This problem should be explored more carefully, before massive housing rehabilitation programs are started, risking failure.

Equally important are socioeconomic programs to provide better jobs and higher incomes to those living in historical districts, without forcing them to leave.

This aspect of the problem is entirely absent from the "Special Act" for Venice, while there is great awareness that without specific, careful socioeconomic policies, programs for the survival of Venice will only contribute to speed up its death as a balanced social organism.

Given the present political situation in the country and in Venice, it is now necessary to ask, are these policies and programs likely to be implemented? A fair answer is no.

The only alternative to the political gambling about Venice, the arrogance of its bourgeoisie, the stupidity of most of its defenders, is still the militancy of the lower classes and their fight to avoid eviction and to demand better, modern, permanent jobs in the place where they have always lived. And as you know, many times it is the common, ignorant, poor people that at the very end win long and bloody wars.

Notes

1. In the June 15, 1975 elections, a Communist-Socialist coalition government was elected to the majority in Venice. Francesco Bandarin reported from Venice in 1978:

The situation inherited by the leftist coalition (Socialist and Communist parties) which took over the city government in June 1975 showed a complete disorganization of the bureaucratic structures and the inadequacy of the plans that had been previously designed. The first three years of the term have been dedicated, therefore, to improving the quality of the administrative work and to the design of an implementation plan for restoration. New planners, coming from other experiences of restoration of historic centers, have been hired, and a new analytical methodology has been applied. The major effort of the new administration has been directed at overcoming the complexity of the planning and financial mechanisms included in the Special Law for the city, which is still the major financial source for housing renovation. Although many of the funds provided by the Special Law for the construction of antipollution devices, for experimentation with a new sewage system, for public works on the canals, and for the restoration of monuments have been spent, nothing has been invested yet in the restoration of residences. In February 1978, the Administration approved the first three *Progetti di Coordinamento* (detailed plans required by the Special Law), based on an analysis of historical typologies, and including about 400 apartments with 1,200 inhabitants. While intervention in these three areas has already started, the planning division is beginning to extend the analysis of typologies and of the property structure to the entire city and to design plans for new areas (about eight plans are scheduled to be completed by the end of 1978).

2. In Italy, there are many political groups with not insignificant impact which operate outside the normal electoral channels. This is sometimes by choice and sometimes not; many groups on the left disdain the electoral process, however, and are therefore called "extra-parliamentary," or outside the parliamentary arena.

The Communist and Socialist parties are, obviously, not of this grouping. *Ed.*

2 Utrecht: Den Hoog Catharijne

J. P. Barendsen

Den Hoog Catharijne, Utrecht: aerial perspective of the entire project with the historic center at bottom right. From Den Hoog Catharijne publicity brochure.

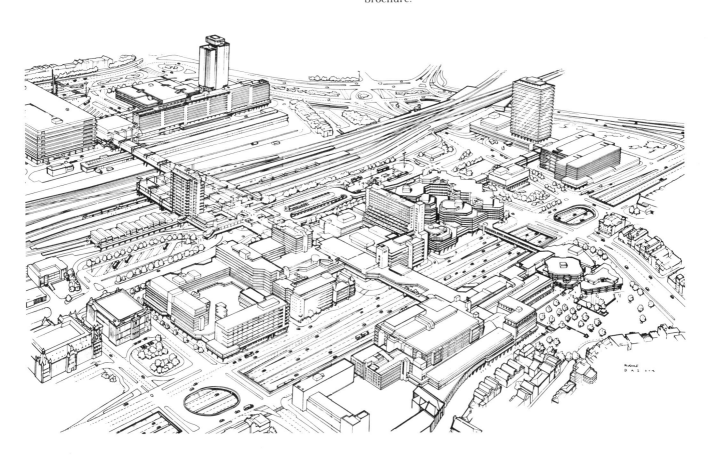

A view of Den Hoog Catharijne
with the historic center in the
foreground. From Den Hoog
Catharijne publicity brochure.

The city of Utrecht, which is one of the oldest cities of the Netherlands and in the early middle ages occupied a leading position in the commercial, cultural, and religious life of these "low countries by the sea," is now once more going through a period of activity after many centuries of relative quiet.

Utrecht's history goes back to about 50 A.D., when the Romans built a fortress on what was then the bank of the river Rhine. The remnants of this fortress are still in evidence in the very heart of the city.

From the seventh century onward christianization of the northern part of the Netherlands emanated from Utrecht. The great era of prosperity, however, did not commence until the twelfth century. By that time the city acquired the size it retained until the middle of the nineteenth century. The period of prosperity did not last particularly long and it took until the seventeenth century before Utrecht once more gained in significance through the foundation of what is now the largest university of the Netherlands.

For Utrecht as well the industrial revolution in the nineteenth century did not pass by unnoticed. Different branches of industry were established here, of which the metal industry occupied a prominent position. The improvement of the means of transport (rail, road, and water), the increasing number of educational institutions, the cultural activities and the development of industry, and later more especially the so-called tertiary sector, enabled Utrecht to give even greater content to its position as the "center of the country" than could be derived from its geographical location alone.

In this respect the Industries Fair, a commercial institution of national and international significance, was and still is an important object of attraction.

After the Second World War Utrecht developed substantial building activities in its extended territory. Three new, large neighborhoods were laid out. In addition, attention was directed to the city center. This is the subject I should like to go into a little more closely.

To this end it is helpful to know what this old city looks like.

In the nineteenth century beautiful public gardens were laid out at the point of the old city walls and ramparts: the moat encircling them has been maintained as a fascinating, historical boundary. The street pattern is still largely medieval and is characterized by two canals running in the longitudinal direction of the city, with the—for Europe—unique, low-lying quays with basements and a multitude of streets and alleyways at right angles thereto.

The actual city lies to the northwest of the old town and in some places is on a larger scale and more spacious. But for the rest the shopping amenities have found their place along the old streets and canals. Developments in the first half of the fifties presented the Utrecht Municipal Authorities with an unusually large number of problems. Stresses had built up between the physical immobility of the city on the one hand and the social mobility on the other.

To the municipal authorities the modern traffic requirements, the changed housing needs, and other shifts resulting in increased prosperity constituted as many signs of the need to adapt the city center to these social developments.

The starting signal was given for an extensive investigation. The main query that had to be answered was, "How do we keep our old city open for traffic?"—Utrecht was screened and laid on the examination table. Town planners, traffic experts, architects, financiers, administrators, and many other experts bent over the results of the investigation, analyzed them, made diagnoses, and ultimately gathered round the operating table to provide the city with a new nervous system and a larger and better heart. In doing so careful attention was given to plastic surgery, because all the new elements that would have to be introduced also had to make a perfect match with the characteristic, historical features of Utrecht. However necessary it may have been to keep the city open for modern and steadily increasing traffic, the greatest possible care had nevertheless to be taken to ensure that what formed a whole at the time would also continue to do so in the future.

First traffic studies were carried out and later supplemented by a basic town plan. However, all these studies did not come to much, partly on account of the long time and the great cost that would be involved in realization and partly because a gradual change occurred in the views on what could be regarded as desirable and effective action on behalf of the old city.

During this municipal planning phase an entirely new dimension was added by private enterprise. A large construction company established in this city, Verenigde Bedrijven Bredero N.V., arranged for its recently founded subsidiary—the Empeo Project Development Company— to draw up a plan in 1962 for a new section of the city center adjoining the old city in the area around the Central Station and submitted this plan to the municipal authorities.

The plan was in line with the desire entertained by the authorities to extend and reinforce the heart of Utrecht and consequently it was well-received—not just by the municipal authorities for that matter—but equally by the Utrecht shopkeepers and the remainder of the population, as well as by town planners and experts representing other disciplines.

It is about this project—known as the Hoog Catharijne Project—that I should like to tell you a little more, seeing that as regards size and realization the project was unique for the Netherlands and still is today. The Hoog Catharijne Project comprises the total reconstruction of an area covering 24 hectares, situated between the heart of the old city and the Central Station located outside this central area. From the point of view of the buildings it contained the area was not of particular interest, seeing that it consisted of a nineteenth century station neighborhood of housing and business and a barracks site, while in addition there were some out-of-date buildings, such as the Industries Fair building and a number of offices due for extension or replacement. Public transport, train and bus accommodation, clearly required improvement. The plan offers instead: a renewed central station, new greatly enlarged stations for local and long-distance bus transport, and an entirely new city area comprising shops and a department store (approximately 66,000 square meters in all), offices (117,000 square meters), showrooms, café-restaurants and hotels, assembly rooms, etc. (31,000 square meters), with in addition a new

Industries Fair building, providing 75,000 square meters of exhibition and assembly area.

Furthermore, the plan includes a large, multifunctional sports hall. The accessibility of all this—already ideally ensured by the most favorable location of the Central Station, the largest railway junction of the Netherlands— is completed by the building of seven parking garages capable of accommodating 5,000 motorcars in all.

It will be clear that this adds an entirely new dimension to Utrecht. The floor areas mentioned were only partly available or not at all in the existing buildings. This combination of accessibility on the one hand and offices, assembly rooms, and hotel accommodation on the other will have a great external influence, which is already clearly noticeable even now. Quite recently, for example, the Central Committee of the World Council of Churches held its meeting in the new Industrial Fair Congress Centre.

From a town planning point of view the plan is characterized by highly intensive and interrelated building. The need for this lay in the high level of the costs of acquisition, as a result of which a sound profitability basis could only be achieved by applying a high building density per square meter. Furthermore, the plan has been put into a highly integrated form and consequently, through its unity, makes a very powerful outward impression.

Another feature of the plan is that the shopping and pedestrian traffic are elevated above street level, i.e., pedestrian traffic and motorized traffic have been separated.

Naturally, a project of this kind always tends to give the impression of a large concrete colossus. From the point of view of finish and presentation this difficulty is encountered in connection with this plan as well, although the art of kneading concrete is gradually being mastered. Yet, there is every reason to believe that due allowance has been made in the plan for sufficient vegetation and immaterial forms of presentation to force back the "lifeless" concrete, thus enabling "communicating man" to experience Hoog Catharijne as a whole together with the old and varied city center.

After its presentation by Empeo in 1962 the plan was subjected to a close study by the municipality. It was necessary to obtain the approval of many and the fulfilment of numerous conditions had to be feasible in principle before the municipality would give its cooperation. It did not take more than a year before this cooperation could be granted.

To this end an agreement was concluded between the company that would realize and operate the project and the municipality, laying down the main outlines of the plan and more especially a number of financial and legal arrangements.

I would mention a few of these main points:

1. The realization of a project of this kind involves a great deal of money. The surveyability of the project is seriously obstructed by the long duration of its realization. The project lasts fifteen years and will not be entirely completed until 1980 or 1981. With a long duration such as this it is absolutely essential that the solvency of the entrepreneur be guaranteed not just at the start alone, but also during the period of realization. For this reason "the parent company," Verenigde Bedrijven Bredero, had to guarantee the work of the Project Development Company, while guarantees for the realization of the plan as a whole have been ensured via the issue of land.

2. Because the plan involves the sum of a few hundred million guilders, it had to be made certain that no stagnation was likely to occur during realization owing to a lack of funds. To this end the participation of a bank was ensured and a guarantee obtained from this bank to furnish 75 percent of the building costs via mortgage loans.

3. A separate company was founded (N.V. Hoog Catharijne) for the realization of the project and its subsequent operation. The partners in this company are the bank and the building company (Bredero); the municipality does not participate. The municipality did not undertake any form of participation, because it cannot run the risks of an entrepreneur and because in the Netherlands, as in so many other countries, the separation of the responsibilities of the entrepreneur and government authorities is a sacred dogma.

It is true, of course, that the municipality has a very important voice in the preparation and realization of the project via the agreement and the associated leasing terms.

4. The municipality acquires all the land and subsequently leases it out. This ensures that the valuable land will remain in the hands of the community itself, while the revenues will also go to the benefit of the community. What this means is that the municipality acts as a land operator.

The acquisition of the land will involve a sum of 150 million guilders (1971 figures). The municipality finances this amount and recovers it by means of the ground rents. The basis for calculating the ground rent is made up of the actual costs of acquisition, demolition, preparation for building, etc. Administratively, a separate account was opened for this purpose. Hence, the ground rent can only be fixed after all the land has been acquired and leased out. For this reason an interest of 5 or 7 percent is credited annually to the balance of this account.

After the last plot of land has been issued the ground rent is increased once every 15 years in relation to—and this is important—the gross rent proceeds.

5. The project comprises a number of public amenities which are hard to finance in the private sector, such as parking garages and elevated pedestrian facilities. They are so closely associated with the project as a whole, however, that the private contractors will realize these amenities as an integral part of the overall plan. For these elements also the municipality was prepared to undertake the financing.

The sum of 25 million guilders involved is likewise recovered in the form of annuities forming part of the ground rent.

6. The other public provisions, such as roads, sewers and similar projects, are for the municipality's account and are also realized by the municipality.

The amount required for this will run to about 30 million florins, which sum does not form part of the ground rent, but constitutes a direct charge to the municipality.

7. The building costs—estimated in 1975 at 400 million florins—are for the account of Hoog Catharijne N.V., with the exception of the Industries Fair Building and the department store, which however were actually also built

by Bredero. The procedure continues to be that Hoog Catharijne N.V. constructs the buildings and lets them on completion. In addition, the Netherlands Railways built and financed their own new station building.

These are in brief the main arrangements of the plan between parties. Further, the agreement contains extensive terms in respect of the provision and the issue of land. It also contains provisions concerning typical public matters, such as those whereby the municipality undertakes to make an effort on behalf of the realization of traffic measures *elsewhere* in the city and those whereby parties undertake to ensure a sound town planning development around the project area. The final provisions concern the procedure to be followed in case of disputes.

One of the most urgent policy problems in the development of the plan still is—and with greater urgency than ever before—the competitive position vis-à-vis the old city. The new may not be realized at the expense of the old. This means that Hoog Catharijne may not be regarded as a transplantation in the true sense, but should be seen as an expansion, renewal, and reinforcement of the heart of the city. There should be no artificial barriers between the two, but instead there must be a true identity. The municipal authorities are making every effort to keep the old city center alive in the economic sense. The difficulty in this respect is, however, the accessibility. Parking garages do not fit in easily with the small scale of the old city, which should as far as possible be retained in its existing town planning form. We are endeavoring to enhance the attractiveness of the old city by providing a properly laid-out pedestrian area.

Furthermore, binding arrangements have been made with N.V. Hoog Catharijne concerning the nature and the number of the shops that will be allowed to move from the old city to Hoog Catharijne.

One of the important principles is, of course, that Hoog Catharijne will provide an extension of the existing range of shops. Realization of the plan was taken in hand in 1968. The initial phase—opposite the station—has been completed and has now been functioning for some years. The

department store with surrounding shop buildings is near completion, as are also the new station and the pedestrian facilities in between, with adjoining offices, shops, parking garages, and housing.

In general, realization is proceeding entirely in accordance with the predetermined time schedules. In this connection one of the most important advantages mentioned when the plan was approved, namely to have a project of this kind realized by private enterprise, still applies. Although, when looking back, it might have been more desirable for certain aspects of the relationship between the municipality and Hoog Catharijne N.V. to have been arranged differently, the motivation underlying the realization of this project has not lost any of its validity. It is not to be wondered at, of course, that the appreciation of the project as such and of the building and development company is no longer quite so unanimous as in the beginning. This is associated with the greatly increased and sometimes highly romanticized attention devoted to anything that is small-scale and to anything old, and with an aversion to anything that resembles concrete and commerce.

Apart from this some people consider the influence of the building company too great and the municipality too closely tied to this company, as a result of which there is supposed to be insufficient possibility for adaptation to changing social requirements.

Although the municipal authorities are fully aware of the fact that the initial lyricism, which—it must be admitted—sometimes acquired the nature of a chauvinistic chest-beating, has turned into a more critical prose, the authorities still fully back the project, admitting at the same time that what was agreed upon ten years ago cannot now invariably be regarded as the best possible solution. It should be realized that in a period of demolition and construction it is difficult for a lot of people to recognize at the present time the excellent results which are definitely expected to materialize. As regards the relationship between the municipality and N.V. Hoog Catharijne it is true that the collaboration is good and that this situation is not expected to change, despite the fact that there have been and there still are problems from time to time.

3   The Sack of Bath   Adam Fergusson

Map of Bath showing areas
which have been destroyed
(black areas) or redeveloped
(dotted areas) since 1949. From
Adam Fergusson, *The Sack of
Bath* (Compton Russell:
Salisbury, England, 1973),
back end papers.

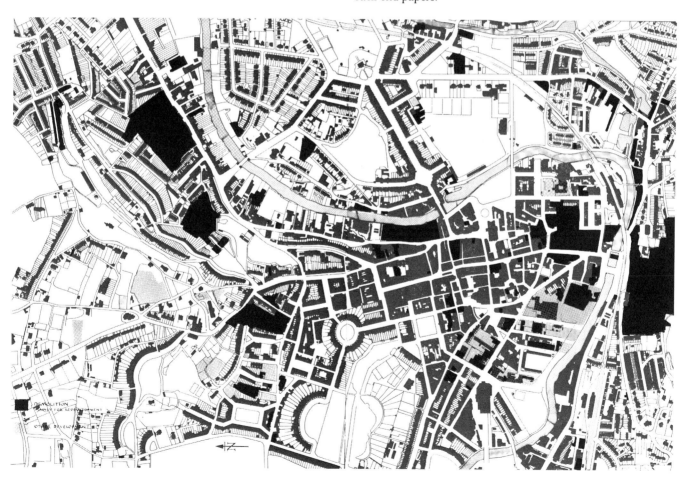

"Here, in 1970, with North-
wick House behind, is the last
public appearance of Philip
Street." From Fergusson,
The Sack of Bath, p. 19. Photo by
E. L. Green-Armytage.

"The view from Beechen Cliff. The College, center left, was designed by a member of the Royal Fine Arts Commission." From Fergusson, *The Sack of Bath*, p. 22. Photo by Snowdon.

"The replacements, built by
the mile and cut off by the yard.
The end of Marks and Spencer
can be seen behind the left
end of Woolworth's." From
Fergusson, *The Sack of Bath*, p.
25. Photo by Snowdon.

The classic picture postcard view of Bath's Pulteney Street Bridge, just two centuries old, in its setting for the 1970s. From Fergusson, *The Sack of Bath,* p. 57.

"Under Pulteney Bridge—the multideck car park is one of Bath's newest riverside amenities." From Fergusson, *The Sack of Bath*, p. 57. Photo by David Brain.

Bathwick Hill: "The redevelopment . . . lurches inelegantly down the slope, like a juggernaut with a flat tire. As the chairman of the development committee said of the Ballance Street area: 'a difficult site, being on a hillside.'" From Fergusson, *The Sack of Bath*, p. 70. Photo by E. L. Green-Armytage.

"Georgian architects made virtues of their hillsides. Directly across the road, on Bathwick Hill's north side, Dunsford Place swings downhill with the grace of the bird." From Fergusson, *The Sack of Bath*, p. 71. Photo by Snowdon.

Reprinted from *The Sack of Bath* (Salisbury, Wiltshire: Compton Russell), 1973.

Until the 1950s Bath remained among the two or three most complete period cities in the world. Planned and constructed within the short space of the century which spanned the reigns of the four Georges, it had a harmony of style and grace unmatched on such a scale anywhere else; and because it was built by a handful of rare architectural geniuses, it had a beauty unusual even for its time.

Other cities in different ways as splendid as Bath grew up normally over several centuries. In many instances the juxtaposition of buildings of different periods gives them their distinct characters and charm. Most old cities, moreover, have had extensive poor quarters, generally down-wind of the town: the "east ends" which have fallen historically further into decay as fashion and money moved elsewhere.

Here, then, is why Bath is so remarkable. The Roman spa is the tiny core of the City. The medieval town immediately around it disappeared with the Georgian development, surviving only in elements of the street pattern. Some seventeenth-century survivals apart, to all intents and purposes Bath was a "New Town"; and practically all the artisan housing—the "poor quarters"—was planned and built in conjunction with the big set pieces which made Bath magnificent. Eighteenth-century Bath had virtually no decay in it. The terraced cottages of the grooms, the ostlers, the stonemasons, the buhlcutters, the roadmakers, the porters and the Sedan chair carriers—and of the pimps, the pickpockets and the whores—were of brand new Bath stone. In their often simple way they were as perfect and graceful and as harmonious as the Bath of the middle and upper classes. All Bath grew old together. It was unique.

Bath went on expanding when Brunel's railway station and viaduct brought the early Victorians crowding to the Spa to dance, gamble and womanise as their forefathers had done. Almost always, however, the new Victorian developments respected the existing architectural style, with the result that the totality of Georgian Bath survived, and was moreover to survive into the second half of the twentieth century. Certainly some clearance of the seediest areas like Avon Street and Peter Street was started between the wars—the Dolemeads actually before the First World War. Certainly the severest war bomb damage, principally in the south of the town, necessitated some large-scale reconstruction where renovation was impracticable. Yet when the 1950s dawned the City's appearance was virtually unchanged. A bit battered, her stone worn and blackened, her basements often damp, her mansard roofs sometimes leaking, and many of her houses, well-to-do and artisan alike, below the new housing standards of the post-war world, Bath had none the less won through to the era of protective legislation for period architecture. There was every reason to expect that, with the new, growing consciousness of Britain's architectural heritage and the value of Bath in particular, her survival was assured.

Today "artisan Bath" is largely rubble. Acres upon acres of the Georgian City's minor architecture have been flattened in the course of a decade and a half, most of it during the past five years. The set pieces—Royal Crescent, the Circus, Milsom Street, the Pump Room, and so on—stand glorious and glistening (some have been restored and cleaned) for tourists to come and see in their thousands every year. But now, more and more because the devastation goes on, they have become like mountains without foothills, like Old Masters without frames. The Bath of the working classes, the Bath which made Beau Nash's fashionable resort possible, has been bodily swept away. Irreplaceable, unreproducible, serendipitous Bath, the city of period architectural vignettes with a myriad tiny alleys and corners and doorways, is either being wrenched out pocket by pocket or bulldozed in its entirety. In few places has the notion of "urban renewal" been applied with such destructive vigour as here, or with such callous disregard for the finer subtleties of urban charm.

It has not been for want of being told. The 1947 Act which first established the lists of Britain's buildings of particular architectural or historic interest gave statutory protection to nearly 2000 in Bath alone: Grade I and Grade II buildings, respectively defined as being "of outstanding interest" or "of special interest which warrant every effort being made to preserve." The provisional lists of 20 years ago also included a third grade of buildings which were "important enough to be drawn to the attention of local authorities and others, so that the case for preserving them can be fully considered."

Bath once had some 1000 of these Grade III buildings, as well as many hundreds more unlisted which would certainly have been considered for statutory protection in almost any other town. In no case before 1972 has Bath City Council shown itself anything less than merciless towards Grade III or unlisted houses which stood in its way. Nor has it been notably reluctant to knock down Grade II buildings, or to permit their destruction, when some reason was advanced to do away with them.

Enter the Packing-Case

Regrettably, that is but one side of the picture. The most wilful vandalism may be excused if that which is destroyed is replaced by something as appropriate and unquestionably as good or better. In the event, almost every original construction for 20 years in Bath has to some degree been an environmental calamity, a few less catastrophic than others but not one a positive embellishment to the City. Asked in 1972 of which buildings in the modern idiom the Corporation was really proud, the then Chairman of the Development Committee of Bath Council answered "None."

It is doubly unfortunate that the buildings in which the Corporation thus admitted to no real pride are quite unusually obtrusive. A local regulation specifying the use of Bath stone for facing all new construction has had many unhappy consequences. Bath stone is well suited to the classical style; but when applied to modern elevations built on a larger scale it serves principally to emphasize their functional nature and causes them to stand out aggressively from their surroundings. Reconstituted Bath stone, furthermore, neither weathers exactly as the fresh-cut material (whose supply is now very short), nor permits the same closeness of fitting. Although it has its uses, it actually contributes to Bath's uglification when clothing, for example, a bus station, a tower block, a motor showroom, a public lavatory, or a multi-deck car park.

Bath's contemporary developments in any case present a sad and repetitive tale of architectural discord. The stark redevelopment of Snowhill, above the London Road, seems to have launched the new era: it incorporated a tall block of flats no more appropriate to the City's style than a pop group in a symphony orchestra. In 1958, the squat nastiness of the bus station followed. Then the building of Rosewell Court (1960) began the physical and psychological isolation of the southwestern part of the Georgian town: the first but not the worst of a cordon of packing-case constructions strung around the Kingsmead area. In 1961, Northwick House, now used by the Defence Ministry, did the same thing for southern Bath—the area between Abbey Green and the station. Although faced with natural Bath stone (some of which fell off a few years later), Northwick House brought a new measure of soullessness right up to the edge of the former medieval City.

Yet in truth the Corporation was managing very well on its own; and by 1965, deliberately or not, the practice was becoming marked of separating the less spectacular expanses of period architecture from the centre, and then mopping them up quickly as soon as their relevance to the totality had gone. That bridgehead of philistinism established by Northwick House was strengthened and greatly enlarged by the spread of the Marks and Spencer and Woolworth development across the south of Abbey Green, behind a neo-Georgian frontage whose very length insults the recognized unities of the past. The pincer movement which isolated the Georgian town in the south, together with the Victorian station group at the end of Manvers Street, was completed with the construction of the new police station, to the designs of the Corporation's Planning Department, as rectangular and plain as a biscuit tin, on orchard land not far from the old Bath Oliver factory. The encircled period quarter beside Southgate Street received the *coup de grâce* by being declared a comprehensive development area. Further west, beyond Rosewell Court, there sprang up next door to one another an old people's home, the Bristol Avon River Board building, the Salvation Army Citadel and Kingsmead House (a Crown property). The discord of this group completed the desolation of south-western Bath, isolated the Green Park river terrace from the centre, and pointed to the eventual redevelopment of the adjacent Georgian streets leading to Norfolk Crescent.

At that point the Corporation planners and the developers got the bit properly between their teeth. The 1960 revised version of the City Development Plan had spelt doom for the Calton Road and Holloway district by declaring it the first comprehensive development area. On this extensive salient directly below Beechen Cliff and governing Bath's southern prospects, the old terraced houses and cottages were hacked down, and replaced after a few years by houses whose modernistic roofs give them the appearance and aura of hencoops. The 1960 plan also showed that the Council had abandoned the (scarcely credible) idea of developing for educational purposes the open space in front of the Grade I Norfolk Crescent, and instead decided to build the new Bath Technical College on ground already cleared at the north-west end of St. James's Parade. The edifices raised there today are to the designs of Sir Frederick Gibberd, the same architectural knight who built some of the terminal buildings at London Airport, of which these might just as well have been part. It was not to be the last time that a member of the Royal Fine Art Commission would contribute to the erosion of Bath's period character.

Rearguard Successes and Defeats

The late 1960s and early 1970s saw Bath's preservationists in a series of skirmishes and pitched battles with the Corporation. After public inquiries, they won the battle for Beauford Square, behind the Theatre Royal, in as much as its east side, if no longer all original, is at least constructed in the classical style. They won the battle for Abbey Church Yard, where the Development Committee had assented to the construction of a glass and concrete office block immediately beside the Abbey itself ("It would have been a magnificent building," protested the committee's then chairman). Backed by the Georgian Group, the Society

for the Preservation of Ancient Buildings, the Council for British Archaeology, and the Bath Preservation Trust, they won the battle for Kingsmead Square, the last bastion of the Georgian centre in the southwest. The City fought hard to bring the square's south side down; and its defeat was later described by the Chairman of the Development Committee as "a Ministerial decision which had no common sense linked to it—no financial common sense." After another public inquiry they won, too, a 12-month respite until the spring of 1973 for the "soap and soda" cottages[1] at Church Road, Weston, where an architect member of the Bath Preservation Trust showed that houses condemned as unfit could be adequately restored for less than £3000 each.

But they failed to save Fielding's house in Twerton where he wrote much of *Tom Jones*. They failed to preserve the west facades of the old High Street where today the hideous sham mansards of painted aluminum and ill-spaced windows of the out-of-scale "Harvey" block disgrace the heart of the City. And they lost the fight in Trim Street, where General Wolfe once lived. The removal of the roof of No. I Trim Street (a listed house) at the west end for purposes of reconstruction led instead to the serving of a dangerous structure notice and finally, after a fruitless three-year wait for permission to rebuild within the shell, to demolition of the facade. Then, in autumn 1971, after another public inquiry they lost the fight to prevent the demolition of the Grade II south side of New Bond Street which the Corporation wanted to be rid of, among other reasons, as its Counsel said at the inquiry, because of its "age."

This quietly beautiful row of shops still stands very much as Jane Austen must have known it, its curved end at Northgate Street forming a pleasing foil to the view of the Abbey from the north. The Government inspector took the view that the existing facade, "exhibiting a graceful accommodation to the slope of the street in sensitively detailed steps," was important "more for its contribution to the harmony of the street scene than for its particular architectural merit, although its connection in time with the era of elegance is not to be overlooked."

The inspector then proceeded to overlook the connection, and thought that the council after 35 years of trying should now be allowed to pull down the whole block between New Bond Street (as far as No. 10) and Upper Borough Walls. Even if that decision was slightly mitigated by the Secretary of State's insistence that the replacement must echo very closely New Bond Street's Grade II north side, in the context of Corporation policy it was a very dangerous one. As the now condemned buildings lie immediately adjacent to the "Harvey" block, the erection of more neo-pseudo-Georgiana in their place will contrive severely to widen the breach in the historic core of the Georgian City, today at this point barely a couple of hundred yards across. To preserve the New Bond Street facade as it is—trade clearly flourishing behind it—may cost more in maintenance than would a new construction. Yet here supremely is a place where the introduction of the *ersatz,* however faithful to period style, is bound, as it was in Trim Street, to be at the cost of priceless atmosphere and character.

The Lansdown Clearances

While these and other critical struggles were going on, the redevelopment of two other enormous areas of the Georgian City was proceeding at speed. The first lay prominently on Lansdown Hill above Julian Road, where six long rows[2] of stepped-up terrace houses, a few dilapidated alleys, a Georgian riding school, and Britain's only eighteenth-century royal tennis court (in sound condition and then in use as a trunk factory) were chosen for comprehensive redevelopment. The three streets of artisan dwellings, Ballance Street, Lampard's Buildings and Morford Street, were declared "unfit." The City Architect asserted that the royal tennis court lacked the glamour of the one at Hampton Court and that rather than preserve it "the needs of history would be better served by putting up a plaque on the spot." (There is only one other eighteenth-century court in the world, at Bordeaux. All other courts appear to date from the fifteenth and sixteenth centuries, or from the nineteenth-century revival of the game.)

The Ballance Street scheme, as it is now called, is after all to incorporate a handful of the artisan houses in Morford Street, now listed Grade II. Yet even this late conversion to cultural reason has its sickening side. Since the listed buildings were in much the same condition as those demolished, it makes the point that all could have been saved. Anyway, whether they will truly survive is another question. The Council may have exercised its rights by applying to the Historic Buildings Council for a renovation grant. But the size of that grant, if it comes, will now reflect the Council's having allowed the Morford Street houses to deteriorate in the few months since they were last occupied almost to the point of hopelessness. By Christmas 1972, nearly every pane of eighteenth-century glass had been smashed. Roofs and ceilings had fallen in. The backs were open to the elements. The ground floors were the haunt of tramps.

As ever, what has so far gone up in the first phase of the Ballance Street development manifestly lacks the charm of what came down. The tall, angular, inappropriate, overbearing apartment blocks, crowned again with frowning sham mansards and, to boot, a sheet of water on top of each to cool and condition the asphalt, can be seen from almost any vantage point in and around the City. They demand our attention and insult our senses. Standing beside the splendid Grade II elevations of Portland Place, they are ugly, intrusive, and tasteless; out of character and scale and harmony. The chairman of the Development Committee said that he did not like them, and that it was a difficult site being on a hillside. He explained that it was "very difficult for the layman to interpret architect's drawings," and added that part of the trouble was that the Housing Committee and the Estates Committee had had a hand in them as well. In 1972, they were perhaps the most detested new addition to the Bath scene.

It is not suggested that in design or construction those buildings fall short of the standards generally prevailing today: anywhere from Brasilia to Bracknell New Town they might very well prove admirable. Neither is it argued that Bath Corporation, its officers and its advisers, in building things of this kind are motivated by anything other than the pursuit of the public good as they see it, repudiate their works as the public may. In Georgian Bath, however, their zeal to redevelop has been tragically misplaced; and it remains the case that the old terraces were saveable almost certainly at a cost comparable to that of putting up the new blocks; that the housing situation in Bath is not so serious that the Council has yet spent money on converting the many empty storeys in central Bath (enough, according to the Buchanan Conservation study,[3] to provide about 350 flats in the study area alone); and that explanations about housing density requirements are simply not applicable in Bath's context. The houses which the Ballance Street flats replaced were homes. The flats will remain, in the words of the development plan, "units of accommodation": in appearance grotesque products of bureaucratic minds fuddled by an architectural challenge they have never understood.

Blight at the End of the Tunnel

Christmas 1971 saw the last of the Georgian town south of Abbey Green and Stall Street. Already the west side of Southgate Street had been rebuilt as a long, bald- neo-Georgian facade. Now more than five acres of mostly Georgian shops, houses, and inns (none, the Corporation pointed out, even on the supplementary list of buildings worthy of protection[4]) were bulldozed before the startled eyes of the Bathonians. These lucky citizens who were at last to be blessed on this plot with a brand new comprehensive shopping centre, now saw more of their city laid flat than ever before.

The Corporation explained that the rising tide of public indignation was attributable not to Council policy but to the fact that so much of the redevelopment in Bath happened to be coming to a head at the same time. Indeed, in 1972 cranes and bulldozers could be seen in almost every direction one looked. But that was reckoning without the Buchanan plan.[5] Public opinion hardened and crystallised over the Corporation's version of the proposal made (in 1965, based on even earlier data) by Colin Buchanan and Partners to drive a tunnel under the Georgian heart of the

City in order to solve Bath's traffic problem which, warned the Corporation, might easily get really serious by the turn of the century.

The essence of the Buchanan tunnel scheme was to bring the diverted A4 over Bathampton Meadows and through an Edwardian part of Bathwick, take it over the river upstream of Grove Street, send it through a tunnel from below the Paragon all the way to the bowling green above the Upper Bristol Road, and so speed it on its way to the West Country and the south. Whatever its merits as an antidote to Bath's traffic problems the scheme was certainly expensive; and, along with other projects which included a cut-and-cover route just outside the medieval area, it might have supplied a great deal of business to contractors and ancillary industries for a long time to come. The Buchanan study's principal deficiency, however, was that its terms of reference were cramped, and its proposals were therefore governed, by the Council's own savage development intentions. The Buchanan reports were not examinations of, still less substitutes for, the City's development plan: rather they were suggestions as to how it might be implemented. To that plan and to its impact on Georgian Bath as a whole we shall return in due course.

At any rate, by the time the Corporation's Planning Department had processed the Buchanan plan and fitted it into an immense putative network of thoroughfares from all the surrounding countryside as well as the new circulatory routes within the City, the tunnel itself was about all that remained of Buchanan's ideas. At its east end, a new A4 built to motorway standards, with approach roads and service areas and everything else, was to run beside the river—a route so destructive of Bath's amenities that Buchanan[6] had specifically rejected it. In the process, one street of Grade II buildings and a considerable number of individual ones of equal value were to go.

The street, Chatham Row, includes at its river end a building whose curious Venetian window is particularly mentioned in the lists. Yet it was used in 1967 by the Corporation's Fire Department to test the fire-resistant qualities of Georgian architecture! According to the report dated March 2, 1967, it withstood the flames for ten minutes longer than the regulations required. As a top official of the Fire Department affirmed, there would have been no point in the test had the house not been in reasonable condition. Since 1968, the penalties for deliberately destroying a listed building without ministerial sanction have been an unlimited fine and up to twelve months' imprisonment.

At the west end of the tunnel, below Royal Crescent, there were to be two-level traffic interchanges, slip roads, and all the usual paraphernalia when roads of this size and quality are made to intersect. It would necessitate large-scale demolition of Georgian property, much of it listed, and the complete severance of Norfolk Crescent from the City centre.

The arguments were endless about the need for a motorway (for such it would be), the amount of extra traffic it might draw to it, its obvious attraction to business interests in the City, the amount of damage it would do to the City's character by night as by day, the pollution and noise it would cause, and, of course, whether a ring route around the City would not in spite of the difficulties of the terrain be more desirable. The Corporation managed to split over it on party lines, of all things—the Labour minority opposing the scheme on social and financial as well as amenity grounds. Bath became a national, indeed an international scandal.

And *still* the ruin and uglification went on. On the Walcot Street site, another comprehensive development area spanning the river north of Pulteney Bridge, rose, first, a multistorey car park. It was to be topped with a pedestrian concourse or podium, so that people coming down New Bond Street could see and walk out to a balustrade overlooking the River Avon—in itself an acceptable idea. But it did not work out that way. When the concrete grew so high that it began to rob New Bond Street of any outlook whatever, this came as a surprise even to the Development Committee itself. And the slab and metal parapet which sits above the pedestrian deck today brings the total effective height of the podium to well over nine feet above the street.

Then on top of the car park there sprang up, in Bath stone and gravel panels, a rectangular hotel in architecture of the usual packing-case persuasion. Before work on the main structure had begun the Chairman of the Development Committee described it as having "a Georgian type of facade" which would harmonise "to some extent" with its surroundings which, he agreed, were of the highest importance. Its appearance today confirms that Bath never learnt the lesson of the Empire Hotel, built in 1901 a few hundred yards downstream, whose obtrusive unsuitability on such a riverside site now pales into comparative insignificance. Taken in conjunction with the top of the car park's free-standing lift shaft-cum-fume extractor, which was designed in complete isolation from the hotel although erected directly in front of it, the effect is of square hunks of cheese adorning at random what must have been the finest urban site in the West Country. Yet there is more to come: new law courts, just south of the hotel and a hundred feet from Robert Adam's Pulteney Bridge, one of the most beautiful bridges in the world.

The Drive to Redevelop

In 15 years Georgian Bath has been terribly defaced. That she is not quite a total loss at the beginning of 1973 is reason for trying to see what went wrong, who was to blame, and why they did it, so that such vandalism may cease. A few rows of artisan houses still stand, still saveable although under threat—along with a host of other beautiful although minor architectural items or groupings which have no relevance to minds concerned with giving Bath the amenities of a Birmingham: the Royal Tennis Court, the Riding School, St. Anne's Place, Allen's Row, Grove Street, the Corn Market,[7] Green Park Station,[7] Ladymead House,[7] Guinea Lane, and many more. There is scarcely one which would not have occasioned a major environmental battle anywhere else but in Bath, and which would not have been statutorily protected.

Let it be accepted that Bath 15 years ago had become an ancient City lacking certain advantages of modern or more modernised towns; that many houses were "unfit"; that the streets were unsuited for unlimited traffic circulation (or at least for an unlimited amount of "through" traffic); and that a great deal of the period architecture called for conversions. Let it be said, too, that Bath in 1970 had nowhere nearly enough money to put even her 2000-odd listed buildings into proper order, and that an £8 million programme lasting 10 or 15 years could well have been a reasonable estimate at that time for renovating them alone (a figure less daunting if it is assumed to include private capital). And for the sake of argument let it be agreed that it was sometimes hard to attract developers to Bath while giving them a whole range of "design" restrictions which did not apply elsewhere.

This line of talk, sometimes defeatist and sometimes simply specious, has been common among the Councillors and their Planning Department, persons who acknowledge the importance of Bath's grandest architecture, not least to the tourist trade, but do not seem to have seen the point of preserving anything else. So far as non-listed Georgian Bath is concerned, their urge is to develop. In the City Architect's Department, more unhappily in view of the designs which have come out of it (the Police Station, Ballance Street, the Sports Centre), it seems that the urge has been to redevelop to its own designs. Neither Development Committee—usually known elsewhere as a Planning Committee—nor City Architect's Department has shown any wish positively to preserve where preservation was possible. Their drive to redevelop apparently for redevelopment's sake is accompanied by vigorous declarations that it is wrong to preserve for preservation's sake. They say that Bath must not be allowed to become a museum (but whoever said it should?). And simultaneously they protest that in conservation matters Bath has always been in advance of any other community in the country—a trendsetter, as a leading Bath Alderman once put it, where historic towns are concerned.

That is paltering with the truth. Bath is only exceptional in having been among the first to take advantage of the Historic Buildings Council's grants scheme for restoring listed buildings; and yet Sir Colin Buchanan[8] stated in 1968 that since 1954 some £105,000 which could have been used had not in fact been spent. One wonders why not. Buchanan suggested that conservation in Bath had been hampered less by shortage of funds than by "administrative difficulties." In January 1973, writing about Bath in the *Journal of Planning and Environment Law*, the City Architect asserted that "there are limitations upon the new conservative grant facilities which may well prove unexpectedly and undesirably restrictive. The most important is that they are available only in conservation areas of 'outstanding architectural or historic interest.' "

Why does he write that sort of thing? Only Bath Council and his own Planning Department have ever stood in the way of enlarging Bath's conservation areas. As he knows perfectly well, the Parliamentary Under-Secretary at the Department of the Environment, Lord Sandford, specifically stated six months earlier that the Town and Country Planning (Amendment) Act 1972 would extend grants "to cover any expenditure on the conservation of *outstanding areas* such as Bath," and that they could be used for "the conservation of the *whole* of Bath's heritage."

Thus property which could and should have been modernised has been declared unfit and allowed to fall to pieces. Outwardly tumbledown buildings which needed only some attention to roofing, new plumbing, and a coat of paint have been cleared away as soon as they could be acquired (and sometimes even before their Compulsory Purchase Orders were confirmed by the Minister). There is no evidence that renovation and modernisation of any area has ever been seriously contemplated, if considered at all, as an alternative to comprehensive redevelopment: and yet surveyors' and architects' opinions are that it would often have been much cheaper per housing unit to have gone for restoration. "The emphasis," said the Buchanan conservation study in 1968, "is on closure with a view to eventual demolition." It is still so: nothing has since been acquired by the Council in order to save it.

The point is that a damp house may have a damp course inserted; that an unfit house may be made fit; that those who live in and enjoy the beauties of an eighteenth-century town should not expect the amenities of Harlow New Town or Hemel Hempstead; and that if they want them that is where they must go and live. And what if restoration is sometimes more expensive than rebuilding? If it costs more to preserve beauty, then the price must be discovered and, when possible, paid. And if developers are not prepared to take a somewhat smaller profit in Bath than in, say, Middlesbrough, then they must be told to go to Middlesbrough and get on with it.

That has not been the attitude of Bath Corporation. Living amid so much splendour, they have become contemptuous of anything less than magnificent; bemused by the traffic and the higgledy-piggledy shopping, and seeing from time to time how modern cities at home and abroad may be ordered, they have become less than ever able to appreciate what they possess. "Such facts and opinions as are available," stated the conservation study,[9] "lead us to think that the benefits to Bath which would derive from the tourist trade as a result of a vigorous conservation policy for the City have not yet been fully appreciated." The Councillors and their officials, lacking the advantage of an outsider's point of view, unable to see the wood for the trees, confused by local politics, have not significantly changed course. It is the kindest thing that may be said: for otherwise only bottomless philistinism appears to explain what they have done.

For a Council which claims pride in its historic heritage, there is an odd relation between the scale and timing of the City's destruction and the legislation passed at Westminster over the years intended to prevent it. In 1947, when Section 30 of the Town and Country Planning Act demanded the compilation of lists of Bath's most important buildings, the city was nearly unspoilt. For a dozen years thereafter, the public remained practically unconscious in environmental terms. To look at it another way, it was the appalling encroachments on Britain's architectural heritage made by land and property speculation during that period that awoke us to what we were losing. At any rate the listing process, though successful up to a point, could not cope with the country-wide spate of human greed let loose. The

Town and Country Planning Act of 1962 and the Civic Amenities Act of 1967 went some way to improving control of listed buildings—the latter particularly obliging Planning Authorities to designate conservation areas and to consult local amenity societies, before allowing their appearance or character to be changed.

Shortly afterwards, the Ministry of Housing and Local Government's Circular 53/67 enjoined those Planning Authorities to require detailed (as distinct from outline) applications from developers, a move which if followed in 1971 might have prevented the turning of the Southgate Street development plans into what the Chairman of the Development Committee called "an abortion." By that time the sack of Georgian Bath was well under way. True, conservation areas were duly designated; but in the event they included only those parts of Bath whose destruction not even a Planning Authority could conceivably get away with. More seriously, as the terms of reference given to Buchanan showed, they excluded everything which the Council felt it might one day need or like to develop.

The brief given to Buchanan nearly a decade ago is, indeed, highly revealing. His maps of Bath buildings of architectural or historical interest[10] included neither the Grade III buildings nor all the Grade II ones. The City's self-declared conservation areas coincide almost precisely with the "fixed areas" given to Buchanan and around which he had to work: the fixed areas in fact were slightly larger, as they included various recent developments like the Technical College. Anything outside those fixed areas, Buchanan was led to understand, comprised "potential development areas, existing proposals," or "additional areas which could be considered for redevelopment by the year 2000."[11] In other words, Bath has not moved a step forward in conservation terms over these years: it has merely taken some extra control over buildings already protected once.

A series of governmental measures in the meantime, including the Historic Buildings and Ancient Monuments Act 1953 and the already mentioned Civic Amenities Act 1967 (which amended it) made money available in loans and grants to make preservation possible. Thus Bath Council was able with pride to point in its 1960 revised development plan to the cleaning and restoration of 11 Circus properties, with another six then being worked on, "since the scheme first commenced in 1955." Two pages earlier, however, the same report was noting that 480 dwellings had been demolished or closed since 1951, and was sounding the death knell of some 1370 other "unfit dwellings which cannot in any circumstances be made fit at reasonable expense." Others of Bath's unfit properties, the report went on, "are being and will be modernised and improved" with recourse to the Government's standard and discretionary improvement grants. It was noted that already 400 units of accommodation had been provided since 1952 by converting Georgian buildings. And it was hoped that a further 800 might be provided by further conversion.

This presentation was disingenuous. The 400 units provided by conversion did not indicate the recovery of a like number of houses: they included, for example, the 26 self-contained flats and maisonettes converted alone from the five Corporation properties in the Circus. And the figure of 800 units was hedged with the possibility that it was "too optimistic because of any change in conditions." Further study of the figures, moreover, showed that Bath's expected housing deficiency in 1960 was considerably worsened by the prospect of the loss of another 1241 houses "not unfit" but which were "to be demolished for road proposals," or "included within existing and proposed industrial zones," or "required in connection with miscellaneous planning proposals."

The worst fears and suspicions that this section of the report engendered were duly justified. The fact is that it was the intention of Bath Corporation in 1960 to sweep away within a decade more than 2600 of the Georgian houses in the City, to join the 500 which had already gone since 1951; and that at that time only one comprehensive development area had been declared. Amendment after amendment was to follow, progressively robbing the city of its countless smaller treasures. The scale of intended destruction went far to explain the selective and irrelevant nature of the City's conservation areas when they were at last declared.

The use of the word "sack" to describe destruction of this kind is not exaggeration.

The 1968 Town and Country Planning Act brought those of 1947 and 1962 up to date, giving a greater measure of protection to listed buildings especially from private developers and, as the lists were about to be revised (a process which would bring many more Grade III buildings within statutory protection), suppressed the supplementary lists which had been such an invitation to developers to knock down Grade III buildings while the knocking was good. Unfortunately, if a Local Authority is not preservationist-minded, in the long run there is little that the Department of the Environment, to say nothing of the amenity societies, can do. The otherwise laudable policy of devolving more power on local government becomes merely lunatic when the national heritage is at stake.

The 1972 Town and Country Planning Amendment Act not only greatly increased the power of Local Authorities to control developments within their own Department-approved conservation areas but provided a fund for renovating old buildings which, because it can always be replenished, in practice could be virtually limitless. The Act in effect challenged Bath City Council not only to draw up a long-term conservation programme, but to solve the considerable problem of planning and carrying out conservation and restoration schemes at the kind of rate made possible by the increased amounts offered.

The unhappy conclusion to be drawn is that as the country has become progressively more worried about its ancient buildings and as sterner measures have been taken to persuade and to help Local Authorities to protect what was in their charge, the destruction occasioned and permitted by Bath Corporation has increased in full proportion. In 1972, it was as unbridled as it had ever been. That statement is not lightly made. By September that year, when the City's Planning Department received official notification of about 760 Bath buildings, not to be listed by the Ministry, but nevertheless eligible for local protection and control as being of local historic and architectural interest—as would now be possible under Section 8 of the new Act—106 of them had already gone.

The City Architect seems already to have found Section 8 impracticable. "It seems unlikely," he wrote in January 1973, "that proper use can be made of a Section 8 Direction in the 1972 Act to control demolition of unlisted buildings in conservation areas, because of the enormous task posed by the serving of notices upon the owners and occupiers of all such buildings in such an extensive area. This, and even the process of serving notice upon the owners and occupiers of buildings in a revised Statutory List, represents one of the embarrassments due to the exceptionally large number of listed buildings in the City."

To these breath-taking pronouncements there are some short answers. No time limit is imposed on a local authority for serving such notices—and the Department of the Environment is adopting the practice of impersonally informing the owners or occupiers of newly-listed buildings before the statutory notices are issued, purposely to thwart the dilatoriness of councils who haven't time or won't care. Further, the "enormous" task only happens once, and is no greater than that of collecting rates. As the local authority is also the rating authority to which the relevant names and addresses are known, the same envelopes might even be used. (And one might add that the *number* of Bath's listed buildings has nothing whatever to do with controlling the demolition of unlisted buildings in conservation areas or anywhere else; nor, in any case, is the serving of listing notices the business of the City Architect's Department.)

Designers and Advisers

There has been nothing particularly covert about the Corporation's intention to pull down and redevelop Bath so far as broad principles go. What the preservationists have lacked for many years has been the detailed information about where the destroyers would strike next, and of what would go up instead. An important example is the new Law Courts, proposed for the site between the new hotel and Pulteney Bridge. The City Architect's design was kept tenaciously in his own hands and stayed a Council secret until the middle of 1972—and by then the substructure of the Courts (comprising the south end of the Walcot Street car

park) was actually completed. Requests from the Bath Preservation Trust for information had been rejected since 1970.

In the spring of 1972 it was rumoured that the City Architect's Law Courts were so little in tune with the character of Georgian Bath that they were windowless. Then it transpired that designs had been submitted to the Royal Fine Art Commission. The Trust's Annual Report recorded in November 1972: "The Royal Fine Art Commission expressed the view that it should have been consulted at a much earlier stage over the whole development of the Walcot Street area including the hotel, the multi-deck car park and the new Law Courts building. It said that the Law Courts building in relation to New Bond Street and Pulteney Bridge demanded architecture of the highest quality. This was not to be discerned in the designs submitted to it. It was felt that the City Council should put the design of the Law Courts out to competition or appoint an outside consultant before anything further was done. On October 12 the Development Committee of the Council reconsidered the position and decided to ask the President of the Royal Institute of British Architects to submit a short list of names from which the Committee could select a consultant architect." The Corporation already employed one consultant architect, Sir Hugh Casson.

The City development plan, to which reference has already been made, laid down the Council's general strategy as long ago as 1952 and reconfirmed it in the amended version of 1960. This latter document, like the official Written Statement of 1966 (a summary for Ministerial use and approval), contains the word "Georgian" precisely twice. On the first occasion in the Written Statement, it is simply noted in the context of residential development that, as the reputation and prosperity of Bath is linked with its Georgian architecture, "one of the Corporation's *problems* is the preservation of *fine* examples of this period in the City" (italics are mine). The other is in the context of the proposed east-west route—"to direct through traffic from the existing A4 which passes through the heart of the Georgian area of the City."

One searches the Written Statement in desperation for any other recognition by the City Fathers of what Bath is. Under the heading "Character and Function of Bath" we learn that it was their intention to "retain and improve" the City as a spa and a tourist centre; as a cultural and educational centre; as a regional shopping centre and a centre for the Admiralty; as a residential City for retired persons and for professional classes; and as a small and well-balanced manufacturing City.

There follows a vigorous summarized account of how all that—some of it obviously unexceptionable—was to be achieved. There were to be a new Police Station, a swimming bath, and multi-deck car parks on land compulsorily acquired. Existing residential areas were to be "substantially redeveloped." Fifty more acres along the river bank and elsewhere were designated for industry. There would even be a helicopter station. The purpose of the one comprehensive development area of Calton Road/Holloway was "to deal satisfactorily with the conditions within this area of obsolete development, dereliction and vacant sites." It was envisaged that more than 300 dwellings would be demolished there alone before 1973, with a further 79 to be considered thereafter. So vanished "satisfactorily" another 28 acres of Georgian and pre-Georgian suburb.

It is easy, tempting, and technically right to blame Bath City Council and its Development Committee over this period for what has happened there. At a remove one might blame the electorate of Bath for putting and keeping these men and women in power. But local electorates are notoriously apathetic, and matters are more complicated than that. Although apparently blind to the importance of the preservation of as much of the whole as practicable, and sadly unimaginative when it came to finding new uses for old buildings, the Council has shown itself conscientious about the set pieces, and fully conscious of the poor impression bad planning and bad building made on the world.

Thus the Council some years ago became a great consulter and employer of the biggest names in the architectural and planning business. Notable among these, and retained as adviser is Sir Hugh Casson, a member of the Royal Fine Art Commission; and Sir Colin Buchanan, now also a member of the Commission, whose "tunnel scheme" was accepted by Bath Corporation but most of whose detailed recommendations for conserving the City (including notoriously the routing of the tunnel's approach roads) have so far been ignored or rejected. Sir Frederick Gibberd did the Technical College, and Mr. Owen Luder the second lot of designs for the Southgate Street site, Sir Basil Spence's having been abandoned.

With a member of the Royal Fine Art Commission, Sir Hugh Casson, to guide its aesthetic sense, what more could the Council have been expected to do? In fact as their City Architect and head of the Planning Department they appointed a university architectural lecturer, recently author of an exhaustive book on Colen Campbell, a Palladian architect of the earlier part of the eighteenth century in England. But alas, it brought no respite for Bath in the destruction of the Palladian City's period architectural undergrowth. And it has thus been with the advice, guidance, and approval of two highly qualified men that Bath Council has wrought the devastation of the past seven or eight years.

In 1972, the restlessness in the City about what was going on began increasingly to be reflected in the Guildhall. Although approved by the Development Committee, the Cavendish Lodge scheme to build three blocks of flats below Lansdown Crescent was rejected in March by the full Council who balked at accepting the justification proffered by a member of its Development Committee that "anyway in summer it would be almost hidden by the trees." The same fate awaited the Development Committee's approval of plans for development of Springfield Gardens, a unique site behind Lansdown Crescent. At some point doubt, too, must have assailed Sir Hugh Casson himself, for in September, a mere fortnight before the first piles were to be driven, he submitted the plans for the new £930,000 sports centre on the Recreation Ground to the Royal Fine Art Commission. Sir Hugh's own colleagues on the Commission found the architecture "heavy and monolithic" and the choice of the site "most unfortunate," but when they asked the Council to reconsider its proposals the request was immediately turned down.

One should not underestimate the extent to which a local authority Planning Committee is in the hands of its professional advisers and employees. Architecturally untrained, most of them, Councillors have the greatest difficulty in visualising what a finished building will look like with no more assistance than an architect's drawing prettified with trees, shrubs, and falling water. To judge by what has been built in this country by the best-known architects, one might guess that the architects themselves hardly know what they have done until it is finished. Councillors find it embarrassing to argue with professionals who declare a building unfit, or dangerous, or too expensive to restore; and who assert that the obviously hideous and unsuitable is a work of merit and art.

In other words the responsibilities of a Local Authority's full-time Architectural and Planning Department are enormous; and if it interprets them in terms of redevelopment, and of reconstructing an old City in a modern idiom, that is how it will go—build in reconstituted Bath stone as you may. As the City Architect said of the 1777 Royal Tennis Court in Morford Street, "if the university needs one it would be as easy to build them another"; or to quote him again: "If you want to keep Georgian artisans' houses, then you will have to find Georgian artisans to live in them." How does one answer such remarks? They prevent sensible consideration of conservation problems and, worse, render the necessary process of careful, essential civilised redevelopment far more difficult to contrive.

"It is cherishing all the features, from buildings to atmosphere," wrote Sir Colin Buchanan, "which gives a historic town its value, whilst ensuring at the same time that the town does not become a dead museum piece."[12] As the City Architect has it, however: "The hard realities of the situation are that when the economic life of a building is over there is no good reason for preserving it." So far the two approaches have not been reconciled. The City Architect described the proposed Southgate Street complex as "a fairly straightforward, unaffected, efficient solution in terms of providing a machine in which to shop." The *Bath and Wilts*

Evening Chronicle early in 1972 quoted a local estate agent as saying: "If people realised what Southgate Street is going to look like, they'd have been marching down there to pull the demolition men off their bulldozers."

When Enough Is Enough

What ought to be done? Bath Council is still bent on implementing a 20-year-old development plan which, amendments and all, ought never to have seen the light of day. Its purpose was to transform a unique architectural entity, built as a "fun" city, into a modern urban complex in which all but the finest pieces of Georgian architecture would be mere encumbrances. Almost uncomprehendingly, Sir Colin Buchanan wrote to *The Times* on June 3, 1972, to ask: "Have attitudes to comprehensive development changed? If so with what justification and with what results? When we approached our task originally we found that a number of areas had been designated for comprehensive redevelopment and we made use of these proposals. No one questioned those areas at that time. What has happened?"

It is only too obvious what has happened. People have seen dearly-loved townscapes disappearing before their eyes, only to be replaced by hulking buildings so awful that no one without a direct interest has a good word to say for them. People have had enough.

What credit is left to Bath Council and its Officers for making so many "right" noises and consulting so many "right" people? The noises—some of them recorded in these pages—have barely muffled the crash of falling masonry. When the "right" people's advice has not coincided with the plans of the Architect's Department it has often been ignored. Sir Colin Buchanan specifically said that the Recreation Ground should not be considered for roadworks[13] (but the Council is putting its Sports Centre on it); that neither river bank should be spoilt by a tunnel approach road[14] (but the Council wants to drive a motorway along the north bank); and that the Grove Street area beside Pulteney Bridge should be used for riverside recreation (but the Council has recently considered plans for a number of multi-storey blocks there).

This is no place to examine the quality of local Councillors, nor to digress on the pressures to which they are subject. Suffice it to say that in Bath (as in many other towns with aesthetic problems of any size) the Council and its Officials show no sign of becoming equipped with either the sensitivity or the determination to solve the town's conservation and preservation problems in a cultured manner. They are still asking "why?" instead of deciding "how"; and it is getting too late. In these matters they have not understood and do not understand their responsibilities to Bath and to the nation.

Those who have struggled to preserve Bath have had an unenviable task, and have fought a mainly losing battle. Often, no doubt, they have not fought hard enough. "The destroyers," as I was told many months ago, "work from nine to five every day, sitting in comfortable offices, figures and plans and projects at their finger-tips or simply in their minds, and they get paid for what they do. The preservers have to make their own time, usually in the evenings or at weekends when they would prefer to be with their families, acquiring what facts and figures and plans they can get hold of, often finding that action is too late, too difficult, or too expensive; and they have to raise the money for it themselves, organize petitions, and pay for legal and architectural expenses out of their own pockets."

The illustrations in this chapter have been carefully assembled. They show the tragedy of what has gone in the recent past and the hopeless incongruity of what has taken its place. They show some of what is immediately threatened, and the dangers of further losses. It is evident to those who have studied the problem at first hand that until Bath's conservation areas have been redrawn to take account of the whole of Bath—of its surrounding landscapes as well as its townscapes—a halt should be called to further demolition and redevelopment.

Has not this national treasure, so terribly abused, at last to become a national responsibility? Bath could still develop as a residential, tourist, and university town of unique beauty and charm, and a joy to its inhabitants as well as to its visitors. If it continues on its present headlong course it will become a modern semi-industrial city, shredded by urban motorways, in which all but the very finest period architecture has been cleared away. That course might be of benefit to some commercial and financial interests within the community, and might bring material advantages of a sort; but it would be at an architectural, historical, sociological, and cultural cost that the City and the nation need not and should not pay.

Postscript

Since the essay was written the prospects for the city have changed beyond recognition. With new men in charge,[15] supported by new Government legislation, Ministerial interest and generous finance, and by means of greatly extending those areas of Bath eligible for conservation aid, the city authorities have set about preserving for posterity those very elements of its fabric that were being so rapidly lost by demolition and decay.

The scrapping of the plan for the tunnel under the Georgian centre led eventually to the removal of planning "blight" from many threatened areas. Of the buildings mentioned in this story, there is new hope for the survival of such gems as St. Ann's Place, New Bond Street, Chatham Row, Hampton Row, Allen's Row, Ladymead House, Grove Street and many others. The building of the new Law Courts was stopped, but not the further housing schemes below Beechen Cliff, nor the sports complex on the recreation ground, nor the third stage of Ballance Street, where the Georgian Riding School, neglected, simply fell into the roadway.

The physical and financial problems of rehabilitating an entire city, of finding new, viable uses for all its old, preservable buildings, mean that there must still be far to go before Bath can be declared truly safe. New developments there must be, which will rightly continue to be the subject of great local controversy. But the will to succeed and to preserve is there at last; and despite the wounds inflicted in recent years Bath will remain a city like Edinburgh, Venice, Rome or Constantinople, though smaller than any of them, still worth crossing the world to see.

Notes

1. They were originally occupied by servants from the large City houses, who brought their employers' laundry home to wash.

2. One row, Lampard's Buildings east side, was in fact Victorian and among the first council houses built in Britain.

3. *Bath — A Study in Conservation,* H.M.S.O., 1968, Para. 84.

4. But in the New Bond Street inquiry, the Corporation put forward in support of their case the fact that some of the buildings had only recently been listed Grade II, raised from Grade III: an interesting example of how third grade *invited* demolition, as though that classification denoted inferiority.

5. *Bath — A Planning & Transport Study,* 1965.

6. *Ibid.,* para. 228.

7. Grade II in the revised lists (1972).

8. *Bath — A Study in Conservation,* 1968. Para. 114.

9. *Ibid.,* Para. 81.

10. *Bath — A Planning and Transport Study,* 1965, figure 5.

11. *Ibid.,* figure 27.

12. *Bath — A Study in Conservation,* 1968, Para 8.

13. *Bath — A Planning and Transport Study,* 1965. Para. 28, 225.

14. *Ibid.,* para. 225, 253, 228.

15. Editor's note: Roy Worskett, author of *The Character of Towns* (1969) is now the city's planning director, and a unique study of the economic implications of "minimum physical change" has been carried out by Nathaniel Lichfield and Partners (1976).

4

The City Center of Istanbul: Its Past and Its Future Problems

Turgut Cansever

Istanbul: the monuments.
Courtesy of Professor Nezim
Eldem.

Istanbul: the wooden houses.
Courtesy of Professor Nezim
Eldem.

Istanbul: working-class quarter
of wooden houses in poor condition. Courtesy of Professor
Nezim Eldem.

From the sixteenth century onwards the Ottoman Empire had been losing, step by step, its geographical superiority on the trade routes between the prosperous eastern countries and the West. Failing to keep up with the western phenomenon of industrialization, the Empire was definitely falling into an inferior position. The desire to regain superiority led to attempts at importing re-evaluated western cultural and technological developments into the country and seeking to create new syntheses.

The most important influences came from France, a country which had developed a notable example of centralized administration. The old Ottoman state structure, which was generally decentralized, was replaced by a gradually strengthening centralized state.

Another significant change is related to the place given to technology. The Ottoman world outlook which had given priority to developing the balance of man with his environment was replaced by solutions which depended on pragmatic approaches, and on technology.

For five hundred years, up to the end of the nineteenth century, Istanbul developed as one of the most important cities in the world. The approach of the Ottomans in reorganizing the city aimed at re-evaluating the Roman-Byzantine heritage with an Eastern attitude.[1]

At that time the city consisted of three main independent centres, being separated from each other by the Bosphorous and the Golden Horn. These were Istanbul (Darüssade — city of Happiness), Galata, and Uskudar, the Holy City of Eyup, and the small Bosphorous villages. However, through the construction of two bridges over the Golden Horn connecting Galata with Istanbul and through the foundation of the Sirket-i Hayriye company, which was responsible for connecting the Bosphorous villages, Uskudar, and Kadikoy to Istanbul, as well as for developing and managing urban ferry crossings, and extension of the railroads up to Sirkeci, destroying important buildings of the Topkapi Palace in the process on the one hand and eastwards from Haydarpasa on the other, separate sections of the city were connected to one center, the central areas of Sirkeci, Eminonu, and Galata.

During the same period immigration, caused particularly by the collapse of the Anatolian manufacturing system as a result of the 1840 Anglo-Turkish Trade Agreement, affected Istanbul and consequently the population of the city rose in the period of approximately 30–40 years from 500,000 to 850,000 in 1870.

In this period, the group of new rich levantins created by foreign trade built up new quarters in Beyoglu with new techniques and styles. The contrast between the permanent construction forms consisting of religious and community buildings of the quarter centers and the temporary character of the wooden houses, the separation of the community facilities from the privacy of the internal courtyards of the houses and the balance between the buildings and nature, all characterizing the Ottoman urban structure, were replaced by eclectic construction forms and imitations which disregarded this sense of balance and these relationships.

Also in the same period, there developed new groups of buildings which were not connected to the culture and technology of the past, in and around the historical commercial and staging districts and areas of inns of the Istanbul peninsula. The area rapidly became concentrated and the roads once walked on by Suleyman the Magnificent on his way to the mosque were torn up and expanded in order to facilitate passage of horse carts and later the horse drawn trams.

The new centralized, military government established its dominance over the old structure and destroyed the whole hierarchy of humane cultural values. To locate important structures in new directions and to liquidate the historic Ottoman and Islamic values became the main attitude. After the 1900s, the destructive results of this attitude emerged in the form of changing historical land use forms. The Golden Horn was opened up to slaughterhouses, warehousing, wholesale markets, and other industrial uses.

After the foundation of the Republic, the population of Istanbul remained constant for a certain period. However, we can observe the rapid demolition of the old quarters of wooden houses and the construction of degenerate architectural imitations inspired by western cubism as a result of the westernization drive of the Republic.

The future of Istanbul, which again became the focus of attention around 1935, was envisaged as a city of 500,000–600,000 population living in 5–6 story buildings with internal courtyards, built according to the continuous row system, similar to Paris.

Particularly in the years following the assignment of the French architect, H. Prost, with the task of preparing a plan for Istanbul, attempts to give a western appearance to the city dominated all enterprises of different sources and foundations. Here, westernization was generally understood to mean Paris; the demolition of all existing structures and their rebuilding (on the lines of the French Revolution) following the example of Baron Haussmann. This line of thought was put into application once around 1938 with the construction of the Ataturk Boulevard which once more changed the historical bridge and road network connecting Istanbul to Galata and for the second time in the period 1957–1960, in connection with Prime Minister Menderes' activities of opening up wide roads in the Historical Peninsula which were the implementation of Prost's proposals. This eased access of vehicle traffic into the city center, and was accompanied by the construction of Salipazari and Haydarpasa cargo terminals in the historical central districts in the same period, the introduction of industrial areas in the Golden Horn and to the west of the historical city center, and the development towards the north of center functions which could not be accommodated in the Istanbul Peninsula.

After 1950 the population of the city grew rapidly as a result of internal immigration. The population of the city was 570,000 in 1937, 900,000 in 1949, 1,800,000 in 1960, and had reached 3,800,000 by 1974. Actually we know that the population will be at least 7.1 millions or might possibly reach 9.2 millions in 1995 and that there is the danger of the city population topping the 12 million mark at the end of the present century.

The question of how to settle the new population in and around the city will affect to a large extent the possibility or otherwise of preserving historical Istanbul, the Bosphorous, and Uskudar, which are full of the most precious cultural values of human history, to continue to transmit the message of these values to humanity.

Two important mistakes were made in the past concerning these areas and values, first in thinking that the Ottoman cultural values and the historical existence of Istanbul were insignificant and in then believing that the city's future could be saved by undertaking resettlement and reorganization in these areas.

We are now faced with the task of clarifying these two points. The attitude of the last Ottoman cultural layer, which developed by integrating with the Roman-Byzantine tradition of historical Istanbul, as regards the culture of the past ages, reflects a very special historical consciousness.

The techniques they used for supplementing Roman-Byzantine structures with their own cultural values; the forms of particular relationships they established between the temporary and the permanent, the universal and the individual and local; the variety they achieved in a sphere of standards; the nature-man relationship of the world they established—the originality of all these solutions they developed lay in their combination of the pure, the dignified and the great with elegance.

Parts of the city, which consisted of fragile wooden structures built around the mosques (community buildings), markets, and such facilities as inns and public baths and which were kept up through constant maintenance, were abandoned to destruction as a result of changes that took place in the socioeconomic structure and the urban land use system. The opening up of the Golden Horn to industrial development, the establishment of the Topkapi Industrial Area in 1954, and the *gecekondu*[2] districts, which developed around the historical city, caused the old inhabitants of the historical city to move out. The districts of inns of the historical city center were abandoned to warehousing and similar low level uses.

The attainment of a level which would enable the regeneration of the cultural values of the whole of this area is one of the fundamental goals of present planning activites.

It is necessary to consider this subject with a view to the resources and dimensions of the twenty to twenty-five years in front of us. The main problem is how to distribute the population to the east and west of the axis formed by the Bosphorous in a city which will accommodate a population of 7 to 9 million people. The equal distribution of the population to the east and west of the Bosphorous will be a continuation of the policy of concentration in the historical central area and will lead to the complete elimination of the historical city. Therefore the strategy of resettling the new population in metropolitan Istanbul will necessarily include the reorganization of center functions.

It cannot be conceived that all of the center functions necessitated by the growing population can be met in the historical center. It is also clear that the historical city will be destroyed by the effects of such concentration and land use form. It is necessary to use the historical city as a cultural area in the new system of centers to be established, and to reconsider railroad, port, and industry relationships which account for the present situation.

The line of thought established by Prof. Piccinato concerning the achievement of linear development for Istanbul, and attempts to establish a new hierarchy of centers which go as far back as 1957 have come to supplement each other today. Unhealthy conditions caused by the separation of Istanbul, Galata, Uskudar, and Kadikoy from each other by the Bosphorous, and also the existing structure of these areas, are posing a serious threat to redevelopment.

This fact, as well as the additional functions Istanbul will have to accommodate within the context of the whole Middle East, necessitate the creation of a new system of control functions.

Istanbul is faced with the task of solving the housing and employment problems of nearly 200,000 new population each year on the one hand and restoring the historical urban areas which are focal points of historical and cultural values on the other.

There is consideration of making use of the new transport system, as well as organization and control of land use forms, in improving the unhealthy structure and to achieve the transition to this new land use and settlement form with an action orientated approach. Also of implementing a regional decentralization policy to protect Istanbul against new industrial and demographic pressures.

A balanced development is foreseen for Istanbul through the introduction of regional measures to protect metropolitan Istanbul from the pressure of population, through the containment of industry and the new population in new cities to be developed in the region, and through new poles and axes of development on a national level. Consequently, urban planning in Istanbul has been directed to the twin aims of developing the new settlement areas of the expanding city around a new system of centers, and maintaining, preserving, and restoring the historical quarters.

Assuming that a population of 500,000–800,000 will inhabit the historical urban areas, that is, about 5 percent of the total future metropolitan population of 8–10 million people, it can be seen that, on the whole, the preservation of cultural values existing in these areas will present a relatively limited problem.

Naturally, the above mentioned general strategies would not be sufficient for the preservation of historical areas and of the traditional sector. In practice, the problem of preservation directly relates to two necessities. In order of priority these are, primarily, the necessity of reorganizing the environment of works of art and monuments crowning the historical areas, in order to maintain and develop them as the focal points of the citizens' interest and value system, and, secondarily, of transmitting to the coming generation the solutions found and experience lived in organizing the cultural environment by other cultural eras.

Planning should assist the movement to new locations of manufacturing; warehousing; trade and administrative functions; land use forms which are responsible for damaging the historical areas and which are in turn hampered in their development because of such limitations as prevention measures; transport difficulties; and land costs. Attempts are already being made to direct in a planned way cultural institutions with relevant needs to locations vacated by the above mentioned activities.

The quarters of Eyup, Zeyrek, Suleymaniye, and Kucuk Ayasofya, which partially escaped damage, should be restored and the problems of the present inhabitants of these quarters arising from the conditions brought about by restoration should be solved.

In addition to the matters explained above, I would like to point out the international importance of the following questions: the preservation of the Bosphorous historical site and the restoration of the Golden Horn; Kagithane; Alibey picnic grounds of Eyup, Zeyrek, etc.; the environment of the Byzantine walls and the coastal strip of the historical city; and the archaeological area of the Roman-Byzantine palaces, as well as the district of inns.

It is evident that internationally standardized conventional architectural practice should be discarded. To accomplish the mission of sustaining the traditional sector necessitates a new, different approach to the problem. This approach, being the source and reflection of architectural achievement, necessarily will be similar to, or a continuation of, the attitude which is the source of the traditional.

In the case of Istanbul and Ottoman city culture, the problem was the resolution of the dichotomies of the individual and the universal, of variety and standardization, of the large and small, of the austere and gentle, of the eternal and the temporary, of the solid infrastructure and the independent superstructure, of the freedom and control of the personal experience and sensibility and scientific objective research. All this in the context of the attempted efforts for the resolution of historical contradictions between the past and present cultures.

The fundamental principle in carrying out this task will be "not to change until the old can be replaced by something better."

Notes

1. There are numerous examples of this approach of the Ottoman view of history which sought to establish new relationships between separate entities. Let us point out here as an example of this attitude, the redevelopment through such Ottoman additions as support walls, minarets, mausolea, etc. of the Ayasofya (St. Sophia).

2. *Gecekondu* means almost literally "fly-by-night." It is derived from *gece*, and refers to a law allowing houses to remain up if a roof could be put on by dawn of the morning following their construction, that is, overnight. Needless to say, such districts are for poor working or unemployed people, usually slums.

5 An Urban Renovation Experience in the Center of Brussels: The Manhattan Plan

Nicole Brasseur

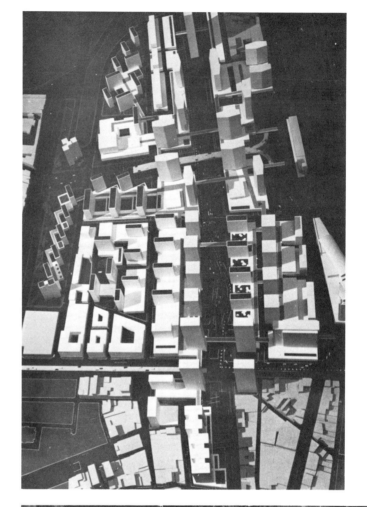

The Manhattan Project, Brussels: the plan includes the pulling down of houses accommodating about 12,000 lower-income families (1967 figure) and the construction of thirty skyscrapers, residences for 13,000 persons (for whom?), car parks for 16,000 cars, and employment for 100,000 people. From *Wonen–TA/BK,* August 1975.

Angry demonstration outside the Collège Echevinal de Bruxelles. Photo Comité d'action local.

This material appeared originally in *Clearing House Abstract* (The Hague), No. 4, October 1972

Introduction

For some years past the center of Brussels has changed very much. Impressive constructions, such as the "South tower," the "Madou tower," the Philips Complex, and the Mint center, were built. Several main traffic roads have lost their trees, are crossed by several subterranean roads, tunnels, and train and underground lines, or are bridged by provisional or definitive viaducts.

In short: Brussels is and will be an enormous building site during the next few years. This large setup of town planning has a twofold purpose: on the one side to give the city center its administrative and commercial status through a concentration of office buildings, quick and direct connecting roads, easy and money-producing parking places, and on the other side to facilitate the flight of the more well-to-do inhabitants to places with clean air and quiet. Because of an efficient cooperation of private and public men in power this setup can be realized. With all this the inhabitants of the neighborhoods in question are overlooked. An arrangement with those inhabitants, or even their having a say in the plan, is out of the question. The "rebellion" in the nineteenth century in the "Marollen" quarter, or the unsuccessful opposition to the tower of the ITT (near the abbey of Ter Kameren) are still fresh in everybody's mind.

It should be worthwhile for people to think about the import of the vivisection which is being carried out at the moment on the Belgian metropolis by the construction of motorways that cut through old neighborhoods and create noise and air pollution. There are the consequences of seting such skyscrapers in one line (such as sudden gusts of wind, increasing noise, daily concentrations of working people). And finally the doubtful effectiveness of repopulation of the metropolis through such a project. A reply to this question is outside the scope of this chapter, but it is high time that these questions were raised by independent specialists of the various sciences.

I will, from my side, limit myself here to the fate of the inhabitants, who were confronted by a "town plan" for which they were not prepared. The inhabitants of the so-called northern quarter, situated on both sides of the North Station, are meant here.

These people are at the moment involved in a new building plan called "Manhattan," which was approved by Royal Decree in 1967. Involved are 53 hectares, the greatest reconstruction area up till now in the whole of Europe, scattered over the municipalities St. Joost-ten-Node, Schaarbeek, and Brussels (Brussels is divided into a number of smaller municipalities).

The Quarter Itself

From the Second World War on there has been some talk of—a necessary!— modernization of this quarter. The business activities in this quarter have, since the beginning of this century, been declining rapidly.

As a result the various house-owners neglected their premises. Near the station, hotels and pubs came into being. Narrow little streets and slums without sun, houses of the last century, badly kept and often unhealthy, surround the big street which crosses right through the quarter.

In 1967, 8,000 to 10,000 people were living in this quarter, of which 25 percent are older than 60 years. Many people have a shamefully low income and are dependent on relief. About 90 percent of the families are laborer families, often foreigners (especially North Africans, Greeks, Portuguese, Turks, and refugees from Eastern Europe, Spaniards, Congolese, and people from Common Market countries). The easy accessibility of the quarter, the low rent (although that is only because of the condition of the houses), the discrimination in other neighborhoods, explain the concentration of foreign laborers. Mostly they have large families, so that half of the houses are overcrowded.

Less than 10 percent of the inhabitants are owner-occupiers; 85 percent pay less than 1500 Belgian francs rent per month; 45 percent even less than 1000 Belgian francs. More than 15 percent of the houses have no running water or electricity. More than 60 percent of the families do not have their own toilets.

With those figures the miserable condition of the houses is made clear. One can also come to the conclusion that the land value is, relatively, not very high and that therefore the building of department stores on this land is very attractive. Moreover, the long lease terms which are agreed on with the businessmen and authorities of the municipality make this enterprise doubly attractive.

The Plan

The physical development plan includes the pulling down of houses and the construction of a pedestrian walkway 13 meters high, besides 30 skyscrapers; namely, 684,000 square meters of office buildings and hotels, 405,000 square meters of residences for 12,000 persons (for whom?), 375,000 square meters of storage, 554,000 square meters of parking space, and carparks for 16,000 cars. There should be employment for 100,000 people, with working conditions, which—according to the brochure "Manhattan-Center"—should comply with the highest European standards.

Compared with the quarter as it was in 1967, a cancerous tumor in the city, the Manhattan project is very attractive. Therefore, one of the promoters said proudly in an interview: "Look! What do you prefer, gentlemen of the press, Daddy and Mummy in their apartment in front of their television set or a building like this?"

And that is the crucial point. What will happen to Daddy and Mummy, who depend on relief and have no television set, and what will happen to their neighbors, Mohamed ben Mohamed blessed by Allah with numerous offspring. *How* will they find other houses and *where* will they find other houses?

Hard Reality: Expulsion

Belgian law authorizes the burgomaster of a city to evacuate or to pull down slums in the public interest. However, the law does not make him responsible for taking care that expelled people will get new houses. Doubtless they reckon on the social feelings of the aldermen. But those aldermen only signed the contracts with the businessmen, who were interested in the conditions of the plan. The government binds itself to have the area cleared by a fixed date, a task which they complete with due speed. It is estimated that already half of the inhabitants have left the quarter and that the rest will undergo the same fate within a short time, before even one new house in this northern quarter has been finished as a substitute for the slums. Under pressure from the population the city council of Brussels decided that a complex of 152 houses should be assigned to these people. This building, named "Harmony," would not be finished before October 1972, that is, four years after the first eviction. The municipality of Schaarbeek considers building cheap houses. The municipality of St. Joost-ten-Node will start with similar plan about 1982. It is senseless to speak of public housing authorities; they show you waiting lists with thousands of names.

One of the public housing societies, for example, wanted to build 720 homes. They would have started in October 1970 but, although the land has already been free a long time, the fallow land in which, at the beginning of 1971, some piles were driven, is still undeveloped. They are waiting for funds from the National Society of Housing. A project in the center was not carried out, because no candidates came to two successive public tenders. The city council of Brussels then decided to have one building built. Thus they spent 2 million Belgian francs in order to rebuild a garage into a temporary church in order to clear the area of the old St. Rochchurch. The temporary church would have to be pulled down after some years. The three municipalities, which could not give houses to the expelled people, then decided, under certain conditions, to pay a premium of 500 Belgian francs, which often was paid months after they were moved. The inhabitants replied that no better accommodation could be found with that sum.

Who Is Building What?

In the mad noise of the bulldozers, the old quarter surrounding the North Station dies. Pulling down houses and dramatic evictions make rapid headway. Against all this the Manhattan-Centre raises itself proudly. According to the brochure: "as basis a commercial foothold of 5 floors, to contain storage-rooms, shops, restaurants, discotheques, bookshops, hairdressers, tearooms, beauty parlors, night-clubs. On all that three towers will arise. Two of those will be luxury hotels. Together they offer travelers 1,100 rooms and suites, restaurants, bars, indoor swimming pool, dining rooms. The third tower is an enormous complex with a total of 35,000 square meters of luxurious office space equipped with the latest conveniences." Parking space and underground transit lines complete this whole affair as "a center for relaxed, happy living, pleasant living, a life that goes on without striking a blow, a life that lets itself be lived—the life of the year 2000."

In the center of this construction plan, at the crossing of the motorways Aachen-Liege-Ostend-London and Amsterdam-Antwerp-Paris, will arise the World Trade Center with eight towers, each 102 meters high. The first tower is already finished, and they have started with the second one. The Belgian Minister of Public Works promised that before that time the large internal traffic road—8 meters wide—of the World Trade Center will be ready. One could wish that his colleague in housing were just as energetic in finding funds for a public housing project.

Attachment to the Quarter

However, public housing projects would only partly resolve the problem of forced eviction. The population should be prepared for living in those modern houses. There should be enough room for the big families and foreigners, and the rent should be reasonable, which is not the case at present. Because the problem of financial means was not studied in time, and these means are now used for something else, the population are left to themselves in spite of some well-meaning municipal officials.

The population is very attached to the quarter, where good schools exist and there are day-care centers for all and since 1960 a good working Social Service, set-up by the Catholic Church. The Social Service specializes in obtaining permits to look for employment and the housing of expelled people. In the quarter the aged people were visited regularly and cared for; twice a week they went to their club to talk a bit and to play cards. There was care at home; hot meals "on wheels" were supplied and coal was available for a cheap price, while some weeks in the Ardennes and a yearly pilgrimage to Lourdes made the holiday months attractive. There is a service for clothes and a furniture store where things can be bought dirt cheap. Because of this sort of work a thread of human contact is woven through the quarter, which now is totally ruined by the new construction plans.

The foreign laborers got a good reception in the quarter, which made their "being foreign" easier: supplementary education for children, courses for boys and girls (creative and cultural occupations), cooking and sewing classes, courses for adults in the French language, reading and writing, etc. Cafes and little foreign shops were opened soon, mostly run by wives of retired miners, who already have done their part for the economy of the country. The deep attachment to the quarter, the financial difficulties, the discrimination with regard to the big families, the prejudice of house-owners against foreigners, adaptability difficulties, the lack of a protective policy for the expelled people, were all reasons for those expelled people to stay in the quarter, often even within the project area, in houses which were already fallen into disrepair or would get that way in a very short time. For the expelled people nothing has changed except for an increase in rent and a tiresome chase after a new home. The living conditions and the housing are still the same. Thus the new construction plan has almost failed completely. Who profits from all this? "The expelled people will starve," one could read on one of the banners which were put up during an eviction. The government thinks that it can solve the human problems with financial assistance. But what is the use when human relations are being ruined, the slum problem is not solved, and the living conditions of foreigners and those in small houses are not improved?

From Social Service to Social Action

The origin of the Social Service in the quarter can be found in the parochial structure. At first it was more suitable for taking steps in the field of social security than for mediation in labor affairs; now the Social Service has become the central point in the quarter. Because of construction plans and related evictions, the Social Service also found work to do in the housing field. The Service had to expand its competence and has organized a permanent service for solving housing problems only. At first the Social Service tried to find a way to solve individual problems.

The related aspects which demand all the attention of the social worker are: to inform the client of his rights and the existing housing and other allowances in this field, to help him to find an adequate house, to help him deal with the unavoidable expulsion. This support does not limit itself to the period in which the expulsion is effected, but should be continued during the removal and the adaptation period in the new house and the new quarter.

Those forms of assistance appeared to be insufficient in the northern quarter. The number of persons for whom the Social Service found a house was rather limited. However, it appeared that people who were assisted by the Service were much more motivated to look for addresses themselves, besides those they got from the social worker. They came back to the Service to talk about their problems. At that moment it was clear that they were not only confronted with the problem of expulsion from their old home, but that there were other problems also. From this a spontaneous feeling of willingness to assist and solidarity came into being.

Therefore, besides the more individual assistance a more collective assistance came into being, which was directed at the social roots of the individual problems. The assistance at the level of the community was on one hand the work of social education, on the other hand, of social action. In other words, action directed at social structures in view of a redistribution of power and influence and in order to establish even chances for everyone, including deprived groups.

In the first place the social worker tried to make the population conscious of the problems which they meet or will meet in the near future, and which they themselves must tackle. Before an active and a real participation of the population comes into being, they must be informed about their rights. They must be sure that all inhabitants are aware of the problems surrounding the Manhattan project and the evictions. In this respect the Social Service organized meetings for the population, sometimes according to nationality, in order to inform the various groups about their rights as evicted people. Those meetings have, for example, resulted in a joint delivery of a petition to the municipal authorities in order to call their attention to the problems, also for special groups (bachelors, large and/or foreign families).

Another problem was presented in a similar manner to the Social Service. Here it was the question of adaptation of the population in new houses to be built in the quarter itself, which should stimulate and make possible the return of a part of the original population. The Social Service organized an information campaign in order to have people who were on the list for those new houses become familiar with the problems of a large group of people in a similar small housing-area. The Service has also tried to acquaint the various groups with each other, to overcome existing prejudices and to start a discussion in order to establish human relations.

The Contact Committee

As social action, the people needed to be mobilized in order to give them the opportunity to take an effective position against the municipal authorities, so that they could "live" in a normal way in the new neighborhood. It was clear that such a process would crystallize very slowly and with much difficulty with such a heterogeneous population as in this quarter. Thus there was a need for a catalyst, which, with regard to the city of Brussels, was the Contact Committee. This Committee consists of citizens whose most important interests involve the problem of new housing within the more fundamental perspective of the improvement of living conditions of the population. It acts as intermediary between the population and the municipal authorities and at the same time as the representative of a group consciousness among the population and the will to fight against the housing policy of Brussels. The Social Service works in close cooperation with the Contact Committee. Furthermore, meetings are organized in which people get the opportunity to express their feelings and to show their emotions and expectations, which stimulate the communal sense. It is clear that the population makes progress very quickly, in action as well as emotionally. Now people find in themselves the power which will stimulate the solution of the problem.

The experience of the Social Service made it clear that social assistance cannot stop at being installed as well as possible in another house. It is evident that in the first place the direct task of the Service is to look for better housing, and to do this as much as possible together with the inhabitants.

This material progress can serve as a lever for changing the people as well as for improvement of structures, because it is not only a question of development of the individual, but also of the institutions in which the individual is so deeply rooted.

Postscript (1976)
by Evert Lagrou

Since 1972, the plan itself has not changed, but there is discussion about the execution.

The economic calculations did not turn out as supposed. Many new offices are empty in the few buildings already constructed. Attempts have been made to convince the public authorities to lease or buy these from the private company. Under pressure of public opinion this course of action has been unsuccessful.

Various other attempts to financially assist the private company have been unsuccessful and it went into bankruptcy.

For this reason the largest part of the work has stopped. At present the public streets and the planned subway work are being carried out. After very significant actions by various community groups, the government has dropped for the moment the original plan for the crossing point of urban expressways. Because of the fierce reactions, the "Manhattan business" was temporarily buried without the plan itself being changed. In 1975 the road plan was nonetheless taken up again.

The north quarter committee proposed three objectives for further activities: first, rehousing for residents who quit the area as a result of the plan; second, social support for residents who live in the new high-rises (at the beginning of 1976 700 apartments became available with a capacity of 2,000 people); third, further action in order to modify the original plan, according to a plan proposed by an "umbrella" urban council. In this plan, the office zone was greatly reduced and proposed as lower buildings.

It also successfully pushed for the timely provision of social facilities (above all for children's playgrounds). The municipal and national government became extraordinarily cautious about the further implementation, since the Manhattan plan has become a symbol, via the press, television, folk songs, and sociocultural groups, of the fight against the destruction of the city.

6 Brussels: Urban Transformations since the Eighteenth Century

Francis Strauven

In the foreground the texture of the Ilot Sacre, the heart of Brussels, can be seen; in the middle there is the gap that now functions as a parking lot, with the north-south connection for its border. Along the Keizerinnelaan, which covers the railway, the RTT Building, the Sabena, and the Central station rise above the rooftops. From *Wonen–TA/BK*, August 1975. Photo by Francis Strauven.

To make clear from the start its original intention of restoring the value of the city as a meeting place, ARAU aimed its first campaign at the so-called crossroads of Europe. This is a waste zone in the middle of the city between the upper and the lower city, a triangular gap in the center caused by the breakthrough for the north–south connection.

The area owes its name to its situation in the master plan: the urban motorways had to come together here near the Central Station and the Sabena Air Terminal in one impressive knot. On the lower part of the site there was the existing point where the Vlaamse Steenweg (de Grasmarkt) divided in the direction of Cologne (Bergstraat) and Namur (Magdalenastraat). The latter, which had been the favorite promenade between the upper and the lower city during the first half of the century, evaporated in the merciless monumentalism of the Albertina and was drastically cut off from its extension at the foot of the library's interminable stairs by the north–south connection and the urban motorway that had been built on top of it.

The area still has the air of a battlefield. The Magdalena church is the only remaining bit of the old texture of the area. The remaining walls of the former Berg- and Magdalenastraats look denuded, and on the other side of the Keizerinnelaan (the part of the inner circle completed first) one can see the administrative lumps coming menacingly down from the upper city.

The gap itself was used in 1969 and is still used today as a parking lot (completely in accord with the master plan). This function was confirmed in the Local Plan (LP) made public by the city in March 1969, supplemented with offices and commerce, and covered with a "public green space." As usual, this LP answered to a design already completed (instead of the other way round), which fact was made public in the daily newspaper *La Dernière Heure* of May 17, 1969. This publication clarified that the intention was to continue the grace of the Albertinagarden here, an esplanade included. On top of that the area had to remain a little island in the midst of the flow of traffic, which had been widened. Pedestrians were to reach the island by way of underground tunnels.

When this design was first made public, ARAU had already held its first press conference on May 8 in the café La Mort Subite only a few steps from the area under discussion. ARAU had criticized the LP sharply and pleaded to restore the area as the forum of the city and to turn it into a hospitable connection between the upper and the lower city. Concretely, ARAU demanded that the lower part of the Kardinal Mercierstraat, which had been created in 1926, be abolished and that the Berg- and Magdalenastraat be rehabilitated for pedestrians. This could be done by reconstructing a close urban texture with enough space for encounters and houses.

At a subsequent press conference on July 3, 1969, at which a number of councillors were present, ARAU presented a draft design in which it had given its plan a rather vague, drugstore-like form but which as an object of discussion led to the decision of the authorities to invite designs for the area concerned in the spring of the following year. The jury, which deliberated in June 1970, did not award a first prize, but the design by the planning bureau, which was awarded the second prize, was chosen as the base from which to work out a definite plan.

This design was a compromise between the options of ARAU and Tekhné's LP. It did not go as far as aiming at the reconstruction of the urban texture, and it did not supply houses, but it did retain a kind of roof-esplanade that had the character of a square. This was because it was surrounded by green and a few buildings that kept the denuded street walls out of sight.

Justice was done to ARAU's ideas in the design by F. Terlinden, who proposed a modern version of the old city. Even so, ARAU accepted the design by the planning bureau as a base for discussion. After Tekhné had worked out a "synthesis plan," which it presented as a combination of the ideas that had come out of the competition, but that were in fact an adapted version of its own original LP, the planning bureau made a counterproposal, presenting an urban structure with houses, a correction of its design for the competition. At the moment the problem is still pending (between the options of Tekhné and of the planning bureau), and ARAU is considering a continuation of the campaign.

The crossroads of Europe as
designed by F. Terlinden

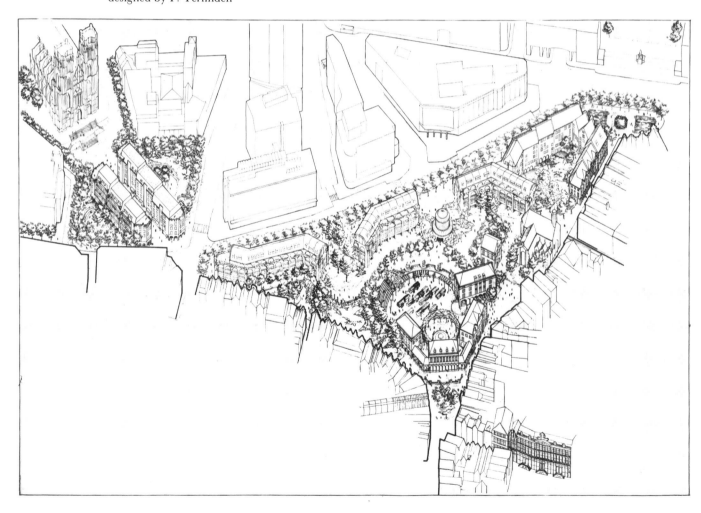

On May 9, 1973, the authorities presented, not without pride, a design for a Museum of Modern Art for which there had been much demand for thirty years. In 1969 the foundation De Vrienden der Koninklijke Musea entrusted the design to R. Bastin, the doyen of Walloon modernists.

After controversies that dragged on it was decided to situate this museum in the 17-meter-deep pit that had been dug in the foundations of the front of the old Royal Library. In itself this was rather a discreet solution, but people wanted to go further than that. "In accordance with the wish of Leopold II to devote this sector, situated in the heart of Brussels, entirely to Art and Spirit," the authorities wanted to turn the new museum into a "key point" of the Mountain of Arts, visually as well as physically.

This went further than Leopold himself had wanted. His architect Maquet had, in his design of 1898, maintained the seventeenth- and eighteenth-century premises between the Hofberg and the Museumstraat as a small scale component of the Museumplein. In 1973 the authorities labeled this texture as "an abscess formed by dilapidated and unaesthetic houses." These same authorities had already expropriated these premises before they gave any publicity to their design. They had left the premises, which still accommodated houses, commerce, and restaurants, to rot in accordance with the well-tried procedure of clearing the site at a convenient moment.

Thus a space was to be created in which the subterranean museum could manifest its presence unhindered by disturbances, by way of a detached "signal." This signal, a vertical vaulted cylinder (a dented section of a column?), formed the entrance to the museum, which literally folded itself toward the unreal monumentalism of the Albertina and the denuded walls of the Museumplein, where it linked up with an indirectly accessible sunken garden.

This (paradoxically) closed entrance was as rejecting and cryptic to the passerby as the Albertina itself, and it did not offer a single starting point for any activity in the empty spaces surrounding it. This course of things contrasted violently with the intentions stated in the official brochure ("a forum closely integrated in the daily life of our society, a profession of faith in our city," etc.).

It was also very strange that the exhibition, which the authorities organized by the way of unofficial public inquiry, was held outside the center and lasted barely two days. Nevertheless, there were numerous quick reactions from various directions, for instance from the Archief voor Moderne Architectuur, which published a counter-brochure in which it presented various alternatives such as the removal of the museum to the crossroads of Europe.

ARAU joined this campaign and later also supported the initiative of the minister of Brussels Affairs, Cudell, who proposed to house the museum in the former department store Old England, a beautiful Art Noveau building. This building had been vacated by the firm concerned, because the prospect had been that all commerce on the Hofberg would have to leave to make way for the cultural monoculture.

The alternative that was finally accepted by the competent authorities, after a deliberative commission had been set up and after a number of conflicts with the foundation De Vrienden van de Koninklijke Musea, was the preservation of Bastin's design under the surface of the Museumplein, but supplied with a discrete entrance as part of the texture that had been rehabilitated and strengthened for housing, shops, restaurants, and cafés.

Museum for Modern Art,
Brussels: Design for under-
ground museum by R.
Bastin—a detached "sign."
In the middle is the entrance to
the subterranean museum.

ARAU's first counterproposal
for keeping the texture of the
area. The residential buildings
have businesses and restaurants on the ground floor, as
well as the entrance to the
museum. Drawing by F.
Terlinden.

Museum for Modern Art, Brussels: The remaining premises of the Hofberg after the completion of the Mountain of the Arts. The authorities expropriated them, and let them rot.

ARAU's proposal to restore street façades.

Existing situation of the
denuded seventeenth-century
Brigittinen church against the
background of "venetian
blinds" facing north

The Brigittinen church is a small seventeenth-century building in Flemish Baroque style that has not been in use as a church since the French Revolution (although it has been used for such varied purposes as storage, slaughterhouse, and ballroom). Originally it faced a little square and was part of a block that had been partly mowed down by the north–south connection and partly demolished after the Second World War.

From 1960 onward some famous Belgian modernists have been at work on a renovation plan long delayed by the highway authority. The little isolated church stands dumb in a background of venetian blinds facing north. The biggest apartment block looks out on the railway (1,000 trains pass through per day) and also on a completely empty esplanade raised above street level.

ARAU proposed to conceal the lack of scale and the discontinuity of the situation by reintroducing an urban texture. A reconstruction of the original configuration was impossible as the local pattern of streets had been altered drastically by the north–south connection. The bureau opted for building in the new Brigittinenstraat which was no longer destined for an urban motorway since at the beginning of 1973 the government had decided to abandon the idea of a tunnel to the Louisalaan. The buildings were to consist of a row of shops that would create a small square in front of the little church, which was destined to become the local center: simple architecture aiming to make people forget the social storage system apartment building behind it.

Proposal by ARAU to conceal the situation and reconstruct the urban texture

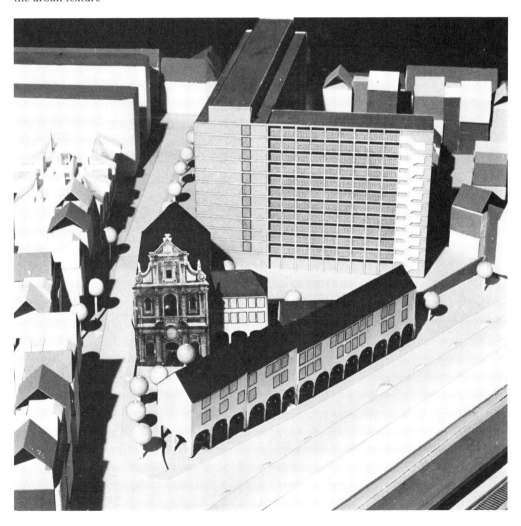

Zavel: A large government redevelopment plan was to replace existing structures in the Zavel quarter of the city. To prepare for reconstruction in the Zavel the government had already patiently bought up the houses concerned, evicted the people in them, and judiciously damaged them (breaking or opening all the windows, damaging roofs) to make them rot as soon as possible. To show up these practices, ARAU organized a symbolic "shutting windows" campaign on September, 14, 1974. The local action committee members of ARAU climbed into the houses that were rotting away to shut the broken windows with black plastic foil.

Renewal of the Rue Royale by
Maurice Culot. This design for
a row of new (!) buildings
monumentalizes the existing
"Dutch 1830" style prevalent
in the quarter, which "because
of its continuous unity . . . will
form an unassailable obstacle
against the motorways that are
still looming there." Drawing
by D. Lelubre.

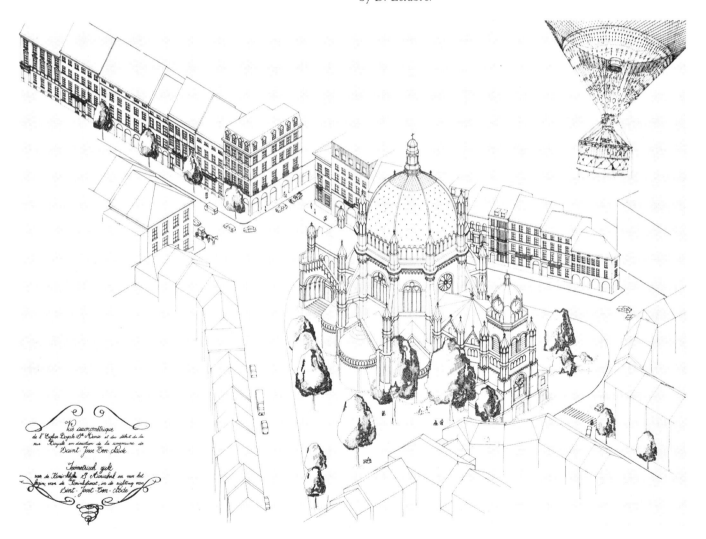

The tale of the completely translucent building: In the case of the ITT tower ARAU clashed with the interests of "capital" and its political pacemakers.

ARAU joined the protest of the local inhabitants to oppose the construction of the tower in spite of everything. ARAU suggested that the tower by its mass and shade would detract from the park and the Abbey of Ter Kameren, that its presence would affect the residential character of the neighborhood, and that the parking space that went with it (constructed partly under the public road) would not only destroy a number of trees of the Louisalaan, but would also produce considerable obstruction of traffic in the neighborhood.

When a number of inhabitants made these objections known to the mayor of Brussels, they received an answer as presumptuous as it was unlikely from alderman Vanden Boeynants, who presented himself as defender of the architectural qualities and townscape of the tower in question. It had been designed, he said, by "one of the greatest names in modern architecture, Walter Gropius from New York, whose name and qualities have never been under discussion in modern architecture."

The fact that the alderman of Brussels was confusing Walter Gropius and the Antwerp architect Walter Bresseleers made his fencing with thoroughness and professionalism already quite questionable. The most sensational thing, however, was his foolhardy argument that "the perspective of the Abbey of Ter Kameren will in no way be spoiled by the tower which has been planned. In fact, here we can speak of a construction which is completely translucent and which will certainly in no way spoil the perspective."

Although this campaign turned out to be completely impotent as far as its immediate aim was concerned—the tower is there, as translucent as the process of town planning from which it resulted—and must thus be seen as a failure, it did produce a number of rather important side effects. It made the bourgeois press realize the connections between the authorities and trade and industry, and it clarified that town planning in Belgium is not carried out from a viewpoint of detached academic neutrality, but is glued to private and political interests.

Since Vanden Boeynants has become known in Belgian politics as "the man of the translucent tower," he has not dared to promote openly the construction of any more towers.

The campaign also produced an administrative benefit. The Order in Council of February 13, 1971, concerning article 63 of the law of 1962, contains a clause which in some cases compels the applicant for a building license to make the character of his plans known by way of posters in the place concerned within ten days after he has submitted the application.

Before and after pictures of the
park at Ter Kameren and the
"translucent" ITT tower.

Editor's note: The August 1975 issue of *Wonen-TA/BK,* a Dutch planning and architecture journal, was devoted to case studies of over fifteen development conflicts in which the Atelier de Recherche et d'Action Urbaine had been involved. The chapters by Francis Strauven and René Schoonbrodt describe the history and future prospects for the city of Brussels.

Up to the end of the nineteenth century, Brussels was a vital, attractive city. In 1893 it was still described by W. Shaw Sparrow in *The Studio* as "this delightful little light bright city." The public and civil works of the eighteenth and nineteenth century had locally intersected and "normalized" the old inner city, but even so they had produced quarters which, visually as well as functionally, could be seen as complements of the medieval texture. They had left this texture, which continued to constitute the residential component, untouched in as far as that three years before Shaw Sparrow wrote, the 416 hectare inner city still contained the never equalled number of 159,374 inhabitants.

The large-scale transformations which took place under the Austrian government at the end of the eighteenth century, the government district (parliament, royal palace, and park) and the Koningsplein, were executed in a place where from early days the men in power had been established in equally large-scale structures: that is, on the eastern plateau of the inner city, which is 40 meters higher, the so-called upper city. The Martelarenplein, which was constructed at about the same time in the lower city, also did not cover more than an existing mesh of the texture in which it took the place of a bleachery no longer in use.

In the nineteenth century the city underwent transformations which were more radical. These were not only connected with the inevitable functional and hygienic needs caused by the industrial revolution and the demographic growth that went with it, but just as much with the fact that the bourgeoisie and the authorities wanted to give Brussels the equipment and the appearance of a modern capital.

As early as 1810, on the orders of Napolean, the old city walls had begun to be replaced by broad boulevards, after which, following upon Belgium's independence, slum clearance and infrastructures especially were carried out: water and sewage-works, sidewalks, and the construction of a number of new streets through districts which had been declared unhealthy; the Begijnhof and the old St. Jans-hospital had to make way for new allotments, and through the Marollen district the Blaesstraat was built to run parallel with the Hoogstraat.

But it was especially the construction of the South and North stations in 1840 and 1841, respectively, that brought drastic and far-reaching changes. The implantation of these stations did not take place outside the texture, but the field of force which grew between the two was repeatedly to leave deep and lasting traces later on. Traditionally the lower city had no clearly direct north-south connection so that traffic between the two stations at first had to finds its way through the old intricate pattern of streets. To remedy this the authorities created a number of thoroughfares in the course of years. the first one was still rather discreet: it consisted of the extension of the Nieuwstraat, which up to then had been an entirely residential street, but with the Zuidstraat to become an axis which was soon to grow into a prosperous shopping center.

Leopold II, the Zenne, and the Kunstberg (Mountain of Arts)

The changes were not to assume larger proportions till the reign of Leopold II, the "urbanist king" who wanted to extend Brussels, after the example of Napolean III in Paris, into a prestigeous capital of a state he wanted to be organized centrally. His reign coincided with the economic growth which took place in most European countries from about 1860, and just like Napolean he coupled his passion for architecture and town planning with a pre-Keynesian economic policy, which implied great public works. It was with such works in mind that Belgium passed its first bills concerning town planning: the legislation of 1858 and 1867 made it possible to expropriate "for all construction works which form an entity, destined to reconstruct an old district to improve or to embellish, or to create a new district."

The first large-scale change which Brussels then underwent consisted of the alignment and overarching of the Zenne, the river on which Brussels had originated and which up to that time had meandered picturesquely through the inner city. The construction of the sewage system in 1840–1850, however, had transformed it into an open sewer which frequently overflowed its banks and to which the cholera epidemic of 1866 was attributed. (Baudelaire saw the river as "*une Seine obscene, un excrément qui coule.*")

At the same time this clearing-up created space for an alternative north-south connection, that is, the central boulevards (Max, Anspach, and Lemonnier) which in the manner of Haussmann brought about a linear connection between the key civic functions, such as the Exchange, the Halls and the Zuidpaleis, and which were lined with tall apartment buildings with ground-floor shops.

Just as in Paris these boulevards met various needs: they were not only a solution for the problems of hygiene and traffic, but they also fulfilled the urge of the bourgeoisie to occupy a central position in the city center where it could exhibit the signs of its economic expansion and from where the old intricate texture became more clearly outlined and more accessible. But however drastic the measures of this civic planning were, so far they were limited to a through street and did not tend to destroy the texture, which was kept alive as a vitally important matrix for the new "arteries."

This was not so much the case for the upper city, where the number of residential buildings was traditionally smaller and of which the authorities wanted to strengthen the official character. Thus around 1865 part of the Marollen had to make way for the construction of the Palace of Justice, the titanic masterwork of the architect J. Poelaert, which was to dominate the entire city skyline because of its situation on the former Galgenberg.

Even more monumental, if possible, was the Kunstberg (Mountain of Arts) the king then had designed by the architect Maquet. On the slope between the royal palace and the lower city a gigantic string of buildings had to be built for a link between the two, in which the Royal Museums were to be housed. For this design the most elegant shopping district of Brussels had to make way, which shows that Leopold was not so much interested in the reconstruction of supposed slum areas but rather in the grandeur of his capital, for which all existing structures had to make way if necessary.

The necessary expropriation and demolitions had already been executed when public opinion at the very last moment turned against the plan in 1908. People had begun to realize from the dimensions the demolition had taken in the stricken St. Rochus district that this was a "cyclopic" design ("in no proportion to the surrounding buildings and of a discouraging severity which will cause the Mountain of Arts to be deprived of all joy and all commercial animation"). The design consequently suffered shipwreck in the senate, which refused to give the necessary funds by a majority of one vote.

Maquet's design also contained a solution, however, of a problem which had grown into a real obsession during the second half of the century: a modern, quick traffic connection between the upper and the lower city. This connection was already there to be sure: it was the oldest road of Brussels, the so-called *steenweg* (stoneway), the east-west trade route at the crossing of which with the Zenne Brussels had originated in the Middle Ages. It penetrated the city via the Vlaamse Poort and followed the course of the present day Vlaamse Steenweg, Kiekenmarkt, Grasmarkt and Magdalenastraat after which it mounted directly to the Koningsplein via the steep slope of the Hofberg. (That is why the Koningsplein is sometimes called the capitol.) From there it ran on into the Naamsestraat.

This road remained the most important shopping street of Brussels until the central boulevards were constructed perpendicularly to it. The Hofberg housed the most distinguished shops and was the meeting place of the elegant bourgeoisie. But the steep slope of this street, "la bosse du dromadaire" (the dromedary's hump) turned out to be such a hindrance for the ever-increasing traffic that in the second half of the nineteenth century more than 200 designs were worked out to lessen this slope. Maquet's Mountain of

Arts was not realized, but on the other hand the necessary demolition had already taken place at that moment to construct the esplanade which was to have shown up to its full advantage the monumental entrance to Maquet's edifice. The north flank of the Hofberg and the entire St. Rochus quarter, which bordered on it, were wiped off the map for the purpose. The space which was created this way rendered enough space for the curved line of a new street, the Coudenberg, which temporarily solved the problem of the connection between the upper and the lower city.

At the occasion of the World's Fair of 1910 the demolished area between the Coudenberg and the Hofberg, which still existed, was filled up with a temporary garden designed by the Parisian architect Vachérot. This charming garden, which soon became the favorite connection for pedestrians between the upper and the lower city, held its ground until 1954. Then it had to make way for the postfascist Albertina, which in all its chilling monumentalism was only a weak reflection of Maquet's design.

The North-South Rail Connection

The presence of the North and South stations and the hindrance of the traffic up and down finally necessitated the construction of the railway connection between the two with the Central Station in the middle. This then was the last of the three north-south connections. Numerous designs and controversies were once again dedicated to this problem, which was also close to the heart of Leopold II. Finally a very drastic change was decided on. The railway was constructed in the flank of the mountain between the upper and the lower city, right through the old texture, which this time did indeed contain a number of working-class quarters.

The fact that this solution was chosen, and that this rail connection had not been combined with the normalization works of the Zenne and the construction of the central boulevards in 1867–1871, was perhaps connected with a pre-Keynesian urge to spread public works. It may also

have been connected with the wish of the authorities to extend the official and the administrative area of the upper city into the lower city. (Even so, today an underground line is under construction even though the Zenne still flows there.) The demolition which the new railway line necessarily caused gave ample opportunity for this.

This last north-south connection destroyed all working-class quarters it met on its way. The works were started in 1903 but they were interrupted repeatedly because of the two world wars and disputes which kept on flaring up. These dragged on for more than half a century, so that the entire area between Kruidtuin and Kapellekerk looked like a disaster area for scores of years, a situation which was hardly changed with the filling up of the rifts in the fifties. The disaster only produced more disasters. From the strange boulevards which covered the railway, there sprang up around the stripped cathedral the equally strange organs of a central state: the National Bank, the Central Station, the Sabena, the Mountain of Arts already mentioned, the RTT, and last but not least the Government Administrative Center.

The Government's Program of Town Planning: Regional Plan and Sector Plan

In accordance with the liberalistic traditions which have characterized Belgian society from the start, the Belgians have never attached much value to town and country planning, an activity in which they saw nothing but an attack on their sacred proprietary rights as embodied in the Code Napoléon. The initiatives taken by the government in the field of town planning, the laws of 1915 and 1940, have for the greater part remained a dead letter. This legislation was directed mainly at compelling war-stricken municipalities to draw up a Municipal Plan for their reconstruction. Of the 2,663 Belgian municipalities, only 1,891 came under the head of the application of that law, but by 1960 only 186 had produced a Municipal Plan.

This law did not apply to Brussels, which had not been stricken by the war but rather by public works. And as not a single one of the 19 municipalities which constitute the agglomeration of Brussels had got as far as drawing up a Municipal Plan, the government's program for town planning remained decisive for this whole area.

The vision, or rather the absence of vision, on which this policy, drastic as well as monomaniacal, is based, is revealed clearly in the Regional Plan (1948–1957) and the Sector Plan (1962) of the agglomeration of Brussels, which was designed by the bureau Alpha commissioned by the government. In these plans no stand is made against urban deconcentration, "*le déserrement*," mentioned in the survey that went with it. The capture of the center by offices and recreation at the cost of residential houses which are banned to the periphery, and the necessity of a functional traffic system between those two separated functions, are accepted without any criticism as an inevitable evolution. The authorities had no vision of what could be a livable city to set against these "lines of force." On the contrary, they did nothing but accompany and reinforce these lines of force with public works. The present day structure of the agglomeration of Brussels was not born from a vision of living together but from an urge to drive together. The vacuum left by the Department of Town Planning was filled by the Department of Roads (both departments of the Ministry of Public Works). The Department of Roads steered the development of town planning in the capital (and of the whole country) into new channels. This is stated very clearly in the draft district plan of January 1971: "We must establish that the capital needs to be adapted to motorized traffic; as the Buchanan report says: it is no longer possible to live in peace with the car without making a new kind of city. The new road system supposes a restructuring of existing space. Its dispositions make a profitable use of the necessity of renovating the oldest quarters: they strongly contribute by injecting the necessary transformations."

The Master Plan

In accordance with this policy and after the example of other European cities, Brussels decided in the middle of the fifties to draw up a master plan for the "pentagon" (the inner city within the former pentagonal walls). It was made to do so by the "lines of force" mentioned above which were beginning to make their pressure felt at that time. First there occurred an increasing need for office space which was soon no more to be gauged. Brussels was not only to be the center of all (bilingual) government services (this was done mostly to stabilize the unitary structures of a country consisting of two communities), but also there was at that time already mention of this city as the seat of the European Communities, a prospect which was to be verified later on.

Then there was the fact that Belgium was one of the European countries in which the American consumer society and the investments that went with it had taken root very early. At the beginning of the fifties the Belgians already owned a large number of—predominantly American—cars, of which the capital soon began to feel the pressure to a point that it was even expected that public transport would be superfluous in future.

And finally there was the fact that the population of the inner city had declined gradually and linearly from 1890 on. While the number of inhabitants of the pentagon was still 154,732 in 1900, it had decreased to 64,535 by 1962 and is now about 50,000. More than half of the population had already fled before the so-called "city-forming" ("slum clearing" followed by the advance of offices which sent the cost of land and rents soaring higher and higher) and they had settled in the suburbs.

The authorities expected a solution from the master plan, "to lure around 35,000 new inhabitants to the pentagon in order to increase the number of inhabitants to 100,000." (This was practically the population figure the inner city had numbered at the time Belgium's independence had been declared.) Strangely enough, the authorities clearly did not blame the "urban deconcentration" on the "slum clearing" schemes but rather on a lack of them. They were convinced that people were leaving the inner city because of the dilapidated and unhygienic state of the old houses.

Slum clearance, which had up to then been performed under the pretext that it was a functional change, turned into an obsession in the fifties. It was as if people were ashamed of the old intricate texture of streets, many of them blind alleys, and they wanted to have done with them as quickly as possible. It was as if they were jealous of cities which had been bombed such as Berlin and Rotterdam, whose reconstruction was a shining example to them.

The city did not entrust its master plan to its own administration, but to the foundation Tekhné, a research bureau which consisted mainly of former colonials who had applied the CIAM principles on a large scale in the Congo. The plan produced by this bureau in 1962 was to be a classic example of simplistic functionalistic zoning. The city was divided up into the familiar large-scale monocultures: dwelling, working, recreation and traffic. Especially to the smooth unrolling of the last function, the plan gave extra great care. Not only did the wooded circular road have to make way for an "urban motorway," fitted out with a complex system of bridges and tunnels (works which had in fact already been started for Expo 58); but also various other urban motorways were to penetrate into the inner city from all directions to come together in an "inner circle" around the *ilot sacré*, the old heart of the city, in order to "open up the city as much as possible."

This system of communication was surrounded richly by spacious parking lots and well-endowed with great overpasses which had to ensure an optimal flow of traffic. Within the large-scale mesh of this net the other functions were spread zone by zone. The upper city was destined entirely for business and administration and the *ilot sacre* was reserved for commerce, which was allowed to stretch tentacularly along the radial roads running into the city. Apart from a few spots in the old west, the function of dwelling was referred to the higher regions. In accordance with the renewal obsession mentioned above, it was not intended to embody these functions in the existing city structure. On the contrary, the intention was to eradicate the old texture entirely, apart from some monuments and the *ilot sacre*, in order to enable the new order to come to its pure expression, free from all pressure.

This can be seen clearly from the town planning competitions which were organized at the time. In 1962 Tekhné, for instance, invited designs to get new ideas for the possible lay-out of an area of about 40 hectares in the southwestern part of the inner city (on both sides of the central boulevards). All youthful and ambitious competitors started with a tabula rasa and they each designed a kind of *ville radieuse*. The jury rated the design by J. H. Baudon the highest: he had left most space between his buildings, which was judged to produce a favorable scale and rhythm.

This design was not executed, however, but it does give an idea of what sort of image of the future modern architects recommended to the authorities at that time. In practice they tried to achieve this bit by bit, by renewing smaller areas. This had already been started before the completion of the master plan, for Expo 58. As far back as 1953, a law had been passed to "organize the clearing of slums," which gave the city the opportunity to expropriate to the advantage of the building companies. Thus the Foyer Bruxellois renovated a large part of the Meiboom quarter and the Pottenbakkers quarter around 1958. The Miniemencomples followed (1960–64), the Papenvest (1964–67) and the Brigittinen quarter (1966).

All these quarters, which, in all their drab grayness are hardly to be told apart, were the works of architects who saw themselves as pioneers of the coming welfare state. For them and for their younger colleagues, too, such large-scale realizations meant the first and true breakthrough of Modern Architecture in Belgium. While before the war it had been limited to some marginal experiments, it now got a firm grip on the urban environment.

The immediate execution of the road plan under the dynamic impulse of the Ministry of Public Works brought this future much closer. Except for the strip along the canal of Charleroi, the ring was constructed completely, with its planned tunnels and junctions. Within this ring the first urban motorway came into being: the boulevards over the north-south rail connection come to a dead end now at the Kapellekerk, at which point the railway comes to the surface to wind its way through the Marollen along a great viaduct. Here the new motorway was to have turned to the southeast via a tunnel, right through a different part of the

Marollen, to be linked to the Louisalaan. The inner circle was not executed, it is true, but from its trace there sprang 5 parking garages in anticipation of its construction.

It is very strange indeed that right up to the end of the sixties there was no criticism to be heard in professional circles either against these realizations or against the whole master plan. The perspective of changing Brussels into a *ville radieuse* after all meant the realization of the architectural eschatology of that time. As P. de Saulnier, alderman of Brussels, expressed it, this was a "policy which tallies with the principles of the Charter of Athens by working on an urbanization mainly at the service of man, that is the inhabitant (*sic*), by building an attractive city for him in which it will be pleasant to dwell, to work, to move and to recreate."

The fact that the principles of CIAM had been put aside by the international avant-garde of architects since the congress of Otterlo in 1959 was not to dawn on the Belgian architectural world until about ten years later, and for some time to come, not at all on the Belgian authorities. (If they go on assimilating the evolution of urban theory at the same rate, the ideas of Team 10 will dawn on them around the year 2000.)

The only protest came from antiquarian societies and the Ligue Esthétique, a protest based on aesthetic grounds only. It had nothing to do with the destruction of the texture but rather with the fact that this also entailed the demolition of a number of monuments.

The reason why public opinion did not produce many convincing reactions was connected not only with the depopulation of the inner city and a certain fatalism of the population which remained, but also with the discretion with which the authorities always managed to surround their (changing) plans. They were enabled to do this by the special statute, or rather lack of statute, the extra-legal character of the master plan.

The Master Plan and the Law of 1962

In the same year, 1962, in which Tekhné delivered the master plan, the new law "concerning the organization of town and country planning" was drawn up. This law, drawn up by lawyers, did not contain a single vision on the policy of town planning to be pursued, but it did institutionalize a procedure in which a very modest place was allocated to participation: it compelled all Belgian municipalities to draw up general and local municipal plans, which had to result from the confrontation of various interests and ideas of the authorities (that is, the government, the municipalities, and the agglomerations), the project developers, the designers, miscellaneous advisory committees of advice (on a national and on a regional level), and finally public opinion.

The law enables the interested public to formulate its wishes and objections (if only in a well-advanced stage of the process) concerning each general and local plan by way of a public enquiry, which has to be published with the necessary publicity every time.

Some people might expect that after the new legislation was passed the authorities of Brussels would have seized the opportunity to use the procedure to legalize their master plan into a general plan, but they knew better than that. The master plan continued to be a shadow plan. It was published in an unofficial technical journal only (the magazine *Wonen*, December 1963), and it was never made subject to enquiries, either by the city council of Brussels nor by the population. Nor was it put down in a Royal Decree, so that it was a "flexible" plan, with which the authorities could maneuver according to the offers made by the project developers.

This was the phenomenon which was to be seen in practically the whole country after the new law had come into force, that is, a feverish increase of speculative parceling in expectation of legally binding plans to come into effect, only took on larger dimensions in Brussels. The only thing was that the function of dwelling, for which the master plan had, after all, left a number of zones, had to make way systematically for offices and parking. This resulted in "optimal use" of the land of the city.

The law was not only a spur for the project developers; it turned out that it worked as an instrument, even as a weapon. Even though there were no general plans (and thus no policy decided on by all parties) it turned out to be possible to draw up local plans, for limited areas, which made it possible, for instance, to legalize the construction of tower buildings, under the disguise of general benefit. In this case it sufficed when the interested project developer was given an agreement in principle by the Minister and the Alderman of Public Works. As V. Buré, chairman of the Belgian Federation for Town and Country Planning, Housing and Development once said: "Real town planning will be born from active cooperation between owners and public authority. To practice town planning, public authority has legal weapons at its disposal, and usually no money. The private sector has the money but no legal expropriation—of all parties they must join hands." When these hands had found each other the "public enquiry" which had to be held in accordance with the law (but as quietly as possible, preferably during the vacation period) was too late to change this relationship. This interpretation of the law was even sanctioned by a ministerial letter of 28 October 1967. It turned out that "participation" was to be limited to just a few marginal details.

The legal weapons of expropriation mentioned by Buré are mainly defined by article 25 of the law, which enables the authorities to expropriate "in the general interest" to the advantage of persons who own 51% of the surface of a certain plan area and who request "to be charged with the execution of the works required. . . ." In practice people have been successful in having plan areas defined in such a way that the surface is exactly 49% larger than the property owned by a project developer eager to build.

The little protest there was could, because of lack of skill, not take a firm stand against the civil servants, who in accordance with technocratic ideology, presented their plans as the inevitable solution of the problems the city had to cope with. When fundamental and pertinent objections were raised, the authorities managed to wipe them off the table with the final argument that in matters of town planning "private interests have to make way for general benefit."

The Origin of ARAU in Brussels

Consequently in Belgium as in other countries, there arose protest and participation movements which turned against the consumer society as well as against the accompanying building practice that went with it. Criticism was not only directed against the procedures of town planning, but just as much against the concepts of modern architecture, and so against architects.

Under this pressure, the societies of architects organized all sorts of meetings and congresses aimed not only at the defense of the interests of architecture, but especially at defending the architect. There was hardly any feedback or self-criticism to be heard at such assemblies. They did not lead to a fundamental analysis of the current building process in Belgium, let alone to critical reflection or theory formation. The discussions were held, based on the strange fiction that every right-minded architect knew what is to be understood by valid architecture and town planning, and that there was a consensus among all right-minded people concerning this issue. The architects did not discuss the (social) contents of their profession but limited themselves as usual to organizational and formal problems. It is not surprising then that all the verbalism of that period produced hardly any permanent initiative. Having vented their feelings about the obstacles which prevented them from giving Belgium a harmonious appearance, the architects went home and continued to build on assiduously. Apart from one or two private initiatives the formation of theories remained nonexistent in Belgium, and it still remains so.

The historical reflection which has to go hand in hand with such theory formation was nevertheless started around the same period. It was not the initiative of any school of architecture or of a society of architects, but of two young architects, Maurice Culot and François Terlinden, who organized and financed the exhibition "Antoine Pompe et l'effort moderne en Belgique, 1890–1940," the first full-grown overall exhibition of modern architecture in Belgium. This event revealed the existence of a rich heritage, of which the modernists of the sixties were hardly aware then. Because of this it contained fundamental criticism of the architectural traditions of that period. The postwar generation tended to found its practice vaguely and implicitly on prewar traditions of which it obviously had no clear picture, and even less of the social traditions which formed their base. The exhibition made clear that modernistic formal ideals had become completely detached from the ideological grounds from which they had sprung before and after World War I, and it showed them up as signs of progress which had not been understood.

The introduction to the catalogue made clear that it was the intention of the organizers to demonstrate this. They inveighed strongly against the picture of the future which had been propagated by the local authorities some time before, in April 1968, at the exhibition "Brussels 85." At the occasion of a trade-fair the city had shown the construction stage which the master plan had to reach in 1985. They had proudly filled a stand of 2,500 square meters with grand models of the complexes it considered necessary "to turn Brussels into a truly great capital, capable of playing her part in Europe and in the Atlantic world."

While practically everyone regarded this whole situation with resigned fatalism (that is, everyone who already realized what a calamity was approaching) and considered Brussels to be a lost case, ARAU was born. At the exhibition at Elsene, Culot met René Schoonbrodt and Jacques Vanderbiest, who shared his aims, albeit not so much from a historical but rather from a sociopolitical bias, to change the urbanistic course of events in Brussels in spite of everything, by waking up the public to the situation and by producing alternatives.

ARAU stands for Atelier de Recherche et d'Action Urbaine, and this shows that the group had a two-fold aim in mind right from the start: theoretical research concerning the nature and concept of the city as well as carrying on campaigns to realize this concept.

In the beginning it was ARAU's intention to revitalize the city as a center of encounter and as spatial condition for political participation by way of democratic decisions. Soon in practice quite naturally there grew parallel to this the aim of raising the political conscience of the public to town planning problems and processes.

Structure versus Architecture

The alternative images which ARAU has launched have never been meant to be ready-made designs to be executed, but rather lucid illustrations of the possibilities in town planning which certain problem-situations still have to offer, in spite of everything.

They are an essential part of ARAU's strategy, which enfeebles technocratic fatalism, not only by showing up the latter's contradictions, but just as much by showing that there are other possibilities—by offering suggestions of which the authorities apparently have no idea.

The reproach made by ultra-left groups, that this way ARAU is just committing an alternative kind of technocracy, is based on an incorrect use of words: ARAU's alternatives do not just tend to a city which functions better. These alternatives are not at all the sum of a number of technical imperatives—they result from a vision of participation of the population in an urban community (as has been set forth in the Charte Urbaine, which was published as far back as 1970).

Not only does ARAU tend to an urban structure which will facilitate this participation, and in some cases evoke it. It has also succeeded in having the population of Brussels participate in determining this structure by way of local committees which are united in the Bond Beter Leefmilieu ("Inter Environment"), and via the official commissions of deliberation.

What forms does this structure take? Especially during its experiences in the Marollen quarter, ARAU gradually became convinced that the historic texture which had grown from coordinated efforts from below gives better guarantees than any other known model for the participation of the inhabitants, during the production process as well as when in use. The treatment in phases of clear, small-scale unities, structured with familiar patterns and building elements, allows a real contribution of the inhabitants. It is also completely opposed to the current production process, which has a tendency towards large-scale monopolizing.

Of course the architectural semantics were not left untouched in this process. The choice of the traditional texture as the model of reference and the criterion for the viability of the city inevitably led to the writing off of the current modern architecture, which was never meant as a contibution to this texture, but which embodies its negation. While modern architecture in its revolutionary origin as a universal language wanted to be a prefiguration of a socialist society, it was soon roped in by reaction, and turned into its own opposite, only to degenerate finally into a stream-lined prefiguration of an air-conditioned consumer society, an antiurban kind of architecture the production of which already supposes the end of democracy, as is illustrated clearly by the history of the Noordwijk.

At first ARAU still tried to link up with the initial intentions of modern architecture. It wanted to set a non-hierarchical structure as well as an authentically contemporary representation of this structure against authoritarian routine functionalism. Thus it opposed "*le mauvais génie des pastiches*" in the Bergstraat in the case of the Europe crossroads. But as it gradually attached more importance to the process of participation, it dropped this ambition (which had been realized very seldom anyway). It started to consider architectural semantics as a separate superstructure, after the example of Venturi, only to use it, not unironically, as just a tactical instrument later on.

ARAU not only presented its alternative structures in reassuringly familiar images; it also began to produce more than one version of form and style in certain cases. Paradoxically enough, however, this strategy at the same time means a return to the traditional diversity of the texture of Brussels. Because in contrast to, for instance, Bern or Bologna, Brussels was never characterized by a homogeneous typology, but by a dynamic diversity which had grown from below. A return to the texture of Brussels cannot consist of the restoration of an imaginary Platonic order, but it must be a contribution to the original urban complexity, and at the same time a pragmatic acceptance of and answer to compromised situations.

Till into the nineteenth century Belgian architects employed such a method as a matter of course, for instance by differentiating various houses of one block in various styles. The resulting chaos—which Van de Velde called "the expression of the corruption of the bourgeoisie," but which is "food for the mind to feast on," according to Dubuffet—in any case evokes more communication than the current modernistic alternative people have learned to associate with the destruction of the city. The plural images of ARAU suggest a renewed execution, "bit by bit," of small-scale unities by individual architects, from whom no exceptional creative effort is expected, but rather an unpretentious, artisan-like contribution to the rehabilitation of the city.

Similar tactics of treatment of architectural semantics become evident from ARAU's attitude with respect to the preservation of monuments. ARAU in its campaigns often insists on the protection and restoration of monuments, because in the first place these buildings obviously function as key points in the texture. Even more than old formulas, authentic monuments are regarded by public opinion as unassailable values, for which in some cases even land speculation has to be worsted. Now that the idea that monuments have to be preserved in their context is winning ground, ARAU again and again uses the available monuments in problem areas as obstacles against the destruction of their contexts.

The other way round, as in the case of the Brigittinnenkerk, a monument which has been spared, can be an argument for the reconstruction of the texture. Sometimes ARAU even creates "ready-made" monuments on its own authority (an initiative which should be taken over by conceptual artists). This was the case in Marollen, and, in a different way, in the Rue Royale, too. The design for renovation made by Maurice Culot for this street not only provides renewal of the "Dutch 1830 style," which is prevalent locally, but not very striking, but also the monumentalizing extension of this style on buildings which are doomed to go because of options already given by the authorities.

Culot's aiming at a virtual, unhistoric homogeneity here, in contrast with what he does in other areas, is not caused by a sudden predilection for unity or for that particular style. It is meant to force the building urge which is present into a monumentalisim which, because of its continuous unity (according to the current norms, that is) will form an unassailable obstacle against the motorways which are still looming there and against the transformation of the adjacent Groenwijk into an office zone. The result of this plan for the time being is that, because of the curbing of the building volume, inherent in the "1830 style," sites concerned have now depreciated.

7

ARAU (Atelier de Recherche et d'Action Urbaine): Balance and Prospects after Five Years' Struggle

René Schoonbrodt

Is it worth the trouble to dwell on the very short history of the Atelier de Recherche et d'Action Urbaine? History will show. Not just the history of the princes and the great of this earth, but the history of the peoples struggling for their liberation. In the eyes of those who hold themselves responsible, all actions of ARAU are aimed at a single goal: to create the possibilities for the birth of a society in which every individual can assert as much power as possible on social life as a whole.

Even though it is focused specifically on the city, ARAU wants to (and does) link up with the numerous forms of social, cultural, and economic fights which take place in this post-industrial society. It would in fact not make much sense to go deeply into the various tactics and the various forms of struggle. This would play into the hands of the adversaries, that is, those who control the economic and cultural power at present. So it is not impossible for ARAU to be contradictory in its campaigns! But these discrepancies will have to be solved within ARAU itself.

Brussels, a Slut

Undeniably, Belgium has an enviable standard of living, and there is great progress in the social field, especially thanks to the powerful organization of the trade unions. Even so, Belgium remains an entirely capitalist country, governed by the almighty multinational enterprises.

Brussels, the capital of the country,[1] is the embodiment of this society. As a bourgeois city, controlled by bourgeois political powers, it lends itself to all manipulations expected from it in a capitalist structure by the economic as well as the cultural powers. Brussels is prepared to sacrifice everything for the demands of "economic growth," whatever the cost may be in the social and human sphere.

Right from the start of its activities ARAU has realized that there are three conflicts which play a part in Brussels:
—A conflict between on the one hand an economic development of Brussels in favor of the international monetary powers, who have their connections in the upper classes of Brussels, and on the other hand the crumbling away of the more local industrial economic structures which rely on the

local population and a rather pithless middle class. The politicians in power and the public services (on a municipal as well as on a national level) have favored the former by creating structures accommodated to them: Brussels was not to be just the capital of a centralizing state, but also the capital of Europe because of its function as the seat of the European Communities.

—A conflict of a regional nature which is expressed in a continuous pressure of Flemings and Walloons to limit and control the development of Brussels, as an agglomeration as well as the seat of the centralizing power, this against the will of Brussels itself, which wishes to retain the advantages that go with the position it has, and if possible to extend them. This conflict becomes obvious in the definition of the boundaries of the agglomeration of Brussels at 19 municipalities, the institution of a strengthened state inspection over Brussels (by the formation of the Agglomeration Council), the formation of the regional organs (revision of the constitution), and by the strengthening of the position of the Flemings in the agglomeration (the 19 municipal administrations are to be bilingual and there will be a committee for Dutch culture).

—A conflict between the adherents of a strict application of the Charter of Athens's principles for town planning on the one hand, and on the other hand those who advocate living in the city and a mixture of socioeconomic functions in creating urban space. In fact, this conflict is really the most striking expression of a much deeper conflict which has to do with the democratization of society. Public authority, town planners, project developers, and the builders have gathered under the banner of the first group, while the committees of inhabitants belong to the second group.

It is of course dangerous to separate too rigidly the fields of power which are in reality closely interwoven. One split leads to another: the monopolistic organization of the economy, for instance, demands town planning in zones. Sometimes oppositions (contrasts) occur within one group, without breaking its unity: thus the development of luxury housing is demanded by those groups who commit the most unbridled speculations.

If we were to situate ARAU within this balance of power, it could be described as a group:

—which situates itself in the perspective of the struggle against capitalist economic structures;

—which fights for the democratization of the organs in which the political decisions are taken;

—which advocates a kind of town planning in which a mixture of functions can be brought about and which demands the right to live in the city;

—which has advocated a high degree of regionalization of the power of the state since 1971, with agglomeration = region for its axiom;

—which is French-speaking, but which does aim at cooperation with all groups and all persons who share its democratic ideals.

Urban Housing, Spatial Structure of Power

Which ideology does ARAU adhere to?

ARAU has formed itself around a twofold conviction: the city is a center of power; the power the city creates must be returned to the inhabitants. The correct analysis of present day town planning needs to be grafted on the following question: in what respect does a certain plan, a certain project, a certain building-license increase or decrease the power of the inhabitants, of the poorest inhabitants, of those alienated most, so of the workers?

Starting from the conviction that the city is the center of power of the inhabitants, the place where they can be themselves, the place where they can get away from alienation, means that people can set themselves against the current theses (the city is unlivable, the country is much healthier). This deep conviction is based on a sociopolitical analysis the key points of which are the following:

—The attraction of the cities for the economic investments (seat of enterprises and execution) can be explained only by the increasing power (market control, international economy, channels for information and renovations, . . .) which results from the urban structure;

—The attraction of the cities for the upper strata of the population can be explained only in the same way: the opportunity for self-determination of the inhabitants in all facets of life increases in the urban structure because it is a structure of choice;

—On the other hand all practices (social practice included) lead to people moving from the city to the suburbs, with the result that there is an increase of social control, which by nature goes hand in hand with the mechanisms of the macrosocial organization, which make society as a whole "repressive." (That is to say that personal and collective creativity are killed.)

So if the city is the road to power for the ruling groups, that is, to the control of their environment, this thesis must be reversed in a dialectic opposition: the city is to be one of the instruments for the liberation of the workers.[2]

This key analysis of the urban phenomenon certainly deviates from a number of others, such as the historic, the legal, and the aesthetic. Or: the analysis put in terms of power (of the people) implies the other. But it radicalizes the various stances, because the crude results of a fatal decision do not become clear in aesthetic terms, to give an example, but in the decline of democracy.

ARAU and the Other Committees of Inhabitants

The radicalization of ARAU's ideology (the struggle for the city is the struggle for power) has taken place gradually. The Charte Urbaine, an ideological document which was drawn up at the end of 1970, indicates the direction. ARAU makes it its object to democratize the process of decision making and to propose a different "image" of the city. Some people have shown surprise about the careful way in which ARAU has expounded its ideology: it looked as if it were waging a purely formal war and that on three levels: administrative, that of town planning, and in the field of architecture; and ARAU has been reproached with too much opportunism in analysis and even in its campaigns.

In the analysis of private or public designs for town planning, attention was mainly directed at the "internal" discrepancies of the plan, and at the negative results it produced for the urban environment: traffic problems,

expulsion of the inhabitants, decay of urban life, destruction of the urban texture, waste. ARAU has not shown up the abuses in land speculation, nor has it brought to light the connection mechanisms between public authority and financial groups. This silence is based on two motives: on the one hand there are other groups (certain political parties included) who do this excellently; on the other hand it did not seem a pedagogical way of acting: in a bourgeois city such as Brussels it is more effective to mention the loss of urban life than to fight against land speculation! Well, the thing that had to be (and still has to be) done, is to show which alternative ways of town planning will allow the inhabitants to recapture the urban spaces.

ARAU's way of acting has sometimes raised tensions. Quick intervention in some decisions, which in some cases were made known very late, the technical character of certain problems, the manner of negotiation with the organs of public authority, have perhaps sometimes created the impression that the ARAU was a bureaucracy which did not keep in touch with the "base," that is, the district committees.

It was on purpose that ARAU has so far not formulated a very clear ideology. Now what are the contents of that ideology?

In present day town planning practice, the functions of policy (in the private as well as in the public sector) are concentrated in the centers of the agglomerations, while the inhabitants—the people who used to live in the center, and the newcomers—are removed to the outskirts of the city: to urbanized districts or to satellite towns.

This procedure, as is well known, results from the concern for finding a solution for the problem of housing. During the whole nineteenth century and in our century, too, the problem of housing has been a continual worry for the public authorities and the inhabitants. Howard's garden city was to solve two problems at the same time: housing the workers and renewing the city centers. But Howard's theses in practice have led to living in the suburbs and to the capture of the city centers by economic forces.

We must remember that the city is not just a geographic spot, but that is is a net of communications, of exchange of information, of renewal; it is a source of power for those who are in it; he who seizes a section of the urban space thus gains a place in that net of exchange, of information: the structure which in modern society reinforces the present day economic powers.

We must also remember that he who has to abandon the city, will be deprived of information channels, of the communication structures without which one is not in a position to take part in the whole collective evolution.

The political meaning of present day practices of town planning in fact comes down to giving the places of political and cultural power to (or allowing them to be taken by) the dominating socioeconomic groups, while the others (the dominated) are robbed of these self-same advantages, and that under ideological pretexts such as fresh air and the green and the peace of the countryside. In the end this leads to a twofold destruction: that of the city centers and that of the countryside.

Every year a part of the population leaves the centers of Brussels because of urban reconstruction (euphemistically called urban renewal) and because of the decrees that go with it: prohibition on performing necessary renewal in time, expropriation and expulsion, and letting whole blocks of houses rot on purpose. The increase of such brutalities promotes defeatism, despondency of the inhabitants and the flight to the suburbs. The departure of the inhabitants can be explained, more than by the intensity of traffic, pollution, and noise, by the manner in which the promoters and the authorities habitually treat the city.

The exodus to the suburbs of people who are trying to find a manageable solution for their plight, affects the suburban areas. City as well as countryside perish under construction. This almost universal problem which is linked up with the development of the capitalist industrial society, in the case of Brussels is sharpened by nationalistic conflicts: the settling of mostly French-speaking inhabitants in Flemish suburbs leads (and led) to the continuous denationalization of the original inhabitants. This slow process—which seems to be slowing down at present—can only be explained as the result of the capture of the center by a capitalist sociopolitical structure, and not as a (devilish or missionary) plan of a number of French-speaking natives of Brussels.

In short, the existence of the peripheral zones as natural and cultural spaces depends on the development of livability of the center. So ARAU wants to give the power of the city to the inhabitants, and in the first place to the workers.

ARAU, a Real Urban Encounter

A group such as ARAU is urban by nature. It is a group of people which has gotten together rather incidentally from various directions, a gathering which reaches further than the divisions of Belgian society, which is very split up indeed. ARAU has been constructed on two levels: a General Assembly, which meets three times a year, and an executive committee, which meets once a fortnight. The by-laws give the executive committee great autonomy in its actions. This committee consists of twelve members who have been elected and it can number ten co-opted members. One is not allowed to be a member of the committee and at same time fulfil an executive political mandate (mayor, alderman, or minister).

A sociological analysis will give a better insight into the reasons for the internal cohesion of ARAU and into the difficulties which sometimes occur in the admission of new members, especially in the executive committee. The history of ARAU and the complexity of the technical problems have turned ARAU into what is called by Sartre *une groupe de fusion*, the members of which take part in operations which are required continually, without any political or personal ulterior designs.

An unimportant little group? It is sometimes called that. But what meaning does such a remark have? ARAU soon realized that the campaigns in the urban environment— besides the campaigns in the district committees—could take another form: that is, informing public opinion by way of the mass media. Here, too, a sociological analysis can be of help to understand the importance of the intention. The city is a network of small district communities in which interpersonal relations, whether they have been realized or not, are predominant. But the city is also a totality, structured on functional grounds according to technical specializations: workers, artists, teachers, tradespeople, etc. The thing was to find a language in which these people could be reached, across the usual barriers, to finally reach the people who are politically responsible.

Formally the mass media, newspaper, radio, and television, have been the means for informing the public, and thus they have gradually also become the expression of public opinion. Of course the fact that ARAU has access to the mass media is to be attributed to the credibility ARAU has gradually built up thanks to the quality of its case studies and by its manner of acting itself.

Looking for Alternatives and the Practice of Deliberation

In the first place people should not be given the impression that ARAU is a group of architects and town planners who try to drive out their rivals by setting public opinion against them. That is why the plans proposed by ARAU are not for sale. Their aim is only to show public opinion an *alternative*: this could be done, or that. Democracy is based on information and the possibility of choice. ARAU is working on the creation of this possibility of choice to break through the idea of the "necessary and only possibility." It is a matter of technical choice, of course, but also of a political one. Public opinion and the politicians know this only too well. There has never been a lack of proposals to buy the study designs from ARAU. This has never been done. This has given ARAU its credibility.

But here the question arises: how do you make a living? How do you exist? The authorities have awarded subsidies a number of times, because of the cultural role ARAU fulfills. For the rest, being a member of ARAU implies a practical involvement, with all it entails in the way of disinterestedness in the financial sphere . . . and in the way of freedom.

The projects illustrated here will enable people to form an opinion about the quality of the case-studies which form the base of ARAU's press-conferences. The same scheme is seen again and again: an analysis of the plans or of the problems and a proposal for one or more alternative solutions. Especially the proposal of alternatives has contributed fundamentally to ARAU's credibility, because thanks to these it is always possible to give an answer to the catch-question: "Well, what would you do?"

Proposing alternatives makes high demands. It expects creativity, it prevents living in soothing utopias, and it demands a sense of reality, common sense, and a continuous reference to the political and ideologic contents of the plans. But it also invigorates and inspires confidence, with respect to the politicians who cooperate with us, and with respect to our adversaries.

So the case studies which have been thoroughly prepared and the financial and professional independence of ARAU have gradually convinced public opinion and a number of politicians of the necessity of putting an end to the old practices of town planning, and have won them over to the thesis that the inhabitants must recapture the urban spaces.

This credibility has placed ARAU in a favorable position to negotiate. The deliberation for the planning of the Kleine and the Grote Zavel, a quarter in the heart of the city, has, after very lengthy negotiations, led to the recognition of certain principles which are much more in keeping with the requirements of modern town planning: retaining the urban texture, continuity of building, functional multivalence, the housing density. It is the first example of a successful deliberation with the inhabitants.

Of course other groups had already been in contact with the competent authorities. But the foundation of a work group in which the public forces (the city of Brussels and the government services), various committees of inhabitants, the foundation Quartiers des Arts, La Ligue Esthétique Belge, and a number of associations of shopkeepers came together—not in the framework of a simple deliberation but with the will to come to a satisfactory agreement—has contributed to the democratization of decision making and besides to the realization of better town planning.

ARAU and Inter-Environment

This practice of deliberation (that is if it is more than simple consultation) has become a demand of all the committees of inhabitants which are active in the agglomeration of Brussels.

This brings us to another form of the "struggle for the city" in Brussels. ARAU is not the only group campaigning. Some groups are older, some are younger, some groups work in certain sectors, others are occupied with the districts; some groups are more politically orientated than others; some groups originate in the working-class quarters, others in the elegant quarters.

Due to the threats which loom over Brussels, especially because of a close net of motorways, a great number of district committees were born. By definition they show the shortcomings of having a very partial view of the problems, and they sometimes think it sufficient to move the problems to the territory of a neighboring district! They also find it difficult to think of alternatives, and they do not know very much about the administrative and political procedures to be followed. The coordination of these committees was necessary if the inhabitants did not want to remain divided in their actions against the unity of the public forces and the solidarity of the project developers.

ARAU has undertaken part of the assistance to the committees of inhabitants. After long discussions it was agreed, however, to entrust the coordination of the urban struggle to a coordinating body, the foundation Inter-Environment Bond Beter Leefmilieu. This includes not only the urban associations but also the protectors of the environment, and groups who are active in the fight against pollution. ARAU plays an active part in Inter-Environment Brussels, in the field of campaign methods as well as in the field of the struggle.

Besides ARAU maintains privileged contacts with the foundation Les Archives de l'Architecture Moderne who support logistics (with plans, studies, etc.) and with the Comité général d'action des Marolles, a collection of the committees of inhabitants of the most working class quarter of Brussels. Then there are the practically continuous contacts with the syndical and social organizations (the ABVV/FGTB—the Belgian TUC—and the ACW/MOC —the General Christian Trade Union).

Besides the many campaigns it carries on, besides the numerous negotiations and press conferences, ARAU within the Atelier des Recherches and in the Ecoles Urbaines organizes possibilities for greater reflection. From its formation ARAU has worked continuously in educating urban activists. Every night for a week urban problems are studied. There are conferences and discussions about the economic, social, institutional, and legal problems of urban development. A few hundred people took part in five Ecoles Urbaines, the operations of which find a response via the mass media. This work in education will be intensified in future. There will be a cycle of two years (60 Saturdays of 6 hours of work) which puts itself in the framework of permanent education, and which will make it possible, at least in part, to prepare militants for urban action (discussion 1975). Then there is an Atelier des Recherches, which pursues a fundamental approach to the problems (youth and town planning).

Balance and Prospects

How can a balance be drawn up for five years of continuous hard work, and of sometimes grim fighting?

The thing ARAU has achieved in the first place is the preservation of a number of districts. The ITT tower has been built, it is true, close to the Abbey of Ter Kameren, but that has been our greatest failure. A number of plans have been slowed down. Most plans ARAU has opposed have been stopped, frozen, or withdrawn for further studies, and in the future all such plans are to be subject to public inquiry.

Even though there has not been any building to the liking of ARAU, its principles have penetrated public opinion all the same, and they inspire the town planning programs of the parties. (Political parties, when drawing up their programs, now often consult ARAU). Everybody is discussing the necessity of developing urban housing; who would dare to censure the renovation of de Marollen? Who still clings to the Charter of Athens? Who still believes the car should have preference over public transport? Here we find the cultural victory of ARAU.

Every idea, every plan can be *disarmed*: its real and original intention can be distorted. If we don't look out, the recapture of the city by the inhabitants will be to the benefit of the richest among them. If we don't look out the internal changes of the agglomeration will hamper the creation of jobs in the secondary sector, while there are skilled personnel available. If we don't look out the aim of the struggle will be betrayed, that is, the dawning of a creative and *freed* society.

That is why ARAU's program must be extended and deepened. It must deepen its political and ideological orientation, propagate it, and educate active militants. More radical demands will have to be made, the labor movements must be convinced of the importance of the struggle in town planning, and we must offer our assistance. The future of ARAU is fighting to give the power of the city to the workers.

Notes

1. In the context of real political and administrative structures Brussels can no longer be regarded as one strictly described notion. The agglomeration of Brussels numbers 19 municipalities to begin with, including the city of Brussels, which all have the same rights and are fairly independent of each other. There are a number of organs of contact (the mayor's convention) and there are some new political structures, too, such as the Agglomeration Council, the Region Council, and the societies for regional development, but all this has not yet made any concrete change in the political organization of Brussels.

2. This thesis is in no way directed against the necessity for the workers to control their means of production. Its starting-point is the manyfold character of the liberation process: raising the standard of living, democratization of education and of culture, workers' control of the enterprises.

8 A Street in Grenoble

François d'Arcy

This chapter is different from the preceding ones, since the neighborhood I would like to discuss, which is located in Grenoble, is a very small one, just one street and two adjacent streets, less than one block I would say, and with buildings which are of no historical interest, no architectural interest, rather deteriorated and in rather poor condition.

All these conditions point to the normal solution, which is just to destroy and to rebuild. Moreover, this neighborhood is now occupied (not inhabited but occupied—I will go back to the difference) by Algerian workers, in other words, people who are considered "dangerous" and "dirty." There is pressure in the city to destroy and eradicate this area. A neighborhood in just the next block, which was about in the same condition, has already been destroyed and new buildings have been built on this site with good, comfortable apartments and middle class flats. This other urban renewal project had been decided on by the former City Council before 1965. In 1965 in Grenoble a leftist City Council was elected, which carried out this project but is now hesitating about keeping this image of urban renewal and would like to do something else. So in 1969, a group of radical students in the department of Urban Planning in the University conducted some research, one could say research action, and tried to investigate the situation in the neighborhood a bit more. The results were different from what people had thought and what the local newspapers described when they were talking about the makeup of Grenoble. What was discovered through this research?

First, some historical facts which are of interest. This neighborhood has always been on the edge of the city of Grenoble and has been inhabited by a marginal population for maybe four or five hundred years: Protestants, rural immigrants, some kinds of "undesirable" people such as prostitutes, robbers, immigrant workers, Italians, Spanish, and now Algerians—all people who are kept on the edge of the city. It has always been the fate of this neighborhood to welcome these people. Today, of course, it is no longer on the edge of the city because Grenoble has changed scale. Until 1930 the other side of the city was developed. Now it is growing all over a large area, and this street is right in the middle of the city though still on the edge of the old city. Moreover, it is a very discreet street, very difficult to find. It is not a thoroughfare. People could easily ignore it or not know that it exists because they cannot see it easily. Who is now living there? A small population of twelve hundred people. That makes about 450 units. Most of them are very small units.

Only 40 percent have families. One-third are people living alone, which is much more than anywhere else in the city, and about 25 percent are nonfamily groups, which is also very different from what you would find in the rest of the city.

What nationality? Single persons are French and most of them are older people. Twenty-two percent are Italian; about 9 percent are Portuguese and Spanish, and surprisingly enough only 25 percent are Algerians, surprisingly because the Algerians are the only people you see on the street. That is why I have said that they occupy this neighborhood, although they are far from being the majority of the people living there. What does this mean for the Algerians, this space, this urban space, this disassociation between the occupation of the urban space and the occupation of housing? Of course these people include a larger proportion of workers than in the rest of the city, and their incomes are very low. As far as the buildings themselves are concerned, all of them are more than a hundred years old, and many of them are two to three hundred years old or more. They are very small apartments; 80 percent of the people live in one or two room apartments very different from what is now built in public housing. And of course the level of comfort is rather low according to all modern standards. Only one of six apartments has its own toilet. But in compensation the rents are very low.

I do not want to give more figures; that is enough from the standpoint I want to express. One thing I would like to stress is that the street is occupied and perceived in very different ways by the different groups I mentioned before.

If you look at the Italians (let us start with them because they are usually the most active population within this neighborhood), they settled there about ten or twenty years ago, and they are really established in Grenoble with no intention of going back to Italy. What they have done is to arrange to buy apartments and usually have bought one room after the other until they had sufficient space for their families; and, if those families are expanding, they will buy another group. It is easy in these old buildings because staircases can be altered so you never know what floor you are on and you can just break through the walls. So they have progressively arranged their apartments according to their needs and they have done all the work themselves; and they are well-arranged apartments although the buildings are usually not so good.

As for the French, usually old people, what they do is just to try to stay in their old apartments, and they don't have any impact on the neighborhood. Their goal is their past, to keep their past, to keep the walls and, with that, to live.

The Portuguese are again very different because the Portuguese are immigrants who come, usually with their families, for a short period of time, usually two years, so what they want is just a place to stay. They don't identify themselves with their apartment, their lodgings, as the Italians would do or the old French people would do. Their need is to find a cheap apartment in Grenoble, but it is very difficult to find this type of apartment through normal channels, through agencies, for instance. So they know that in this area they will find one rather easily, a place where they can settle for a few years even if there is no comfort.

The way these three groups occupy the space is still centered on the apartments they are living in; their urban space and other lodgings are not only the street but also different markets which are two or three steps from there. There are cheap markets where they can find not only cheap goods but also other people of their nationality if they are Italian or Portuguese, or other old people who have been living in the area for years and years.

The last group, the Algerians, occupy the space in a very different way because for them the inner space, their private space, is in a way very unimportant. They usually just have a bed in a room and they might share the room with several people. They come to France without their families; they will stay two or three years and then go back to Algeria. I might add that in Algeria the inner space of the house is usually the space of the woman. The men live on the street. Where they sleep is a very unimportant part of the space they occupy. A much more important part is the café in the street, the street itself. That's why they are the only people you can see.

This gives only a first set of ideas and facts which raises questions. As long as the City Council has decided to keep the people in the area and to stop the previous kind of urban renewal, then it has to take into account all these functions, all these meanings of the space, both outside space and inside space. Is it possible, through the construction of new buildings, for instance, to keep this nice balance and economy of space? In a way it would be very interesting to see a functional urbanism which would analyze these different functions and try to treat them in turn. For instance, the City Council has constructed a center for immigrant workers within this neighborhood where an immigrant worker will be able to find one room. It is not an apartment, just one room in a large building of single rooms, one next to the other just as in other buildings with three- or four-room apartments. Here the function is to lodge bachelors, and so you build buildings with single rooms. But if you try to analyze each function and to answer each of these functions through special-use building, no matter what it is, I doubt that the sum of all these functions will recreate the effect of a space which is organized as it is now, since it can perform a lot of different functions. But, on the other hand, if you try to keep this urban form as much as possible as it is, just by improving the living conditions by introducing more comfort, bathrooms, and so on, then you are going to upgrade this housing in the general market. Then what is going to happen? Right now the street is occupied by this group which cannot fit within the norm of what is constructed in public or private housing: bachelors, patriarcal families in the case of the Italians, families without fathers, all these people who can't fit within norms; people with low incomes. If this space were improved then the area would become attractive to the new marginals of our society, the new intellectual middle class, what many researchers in France have called "the new *petite bourgeoisie*," who also want to escape the norms which are imposed on them, but who have the money to do it. There are many of them in Grenoble, where there is a very important university.

I would like now to take the same problem but from a different point of view, which is not a point of view of urban form, but is more economical and political, and talk about the Algerian workers who are there because this area serves Algerians who come from all the urban areas of Grenoble. What are they going to find there? Well, in the café they will find not only people who share the same mores, but also all kinds of information which is very useful in their daily lives and that they can't find in any other place in the city. In other words, this street plays a very important role of center, urban center, for a marginal part of the population. Some researchers have defined it as a Moslem center within the city. It is very important to try to understand its very central role for the Algerian community within Grenoble, mainly because there are in this neighborhood degraded lodgings where people have quickly found a cheap place to stay for a short period of time: they can be sure they will find it there the very night that they arrive.

This process doesn't go on without some form of exploitation of the Algerian workers by the Algerians themselves, giving the opportunity to some Algerian petit bourgeois to exploit the Algerian worker coming to Grenoble looking desperately for a bed for the night. They usually sublet a room by putting five or six beds in a room and asking maybe seventy francs a month or one hundred francs a month for just a bed. This is a good source of profit. At the same time, these people, who also own the cafés, play a role of social regulation for the Algerian community. Is it possible to have this function filled by public offices, like the Algerian Consulate, the Office for Immigrant Workers, or other kinds of agencies who might take in charge all the problems of the Algerian workers coming into France? In a way it would be possible, except that many of these immigrant workers, and this is true also for the Portuguese, are in irregular circumstances; they usually don't have the proper documents to work, and the work they find is often done under illegal conditions. Is it possible to think that through public agencies you can take away this economic illegality in the way people are working? This is the question of the function of legality in a society, which is very difficult. Although it is usually ignored by most jurists, it might be claimed that illegality has a function in society as well as the law itself.

If you analyze the economic base of Grenoble and the sector in which these Algerians work, you will find and understand what I am talking about. Then you can see that they work, most of them, in sectors which are regressing and none in the sectors which are expanding. But the sectors which are expanding are expanding because other sectors are regressing.

This cheap labor force, working under illegal conditions, has an economic function in the development of the city, and any attempt to resolve this illegality will not provide any solution to this problem. Illegality has a real economic function in the development of the city, and a place like this neighborhood is providing its space and its function.

Now, what about politics and the objectives of the City Council in this area?

First, why should anything be done? There is no pressure from the neighborhood itself. This is important to say because there is talk of mobilizing the population. In this case, the population is so diverse that any attempt at mobilization has failed so far.

Any study of Grenoble has to take into account that many things which are happening there reveal the conflict between the Socialist Party and, until very recently, the P.H.T. (a very small leftist party which has now joined the Socialist Party) and between the Socialist Party, based in the city of Grenoble itself, and the Communist Party, which is very strong in the suburbs. So far no agreement has been possible between the Communist Party and the Socialist Party.

The City Council itself wishes to do something because it built its image on a progressive urban policy, and it really wants to show that it can do things not only in new dwellings, in new public housing, as it has done so far in a rather successful way, but also in the old parts of the city.

However, any solution which tries to restore the old buildings is more costly than any other. Although the exact figures are still confidential, I think that restoration would cost 30 or 40 percent more than the usual urban renewal program of just clearing the space and building new houses.

Not only that, but there is no public regulation which is adapted to restoration. The City Council would need some grants from the national government to do it, but there is no national regulation under which these grants can fit, because the legislation is designed for an area which has a historical and architectural quality, which is not at all the case. Also, the regulations regarding health conditions are designed to demolish and in consequence to build new buildings.

So what they are trying to do now is what they have successfully done many times so far. It is to ask the government to recognize the experimental status of a restoration of that street in that neighborhood. Many times it has happened that the political will of the city of Grenoble didn't fit within national regulations. What they do in such cases is to go and see the minister or his personal advisors and say, "Look, we are going to do something which doesn't fit in with your regulations but we think that it is interesting and that it will give you new ideas and improve new regulations. Give us just a little more money than you give usually for equivalent programs in other cities so that we can really go as far as possible in the experiment, and then when it is finished, we will demonstrate that it is well done, and that it costs less than solutions we have now."

This is something which usually works because within the central administration in France there are a certain number of people who think that their bureaucratic way of acting is inadequate to solve the problems of French society now but who cannot really change them by themselves because they don't have the local contact and they don't know enough about the local situation to change the regulations by themselves.

It is not at all certain that this experimental status will be accepted by the government. In that case, I think that Grenoble may go to some form of classical urban renewal, but in that case liquidation of the neighborhood will force a kind of social planning that is not wished by the City Council. Alternatively they will get the money to do the experiment, and they will try to dig up some kind of social process within this neighborhood to keep the neighborhood as much as possible as it is. But nobody really knows what this kind of social process means.

9   Rome from the Inside: Lisa Ronchi
Inhabitant's Intermezzo

A panoramic view of the ragged roof of the Palazzo Borghese, Rome. Photo by Enrico di Cave.

Skyline of Via di Campo Marzio. Photo by Enrico di Cave.

Construction of an elevator for the *carabinieri*. Photo by Enrico di Cave.

Closeup of the completed elevator shaft. Photo by Enrico di Cave.

Views of an addition to Via della Torretta and the various elegant attempts to disguise it with plants. Photos by Enrico di Cave.

Walls slowly rise to fill the arches of the Altana of Palazzo Fiano. Photos by Enrico di Cave.

An abandoned fruit store on the Via del Prefetti. Photo by Enrico di Cave.

The only remaining *vino e olio* store in the quarter. Photo by Enrico di Cave.

I live in the inner fraction of the 1,000 hectares of the historical center of Rome, the very heart of the city. I have always lived in the inner city, first Treviso, where I was born, then Venice for a long time.

I am an architect and my husband is a *museografo* (a designer of museums); his office is at the Palazzo Venezia.

As newlyweds we lived for two years in my husband's family house, via Paisiello, near via Veneto and the Borghese gardens, the gorgeous entrance to the Parioli: this was at that time the most fashionable residential district in Rome, where, for the wealthy and the would-be, it was a must to stay. We didn't enjoy the Parioli and its aristocratic isolation, its empty streets and their scarce, lonely population of maids, butlers, and well-groomed dogs; we missed the shops and the reality of the people, the contact with the town, though the contact with the Borghese gardens was pleasant indeed.

We moved to via di Campo Marzio, by the Parliament, in the early fifties, to an apartment we rented from a Roman nobleman: the Roman nobleman had just moved to the Parioli.

Our flat was huge, shabby, and sunny and still is: only one bathroom, no heating, electric wires in sight and obsolete plumbing forever under repair, bugs forever chased away and forever reappearing, cracked shutters and irregular, unstable floors. From our windows we looked into mysterious tiny courtyards swarming with children, into the dorms of the *carabinieri*, over the church's roof and its Romanesque campanile, the solemn covered roof-terrace of Palazzo Fiano, the variety of houses, roofs, and chimneys of the Rione.

The flat belonged to a high-density condominium. Each floor of the palazzo housed its good measure of old, middle-aged, and young population as well as cats and dogs and a hens-and-rooster couple on the top floor; until 1945 two or three cows lived in the courtyard and their milk was sold at the milk-shop next door. Other tenants: a janitor, a bakery's workshop, two lawyers, one doctor and one dentist, a dressmaker, a real estate agent, a refined lady, two shopkeepers, an artist, and an elderly former maid of Doris Duke. The upkeep of the building was poor; the large, fine staircase was perpetually smelly, soiled, and scratched and at regular times we were asked to keep our windows shut while the bakery's flue was being cleaned. We fitted into all this with perfect ease.

Campo Marzio was a village whose features and characteristics are common to many villages in the world. Describing it would seem banal were it not in the center of Rome; the long, narrow 5-meter-wide street with the janitors sitting outdoors, the large piazza and the smaller ones, the little dark alleys, the church and the chapels, the schools, the little hotel, the *carabinieri* station, the pharmacy and the tiny surgery, the not distant hospital, the undertaker's, the pubs and the bar, the restaurant and the pizzeria, the cinema, the shops as in a scattered supermarket with their infinite variety of food and goods, some of them known to all Rome, the best whipped cream, the best buttons; the grinder was present too in a man-bicycle solution at the streetcorner, as well as the fruit and vegetable sellers Bruno and Lucia who came each morning from Trastevere pushing their heavy greengrocer's cart. The Bartolozzi's old baker's shop was the core of the village, where everybody found a warm and witty reception and sympathetic credit terms: signora Pina used to say that she had paid for four Campo Marzio generations' births, first communions, marriages, and deaths.

The ownership of the palazzi was in few hands: religious brotherhoods, some old families, some private societies, and only one condominium, ours. But lots of tenants; the local people were as heterogeneous as a Roman minestrone: the poor and the rich, the beggars and the princes, the tailors and the cobblers, the artists and the whores. Each one was familiar to the others, as all of them had gone to the same primary school, vicolo Valdina, and had jobs in the Rione. There were many children in Campo Marzio, and the priest of the parish of S. Lorenzo in Lucina traditionally held, each year, a solemn ceremony for the first communion and confirmation of the children of age. The young men used to meet by the Marangoni bar for endless night talks on Roma-Lazio, the city's football teams.

There were not many cars in Campo Marzio: Mr. Vicerè, who owned a little lorry, often generously gave his help and drove sick friends to the hospital. We had bought a large second-hand Alfa Romeo and parked it in the piazza del Parlamento. Often the guards to the venerable institution used it as a sentry box when it was too icy outside.

In the immediate vicinity only the celebrated piazza di Spagna and the prestigious via Condotti with their exclusive shops were well known to the tourist crowds. The surrounding myriad of narrow streets was an inextricable, lively congeries of shops and trattorie, crowded houses, workshops, and brothels. No remodeled houses and some empty land, the leftover from the fascist dream of "reclaiming" the historical center by leveling it.

The other districts of Rome didn't seem to be very distant: Rome was a large town but not yet a city.

When we came to live in Campo Marzio the postwar exodus, at first a voluntary one, was just beginning. Traffic difficulties were becoming severe, and the decay of the houses became apparent to those who knew of the existence of modern comfort in heating and plumbing and could pay for it. The professionals—doctors, architects, and the like—were the first to go; the affluent residents followed: the former for lack of parking space, the latter for lack of bathrooms.

The large palaces belonging to religious institutions began to empty for lack of vocations.

So did, for different reasons, the whorehouses, owing to a recent provision of the law: these were perhaps the first houses to be converted into small flats and with them the era of miniapartments was inaugurated.

The forced exodus in our area began with the demolition of a whole block which formed the front of piazza S. Lorenzo in Lucina, a block whose interior was an irregular composition of flats intersecting one another like a puzzle: about fifteen families, many of them very poor, shopkeepers, a landlady, artisans, tramdrivers, a colonel of the *carabinieri*, a cook; and a pizzeria, a pharmacy, a second-hand bookshop, a cheap glassware shop, a garbage yard. The owner's administrator offered the tenants a bonus to go; they all refused but one, and the one who accepted was taken for a traitor (he used the three million lire bonus to remodel a nearby flat he had previously bought). The contractor started work and the tenants had to move quickly away from fear of collapsing with their homes. The new building came up on a steel frame behind the ghost of the facade which had been duly left in situ: it housed offices, a furrier's atelier, some more refined shops, an underground garage, and the pharmacy.

The sixties saw chaotic traffic in the old center. The municipal traffic authorities spent their most creative nights designing new circulation patterns for cars and buses while the citizens spent their most miserable days interpreting them. One day in Campo Marzio we found the street one way in the morning and the opposite way in the afternoon. Coming back from school became dangerous for our children as they zig-zagged among the cars and jumped from street to shop entrance to avoid being run down.

The whole large piazza del Parlamento came to be reserved for the Parliament's staff: we had to move our car to the already jammed piazza Borghese, the only parking place available to the area's inhabitants as well as to the crowds coming from the outside. We replaced our car with a much smaller one and used it only when the commuters' cars had gone, when the restaurants had closed, when the cinema had emptied out, and we still do.

We saw the decline of our area; the adjacent, once-flourishing via dei Prefetti was abandoned by both the shopkeepers and most of the inhabitants; some of the buildings were left to decay for years. Also, some of the buildings in Campo Marzio saw the tug-of-war between owners and tenants with an obvious conclusion. Many of the inhabitants were obliged to go; some others died, while the young married couples who had been born there mostly chose to go to better-equipped flats in the suburbs where huge projects were being built, the so-called dormitory quarters. At that time these young people despised their old houses and were asking for better status and supermarkets.

At the end of the sixties signora Pina's shop was in bad need of customers, and the schools were in need of pupils.

The priest could no longer organize mass first communions for lack of children of age. Signora Pina's shop changed hands; the primary and the junior schools were closed.

In the meantime the area around piazza di Spagna was becoming more and more sought after for evident commercial reasons. Via Frattina was the first to be invaded by shiny, steely boutiques with a repetitive display of ready-made clothes. Not one food shop was left. It was the first to accept (and then be happy with) the much discussed "pedestrian island" Christmas experiment, which proved to be highly successful and was maintained permanently. The other, formerly disregarded little alleys followed, some of them more sophisticated and highbrow than others, for mysterious reasons. All of them, little by little, converted into crowded pedestrian areas. All of them, so gay in daytime, were now utterly dead by night.

At the same time the municipal traffic authorities were deciding the division of the whole historical center into sectors accessible only to public transportation and to a fairly small number of cars (inhabitants', of course). The inner city was already an exclusive, secluded ghetto.

The rest of Rome seemed now to be more and more distant: the town had become a city which had expanded outward with dense, large-scale construction.

What did the seventies bring to Campo Marzio? The steady advance of the Parliament's utilities into the rearguard of the street. The so-called shutting down of our area, sector 4, to traffic and the marching in of thousands of cars with permits. The total remodeling of a building on the left side of our house. You can guess its story: programmed decay, sale to unknown company, forced eviction of the tenants, abandon to further decay of the ten-odd apartments. After the treatment, the palazzo houses twenty-seven large luxury miniapartments plus some ground-floor ateliers and shops and a bunch of professionals, politicians, retired, all residents or part-time ones. Same story, vicolo della Torretta, the total remodeling of a modest house. Before the treatment, four families, poor people, worker husbands and landlady wives. Now, twelve duplex miniapartments and a new status: a princess, an architect, a professor, etc. Another case: the shutting down of the small hotel Campo Marzio and its transformation into eight miniflats. And another: on the right side of our house we saw the emptying out of a building where only a couple of families will stay on; the owner hopes to turn it into what? Try and guess.

From our windows we can see new dormer windows, new rooms and additions sprung up overnight like pustules on the old body of the inner city. All of them, of course, illegal.

Many food shops disappeared: two butcher shops, two hand-made pasta shops, Natalucci's bakery, the fish-monger's, the wine shop, and one osteria, the paintshop, the pottery shop, the dyer's, the small hairdresser's, the undertaker's. Lucia collapsed on the street and the greengrocer cart no longer has the streetcorner. Fashion boutiques, silver and fake antique shops took their place.

All this brought new faces to Campo Marzio. By day we meet new, sophisticated, well kept, richly furred ladies. Only a few new children, mostly parked for daycare at their grandmothers'. By night the street is now empty and dark. We don't see much of the new male inhabitants; supposedly their working places are not in the area. As ever, a nice shopping center to the outsiders, and a dormitory district to the newcomers.

The Pariolization of this sector of the center still is in full bloom with the frantic search for "a hole, just a hole in this dear, characteristic old center." Quite a number of highly priced holes have become the much-longed-for nests of more-or-less noblemen and women, members or former members of the Parliament, many of their staff, executives, and others. Some of the natives, who had gone away of their own will, now claim their moral rights as born in the center; their coming back would mean to them, ironically enough, a climb to a higher status.

In our palazzo a private bank, a politician's office, a movie company took the place of some of the old families. It was a natural, non-traumatic replacement. The remaining tenants will stay as long as it will be allowed by a new rent policy and the long-promised social defense of the historical center.

The so-called Comitato di quartiere (district committee), which already is acting in other districts of the city, has not yet taken human form in this area. We hope it will not continue to be an abstract image, but until now nobody seems to have been contacted by anybody; no new social structure has yet taken the place of the old family mutual help and acquaintance.

It will be clear from what I said before that not much physical change is apparent to a casual passer-by. The carefully restored facades and the new, unobtrusive shopfronts conceal, though, heavy and irrevocable changes. The clamor about the inner city made it a privileged but still unknown area, a superghetto detached from the rest of the city. This didn't prevent but helped those changes. The slogan "the inner city to its inhabitants" will not make sense any more in a few years. Which inhabitants? A zoo of a few natives, a few artisans, a few characteristic locals? Why should others from the rest of the city be excluded? And what is this magical historical center; who owns it, what are the names of the houses, of the offices, of the companies? What is the meaning of the huge, empty palazzos that nobody knows what to do with?

This governmental, papal, tourist, international, and national city has impending, serious, urgent problems; its historical center is only one of them and should be seen as a part of the whole. From the inside, from the outside, from the bottom, every citizen can help. Once upon a time, the participation was domestic. Participation should come back with a new knowledge of the real needs and a mutual all-city exchange of experiences, and this applies to both the citizen and the authority. Enough of privileges and the privileged, be it stones or people.

10   A Square in Islington

Jonathan Raban

Reprinted from Jonathan Raban, *Soft City* (Glasgow: Fontana Books [Collins], 1974).

The . . . square is not actually a square at all. It is three sides, each with its own rather odd, cheapskate style of Victorian architecture—one grand with balconies and rotting porticoes, on derelict-gothic, and one orotund fake-Georgian terrace. It looks as if it had been put together by a shady and squabbling trio of speculative builders, while their fourth friend found a more profitable racket: the south side of the square is a cutting, in which the goods trains of the North London Line from Broad Street to Richmond rattle through where the slaveys ought to have been steaming in a line of basement washrooms. In the centre of the square, there is an ornamental garden, mostly grass and flowering shrubs that never seem to be in flower, a children's playground, the superstructure of a bomb shelter which has been turned into a pair of public lavatories, and a padlocked tennis court whose gravelled surface has cracked and subsided as if it had had its own earthquake. It is a square that architectural writers about the area leave conspicuously alone; it shows its own history, of unimaginative enterprises, both private and civic, all too well. Lots of people have had ideas for it at one time or another; none of them have been very bright ones. On the Georgian side, someone thought he would smarten his house up by slapping a coat of gravel-stucco on it three inches deep and painting it nightdress pink; and just by the railway line, on the central space, a truck owner built a large wooden-and-corrugated-iron hangar to unload his lorries in. Floodlit, on a winter evening, it looks as if he is putting on a passion play, a ghostly Islington Oberammergau.

Yet in the late nineteen-sixties, the council put a conservation order on the square—perhaps because it was, almost, a square and squares are in fashion; perhaps because no-one from the council had ever seen it (or maybe because they all lived in it); perhaps because Islington Council has a perversely sophisticated taste in architectural curiosities—and it was this, the most recent idea, which dominated the life of the square while I lived there, skunklike, in a newly-converted basement on the west side.

For eighty years the square had been deserted by the middle classes for whom it had originally been built. They fled north, scared of their proximity to the East End and its suppurating brew of cholera and typhoid germs. By Edwardian times, their only relics were the kept women of gentlemen in the City, who sat out, so people remembered, on the sunny balconies of the north side, waiting for the clank of carriage wheels coming up Liverpool Road from the Angel. But the carriages stopped coming. The houses were broken up into flats. It was a cheap place for immigrants to get a peeling room; and it bulged with Irishmen who had come to London to burrow tunnels for the underground railways, with Greeks who were in the tailoring trade as machinists and hoped to open cafés, with Poles, and West Indians, and the more feckless members of the Cockney working class for whom the square was a vague stopover, a place they had landed up in on the way to somewhere else.

Since 1900, the square, like so many metropolitan districts, had been a shabby *entrepôt,* steadily declining as more and more shipments of people washed up in it for no special reason except that it was cheap and close to the centre of things. That was how I found myself there, too; I didn't feel I had to love it or be randy for its local colour . . . it was just a place to tie up until something better happened, it commanded no particular loyalty. But the conservation order changed that; it slapped a sudden value on all the fungoid stucco fronts, and young couples with a little money to put down on a deposit took to patrolling the square on Sunday afternoons. They stared at it squint-eyed and, after their first blank shock at the mean disorder of the place, they learned to look at it with affection. They saw a uniform line of white fronts, with brass knockers in place of the tangle of electric bells: they put leaves on the trees; they stripped the pavements of fish-and-chip papers; they looked at the people on the streets, thought for a while, and came up with the word cosmopolitan. Tennis in the evenings, dinner on the balcony in the sun . . . the rippling, laden branches of the elms . . . the clicking wheels of smart prams parading on the shady walks between the trees . . . this vision was at a long remove from what one could actually see, but the city is a stage for transformation scenes, and the square was a challenge to the imagination. It had sunk so low that it could only be rescued, restored like one of General Booth's street-harlots to rosy-cheeked prosperity by evangelism and a change of diet.

From then on, estate agents' boards began to sprout from the basements, and builders and interior decorators swarmed round the square, carrying whole walls away from inside houses, pointing the brickwork, painting the fronts, taking long speculative lunch hours in the pub, while Nigel and Pamela, Jeremy and Nicola, made flying spot-checks in their Renaults and Citroëns. The leaves on the trees grew greener; old absentee landlords suddenly started to take an unprecedented interest in the lives of their tenants, shaking their heads gloomily at the absence of bathrooms and the damp patches and the jags of falling plaster, and suggesting that the tenant would be better off by far in a spick council flat in Finsbury Park. For every signboard advertising "Vacant Possession" there had been a flyting game, alternately wheedling and vicious. Some landlords locked their tenants out of their lavatories; some hired thugs in pin-stripe suits; some reported their own properties to the council as being unfit for habitation; many offered straight cash bribes—the going rate for eviction was £200, a large sum to tenants but one that was a fraction of the rising monthly value of the property. (In three years, a typical house on the terrace rose in price from £4000 to £26,000.) The tenants were winkled out; most of them were innocent of their rights, and those who tried to stay were subjected to long, elaborately-mounted campaigns of harassment. Alongside the builders' skips on the pavement, there were handcarts and aged minivans, with a transistor radio squawking pop tunes on top of the roped-together pile of tacky furniture. The local barber told me about the girl-graduates who came to sweet-talk him out of his flat, flashing their mini-skirts and going on about vinyl bathrooms and "conveniences." He had already lost most of his customers, since the council was tearing down several acres of neighboring streets to make way for glass-and-concrete apartment blocks.

It rained eviction notices, but the agents and landlords kept the slaughter out of sight of the prospective buyers, who were all people of principle, staunch Labour voters, dedicated lovers of the working class. They *wanted* the shawled Greek widows, the clowning blacks on the pavement outside the pub, the wise and melancholy Irish and the Cockney wits; they liked the square because it was real, and they found colour and charm where the landlords saw only dreck. And, as the tenants drifted unwillingly away, they left their familiars; lean mongrels and starved cats, who roistered in the alleys and kept the square at night alive with eldritch shrieks and desolated love-moans. There was an old lady with a ruined pram who collected rags and discarded clothes; her business thrived, and she trundled a mountain of furs gone to verdigris and mothballs, and charred demob suits, and plastic basketwork hats with bunches of artificial cherries of an unlikely colour.

I was adopted by an abandoned cat, lean and black as an old curate, with a voice that was uncannily guttural with thirst and hunger. It tottered uncertainly about my flat, took a snobbish shine to the central heating, and bedded down gracelessly, like an evacuee. Pets are forbidden in many council flats, and the ones left behind in the square led a life of ingratiating atavism, battened on to the new wave of middle-class immigrants, and developed sophisticated cravings for cream and chicken livers. They were the real permanent residents of the square, these animals for whom the rest of London, and the wheels of changing social fortune, were not even rumours. The landlord could tear the cat's owner away from the place he had lived in as long as he could remember; but the cat stayed, like the name on the disconnected bell, and the dead-pigeon smell in the front-area—mortal remains, of the kind preserved in old photographs . . . things which survive, but only just long enough for the collector of local colour to record them.

The people went, to Finsbury Park, the darker reaches of Holloway Road, and brazen GLC estates on the Essex border. The people who came in (a disproportionately small number since a single middle class couple and their baby can displace anything up to a dozen sitting tenants) were from Kensington, or the northern outer suburbs, or the Home Counties; and they settled avidly on the land, taking over its shops and pubs, getting up little campaigns to preserve this and demolish that, starting playgroups, and giving small intense dinner parties for other new pioneers. They took tutorials in local gossip from their chars, and talked knowledgeably about "Ron" and "Cliff" and "Mrs. H." and "Big Ted," as if the square and its history were their birthright.

But it was by no means a complete takeover; people still repaired old cars from front rooms along the square, and on the reclaimed east side, the houses seemed to actually swell with an influx of the displaced and the very poor. This part of London responds like a needle-gauge to disturbances across the world, and the expulsion of Asians from Kenya showed up on the square in a sprinkling of faces who looked bitterly unaccustomed to such want and cold, and were determined to move out before they got bogged down in the rising damp and learned to shiver with fortitude before the popping gas fire with half its plaster columns cracked or gone. On the far side, the sunny side, of the square, these unluckier migrants could see a future of a sort; a future of Japanese lampshades, *House and Garden*, French baby cars, white paint, asparagus tips, Earl Grey tea and stripped pine stereo systems—the reward of success is the freedom to choose a style of elegant austerity. It is hard to guess how such conspicuous rejection of the obvious fruits of wealth must have looked to the Asians, who had so recently been forcibly deprived of their money and its attendant powers. ("How much do you have now?" asked a radio interviewer of an expelled Asian businessman at Heathrow. "Two hundred shillings," said the man, speaking carefully, talking of the contents of his wallet like Monopoly money.) They wandered about in second-hand overcoats, glazedly detached from their own dereliction. When stray dogs snuffled at their feet, they kicked them, delicately and surreptitiously, in their bellies.

Both groups of immigrants were innocent of the improvised network of rules which had been evolved around the square. The smart young things trespassed casually, arrogantly, secure in the conviction that the future of the square lay in their hands. The Asians were shy, beadily knowing, and usually wrong. Both groups made themselves unpopular.

On the nearby block of shops there were two opposite, nearly identical grocery stores—one run by a Greek Cypriot, and one by a family of African Asians who had come over some years before. Each shop had its band of regular customers. The Cypriot was liked by the West Indian and Irish women, and kept their local foods in stock. (I tried to buy a loaf of bread there once. It looked ordinary enough. An Irish lady made me put it back. "You wouldn't want to be eating that, it's blackie bread. You go black overnight, if you eat that. Black as sin and too long and big for your girlfriend too."—The shop was full of West Indians at the time; I was the dupe and outsider, not they. They joined in, threatening me with elephantine potency and body-hair if I touched their wonder bread. Alas, I didn't.) The shop opposite was mainly patronized by the respectable Cockney working class; it was full of notices about not asking for credit as a refusal might offend, and piled high with cans of petfood. It was the chief gossip center of the quarter, and sent calendars and cards at Christmas to its regulars. Jokes were the main currency of both shops; facetious insults, usually of a bawdily intimate or racial kind, which buzzed back and forth over the racks of breakfast cereals. These jokes kept insiders in and outsiders out; they reflected—harmlessly would not be strong enough, cathartically would give them too importantly theatrical a function—the tensions in the composition of the quarter. But the immigrants could never get them quite right.

Both the Asians and the young pioneers wandered promiscuously into both shops. Once there they laughed too loudly or not loudly enough at the ritual jokes; they asked for foods which the shop they were in did not stock. When they tried to initiate jokes themselves they were too elaborate, too humorous—for humour was not the point at all—and they were received with wary tolerance. Had they been able to joke about their own peculiar tastes for white paint and thrifty ecologism it might have been different; but

they presumed to a matey all-men-are-equal tone—and the visible untruth of that ploy was all too clear to their auditors, whose own lives were day-to-day struggles with a dramatic inequality (and that made harsher by the presence of these well-heeled young couples), and hardbitten compromises with the other people in the quarter who were their territorial competitors, if not their enemies.

The local pub was carefully demarcated into symbolic territories. The public bar was the West Indian province, with a smattering of white girls with catholic tastes and inclinations. The saloon was for the Irish. There was one black, in a shiny felt hat, who ambled leggily round the saloon bar picking up empty glasses; and in the spade bar of the pub there was a single, very sodden Irishman. These two hostages strengthened the division. In the public bar, the juke box hammered out Reggae records; in the saloon on Friday nights Bridie the Singing Saxophonist carolled about the Mountains of Mourne and the Rose of Tralee through an amplifying system which made her sound like Frankenstein's monster.

On Saturday mornings, the West Indians had the pavement outside the pub to themselves, and called to the black girls coming out of the service at the shout-and-holler gospel tabernacle across the road, in their white dresses and tight curls.

"Rosee!"

"Mary-*lyn*!"

"Gay-*lee*!"

"Oh, man."

A sardonic toast, in rum and Guinness in the sun. Before the pub opened in the morning, you could hear the singing—"Sweet *Jes*-us," languorous and seductive, as if the Saviour was being cajoled out of bed or bar—and the movement of the bodies inside, pile drivers in muslin, stirring and shaking in the thin walls. The Greek church, on the other side of the block of shops, was more decorous, with a subdued trickle of people in black leading pale scrubbed children. But their priest rode like a gangster in a brand-new Ford Cortina; fast, unsmiling, a pack of cigarettes open and spilling on the dashboard like a fan of playing cards.

But the pioneers went everywhere regardless. They stood on the pavement beside the West Indians, pretending they were at a garden pub in Hampstead; they slummed in the public bar, and put the occasional sixpence in the juke box; they investigated the churches; they joined the villainous Golden Star club, a black dive where you drank rum or beer in paper cups and shuffled on the tiny dance floor to records of amazing rhythmic crunch and volume. Wherever they went, they spread money and principled amity. They were interested in everybody, as temporary and ubiquitous as secret policemen. The Polish tailor who had a workshop in his front room in the block of shops grimaced at them as they went by; he, presumably, had prior experience of people who invade places armed with good intentions.

The local paper, the *Islington Gazette,* found its letter columns filling with protests against "the new Chelseaites," with their one way traffic schemes (in Barnsbury, a few blocks south of the square), and their cheque-book evictions. The local Labour Party began to split down the middle, between the soft-accented newcomers—all with honourable theories of workers' control—and the old long-resident trades unionist. It seemed like the beginning of a class war. But the young couples had never conceived of themselves as a class—they had rejected the bourgeois ethic, just as they had rejected the florid display of Chelsea—and were strenuously, idealistically individualist. They didn't see themselves in the stereotypical portraits painted by the angry correspondents in the paper; they were not like that, they *cared* and had scruples. How could sincere socialists be accused of class-exploitation? Or acres of white paint be construed as a vulgar exhibition of financial power? Jeremy and Nicola, Pamela and Nigel, were indignant and troubled; or they took the vindictive portraits to refer to quite other people, and joined in the chorus of execration.

All round the square, more working-class streets came down. Windows were boarded up, and the London Electricity Board put LEB OFF in swathes of paint across the front doors when it disconnected each house's supply. It looked like a sign of a plague or a primitive curse. "Leb off!" As the demolition men moved in, a cloud of old brick-dust hung over the streets, and more frightened cats migrated southwards into the square. Soon after I stopped living there, Lesly Street residents refused to go; they barricaded both ends of the road and tried to sit it out as the bulldozers rumbled closer, taking down their garden walls and flattening flower borders under their tracks. The residents were supported by some rebellious social workers and one sympathetic Labour councillor, and their "No Go Area" got into the national newspapers. But Lesly Street has gone too, now. It wasn't perhaps a class war, but there has certainly been something suspiciously like a class victory.

In the converted house where I lived, privilege and choice, like a thick belt of insulation, kept the destruction of the surrounding streets to little more than an annoying noise that interfered with one's reading. The garden in the centre of the square was replanted; the trees, now we were in a smokeless zone, looked less sorry; the careening streams of after-school kids thinned; the front area was easier to keep clean. It was regarded as a small victory for conservation that the wall at the back of the garden was kept high, so that the tenants of the new council low-rise flats would not be able to watch the sunbathing Brahmins leafing through the *New York Review of Books* on their breakfast patios.

The off-licence which I used came down. The betting shop was served with a surprise notice of demolition. Little back-street businesses shifted or died. Every big city, even at times of desperate property-shortage, has crannies into which the feckless and the transient and some, at least, of the dispossessed, can lose themselves. No-one knows exactly where everybody goes in these upheavals. Municipal housing helps some; but the unlucky have to search out those remaining areas which have not yet been picked out by the spotlight of wealth and fashion or the dimmer beam, which often accompanies it, of urban renewal. Ruinous terraces backing on to the railway tracks in Camden . . . grim apartment houses in east Holloway . . . derelict streets running alongside disused wharves and warehouses south of the river . . . There was a boy with a transistor radio and the scalp of a clipped ferret who sold me a bargain Austin Sprite; by the time the big-end went and the gearbox had exhausted the sawdust he'd added, he had gone too—his house boarded over, his business marked only by a long grease stain on the pavement. He might crop up anywhere.

But the pioneers, the new Brahmins, are there to stay; their money firmly invested, their place assured. The trees grow greener for them; they outlive cats, charladies, sitting tenants, they ride the tides of inflation and depression and mobility just as their parents did. Though they have loftier spirits than their parents, or more innocence. The square is not—will not be—as "real" as it was; but it is coming to be a place of substance, which, on the economic scale of things, is perhaps more important. If the frontier spirit with which it was colonized is fading, it is being replaced by a sense of imminent history—it is growing a pedigree from scratch . . . as if the departed tenants had no more claim on it than the delivery drivers who take cars out to their new owners and put the clock back to zero. The tenants—"temporary people," in the words of a lady Brahmin—will always be on the road somewhere, being passed by.

In its rehabilitation back into respectability, the Islington square was recovered as property; for the middle-class residents it was *place* as something to purchase and own, where for the departing tenants it had been a place to borrow, squat on, or move through. North London is dull and upright at heart; temporariness and mobility are frowned on, and the signals of their existence—cafés, restaurants, bars as meeting points rather than local pubs, take-away food stores, boutiques, bedsitter agencies—are few and dingy. Transients there live a furtive and persecuted existence, regarded as the flotsam of the city; and people hope that they will be swept back to sea on the next tide. The most evident kind of transience is the transience of failure—the shady car dealer, the inept con man, the tramp dossing in the condemned basement, the balding lodger who flits on

rent day—and it is against this that the white city of permanence, property, thrift, and cleanliness is, in large part, a fortress. The exaggerated neighbourliness of the pioneers, their attempt to turn Islington into a cozy village of gossip, play groups, and intimate dinner parties, is a way of rejecting that other city of locomotion, dirt, discontinuity and failure.

II   Conservation Experiments

11 The Future of the Old Sector of the City of Athens: Plaka

Dionysis A. Zivas

Houses of Plaka in Athens, between the Roman Agora and the Acropolis on the hill above. Photo by Dionysis A. Zivas.

Lysion Street, typical of the
existing state of the old quarter.
Photo by Dionysis A. Zivas.

Measured drawing of typical Plaka houses. Students of Professor Dionysis A. Zivas.

One of the series of maps documenting the age and condition of buildings in the Plaka. The Acropolis is in the lower left-hand corner. Shading ranges from black (valuable buildings) to light gray (incompatible buildings). Photo by Dionysis A. Zivas.

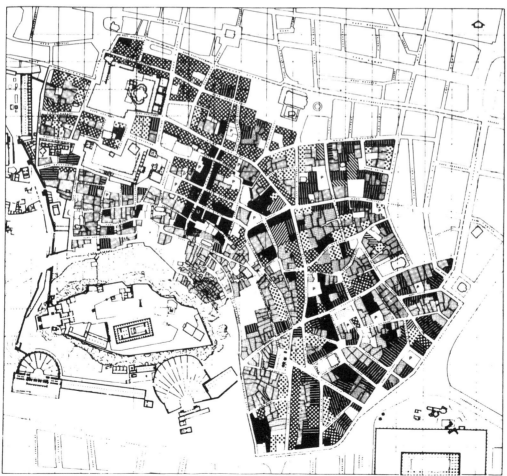

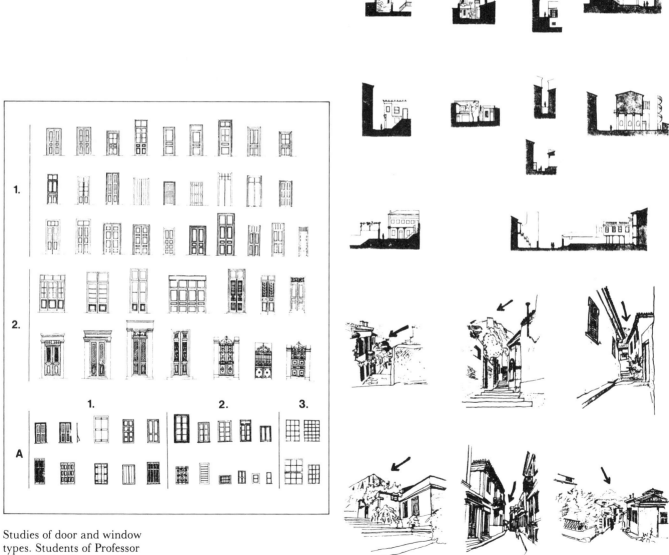

Townscape studies of Plaka.
Students of Dionysis A. Zivas.

Studies of door and window
types. Students of Professor
Dionysis A. Zivas.

1. Plaka, the best known quarter of Athens, is nothing more or less than the oldest district in the modern capital of Greece. It is an area which has been inhabited since the late Neolithic Age, continuously to the present day, a matter of approximately 5,500 years. Its importance, therefore, and problems which today are linked to its preservation are of particular significance. For this reason, in the year 1973, the Ministry of Public Works decided to study these problems in detail and to draw from their analysis, sound conclusions on which to formulate proposals for the future of the quarter in question. A work team was thus set up consisting of Dr. John Travlos, architect and archaeologist, Mrs. Alice Hadjopoulou, lawyer, Mr. P. Mandikas, economist, Dr. Joanna Dimaki, sociologist, and Mr. P. Pappas, an economist specializing in statistics. To this group were added two more archaeologists, three architects, and a number of students. The Ministry of Public Works did me the honor of inviting me to conduct the activities of the work team in question, some of whose results are presented here.

Plaka stretches north and east of the rock of the Acropolis. To the south it borders on the excavation site of the ancient Agora and the Stoa of Attalus, entirely restored by the American School of Classical Studies. The area presently occupied by Plaka amounts to approximately 40 hectares and borders to the north and east on the central section of modern Athens, which hems it in more and more. In order to present some measure of comparison, it should be noted that the city of Athens occupies some 5,000 hectares, while the inhabited area of the Attica basin (Athens, Piraeus, and surroundings) occupies more than 25,000 hectares.

According to the findings of archaeologists, the present town plan of Plaka, even the tracing and location of its streets, is directly related to the corresponding layout of the ancient city. Streets such as Tripodon Street and Hadrian's Way appear to lie exactly upon the lines of the ancient streets, and it seems most probable that the same applies to several more of today's Plaka streets. It is also worthy of

note that the present-day Plaka is the part of Athens which did not cease to be inhabited even during the darkest hours of the city's history. Even after the Herules sacked Athens in 267 A.D. and also during the Frankish occupation of Athens, Plaka, surrounded by the so-called wall of the late Roman period, continued its existence alone amid what had once been Athens.

This fact provides an explanation for the survival of so many monuments in this particular area while, in the course of the centuries, several more were added. Thus it is that, in addition to ancient Greek and Roman remains (and I would note here the Monument of Lysicrates, the Roman Agora, the Tower of the Winds, Hadrian's Library, and others), several Byzantine and post-Byzantine churches have been preserved and also two Turkish mosques and Turkish baths.

All these, of course, are monuments protected by the Greek Archaeological Service, while Greek archaeologists and archaeologists from the American School of Classical Studies in Athens have marked out several other sites where they would like to continue excavations.

Their main ambition would be to uncover, for its full length, the city wall of the late Roman period. They would also like to excavate the built-up areas joining the site of the Roman Agora to that of Hadrian's Library and further the section linking these to the excavated site of the ancient Athenian Agora so that, combined, they could all form a major excavated archaeological site. It is quite obvious that, if this were to be carried out, only pictures of what was Plaka would remain for posterity.

2. Naturally, Plaka not only contains monuments but is a residential area as well. Being one of the more central quarters in Athens, very close to the city's commercial center, its ancient and medieval monuments and the Acropolis, it presents lively activity. In the thirty-odd hectares of Plaka which form the subject of this study, there are at present 992 buildings. These house 1,965 dwellings and 1,825 units of several functions (shops, workshops), 26 hotels, and 193 places of entertainment, such as taverns and restaurants for both Greeks and visiting tourists.

As stated earlier, the town plan of Plaka is closely related to what it was in antiquity, but its present architectural style has emerged from the coexistence of the monuments already mentioned with buildings erected during the period 1833 to 1928, that is, from the time when Athens was once again named the capital of Greece and the time when, for Greece, came the end of the neoclassic style of architecture. It should be clarified that, when reference is made to buildings of the neoclassic style in Plaka, it concerns structures of minor scale and modest quality of construction. It does not mean monumental buildings in the neoclassic style such as exist in the central parts of modern Athens (National Library, University, Technical University etc.) and in other Greek or European cities. To the contrary, the buildings in Plaka belong rather to the category of popular architecture but show, nevertheless, the extent to which the neoclassic style came to be accepted by the Greek people and how it influenced the architecture of dwellings in that period. Thus it was that Plaka acquired and preserved its special atmosphere for the ninety-odd years of this interim, until the period which followed World War II. Until then, the slow rate of development throughout Greece did not expose Plaka to any peril any more than did any other historic settlement in the country. The major problems began to appear—and not only in Greece—when World War II entirely upset the economic and social factors which had been valid until then.

3. Buildings in Plaka can be divided into four main categories:

a) Houses which existed prior to 1833 and have survived to the present day. They are very few but most interesting because they preserve certain rare forms of dwelling in this district.

b) Houses built during the reign of King Otto (1833–1860).

c) Houses of the principal neoclassic era, when the whole of Greece, deeply influenced by this movement, was trying hard to modernize in line with the rest of Europe and to revive the ancient Greek spirit.

d) The truly popular dwellings which, throughout this period, continued to be built in Plaka in the age-old style of the courtyard with rooms around it.

All these buildings blended in with the monuments of various periods which survive in Plaka make up a unique ensemble, and its precisely this which harbors the great peril for the area.

Today, in the small and narrow streets of Plaka, laid out originally for pedestrians, thousands of cars circulate or are parked. Many houses have been demolished and the plots used for open air parking lots.

Several other houses have been converted into taverns; others were grotesquely disfigured and a host of inscriptions in very poor taste were hoisted up on to the facades of neoclassical buildings. At night, the noise from the places of entertainment and from the crowds of tourists who gather there to see old Athens renders life unbearable and drives the residents out of the area.

4. Plaka is literally facing a problem of survival at the present moment. On the one hand are the demands of a modern city, from the center of Athens especially, which weigh on Plaka. On the other hand are the archaeologists who view Plaka as a space where their interests should have precedence. Sandwiched between these two trends is Plaka itself and the people who live and work there. The history of Athens itself lies there while, in addition, there is the Acropolis, for which Plaka forms the immediate surroundings. In all probability, the neoclassic and popular dwellings of Plaka form the very best setting for the Acropolis.

At this point it should be mentioned that these views have already been expressed in the findings of a group of UNESCO experts in 1968. The group consisted of Prof. R. Lemaire, R. Sneyers, and J. Sonnier, who studied conditions on the spot. In their report, after describing the risks now being faced by Plaka, they arrived at the following conclusion: "Protection of the region of the Acropolis is a matter of urgency. It can be achieved only within the framework of a master plan for the area which surrounds it. Inside this, Plaka holds a prominent position. Its preservation is essential because it forms a component part of the region and is also a historic urban entity of quality. A special study will have to be devoted to maintenance, and integration of all that remains of the old city."

In order to approach with accuracy the existing situation and in order to acquire all relevant data, three separate enquiries were instigated:

a) A group of architects compiled an inventory of all buildings in Plaka noting size, number of stories, date of construction, architectural style, degree to which disfigured if at all, architectural importance, and degree of importance in relation to the area as a whole, i.e. whether the building is particularly noteworthy, interesting or not of interest or incompatible with the atmosphere of the whole area.

b) Another group noted down all the functions, showing which were residences, shops, workshops, hotels, places of entertainment, etc.

c) Finally, a third group came into direct contact with the inhabitants through a detailed questionnaire and took note of facts concerning composition of families, monthly income, places of employment, origin of the persons concerned and date of their installation in Plaka, their views on the area, their thoughts about future prospects, etc.

The facts thus collected were used for drawing maps of the Plaka area in such manner as to provide a direct illustration of the present situation and tables were compiled showing the quantitative data of each case.

At the same time, present Greek law was examined in order to see just what it provides for the protection of monuments and settlements of historic value and the extent to which an effort to control the future of an area such as Plaka could hope to succeed. Corresponding legislation in other countries was studied to have certain new ideas from other European countries on the problem before us.

Special collaborators also dealt in detail with the economic and social problems of the area and formulated their conclusions. Presentation of all the data collected cannot possibly fit into the framework of this paper. I will, therefore, limit myself to a certain number only of the conclusions drawn from the analysis. Of the total number of 992

buildings in Plaka, 44 are especially noteworthy, 267 can be classed as interesting, 326 are of no particular interest and 355 are incompatible with the overall atmosphere. This means, in effect, that 35.8 percent of the buildings in the area are old but badly disfigured or mainly new buildings that are out of keeping with the style of the whole area. Indeed, during the 1950–1960 decade very many old buildings in Plaka were demolished to make room for modern blocks of flats which entirely disrupt the scale and architecture of Plaka.

Buildings existing today in Plaka show various disfigurations. Some of these owe their origin to the poor construction of the buildings themselves. Others are due to conversion of the buildings from their original purpose as residences into taverns or other places of entertainment in general. It was found that 23 percent of the buildings in Plaka have been disfigured to a moderate degree, while 15 percent have been badly disfigured.

As regards the age of the buildings, the enquiry showed that half have been built between 1865 and 1924, while 8.5 percent were built between 1834 and 1864. All the others belong to the postwar period. In the case of two buildings, their construction during the period of Ottoman rule was certified beyond doubt and both have been declared as monuments to be preserved. We suspect that there are some more which belong to that period.

From a study of these facts and also from observations in situ, it was noted that the traditional aspect of Plaka is strongest in the sector between Hadrian's Way and the rock of the Acropolis, whereas the nearer one approaches the sectors in contact with the modern city the greater is the alienation from the original style of the quarter. Further examination of the data collected showed that 58 percent of Plaka is built-up plots, 28 percent is taken up by streets and squares, and some 7 percent by archaeological sites. Functionally, 34.5 percent is taken up by residences, 17.5 percent by trade, 7.7 percent by artisan workshops, 21.1 percent by services, 7.3 percent by places of entertainment, and 2.1 percent by educational institutions. These percentages refer to total built area, which is to say, ground floor and upper stories, the total figure being 372,000 square meters.

The distribution of functions in Plaka which gives the use to which ground is allocated today leads back to the conclusion that the residential area tends to concentrate around the foot of the Acropolis and around the church of St. Catherine. It has also been noted that places of entertainment cluster mainly along Lysiou and Mnisikleous Streets although there are also several scattered establishments. It is interesting to note that Plaka hotels total 1,370 beds and that its places of entertainment can seat 18,000. When these figures are compared with the residents, who total 4,485, a pretty clear picture of today's trends emerges. There are four roofed garages in Plaka with a combined capacity for 250 motorcars. Open air parking lots take in a further 670 motorcars while more than 1,100 park in the streets contrary to traffic regulations.

At present 7,690 persons are employed in the Plaka quarter. Of these, 30 percent are engaged in rendering services, 28 percent are engaged in trade, 18 percent in handicraft, and 21 percent in providing entertainment.

Certain conclusions can be drawn from the facts which I have set out in brief.

a) Plaka buildings are either being disfigured in order that they may correspond to the new functions which are invading the district or they are being replaced with new buildings entirely divorced from the architectural style and layout of the particular quarter of the city.

b) Plaka is under increasing pressure from the wave of tourists, and it can be forecast with certainty that it will soon suffer such disfiguration as will destroy precisely that which at present attracts the tourists to it. It must be recorded at this point that all this activity carries with it consequences of another nature also which, on occasions, even provokes police intervention and makes the area more and more undesirable as a residential quarter. Plaka is virtually running the risk of becoming a dead city quarter during daytime.

c) Residences become downgraded all the time, especially in the area of Plaka closest to the Acropolis, this being the section where there is the least renovation of buildings. No doubt this contributes to greater preservation of the original architectural style but it means at the same time that the buildings are aging and becoming less and less fit to meet modern requirements. Typical of this is that in answer to a question on the subject, 54 percent of the Plaka inhabitants declared their desire to leave the district because their dwellings were no longer satisfactory. Of these, 43.5 percent said that their houses did not provide sufficient comforts. It was also interesting to note the replies from inhabitants to a series of questions aimed at ascertaining their attitude to the problems confronting their quarter.

When asked what they considered the most typical feature of their district, 48 percent replied that it was its picturesqueness and thoroughly popular atmosphere.

When asked what they liked most about it, 34 percent replied in favor of its central position in Athens and 30 percent said it was its picturesqueness. Of these 17 percent qualify as upper income, 45 percent as middle income and 38 percent as workers.

When asked what annoyed them most, 53 percent replied the noise and 26 percent said it was the various entertainment centers.

When asked how they would feel if Plaka were transformed into an entirely modern quarter like the others in Athens, it was interesting to note that 66 percent replied that they would feel regret and indignation, 11 percent thought it would be a good idea, and 23 percent had no comment to offer. Still more interesting was the detail that, when that same question was put exclusively to owners of property in Plaka those who expressed indignation and sorrow at such a thought amounted to 77 percent. I should also mention that 47 percent of the inhabitants felt that the presence of tourists in Plaka was harmful for the youth of the district while 32 percent felt that they made no difference one way or the other. In reply to a question given only to pupils in Plaka's secondary schools as to whether they would like to resemble the foreign tourists, 43 percent said they would and 44 percent said they would rather not. Finally, 73.5 percent of the inhabitants were in favor of modernizing the interiors of houses while maintaining the traditional facades, a smaller percentage (26.4 percent) being in favor of building entirely modern buildings.

It seems to be obvious that any problem concerning preservation of a historic settlement, particularly a settlement in the position of that of Plaka, cannot find a successful solution without the cooperation of the owners of property and the inhabitants thereof. The facts that I have just given you permit the formulation of certain conclusions, which supplement what has been said:

a) The inhabitants of Plaka would like to remain there if they could enjoy the conveniences normally expected of a modern home. If something like that were to happen, they would find themselves privileged to be living in a city quarter endowed with modern comforts and at the same time benefiting from the advantages presented by the layout and history of the district. I believe the inhabitants of Plaka are fully aware of this fact.

b) The inhabitants of Plaka have a feeling that their quarter serves as a place of entertainment for other people and that this, in the long run, works out to their detriment. Their attitude toward tourists is, I think, typical of this frame of mind.

With all these facts in mind our team went ahead with the drafting of certain preliminary proposals with the object of defining the following:

a) What could be considered to be the present-day boundaries of Plaka so that the quarter in question can preserve its traditional layout?

b) What measures should be adopted to prevent any further disfiguration of its buildings?

c) By what means could the inhabitants be assisted in repairing, modernizing, and preserving their present homes?

d) How could the quarter be helped to recover its traditional way of life and style, which differs entirely from that of the rest of Athens?

e) How could some of the ambitions of the archaeologists be satisfied without hopelessly parceling up Plaka?

f) What would it cost to preserve Plaka and how could such a plan materialize?

Naturally, the simplest way would be to suggest that the area enclosed between Hadrian's Way and the rock of the Acropolis be designated as that to be preserved. As previously stated, it is the area with the least alteration to its traditional character. On the other hand this is only a portion of Plaka and has the disadvantage that it omits certain very significant sections such as that around the church of St. Catherine, Kydathinaion Street, etc. A second thought would be to attempt to save that sector and Kydathinaion Street as a form of approach route to the main area to be preserved. It is, of course, an ambitious proposal, but we very characteristic Plaka atmosphere and layout. We were finally led to proposing that the whole of Plaka should be preseved. It is, of course, an ambitious proposal, but we believe that only then could it become possible to talk about the "Plaka quarter" in the sense of a real city quarter and not merely a remnant tucked away under the foot of the Acropolis. The proposal is that an institution be set up which would study all cases and would grant owners of property long-term loans at low rates of interest with which to repair their premises and restore them to their original architectural form while, at the same time, introducing modern conveniences and comforts. To restore the buildings would be a matter of detailed study and use of building materials and methods of construction such as were employed for the original structures. The study foresees even rebuilding houses presently in a state of ruin and the construction of entirely new houses in a style compatible with the surroundings. Naturally, each case would have to be judged on its merits and on its possible bearing on the immediate surroundings. It would be equally acceptable to have modern constructions with modern building materials and modern form but displaying a spirit of respect for the surroundings and the overall Plaka scale. In cases where a landlord for any reason whatever were to be unwilling to comply, then he should be given the option to sell his property to the Institute at its current market value. Failing agreement on such a deal, the Institute should have the right to expropriate and use the premises in the manner best suited to serve the overall plan. A major stumbling block will be the entertainment centers. It is our belief that, if we can introduce certain regulations for their operation (such as the abolition of noise, the removal of multicolor signboards, etc.) some sort of result could be achieved. An even greater problem is presented by the circulation of motor vehicles. The study would envisage a total ban of motorcars from the area except during certain hours for supplying shops and removal of garbage and, of course, in cases of emergency. There would also be provision for the construction, at certain points, of roofed garages for the use of permanent residents, shopkeepers, and visitors to Plaka. It is believed that such banning of motor traffic would not throw undue congestion on the peripheral roads of Plaka but the matter would have to form the subject of a special study.

The cost of each of the solutions put forward has been calculated as follows:

For implementation of the first solution, $20 million (1975) would be required for loans to owners of property. A further $15 million might be needed for expropriations.

For the second solution, $24 million would be needed for loans and $18 million for expropriations. For the third solution, $33 million would be required for loans and $23 million for expropriations.

In all three cases it is foreseen that ten years would be required to apply any such plan. The aforementioned sums would, therefore, be spaced out accordingly. During the same period, one should anticipate refund of a portion of the loans granted.

There are no illusions about the difficulties which lie ahead, mainly financial and to a lesser degree administrative and legal. We feel, however, that Plaka merits some special care, seeing that it forms the heart of Athens, the old historic quarter which never ceased to exist and which it would be a mistake, in my opinion, to allow today to become nothing more than a curiosity for tourists.

12 The Methodology Used in the Revitalization of Split   Tomislav Marasovic

Bird's eye view of the Palace of
Diocletian, Split. From *Urbs* 4
(1961–1962), p. 131

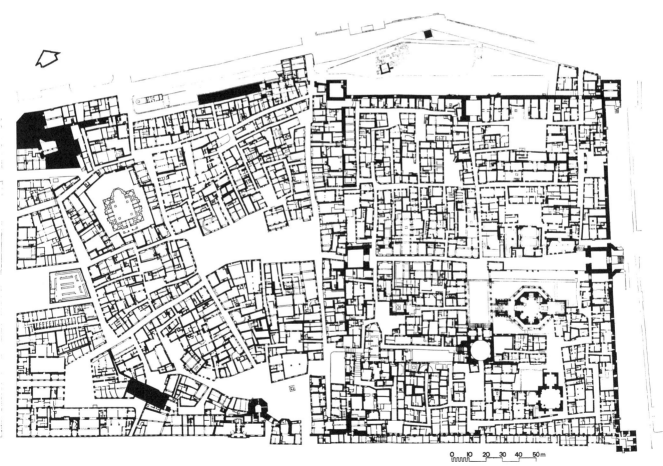

Plan of Diocletian's Palace in
1966. From the International
Symposium, *Urbs, Split* 1970.

0 10 20 30 40 50m

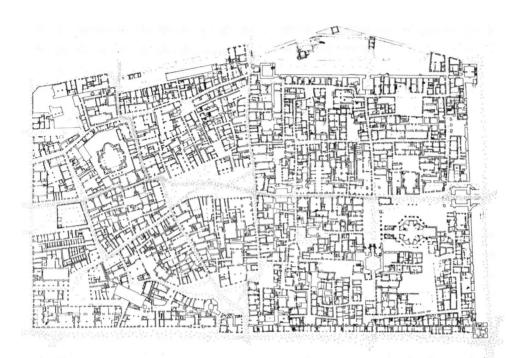

Pedestrian flows in the morning and evening and service access routes. These are part of a series of maps which documented the chronology, function, condition, historic value, height, building type, and paving surfaces of the Palace.

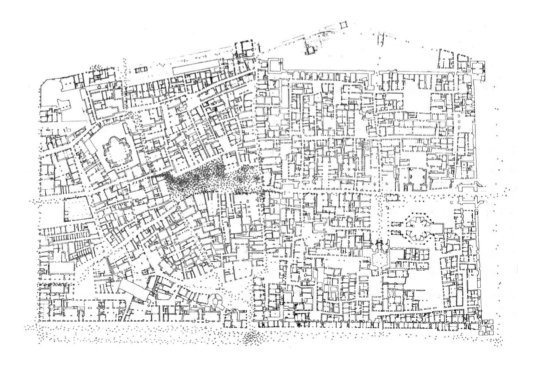

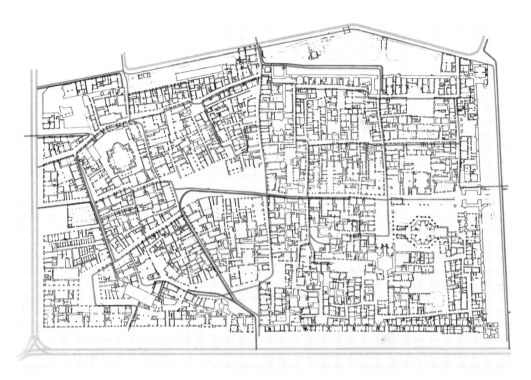

Restored interior of the south-
east tower of Diocletian's
Palace, now the conference hall
of the Split Zagreb Motorway
Construction Enterprise. From
the International Symposium
Urbs, Split, 1970, p. 138.
Restored by J. Marasovic.

Living in Split:

A window peeps through the Roman walls

The only service access

Tourist-crowded streets

A general survey of the methodology and techniques of preservation and revitalization of urban centers at this time can be carried out only on the basis of the publication of the particular experiences of certain towns. Our contribution here is based on the experience acquired during the last fifteen years in the town of Split.

In this paper, we have tried to develop a proposal for a comprehensive methodological approach for the protection, organization, and revitalization of historical centers.

Here we will discuss the methodology used in the preliminary studies, planning, and actual execution of the preservation and revitalization of historical centers.

Split is a town of 130,000 inhabitants, situated on a peninsula in the central region of the eastern Adriatic coast, and is today the cultural, economic, and administrative center of the most important region of Dalmatia.

Split is distinguished among Yugoslav towns by its historical remains and has obtained national preeminence by reason of its present development and construction, especially during the last ten years. The fast-developing economic life of the town depends upon industry, shipbuilding, maritime traffic, trade, and tourism.

The cultural and historical values of the old center, situated on the southern bay of the peninsula, are derived in the first place from Diocletian's Palace, which forms the historical nucleus of the town. This is one of the best preserved examples of late imperial palace architecture, dating from the beginning of the fourth century A.D., and as such represents a first-class monument of Roman architecture. During the Middle Ages and later periods, the town was further enriched with pre-Romanesque, Gothic, Renaissance, Baroque, and other monuments, as well as with objects. Taken all together, these objects today make up the unique urban entity of the historical core. Within the historical center of Split is also included the medieval section of the town, built in the period from the twelfth to the fourteenth centuries and located on the western side of the Palace. This part of Split also contains many historically valuable objects, either individual monuments or elements characteristic of the urban structure of that period. In the seventeenth century, the Palace of Diocletian and the medieval section were surrounded with polygonal bastions, whose remains still enclose the area of the historical center, approximately fifteen hectares, and its 5,000 inhabitants.

I. Methodological Approach

It is quite understandable that such an urban entity has for a long time drawn the attention of experts, not only to investigate its monuments but also to plan their preservation and renewal. In fact, in the historical center of Split we can observe elements of nearly all of the theories of conservation and restoration which developed in Europe during the nineteenth and twentieth centuries. These theories, as applied in Split, ranged from neoclassical concepts of purification, which fortunately remained in the conceptual stage here, to romantic restorations and so-called scientific preservation, first in the passive sense and finally, for the present, in the active sense.

Our contribution to the study of methodology here is based on the concept of active preservation, applied in Split after the liberation of the town at the end of the Second World War, and which is based on the following concepts:

1. The historical center should be considered as a unity, as an area which, in addition to its cultural and historical objects and the consequent problems of conservation, presents many other problems, principally involved with housing and hygienic conditions, the pedestrian traffic and economic life of the area.

2. The preservation and organization of the historical center, as one of the sections of the town, should be carried out according to the principles of urban planning, based on documentation of the existing situation and detailed analyses paying special attention to the historical values present in that area.

3. Special projects should be established for each stage in the preservation, renovation, or revitalization of the historical environment, and all work should be followed by detailed documentation.

4. The most efficient way to protect monumental and historical objects is to include them in the modern living func-

tions of the area. This results in the planning of financial and technical possibilities for their organization and revitalization.

5. During the preservation and revitalization of historical monuments, it is essential to respect in principle all historical periods. When, however, for the purposes of active protection, some monument is to be given a contemporary function, i.e., when it is desirable to present it as a historical monument, it is necessary to make an evaluation of all of the historical elements of that monument and to choose the most significant ones, eliminating in some cases those which are detrimental to the appearance of the object.

6. During the revitalization of the old part of the town, modern and creative architectural solutions are permissable, and sometimes even necessary. However, these must always take into consideration the overall harmony of the historical environment.

7. For the protection and revitalization of the historical center, it is essential to have continual cooperation between the town planning agency and the agency for the conservation of monuments in all stages of the work, from the first analyses to its final execution.

II. Organization of Work

From 1955 up to the present, three town agencies, all professional organizations with specialized interests, have been engaged in the systematic work on the protection, organization, and revitalization of the historical center of Split. These are described here.

1. The Municipal Institute for the Protection of Monuments

This is the institution legally empowered to protect all monuments of cultural value in the area of the municipality. It participates actively in the organization and preservation of architectural objects. In the historical center of Split, the Institute is working on the documentation, analysis, and evaluation of the historical agglomeration as a whole. This involves the development of detailed studies, the presenta-

tion of certain buildings, supervision of conservation projects, and the administration of certain buildings and the use of monuments included in its area of responsibility. In contrast to the practice of traditional conservation institutions which are primarily engaged in administrative protection, this Institute is also operationally involved in projects for the reconstruction of historical monuments in the area of the municipality of Split.

2. The Town Planning Institute of Dalmatia

Through its departments for urban planning, urban design, and architectural projects, this Institute is engaged in a number of projects pertaining to the spatial development of the town, ranging from regional planning to the master plan for the town, from detailed planning to urbanistic-architectural projects. The Institute's department concerned with the architectural heritage of the town has been the chief instigator of the campaign for the rehabilitation of the historical center. This department, on the basis of documentary material provided by the Institute for the Protection of Monuments and its own studies, has produced an urban development program and detailed plans for the organization of the historical center as a whole. In addition to these projects, this department has developed architectural projects for certain objects and areas within the historical center, analyses and projects for the presentation of certain buildings, and, through a special section, has been actually involved in conservation and restoration work.

3. The Housing Enterprise of Split

This enterprise organizes all construction work in the city and administers all of the housing and most of the business areas located on public property. Because the area of the old town falls within its administrative competency, during the past few years this enterprise has been responsible for the organization of the revitalization of the historical center, assigning the work of project development to the Institute for the Protection of Monuments and the Town Planning Institute.

Besides the three above-mentioned organizations, which have been mainly responsible for the work carried out in the historical center of Split, mention should also be made of the considerable role played by the municipal administration in initiating the entire project, especially the Presidency of the Municipality and the Department for Town Planning. The efforts made by the various municipal agencies cannot be ignored either, especially those made by the Town Planning Council and its committee for the historic center in consideration of the broader social ramifications of the different programs and projects. Furthermore, the cooperation of the archaeological and museum institutions in all historical and archaeological investigations was an invaluable factor in the work, and the active participation of the local chapter of the Socialist Alliance considerably helped in solving some very complex housing problems in the old town. Finally, mention must be made of the assistance received from the Split Tourist Association and its commission for developing tourist programs in cultural monuments aimed at reactivating the historical center of the city.

III. Methodological Procedure

1. Documentation, Analyses, and Examination of Existing Conditions

The first phase in the methodological procedure for the preservation, organization, and revitalization of the historical center of Split included the following measures:

1.1. The photographing of the whole historical center and individual monuments and blocks. The Institute for the Protection of Cultural Monuments has made an architectural survey of the whole historical center. The architectural survey of the ground floor of the town was made on a scale of 1:200 meters. Using both classical and photogrammetric methods, surveys of all four town elevations have been made. The survey program also envisages the working out of all the elevations of streets and squares. In the meantime, the Institute for the Protection of Monuments and the Town Planning Institute have made detailed architectural surveys of many blocks, individual monuments, and buildings on a scale of 1:50.

1.2. The inventory of the monuments in the oldest nucleus in the area. In beginning the work on the reorganization of the oldest part of the area, the Palace of Diocletian, the Town Planning Institute made a list of all the buildings in that section, organizing the material under the following headings: registry data, construction data, building materials, state of conservation, living conditions, sanitary conditions, occupancy, property rights, working space, undeveloped space, potential for architectural solutions, historical, cultural, and archaeological data. Included with this inventory was a sketch of each apartment.[1] In future work on the inventory for other areas in the old part of town and in the revision of the list for the entire historical center administered by the Institute for the Protection of Monuments, greater attention will be paid to sociological data, for instance, the origin and occupation of inhabitants, their length of occupancy, etc.

1.3. The analyses of the historical center. On the basis of the material obtained from the inventory and studies of certain individual monuments, analyses were made and presented in drawings on the scale of 1:500 meters. The analyses covered the following fields of investigation:

1.3.1. Historical-artistic and conservation analyses

a. The chronology of buildings with emphasis on the main historical periods (antique, medioeval, Renaissance, Baroque, and nineteenth and twentieth century), showing the historical values in the historical center

b. The evaluation of the buildings within the following categories:

—parts of Diocletian's Palace and medieval buildings of significant historical value
—objects of architectural and ambiental value
—objects of average architectural value and buildings with individually significant elements of historical styles
—neutral buildings and monuments
—objects not in harmony with their architectural environment

This analysis emphasizes the architectural-monumental value of the historical center considered in its entirety.

c. The state of preservation of the buildings according to the following categories:
—good
—partially dilapidated
—dilapidated
—cracked dangerously
—ruined and unfinished parts

This analysis points out the existence of many dilapidated houses, some of which are in danger of complete collapse.

1.3.2. The architectural-technical analysis includes:
a. the height of buildings
b. the materials from which the front walls are constructed
c. the types of roof coverings
d. types of open spaces and green areas.

1.3.3. The housing analysis of living and sanitary conditions. This analysis is expressed by means of a classification system consisting of eight categories, emphasizing the difficult situation prevailing in the historical center of Split, especially in the oldest core within the confines of Diocletian's Palace. Here the very poor living conditions of the inhabitants are presented in a graphic analysis, with the buildings in the lower housing categories being marked in darker shading, or with these figures, indicating that in Diocletian's Palace there were (in 1958):
—no apartments in the first category
—3 apartments, of 0.6 percent, in the second category
—14 apartments, or 2.9 percent, in the third category
—102 apartments, or 2.8 percent, in the fourth category
—104 apartments, or 35.0 percent, in the fifth category
—118 apartments, or 23.8 percent, in the sixth category
—65 apartments, or 13.1 percent, in the seventh category
—21 apartments, or 4.2 percent, in the eighth category.

The analysis of dampness and humidity completes the picture of the different living conditions and indicates that before reconstruction work 77.8 percent of the apartments in the Palace were damp.

1.3.4. Demographic-sociological analysis. This analysis has provided interesting data concerning the relationship between the buildings and the persons living in the area of the historical center. The 1958 census showed that there were 3,056 people, 859 families in 475 apartments, living in Diocletian's Palace and in the buildings connected with its perimeter walls. This density of 1.73 families, or 6.15 persons, per apartment is much greater than the average, that is, significantly below normal living conditions.

1.3.5. The analysis of urban functions and the use of business areas. The following analyses were made for the historical center of Split:
a. the original purpose of the buildings
b. the present function of the buildings
c. a special, and in this case most interesting, analysis of the commercial utilization of ground-floor areas.

The following disadvantages in the commercial utilization of areas within the historical center can easily be seen in the graphic analysis or from numerous statistics:
1) In the old part of the town there is a disproportionately large number of storage areas, most of them neglected, and many of them concerned with business activities outside the historical centre. Inside the Palace itself, in an area of approximately 30,000 square meters, approximately 4,000 square meters are being utilized as storage or warehouse space, $\frac{1}{8}$ of the total surface involved.
2) In some parts of the area shops are very densely grouped, whereas other parts are completely devoid of living functions.

The comparison of the analysis of the commercial use of space with the analysis of sanitary and living conditions has produced some interesting conclusions with regard to the revitalization program. The most dilapidated elements are usually found in the areas without living functions: the basements of buildings are used mainly for storage, whereas shops and other businesses concerned with the active life in the area are located in buildings of the better housing categories.

1.3.6. Traffic analysis. This was made on the basis of pedestrian traffic during:
a. the morning hours characterized by highest traffic density
b. the evening hours.

The analysis of pedestrian traffic has shown the existence of another serious problem in the historical center: the overloading of some lines of communication and the decline in use of others. Because the town expanded westward and because of other reasons I shall mention later, the transverse line of communication through the historical center is seriously overloaded, whereas the longitudinal axis of Diocletian's Palace, before the beginning of the revitalization program, had very nearly gone out of use as a means of communication.

The conclusions from our first comparison of analyses (commercial utilization of space with sanitary and living conditions) may now be generalized on the basis of the traffic analysis, which confirms those earlier conclusions. The intensive flows of pedestrian traffic are connected with the active trade and craft functions located on the ground level in the better and healthier apartments. On the other hand, in the dead areas lacking traffic and attractive functions, the apartments and buildings decay, and with them all of the cultural, historical, and ambient values of the historical center.

c. An analysis has also been made of the method of supplying the shops in the historical center, since all motor-vehicle traffic is forbidden in that area.

1.3.7. Property and legal relationship. This is an analysis of property rights with regard to certain buildings (private, public, and in particular the category of nationalized buildings administered by the Housing Enterprise of Split). The practical possibilities of interventions in buildings and areas frequently depend upon the property rights, that is, the legal processes which have to be attended to before the beginning of work.

2. The Study of Urban Development

The investigation of the urban development of the town has been accomplished by means of accurate drawings showing certain historical phases, within the framework of the region, of the whole town agglomeration, and for the area of the historical center itself, that is, for certain areas and blocks within the old historical core.

2.1. The study of regional development included the following periods:

a. The first prehistoric settlements scattered throughout all of the three geographical belts (the coast, inland, and the islands) without any definite centers; there were the Illyrian settlements, of the tribe of the Dalmatae in particular.

b. Greek colonization, with the main town at Issa on the island of Vis, from which were established other urban centers on the mainland

c. The Roman period, in which the population center was transferred to the mainland, to Salona, which became the leading town of the large province of Dalmatia

d. The time between the twelfth and fourteenth centuries, the period of the medieval communes, when the town of Split was the center of this urban area

e. The Venetian period from the fifteenth to the eighteenth centuries, characterized by the long Turkish wars

f. The period between the nineteenth and twentieth centuries, which was characterized by the growing role of Split as the center of an ever-increasing zone of influence.

2.2. The study of the development of the town agglomeration on the area of the peninsula shows the town's growth in six characteristic phases. There is also shown the growth of the historical nuclei in relation to the entire town area.

a. The antique phase, with Salona being the principal administrational, economic, and religious center, with approximately 60,000 inhabitants in its territory. In the beginning of the fourth century, Diocletian's Palace was built in this territory.

b. In the Middle Ages, the center of activity was transferred to the southern bay of the peninsula, to the town of Split, which included, with all of its suburbs, approximately 5,000 inhabitants.

c. In the period of Venetian administration, from the fifteenth to the eighteenth centuries, the town stagnated and at times even declined in population, to around 3,000 inhabitants at one stage.

d. Split during the Austro-Hungarian administration came out of its historical walls. Before the First World War the town reached 20,000 inhabitants.

e. The development of the town in prewar Yugoslavia, when it became the administrative, economic and cultural center of this area. Before the Second World War Split had 40,000 inhabitants;

f. The greatest development, which Split has achieved in the last twenty-five years since its liberation. The area of the constructed part of the town spreads around the whole peninsula and the population has trebled in relation to the prewar period.

2.3. The study of the development of the historical centers shows in more detail changes in the shape of the center and its nuclei. This is shown through six phases of development:

a. Diocletian's Palace, in the well-sheltered bay of Aspolathos, was the oldest nucleus, constructed in the period from 295 to 305 A.D.

b. In the early Middle Ages, from the eighth to eleventh century, after the destruction of Salona, the Palace received refugees from the destroyed main center of Dalmatia and became a real town.

c. With the spreading of the town westward from the Palace, Split doubled its territory in the period of the autonomous commune. The peasants' suburbs grew outside the walls.

d. The walls, from fifteenth and seventeenth centuries, represented the most obvious building characteristic of the period of Venetian administration.

e. With the destruction of the walls in the nineteenth century, the historical center was joined with the suburbs.

f. The historical center in its present state takes in only a small part of the total constructed surface of the town.

The study of the development of this area was necessary for the regulation of the longitudinal axis of the Palace. The development analysis shows:

2.4. The development of the area between the north and south gates of Diocletian's Palace:

a. The condition of the original form of the Palace showed a clear concept of unbroken communication through the longitudinal and transverse axes.

b. In the Middle Ages the Roman streets were reduced, but communications through the main axes were retained.

c. In the Renaissance-Baroque epoch longitudinal communication was cut by the closing of the western gates and of the passage on the peristyle.

d. In the nineteenth century the municipal government again opened the longitudinal communication.

e. In 1928 the conservation measures resulted again in the closing of the communication on the peristyle, for aesthetic reasons.

f. In the present period of the arangement of the old part of the town, traffic communication has been opened again from the northern to the southern gates of the Palace.

All these phases are analyzed in more detail through the survey of the development of the peristyle itself.

3. Study of the Causes of Decay of the Historical Center

On the basis of studies of the present state from which result many serious problems of the historical center, and the study of historical-urbanistic development, it was possible to find out the main causes of the dilapidation of the old part of Split.

3.1. In general, the decay of the historical center is connected with certain phenomena in the development of the town. Until the end of the eighteenth century, the area within the old walls, today called the historical center, represented the complete town area. Against the medieval outskirts, with a predominantly agricultural and fishing population, in the town, within the walls, were the aristocracy, tradesmen, and craftsmen, who continuously repaired and maintained the housing, shop premises, and basic living activities. With the spread of Split in the nineteenth century outside the historical walls, resulting from the change in methods of warfare as well as from sudden economic development (stronger role of the harbor, beginnings of industries, etc.) it frequently happened that the richer population began to leave the historical center, i.e., there occurred a change in the social structure of the old nucleus. Now this area is inhabited predominantly by the poorer population, mostly from the hinterland, who, not used to a higher living standard, have not been able to maintain their flats and other premises.

The second reason for the bad condition of buildings should be looked for in construction conditions, and in the first instance in bad and uneven foundations, particularly in the southern part of Diocletian's Palace.

3.2. The causes of the greater dilapidation of certain areas in Diocletian's Palace, and particularly along the line from the south to the north gates, are connected also with specific urban development within the historical center itself. With the spread of the town toward the west, the transverse road through the Palace became the main communication in Split, while at the same time the longitudinal axis of the Palace was completely neglected, particularly when the new western approach to the municipal center was opened at the end of the Middle Ages and when the peristyle resumed only the function of the church center. This has been reflected in the neglected state of the complete area around the transversal axis.

4. The Revitalization Program

On the basis of all these elements, i.e., analyses of condition and studies of development and causes of deterioration, the revitalization program was considered in principle.

With the directive plan of Split, adopted in 1961, the basic function of the old part of the town was determined as that of cultural center connected with the new city center.[2]

After all analyses it was possible to determine more closely the framework of the program for the protection and the revitalization of the old part of the town based on the following elements:

4.1. The protection and modern presentation of the series of buildings, facilities, their parts or details, which have a cultural-historical value.

4.2. The reconstruction of old and dilapidated houses and their restoration either into facilities with other purposes in accordance with the envisaged role of the historical center, or into modern-equipped apartments, but in a consider-

ably reduced number in relation to the present density of population and housing area. Some of the dilapidated buildings without historical or ambient value are intended for demolition.

4.3. The removal of the inadequate facilities from the ground-floor areas and creation of new business and other premises for vital functions (trade, tourist offices, catering, cultural and educational institutions, etc.).

4.4. The regulation of pedestrian traffic through the regeneration of dead communications and the relieving of over-burdened streets; the regulation of supply services for shops; construction of parking lots around the old part of the town.

4.5. The organization of basic activities, first in the streets and construction of parking lots around the old part of the Palace; the solution of the sewage problem by using the original sewer system in Diocletian's Palace, the restoration of water system, removal of electric wires which look ugly in the streets and buildings of old Split; the solution of the lighting of the historical center as a whole and of some of the individual monuments.

5. Urban and Architectural Projects and Realizations

During the last 15 years of systematic action for the revitalization of the old part of the town, the Town Planning Institute for Dalmatia and the Institute for the Protection of Cultural Monuments have undertaken a number of steps for the protection, renewal, and arrangement of certain areas, blocks, and buildings in the historical center of the town.

The purpose of this report is to present the methodological experience and not the results; some of the steps are therefore only listed.[3]

5.1. The work in the old part of the Split may be mainly categorized in three main types of interventions:

5.1.1. The renewal and arrangement of the peristyle-wharf area represents a very complex project of planning-conservation nature. The work has started with archaeological investigations, which have made very interesting finds in the peristyle and under the vestibule. They have enabled the elaboration of the urban and architectural project for the improvement of the complete area, which, for the purpose of including the pedestrian communication along the longitudinal axis of the Diocletian's Palace, has envisaged the renewal of the Roman hall in the lower, and restoration of the medieval ambience in the upper part. The works were carried out in a few phases: in the vestibule in 1955–1957, in the peristyle in 1959–1961, and in the central ground floor hall in 1957–1963.

5.1.2. The digging out and arrangement of the ground floor space of the Diocletian's Palace had its archeological significance (the discovery of the substructure of Diocletian's apartment), as well as a practical one (presentation and opening to the public of halls closed throughout the centuries, which may be used today for various contemporary needs of the town, as exhibition halls, music halls, theater and dancing halls, etc.).

The work was carried out here as well in several phases: during 1955–1959 nearly the whole western half was excavated and arranged (twenty-four halls), and is now open to the citizens and numerous visitors of Split. In 1959 the works in the eastern half began. The central hall was cleared and renewed under the project for the arrangement of the area from the peristyle to the wharf. During the last few years the work in this area has been carried out within the program of joint action of the Town Planning Institute for Dalmatia and the University of Minnesota, Minneapolis.

5.1.3. The adaptation and renewal of certain buildings for different purposes contributes to the protection and arrangement of historically valuable buildings, to the revitalization of the old center, bringing in new functions in place of dilapidated apartments. Until now a number of buildings have been renovated, among which the following should be mentioned:

—a series of medieval buildings on the southeastern part of the vestibule, for the Town Planning Institute for Dalmatia
—the medieval building on the west of the peristyle, for the General Education Center of the People's University
—the block of medieval houses near the Golden Gates for the Cultural Center of the People's University

—the apartment building in the street called Usred Geta, place of the collapsed house
—the business facility on the peristyle with a café-restaurant in the ground floor, in place of a house destroyed during the war
—ground floor premises restored mostly for shops, in various parts of the historical center
—southeastern tower of the Diocletian's Palace, renovated and restored as the meeting hall for the Motorway Construction Enterprise Split-Zagreb, one of the last adapted buildings in the old part of the town
—a few adaptation projects underway for some other facilities, among which the project for a big store in the ground floor space of the Palace, and catering premises on the upper floor.

5.2. The methodological procedure for the entire project contains the following elements:

5.2.1. Photography of the existing condition. Detailed architectural photography of the building, which includes precise drawings of each stone and represents the basis, together with the complete photosurvey, of the study of the existing condition and project for renewal. The drawings are made to a scale of 1:50 meters, with details at 1:10 meters.

5.2.2. Research on the buildings. Includes detailed historical, artistic, and architectural analysis with additional investigations (architectural excavation, taking off the plaster from walls, etc.). The investigation is completed with the study of historical sources and other data connected with the origin and development of the building. All this enables the working out of a graphic study the original shape and development of the building, i.e., of the urban entity.

5.2.3. Static analysis. As we are dealing mostly with decayed buildings in the old part of the town, before each intervention a static analysis of the building is carried out, together with the reconstruction proposal.

5.2.4. Project. Afterward, the program submitted by the investor and accepted if in harmony with the general program of rehabilitation of the historic center follows the design elaborated in different stages: sketch, pilot, and final projection. The project is completed to the scale of 1:50 in general and contains all absolute height points, which were found very useful in a complex situation of gradual construction in various historical epochs, particularly because they enable the joining of a number of individual buildings into one entity. Particular attention is paid to reconstruction details of stylistic elements.

5.2.5. The realization. During the reconstruction work in the historical part of Split certain insights were gained about various possibilities for the organization of work (by its own working group, under the supervision of the investigator and project designer, by various construction enterprises with adequate supervision). It was found out that the best way is to have separate working groups in which the workers have gained necessary experience by long practice in excavation and historical restoration.

Notes

1. The inventory sheet has been published in *Urbs*, no. 4, Split, 1965, in an article by T. Marasovic and D. Sumic, "Analiza zgrada na podrucju Dioklecijanove palace," p. 111.

2. Cf. *Urbs*, no. 3, Split, 1959–1960, pp. 9–32, and *Urbs*, no. 6, Split, 1966, pp. 35–44.

3. An outline of the results accomplished in the historical center of Split has been published in an article by J. Marasovic and T. Marasovic: "Pregled radova Urbanistickog biroa na istrazivanju, zastiti i uredenju Dioklecijanove palace od 1955–1964. g.," *Urbs*, no. 4, Split, 1965, pp. 23–54, where other articles may also be found.

13 The Bologna Experience: Planning and Historic Renovation in a Communist City

Francesco Bandarin

Bologna: the medieval skyline. From Giovanni M. Accame, ed., *Conoscenza e coscienza della città*, catalog of the Commune di Bologna Galleria d'Arte Moderna, October–December 1974.

Postwar suburban housing.
From Accame, *Conoscenza e
coscienza della città*, p. 43.

Diagrams of building types

1. Type C: artisan housing, 4–7 meter frontage

2. Type B: palazzi around inner courtyards, 10–20 meter frontage

3. Type B: 21–50 meter frontage combined organically

4. Type B: 21–50 meter frontages combined in series

5. Type A: simple nodal buildings

6. Type A: complex nodal buildings

7. Type A: unique nodal buildings. From P. L. Cervellati, and R. Scannavini, eds., *Bologna: Politica e Metodologia del Restauro nei Centri Storici* (Bologna: Societa editrice Il Mulino, 1973), pp. 114–115.

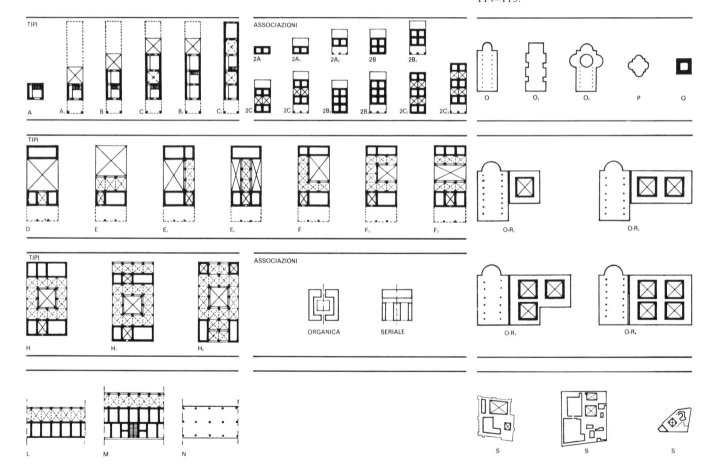

Neighborhood meeting. From Accame, *Conoscenza e coscienza della città,* p. 69.

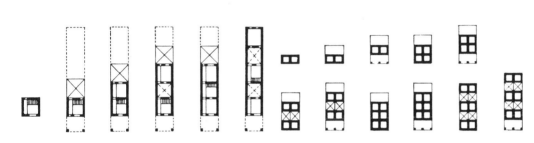

Examples of Type C housing drawn from the original historical documents. From Cervellati and Scannavini, *Bologna: Politica e Metodologia,* p. 160.

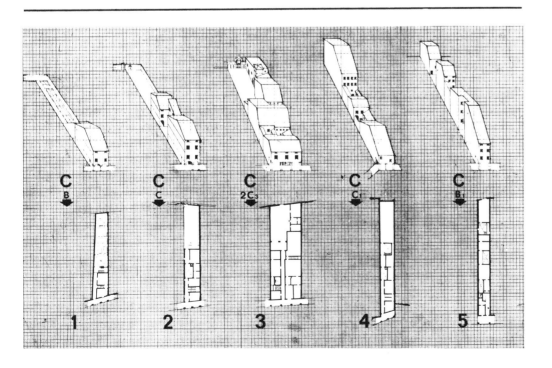

Schemes for the scientific
renovation of Type C buildings.
From Cervellati and Scan-
navini, *Bologna: Politica e
Metodologia*, p. 162.

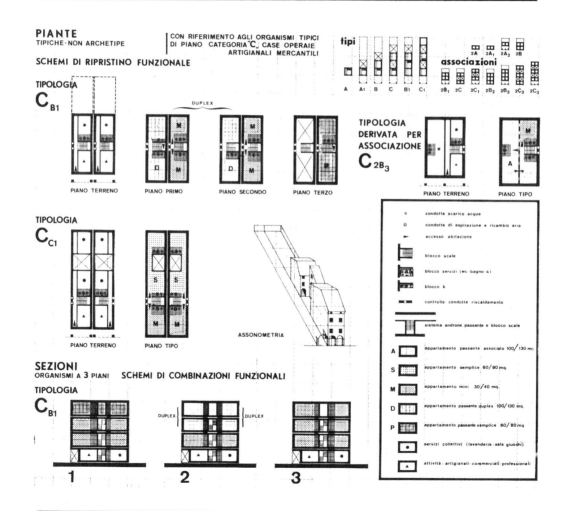

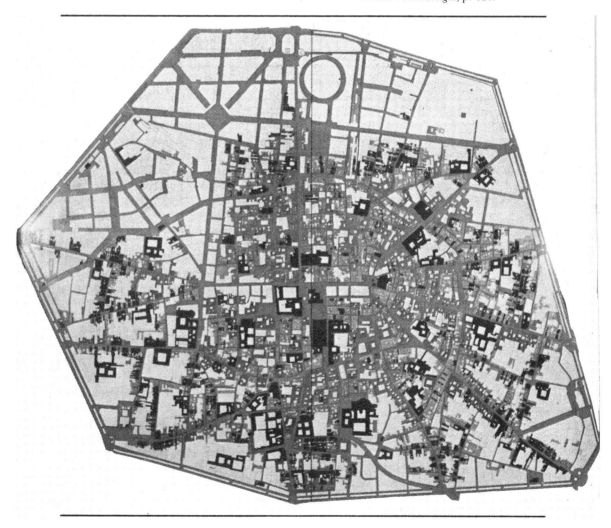

Bologna: Map of historic
building types. From Cervellati
and Scannavini, *Bologna:
Politica e Metodologia*, p. 126.

Exhibit with model of proposed
restoration and explanatory
drawings. From Accame,
Conoscenza e coscienza della città,
p. 99.

Restoration plans for one
quarter. From Accame, p. 86.

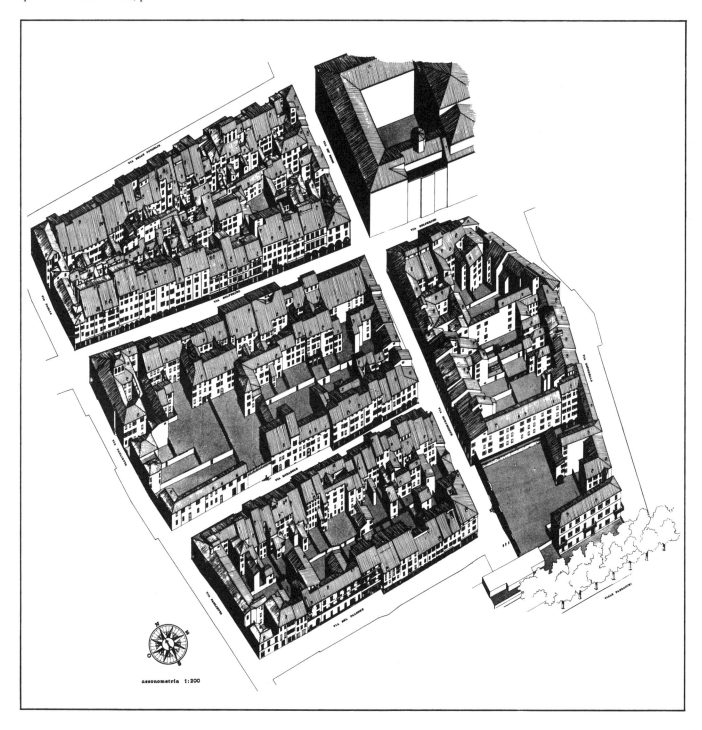

assonometria 1:200

Aerial and ground views of rehabilitation underway. From Piano PEEP Centro Storico.

L'APPROPRIAZIONE SOCIALE DELLA CITTA'

La città antica
non solo era espressione collettiva,
era anche proprietà
dei suoi abitanti.
La stessa presenza di classi sociali diverse,
ma integrate nel tessuto urbano,
era testimonianza,
certezza dell'uso e del consumo comune
indifferenziato della città.
Lo sviluppo del capitalismo,
parcellizzando minutamente
il suolo urbano e mercificando

in modo esasperato i lotti
che ne risultano, determinò,
per la prima volta,
l'effettiva privatizzazione di un bene,
la città, fino allora pubblico ed indiviso.
La città – che diventa,
proprio in quel momento
di accelerata industrializzazione,
centro storico e periferia,
aggregato urbano –
viene venduta alla o dalla speculazione
immobiliare e fondiaria,
e gli abitanti originari estraniati
e le loro attività eliminate.
Pertanto si deve programmare

la riappropriazione collettiva
di un bene che deve e non può essere
altro che pubblico.
Riappropriarsi quindi
del centro storico sottratto
alla collettività dal sistema capitalistico
che lo ha consegnato
alla proprietà privata,
diviene operazione ideologicamente rivoluzionaria,
per la forza invincibile
di questa idea:
CONSERVAZIONE SIGNIFICA
RIAPPROPRIAZIONE SOCIALE DELLA CITTA'.
In questo caso infatti
CONSERVAZIONE È RIVOLUZIONE.

The translation of the caption to this photograph of a demonstration in the principal piazza of Bologna succinctly states the ideology behind Bologna's urban conservation program: "The ancient city was not only a collective expression, it was also the property of its inhabitants. The same presence of diverse social classes, integrated into the urban structure, was testimony to its communal use and consumption. The development of capitalism, minutely parceling the urban land and merchandising the parcels that resulted, created the effective privatization of the city that had, until that time, been public and indivisible. We must therefore reappropriate a good that cannot be other than public. Such reappropriation of the historical center rescued from the capitalist system that has consigned it to private property becomes an ideologically revolutionary act, by the invincible force of this idea: *Conservation signifies the social reappropriation of the city*. In this case *"Conservation is revolution."* From Accame, *Conoscenza e coscienza della città*, pp. 100–101.

Introduction

The renovation of the historic center of Bologna has become widely known, both in Italy and internationally, as an example of what an urban administration can do to prevent the physical decay of its historical architectural heritage, and, at the same time, create the conditions necessary to preserve the sociological characteristics of the population living in the urban center.

All planners involved, in Italy as in other European countries, in the design of a planning and participatory system that allows a reuse of our invaluable urban historical heritage for the purposes of modern life, are facing this question: is the Bologna experience a model that could be applied to other urban centers, or a unique experience made possible by a particular political and cultural situation?

From my point of view, it would be hard to give a single answer to this question, as the experience of planning and urban renovation in Bologna involves many aspects of the history of urbanization in postwar Italy, has had its own evolution, and is still, at the present moment, in progress.

This chapter will try to analyze the history, the issues, the successes, the failures, and the critiques of the Bologna model, in the attempt to evaluate the meaning of that experience and its relevance for other cities.

The Three Aspects of the Bologna Experience

Before proceeding in this analysis it is necessary to make one point clear. The methodology used for the plan for the historic center of Bologna and the system designed for its implementation are not separable from the context of urban and metropolitan planning. In other words, the population and land use development forecasts, and the regulatory system controlling the growth of both the city and its metropolitan area, are consistent with the policy of conservation of the historical housing stock and the existing population in the urban center.

All aspects of planning are inspired by the same concept: that the growth of the city should be limited and be con-trolled by the public authorities using the potential of existing legislation to its fullest; that there should be a balance between residences and public sources involved; that participation and democracy should be enhanced and developed.

This is why, in order to understand the meaning of the Bologna experience, we will have to deal with what I call "the three faces of planning in Bologna":

1. The way in which the city has planned and controlled urban growth during the postwar period, and in which the development of the whole metropolitan area has been coordinated.

2. The development of a decentralized and democratic system of decision making, with the establishment of neighborhood councils. As we will see, they do not have a merely advisory role, but are an effective articulation of the municipal administration, with extensive decision-making powers.

3. The formation of an original methodological proposal for the renewal of the historic center, comprising two parts:
a. the criteria to follow in order to allow the adaptation of the historical architectural typologies to the needs of modern life, without ruining the center's original characteristics.
b. The establishment of the principle that conservation also means *cultural* conservation, which means that the characteristics of the existing population and its culture have to be preserved.

Postwar Planning in Bologna

There is no space in this chapter for a description and an evaluation of the national context in which the plans for Bologna have been developed. It would be enough to say that in the postwar period the city, like many others in Italy, was facing two major problems: (1) the reconstruction of the areas destroyed by bombing during the war, (2) the regulation of a rapid, almost uncontrollable growth due to economic expansion (during the 1950s, in particular) and the large migration of people from the south and from the depressed areas of the center to the north.

Italian planning legislation was not—certainly—among the most advanced in Europe: in fact, the first national legislation, establishing the powers of the local administrations on land use control, was approved only in 1942. The absence of an advanced planning profession (the Fascist regime had closed any exchange with all the planning experiments that were going on in other European countries and the U.S.); the weakness of planning legislation; the lack of fiscal and financial autonomy of local governments; and, most important of all, the pressure of developers, deriving from the huge profits obtainable in land speculation and allowed by the dominant political forces in the country; these are among the factors that contributed to what has been called the "sack" of the Italian cities.

Uncontrolled expansion, lack of services and infrastructures, poor architectural quality: these are some of the characteristics of development, as it has been experienced in most Italian cities. Plans were, and in most cases still are, mere formal documents, unable to shape and control growth and development.

In the period immediately following the end of the war, and during the fifties, Bologna was not very different from other Italian cities, either in its pattern of development or in the inability of the administration to extend its control over it. As Giuseppe Campos Venuti, one of the fathers of the Bologna planning experience, says:

In the postwar period no serious attempt was made in Bologna to change the traditional land policy of the Italian municipalities, essentially dominated by land speculators; on the contrary, a plan was approved that allowed an enormous residential expansion in the periphery, did not plan the necessary services, allowed demolitions in the historic center, favored the expansion of private residences on the "green" open space areas on the hills overlooking the city.[1]

The first postwar plan approved in Bologna, the Reconstruction Plan of 1948 (Piano di Recostruzione) proposed the rebuilding—in toto—of the areas demolished by bombing during the war without any consideration for the new needs of the city, foregoing the possibility of using them for an improvement of urban living conditions.

The first master plan for the city, adopted in 1955 and approved by the government in 1958 (Piano Regolatore Generale [PRG]), did not change these initial choices. Bologna now has a population of approximately 500,000. In 1951, it had 340,000 inhabitants. About 80,000 people live in the historic center.

As in most Italian cities, the plan allowed a large expansion of suburban areas, did not include adequate standards for public services and, with the exception of buildings protected by special legislation (because of their historical value), allowed several demolitions within the historic center. The "model" followed by the plan was essentially one of the two previous master plans of Bologna, those of 1889 and 1937 (Piano Marconi), which did not respect the historical morphology of the city. But this situation did not last very long; the uniqueness of the city's political structure (at that time Bologna was the only regional capital governed by the left, and the Communist Party was close to an absolute majority of votes), the development of a planning profession and a consciousness of the necessity to control expansion and design a balanced growth, led to a rapid evolution in the administration's attitudes, which started an innovative planning experiment.

Schematically, the policies formed during the second half of the fifties and formalized in the new master plan adopted in 1960 (and approved in 1965 by the central government) were intended to

1. Oppose the formation of speculative gains in the land and housing markets
2. Increase the role of public housing agencies in the shaping of development
3. Improve the housing conditions of the working classes and the low-income groups
4. Rebalance the development pattern in the metropolitan area, orienting the location of industries and preserving agricultural land
5. Protect the historical heritage of the urban center. The plan specifically modified all the regulations concerning demolitions in the historic center, and in so doing it opened

the way to the formation of an original proposal for the urban center.

To implement these programs, the Bologna administration used three major policy tools: a public housing program, a service location program, and a new system of land controls.

Traditionally, in Italy, public housing had been located on the periphery of towns, very often in the open countryside, in order save on land costs, and "open" new directions of expansion for private development: Bologna was no exception to this rule. But with the change in urban policy described above, the Bologna administration and its planners started to realize the great potential of public housing construction as a tool of intervention in the housing market.

For the first time in the country, it was decided to use, for public housing construction, undeveloped areas *inside* the city. Using all the powers that a recent legislative reform tool had granted to municipalities[2] a new housing policy was introduced and implemented. The public housing plan (Piano di Edilizia Economica e Popolare [PEEP]), prepared at the beginning of the 1960s, provided for acquisition by eminent domain, of the best undeveloped lands within the city. In addition, large quantities of land were acquired to be used for the construction of public facilities, schools, cultural and social centers, etc.

Although the implementation of the plan did not solve the shortage of low-cost housing in the city,[3] it contributed significantly to improving the situation of the working class, and made Bologna the only city in Italy with a large stock of *newly* built public housing in proximity to the urban center.

The goal of public housing described above was, clearly, to counterbalance the trends that were emerging in the urban development process: the skyrocketing of land prices, the establishment of high, speculative urban rents, the expulsion from the city of low-income groups, the lack of services. It was precisely the lack of these problems, the imbalance of quantity and quality of urban services between the different zones of the city, that the administra-tion tried to solve with its new public services location program.

Most of the public services existing in the city were located in the historic center: the city had been, historically, the service center of the entire metropolitan, if not regional, area. At that time, the new residential areas, both privately or publicly developed, were lacking essential services. In order to re-equilibrate the situation, all the new investments for public services were systematically oriented toward the public housing projects and the periphery of the city.

The new policy of balanced and controlled growth was not limited to the municipal boundaries. Very soon, the city felt the necessity of coordinating its development policies with the one of the surrounding municipalities, which, at the beginning of the 1960s, had started to experience rapid growth.

A metropolitan structure did not really exist before the 1950s. Before then the municipalities surrounding the city were essentially rural communities, dependent, for almost any kind of service, on the main center. Even during the 1950s, this pattern did not change: in fact, the direction of migratory movements was from the metropolitan areas toward the central municipality.

It was only during the 1960s that this trend was reversed, new industries and new resources found their location in the surrounding municipalities, and a different, more complex, urban network started to develop.[4]

The formation of a metropolitan plan for the Bologna area became, more and more, a necessary corollary to the innovative land and growth policy that the city had started. The plan (Piano Intercomunale Bolognese),[5] one of the first experiments of its kind in Italy, and certainly the only one that was successfully implemented, was set up in the second half of the 1960s and approved in 1968. It includes 17 municipalities, a total population of 700,000 inhabitants (500,000 in Bologna), and an area of approximately 390 square miles.

The main goal of this plan was to enhance what appears to be a major characteristic of the Bologna area, as well as of the region where Bologna is located, Emilia Romagna: the existence of a relatively balanced urban network, what the Bologna planners call a "polycentric structure."[6] There are three major policies considered by the plan, in order to achieve that goal:

1. The reshaping of the transportation system, to counteract the tendency of residential expansion to concentrate along the east-west and north-south major highways. This policy is matched by a program extending the network and improving the quality of public transportation.[7]

2. The use of existing land control tools in an effective manner, to orient development trends, avoid scattered urbanization, preserve the agricultural and open space lands around the city (a policy supported by the already mentioned public services location strategy, extended to the metropolitan scale).

3. The transformation of the functions of the main center, Bologna, including preservation of the physical and social structure of its historic center, and improvement of living conditions, open space, and public facilities. This policy was to be carried on by both the master plan examined above and the plan for the historic center, which I will analyze in a later section.

Decentralization and Participation in Bologna

It would be impossible to understand the success of the planning experiments without considering one of the major aspects of planning in Bologna: the decentralization of administrative and political decisions, and the participating structures associated with the plan making process.

The tradition of citizen participation in administrative and political decisions is, in Bologna, much older than in any other Italian city. During the 1950s and 1960s, when the Leftist parties were in the opposition at the national level, Bologna, as the major city run by the Communist Party, became a model of the different way of governing that the Left proposed.

The Neighborhood Councils, to which the city has transferred many advisory and decision functions, were established during the 1950s, and their role has grown continually since. There are now in Bologna 18 Neighborhood Councils (Consigli di Quartiere), each of them representing approximately 30,000 inhabitants. Not only do they express opinions and make decisions concerning local matters, but they are a major component in the formation of overall policies. Their members used to be appointed by the City Council and were apportioned according to each party's strength in the city. A recent reform, though, allows direct elections of each Council's members, by the people living in the neighborhood.

Their major, but not exclusive role is performed in the areas of planning and local housing. In particular, they participated in the formation and evaluation processes of the master plan, the housing programs, and the plan for the renovation of the historic center.

One of the major successes of their action has been a plan for the preservation of the open space in the beautiful hills overlooking the city, which were about to be destroyed by private development. No building permit is granted in the city without prior approval of the local Council.

Besides that, they contributed to the formation of decisions concerning local traffic that resulted in the limitation of automobile access to several areas of the city, in particular in the historic center.

The other functions of the Councils, which I will indicate only schematically, are

1. Discussion and approval of the city's budget, and all public expenditures for social services
2. Regulation of commercial activities in the neighborhoods (new permits, schedules, etc.)
3. The management of child care centers and elementary schools (maintenance of existing structures, expenditures for materials and furniture, admissions, administration)
4. Local libraries and local cultural and educational activities
5. Local hygiene centers, for health care and prevention.

The system of functions, and the role that the administration has attributed to them, make the Councils an important fundamental actor in the municipal policy formation process, and, at the same time, a structure that guarantees the efficient implementation of local programs.

The risk of localism, which is often inherent in any decentralization process, has been, so far, avoided by the administration, which has performed a role of stimulus and coordinator of the activities of the Councils.[8]

The Program of Renovation of the Historic Center: Introduction

We have seen so far that the problem of preservation and renovation of the historic center of Bologna has been, since the formation of the new urban policy during the late 1950s, a major concern of planners and the administration.

The history of the formation of a comprehensive policy for the historic center is a most interesting one. It is no exaggeration to say that the product of that effort represents one of the major achievements of the planning culture in postwar Italy, and, considering the limited financial ability of the city, one of the most efficient systems of public intervention in the urban core experienced in Italy.

Twenty years ago there was no consciousness, among the population, of the value of the historical heritage of the city and of the importance of conservation: the war had left many other problems of physical, economic, and rural reconstruction.

As we have already seen, the plans of the period immediately following the war allowed extensive demolition inside the historic center. The first task of the administration, after its attitude toward the historic center had changed and a conservationist consciousness was developed, was to make an inventory of the historical heritage—the monuments and the "*edilizie minore,*" the architectural and urban tissue inherited from other historic periods. This task, together with the one of formulating guidelines for a correct methodology of urban renovation, was assigned to Professor Leonardo Benevolo, one of the most prominent Italian planners and architecture historians. The result of these studies, conducted from 1962 to 1965, was presented to the population during a conference on the problems of historic renovation in 1966[9] as a methodology and a system of regu-

lations aimed at preserving the original architectural typologies, and at the same time adapting them to the needs of modern life. The essential concept of the Benevolo proposal was that the architectural typology is, as well as the facade or the style of buildings, a characteristic to be preserved as part of the historic heritage. If we think how, too often, in Europe, we see restoration that only preserves the exterior appearance of the building, while what is behind is completely transformed (when not destroyed), we are able to realize the importance of this proposal. The proposal was officially adopted in 1966 and is still in effect.

The impact of the administration's initiative on the development of consciousness about historic preservation was extremely relevant. Step by step, the issue of preservation became a major one in the debates of the Neighborhood Councils, and was discussed and developed in conferences and meetings.

The evolution of the planning process for the historic center could be divided, roughly, in two phases; the one just described, in which a technical knowledge of the problems of the physical restoration had to be developed, together with an enhancement of the consciousness of the problem. The question raised after that process was: "For whom are we going to restore and preserve this historic heritage?"

This question was extremely relevant (for developing working-class interest in the process). It addresses the major problems that Italian (and other European) historic centers face: the so-called gentrification of the urban core, i.e., the change in the class composition of the city, the expulsion of lower-income groups and their replacement by middle- and higher-income groups.

The higher density of services in the historic center, the quality of its environment, its proximity to the location of jobs (especially in the tertiary sector): all these components contribute to make it a highly desirable residential place.

And in fact, this process of "gentrification" is at work, with different intensity, in most Italian cities, including

Bologna. The importance of modifying this trend, not only to gain the support of the working class for the restoration program, but to preserve the original cultural characteristics of the city, led to a second phase of planning. The concept of cultural conservation was developed, in a way that abolished the separation between "cultural" and "physical" conservation.

This is, in a nutshell, the essence of the Bologna plan for the historic center: an ability to function as a good (methodologically correct) restoration plan and an intention to protect the interests of the working classes living in the historic center, and, in so doing, to be a program of integral conservation of the social, cultural, economic, and artistic characteristics of a city.

The studies for the restoration of the historic center, started again in 1967, led to the formation of a plan for the historic center, approved in 1973 (Piano per l'Edilizia Economica e Popolare/Centro Storico). Based on the analysis and the methodological structure of the Benevolo proposal, and using the new powers that a housing reform had granted to the municipalities in 1971,[10] this plan establishes a program of public intervention in the process of historic renovation, which is probably the most interesting experiment of its kind in Italy. As one of the major contributors to the formation of the plan, Pier Luigi Cervellati, Assessor for Urban Planning (Planning Director) of the City of Bologna, says:

An intervention like the one proposed in Bologna clearly opposes all the ideological principles and the speculative aims of the dominant classes, since, while it plans a conservation of the historical urban structure, it established the necessity of public control of the renovation process as a condition to preserve the social classes that now live in it.[11]

The Methodology of the Plan: Concepts

The transformation of the structure and the functions of the historic center of Bologna (but this could apply as well to many other cities) originated in the industrial revolution during the last century. As the structure of the economy changes, and as the center of economic power moves from the city (commercial and financial) to the work places (in-dustrial), the urban center progressively loses its function, and with it, the formal unity that has characterized it historically.

The first "attack" on the physical integrity of the historic center of Bologna dates from 1861 (year of the unification of Italy) to 1898 (first master plan for the city): during this phase part of the urban tissue was destroyed to allow construction of the railroad and the major communications network.

In a second phase, with the strengthening of capitalism and the entrepreneurial bourgeoisie, the city became subject to the same law that regulates industrial production: the maximization of profit. Land and building speculation, focused in particular in some areas of the historic center, were the forces that, from 1889 to 1918, shaped the city; the object was the creation of residences for the new dominant class, the bourgeoisie.

A third phase, from the beginning of this century until now, saw the transformation of the role of the urban center and of its relationship with the periphery. Most of the urban center became the location for new administrative and commercial activities, while the existing population was progressively evicted. At the same time, the process now known as gentrification continued and increased the pressure of the new bourgeois classes to move into the center, which offered higher environmental quality and better services than the peripheral areas.

The conservation program proposed by the Bologna Administration is aware of this historical reality and of the nature and interests of the economic forces that are shaping the city. Its first goal could be defined, therefore, as a modification of the "logic" underlying the capitalistic intervention in the urban center, i.e., the maximization of profit, irrespective of the values of the historical heritage.

The methodology developed in Bologna is not, therefore, a neutral, technical proposal because it opposes the ideology and interests of the bourgeois economic forces.

A first study, conducted in the early 1960s, provided for a "census" of the architectural heritage of the historic center and became the basis for the development of the central ideas of the methodology: the concept of *typology*.

A second phase of the analysis was directed at studying the forms and evolution of architectural structures and was aimed at classifying the buildings in the historic center according to the way in which architectural forms had been developed and aggregated.

In this way, traditional analysis based on the function and use of the architecture was abandoned, and building typology was chosen as a measure of the process of aggregation of the morpholological units. The concept of typology, as used in the methodology of the Bologna plan, is not an exclusively analytical tool. Its goal is to provide an understanding of the rules of formation of the architectural structures to be finalized in the process of active conservation. Its goal is to provide criteria from which it is possible to derive indications and regulations for the renovation work.

Furthermore, it is a concept related to the history and evolution of the city. A typology is nothing but a similarity of the forms of living, working, and operating, materialized in architectural structures. In dealing with the problem of renovation and reuse of historical typologies, two aspects are always present: a "constant," which is the original structure, and a "variable," which is the way of using it, the type of life and use of the structure through the centuries.

The use of typology as a methodological tool allows us to separate the elements in a building that are constant from those that are variable. Furthermore, it allows identification of those buildings with homogenous typological characteristics; this identification is a fundamental step in a program of conservation.

Finally, the use of this analysis has shown the relationship between the residential tissue (*edilizie minore*) and the great architectural works (palaces, convents, churches). The morphological unity of the city of Bologna is composed of the residential tissue and those architectural elements that have historically performed a role of "aggregation poles," both in a physical and symbolic way (the towers, the church of S. Petronio, the palaces, the portici, the squares).

As Cervellati says:

The relationship between the residences and these "emergent" elements corresponds to the separation of public and private life. The emergent elements, as characteristic of the formation of the urban structure, could be renovated in a revitalization of the historic center, changing its relationship with the rest of the city and the region.[12]

The Conservation Program

The analytical work developed by the Bologna administration led to three major products that represent the substance of the plan and the conservation program for the historic center:

1. Definition of architectural typologies
2. Indication of allowable uses of each typology
3. Indication of the kind of renovation allowable for each typology, later formalized in technical regulations.

In the physical structure of the historic center, four major typological categories and many subcategories have been identified. They are not theoretical models, but a useful tool in the process of deciding what use the old buildings should have in contemporary society. Each category has a use destination for the future, according to the typological, structural, and organizational characteristic of the building.

The four categories are:

A. The large "*contenitori*" (containers). These include palaces, convents, churches, baptisteries, towers. They also include special architectural organisms like old depots, etc. Given the structural characteristic of the space of these large *contenitori*, their prescribed use could only be one of public or collective structures, both for the city and the neighborhoods: schools, research centers, libraries, theaters, exhibition halls, civic clubs, laboratories, sanitary centers, and, in general, services for the neighborhoods.

B. Buildings organized around one or more courts. In Bologna, there are two different groups of such architectural organisms:

1. Buildings with a facade (front) length of 10 to 20 meters, formed by aggregation of two combined half-courts.

2. Buildings with a front of 21 to 50 meters, characterized by a complete court, delimited by four principal architectural structures. The organizational characteristics of the spaces do not allow, especially at the ground floor, uses very different from the original one. Convertible functions are cultural activities, both public and private.

C. Private buildings with typological characteristics deriving from the socioeconomic structure of the sixteenth to the eighteenth centuries. This typology, very common in Bologna, and typically associated with the life and activities of workers and city dwellers, usually consists of buildings with a very narrow front (4 meters to a maximum of 8–10 meters) and a deep coverage depending on the morphological characteristics of the lot. The large variety of typologies deriving from the association of one or more of these structures allows a wide range of uses, all of them residential: apartments for students, single persons, retired and old people, young couples, etc. This typology is, therefore, the one that best corresponds to the goals of public housing programs for low-income groups that the administration has been proposing.

D. Private buildings of typologies derived from the other types, at a different scale, or else without peculiar typological characteristics, to be used for private residences, or similar use, provided that the organization of the spaces and volumes remains untouched.

Each building in the historic center has been studied and included in one of these categories, which provide, in a simple but workable way, the basis for the conservation program and a correct use of the historical heritage. In addition to that, Bologna's planners have developed a set of criteria and regulations pertaining to the way in which physical renovations of a historic building are to be carried out.

These criteria are organized by groups, each one of them indicating the kind of transformation allowed, the materials to be used, the functions of the architectural organisms. Some of these prescriptions are very technical and are not relevant for the purposes of this presentation: I will only give, therefore, a schematic description of them.[13]

Group 1: Restoration
Category 1a: Strict Regulation—Category 1b: Partial Regulation   This group of criteria concerns the buildings to be integrally preserved or to be modified only with restoration methods. The intervention will have to pursue the restoration of the building's historical values: additions that have no relevance to the history of the monument (as determined from the historical and typological analysis of the building) should be eliminated. It is important to clarify what is meant by restoration of the historical values of a building. What the Bologna plan wants to avoid is a restoration practice aimed at the recreation of what our aesthetic taste presumes to be the original characteristics of a building. What has to be preserved, in an act of preservation for transmission to the future, are the typological and stylistic characteristics of the building as it has been evolved through time. This is based on a historical consciousness that, unlike the consciousness of other historical periods, forbids any intervention with the monuments of the past which is not physical reinforcement and restoration.

Group 2
The concept of typology I have described could be divided into two kinds: "urban typology" and "building typology." The building typology originates from the characteristics of human living. The urban typology is the aggregation of buildings through the centuries, and is also a testimony to the social organization of the past. As such, it has to be preserved: artificial reduction of densities, or the arbitrary weeding out of some buildings (*diradamento*), as an alteration of the urban structure, is therefore to be banned.

This group of criteria is subdivided into two categories.
Category 2a: Renovation and Conservation   The interest of conservation embraces all the external elements (facades, portici, courts, loggie, windows); and the structural and functional characteristics (structures, stairs, corridors, etc.). This allows the preservation of the original typologies, and the stylistic characteristics of the buildings.

Category 2b: Restructuring within Limits This category allows a partial replacement of old organisms, provided that the typologies are preserved and, eventually, restored to the original configuration. The conservation of the facade must be accompanied with the redesign of the typology, to avoid a "standardization" of residential typologies concealed behind stylistically differentiated facades.

Group 3
Category 3a Reconstruction of buildings that do not have to be preserved, and can be demolished and rebuilt.
Category 3b Demolition without reconstruction of buildings occupying areas that used to represent, in the historical urban structure, essential open spaces. These areas should be used for public open spaces; buildings of comparable capacity could be rebuilt with the same volumes in other areas of the city, or as prescribed by the master plan.

Methodology of Intervention

The methodology described so far was included, and detailed in technical regulations, in the master plan for the historic center, which the city approved in 1969. Although this plan was not a tool for direct implementation of the renovation program, [14] it certainly provided the technical basis for the development of the restoration and renovation programs that came afterward. In fact, the master plan, in addition to the development of a methodology for preserving and revitalizing the old architectural structures without destroying their original stylistic and typological character, included detailed prescriptions of the methodology of intervention that the implementation scheme would have to observe.

The master plan considers two kinds of intervention:
A. Intervention involving single building units, allowed only for the architectural structures included in the 1a, 1b categories examined above.
B. Intervention involving several building units, areas (*comparti*), and subareas. This kind of intervention has to be used for all the remaining building categories with the exception of the units located outside the areas defined by the plan. The aim of this provision is to guarantee the achievement of economic, social, and planning goals of the renovation program that an intervention by single housing units would compromise.

The master plan defined 13 planning areas in the historic center of Bologna on the basis of their functional and morphological unity and identified within them the units to be included in the single-building renovation programs (blocks, sub-blocks, etc.).

For the definition of these units, two other criteria were used:
1. The degree of physical decay of the typological structures
2. The degree of decay and obsolescence of the socioeconomic structure.

These criteria were used to distinguish the areas to be included in the planning units, and those where intervention involving single buildings was allowed, given the better physical and socioeconomic conditions. The planning areas (*comparti*) will be used for the design of collective structures, like open space, services, etc. In the subareas (*sub-comparti*) instead, architectural interventions (restoration, renovation, etc.) will be defined.

The Housing Program for the Historic Center: Concepts and Methods

Once the methodological and operational structure of the renovation program was defined, the administration started to develop an active program of intervention for public housing in the historic center. The 1969 master plan for the historic center provides a rather detailed regulation of the way in which renovation programs have to be carried out. It is a good tool for "indirect" control of uses, but it is not able, by itself, to modify the socioeconomic trends existing in the center, in particular the process of eviction of low-income groups and their replacement by bourgeois classes.

This is why the administration developed the Public Housing Program for the Historic Center (Piano di Edilizia Economica e Popolare, from now on PEEP). This plan, adopted in 1972 and formally approved in 1975, was aimed, for the first time in Italy, at the provision of public housing through the renovation of old historic buildings. PEEP furthermore coordinated the financial efforts of the city of Bologna and the National Agencies for Public Housing. [15]

Before reviewing the methodology used by PEEP and its achievements up to now, it seems useful to present the three major concepts on which this proposal is based. The importance of the Bologna plan for other Italian and European situations and experiences largely derives from these "theoretical" premises.

1. It is necessary, in order to re-equilibrate the imbalances generated in the fields of housing and land use by the development of capitalism in Italy, to shift construction activity from new construction to restoration of the existing housing stock.

This statement is based on an evaluation of the housing situation in Italy. While, in a country with a population of 55 million, there are approximately 65 million rooms, the housing shortage, especially for workers and low-income groups, is dramatically increasing. This reflects two phenomena: the abandonment of many cities and villages in the depressed areas of the country that paralleled the large migrations of workers toward northern Italy and Europe in the fifties and sixties, and the fact that most private building activity has been concentrated in higher-income housing and second and third residences. At the same time the percent of public housing in the total number of units built every year has declined from 25 in 1950 to the current 3–4.

The idea of the Bologna plan is that, to reverse this trend, it is necessary to reuse the existing housing stock (the old historic center to provide low-cost housing for the working class.

2. The second idea concerns the nature of public housing, which the Bologna plan considers to be a public service. The importance of this definition is less trivial than it may seem because of its legal implications. As we will see in a short while, the proposal of expropriation of land and buildings contained in an early version of the plan was based on an extended interpretation of a reform law regulating expropriation.

3. Although the Bologna administration thinks that direct and indirect intervention in the market processes, under the control of the Neighborhood Councils, is the principal tool to guarantee the achievement of its planning goals, this does not mean that private activity is banned from the historic center. On the contrary, the intervention of building cooperatives and private developers has been encouraged, with subsidies and other financial guarantees, provided that certain conditions, agreed on in a covenant (*convenzione*), are respected. This procedure, which constitutes one of the most original innovations in planning in Italy, will be described later on.

Architectural Typologies

PEEP, adopted in 1972 and started in 1973, includes only five of the original thirteen planning areas (*comparti urbanistici*) designated by the plan for the historic center; these were selected for the first phase of implementation of the plan because of their typological and social homogeneity and because their structural conditions were extremely precarious. [16]

For the purpose of renovation, the architects working with the planning department of the city have designed a large variety of possible ways of reusing the old typologies for the needs of the existing population.

I will present here only an illustration of these designs, in particular for the most common housing type: the artisan house.

An analysis of the historical buildings had led to the definition of different typologies, according to the number of stories, the width, length, the presence of courtyards, back yards etc. Each of these typologies allows the design of one or more possible combinations of apartments.

These variations all respect the original historical typology and are reflected in the implementation phase, according to the structure of the population existing in the *comparti* to be renovated. As an example, category CB1 (shown on p. 180) allows the following variations:

a. Four small apartments for students, two on the first and two on the second floor; one apartment on the third floor
b. Two small apartments at the first floor; one maisonette (duplex apartment) on the second and third floor
c. Six small apartments

The only typologies designed by the architects provide a similar flexibility with respect to the needs of the population.

As mentioned earlier, one of the major goals of the plan is to improve the quality of services for the public housing projects. This is true not only at the urban level (neighborhood services), but at the architectural level as well. The design of the *comparti* includes, consequently, a number of collective services: child care, collective areas, playrooms for children, open space, collective restaurant (especially for students and the elderly), and central heating. On a larger scale, other services must be located outside the area of the *comparto,* if not feasible inside, including elementary schools, social centers, and parks.

Political and Legal Aspects

Let's consider, now, the plan's most challenging and important aspect: an implementation structure, based on political, legal, and financial agreements, which is able to start and carry through the physical and social conservation program initiated by the administration.

As anywhere else, the problem is an extremely complex one, far from a definitive solution. In spite of this, the system proposed in Bologna, if sustained by adequate financial backing, can allow renovation of the historic center and, at the same time, guarantee the interests of the low-income groups living in the center. In fact, the idea of the "covenant" (*convenzione*), proposed for the first time in Bologna, proved to be such an interesting concept, that it was incorporated in a National Housing Reform Law approved in early 1977.

There are two factors, both outside the control of the Bologna administration, which influence its ability to carry out the renovation program:

1. The state of national land-use and planning legislation, which, in spite of some recent important innovations,[17] is still inadequate to prevent the most disruptive phenomena that have shaped the Italian process of urbanization since World War II: land speculation and the concentration of building activity on new construction instead of renewal.
2. The financial situation of local governments. In Italy, local governments do not have fiscal autonomy. All the revenues are collected by the state, and then redistributed to the municipalities. Besides this lack of autonomy, the economic crisis which has shaken the country since 1973 has severely impaired the ability of local governments to finance housing programs.

The existence of these factors has necessitated the design of a system of agreements with private owners for the purpose of renovating historic buildings. In this way, the impact of the limited financial means available to the city can be extended, without losing control of the development processes in the historic center.

This approach represents an evolution from the plan first developed by the Bologna administration, which was based on two proposals:

1. Use of a recent housing reform law (no. 865 for 1971; see note 17) for the expropriation of buildings in the historic center. The legislation, in fact, allows the expropriation of land and buildings in urban centers for schools, open space, and public services in general at a price corresponding to the value of agricultural land multiplied by certain coefficients. The Bologna plan gives an extended interpretation to this legislation and considers public housing as a public service, sustaining, therefore, the legality of expropriation for public housing. The price that the administration would pay is, obviously, much lower than the market price, because it would be "purified" of all speculative values. The impact of the funds available to the administration would consequently be much larger.
2. The buildings were to be expropriated, renovated by

the administration, and then returned to the tenants' cooperatives. This form of cooperative management of buildings was seen as the most flexible one. Its characteristics are:

a. Collective ownership and management of the entire planning area (*comparto*)

b. Guarantee of the security of an apartment to each member of the cooperative for the duration of his lifetime

c. Guarantee of fair rent, according to the amount of space used

d. No obligation of capital investment in the buildings. The cost of acquisition and restoration would be paid with the rent, over a very long time span.

e. Mobility of the tenants within the renovated area, according to family-connected needs. This would ensure, at the same time, the efficient use of space and preserve the social links and structure of the neighborhood.

This proposal, submitted for discussion to the Neighborhood Councils and to all the political parties represented in the City Council, was the subject of long debate, both on its technical and political aspects. The evaluation process of that proposal revealed its major difficulties:

1. The use of the extended interpretation of the expropriation law would have generated countless appeals to the courts, stopping for years the process of renovation initiated by the city. Furthermore, despite the fact that well-known scholars of constitutional law had supported the interpretation used by the Bologna plan,[18] it was uncertain whether the Constitutional Court would have confirmed it.

2. There would have been political opposition from most of the property owners involved in the renovation plan, and the center and right-wing political parties.

Not only was the program seen as discriminatory against a group of small owners who just happened to be in the historic center, but also it would have lacked the cooperation of the other political forces in the city. The administration decided, consequently, that it was not worth destroying the whole program for a matter of principle, and that the unity and cooperation of all the political parties was a necessary condition for the achievement of the plan's goals. The compromise solution that was reached and approved in 1975 is the proposal of the Covenant (*convenzione*) between the city government and the private owners.

The Covenant

As the product of a City Council Commission and all the Neighborhood Councils in the historic center, the covenant has been approved by all the political groups existing in the city.[19]

Although it represents a compromise solution, in comparison with the previous proposal, it guarantees the achievement of the plan's original goal: initiating a process of urban renovation capable of protecting the interests of low-income tenants. In fact, as we will see, the relationship between landlord and tenant has been drastically changed by the adoption of the Covenant.

But let's examine, in detail, the scheme of the Covenant adopted by the administration.

A first point, coherent with the physical conservation concepts examined earlier, is that the owner signing the Covenant agrees to use, in the building's restoration, the criteria and methodology established by the plan. The Commune, nevertheless, is to reimburse the owner for the value of the building, or part of it, that has to be demolished according to the prescriptions of the plan.

The Commune of Bologna contributes to the renovation with grants, totaling up to 80 percent of the total expenditures, according to the owner's income. The subsidies can have three forms:

a. Grant for capital expenditures

b. Grant to cover part of the interest on mortgages

c. Combination of the two.

The Commune can award grants covering the entire cost of restoration in the case of owners in extremely poor economic conditions.

The Covenant, with the purpose of excluding any possible speculation on the renovation process, excludes private developers and development corporations from renovation contracts. The duration of the Covenant varies from fifteen to twenty-five years; if, at the end of the period, the owner wants to sell the property, the Commune has the right to be the first buyer at the price indicated by the State Offices for Land and Building Estimation.[20]

If the owner wants to sell the property before the end of the contract, he is obliged to reimburse the entire amount of the grant to the municipality, with the addition of the interest on the capital for the years he has used the property. When the owner dies, his heirs have the right to use the apartment and to acquire the property by paying back the grant. If they do not want to acquire the property, the Commune can purchase it at a price corresponding to the official estimate of its value, less the amount of the awarded grant.

The owner signing the contract, and not using the property for himself, has the following obligations:

1. To keep the tenants on in the apartments
2. To allow the continuation of existing economic activities on the property
3. To agree on the rent with the administration. The agreed-upon rent is based on a combined evaluation of the subsidy awarded, the duration of the Covenant, the tenant's income, the owner's expenditures, and the rent levels of public housing apartments (on the average about twelve percent of the tenant's income). All these obligations are transferred, in the case of the apartment's sale, to the new owner.

When a tenant moves out, the new tenant has to be selected among those on the public housing list. If the new tenant does not have an income level sufficient to pay for the apartment, the Commune has the right to rent it, and sublet it to the tenant at a lower cost.

If an apartment is empty and is not rented after four months, the administration has the right to purchase it, by the procedure outlined above.

Any violation of these obligations allows the Commune to expropriate the building or the apartment, using law no. 865 of 1971.

Finally, the administration is responsible for the construction of temporary housing for the tenants living in apartments to be restored. The temporary housing must be located in the same neighborhood.

This system is clearly designed to protect the interests of the small owner, those who live in the buildings they own, as well as the tenants. While any possibility of speculation is excluded, the system allows for the conservation of the city's social structure, including the small artisan enterprises still using the historic center.

Achievements and Future Developments

The housing plan for the historic center has now been in operation since 1973. The Covenant was approved only in 1975. As of 1977, there has not been enough time to achieve such an ambitious goal as the renovation of the urban center of Bologna and the reversal of the gentrification trend.

Nevertheless, it is important to examine what the administration has been able to accomplish, taking into consideration all the problems and difficulties the program has encountered in the current Italian economic situation. It is even more important to understand how the administration is trying to develop and extend its programs in the future.

In the five *comparti* included in the Public Housing Program (PEEP) the following projects have been completed:

1. Acquisition of land and buildings from private owners, for a total expenditure of 2 billion lire (approximately $2.5 million, 1977)
2. Renovation of approximately 200 apartments, for 500 people, partially financed by the municipality, partially by the National Housing Agencies
3. Construction of social services (schools, sanitary facilities, open space, etc.) for a total expenditure of 2.5 billion lire (approximately $3.2 million)
4. Restoration of historic monuments, for a total of 750 million lire (approximately $1 million).

In the view of the Bologna planners, these achievements are to be considered only the beginning of a process that has to extend public control over most of the areas of the city inhabited by low-income groups. The experience of the first phase of the renovation has revealed some of the problems that the second phase will have to solve:

1. The limited number of apartments available to be used as temporary housing
2. The absence of adequate legislative support for renovation programs
3. The technical difficulties associated with work organization and the need for particular skills in renovation work
4. The length of the bureaucratic procedures

But the new phase of the program is not intended to deal only with these problems; the intention is to expand the intervention, step by step, to include the whole city in a program of urban renovation under the administration's control.

The first step is the renovation of all the public housing existing in the city. For this purpose, agreements have been signed with the local housing authority for the renovation of 130 apartments.

A second step will be the creation of more temporary housing, to allow for intervention in many other city areas.

A third step will be the elimination of all the substandard housing (such as that occupied by squatters), of which there is a limited quantity in the city.

But the major goal of this phase is to include in the renovation process all property belonging to public institutions, and all the collective ownership cooperatives which exist in large numbers in the historic center.

Conclusions

The proposals contained in the Bologna plan certainly represent one of the most interesting innovations in Italian planning practice. Many cities, in this decade, have adopted programs and a methodology inspired by those of Bologna[21] and have shown interesting results. The question I posed when I began this presentation (that is, is the Bologna model exportable to other cities?) deserves a conditional answer.

It is possible to initiate and carry out a program of physical, cultural, and social conservation if there are a political will to fight land speculation; a capacity for organizing the democratic participation of citizens; and an understanding of the historical, economic, and social process that have shaped the city's structure. And it is possible to do it without special powers, using only available financial resources.

Certainly, it cannot be said that Bologna's achievements are extraordinary or that all the problems have been taken care of. But no city in Italy can show similar results.

The example of Venice, often considered the other side of the coin, is indicative. Before a leftist coalition took power in 1975, and in spite of special legislation giving extraordinary powers and a large grant (approximately $120 million) for renovation, not much had been accomplished.

Planning for Venice's historic center has been inaccurate, complex, and substantially unable to address the city's major problems. Democratic participation structures were underdeveloped. In two years (until 1977), the leftist administration has not accomplished much more. Two years are not even enough to repair the damage of thirty years of bad management and bad planning, or to reinforce the trust of the citizens in what the administration proposes.

Bologna need not be a model for Venice, or for any other city; each of them has a particular structure, deriving from its history, its particular problems, and its own social and economic situation. Bologna shows simply that a coherent methodology and a democratic decision-making process can do something to save the invaluable character of the historic center. Bologna shows that the battle for a better city is not lost.

Notes

1. Giuseppe Canpos Venuti, "Quindici Anni di Esperienze Urbanistiche a Bologna" (Fifteen Years of Planning Experiences in Bologna), mimeograph, December 1974.

2. The law, well known in Italy as the "167" approved in 1962, was one of the first products of the new center-left government formed at the beginning of the sixties. It allowed the municipalities to acquire land for public housing projects at what it had cost

two years before. This provision, designed to avoid the accumulation of speculative windfalls, was later repealed as unconstitutional by the constitutional court. This did not prevent the city from implementing a totally new housing policy.

3. In Italy at the time, most of the funds for public housing programs were provided by the national government and administered by several housing agencies. The relative proportion of public housing to total yearly housing construction has been constantly declining, from 25 percent in the postwar period, to the current 3–4 percent.

4. During the 1951–1961 period, 168,000 people moved to Bologna; 70 percent of them came from the metropolitan area. Employment in the industrial sector increased by 61 percent in the city (from 50,000 to 82,000). In the second phase, during the sixties, the metropolitan area led the growth process: 50 percent of the new population (approximately 70,000) found residences in the metropolitan area.

5. Technically, the plan is not a metropolitan plan, in the sense that there is no metropolitan government. The urban legislation of that time (modified in the early seventies with the introduction of the regions as an autonomous level of government) allowed only for the formation of intermunicipal plans (*piano intercomunale*). The participation of local administrations had to be voluntary.

6. See P. Maldini, R. Mazzanti, U. Pallotti, and F. Tarozzi, "Linee Generali dello Schema per la Pianificazione Urbanistica nel Comprensorio Bolognese" (General Outline of the Planning Scheme for the Bologna Metropolitan Area), in *Urbanistica*, no. 54–55, September 1969.

7. Long before the energy crisis, the Bologna administration started a program to provide free transportation to all citizens during rush hours.

8. See Comune di Bologna, *Per un Ulteriore Sviluppo del Decentramento e della Partecipazione Democratica* (Contributions to a Further Development of Decentralization and Democratic Participation), Bologna, 1974.

9. *Convegno: Centri Storici a Confronto* (Conference: Historic Centers Compared), Bologna, 1966.

10. The law, known as "865," allows for the acquisition of land and buildings inside the historic center for public housing projects at a price linked, with some multipliers, to the value of the agricultural land in the area.

11. See P. L. Cervellati, and R. Scannavini, *Bologna: Politica e Metodologia del Restauro nei Centri Storici* (Bologna: Politics and Methodology of Restoration in the Historic Center), Bologna, Il Mulino, 1973.

12. Ibid., p. 113.

13. See Comune di Bologna, *Norme Tecniche di Attuazione del Piano per il Centro Storico* (Technical Regulations for the Implementation of the Plan for the Historic Center).

14. Master plans in Italian legislation have never had a direct implementation power. This pertains to detailed plans or other implementation plans, such as public housing programs, etc.

15. At that time they were GESCAL (Gestione Case per i Lavoratori), later suppressed by housing reform, and the IACP (Istituti Autonomi Case Popolari).

16. The *comparti* are S. Caterina, Soferino, Fondazza, S. Leonardo, and S. Carlo.

17. The most interesting innovations produced by the 1942 Planning Act, besides the 1977 legislation already mentioned, have been the law of 1967, which for the first time transferred to the developers the cost of "primary" urbanization (roads, power lines, sewerage, etc.), the law 865 of 1971, which reorganized the National Housing Agencies and regulates land expropriation for public services provisions, and the law 10 of 1977, which introduced for the first time the concept of phased development in Italian planning legislation. In addition to that, the new legislation forces private developers to pay for all the urbanization costs.

18. See A. Predieri, *L'Espropriazione di Immobili nei Centri Storici per l'Edilizia Residenziale Pubblica Secondo la Legge No. 865 del 1971* (The Expropriation of Buildings in the Historic Center for Public Housing, According to Law No. 865 of 1971).

19. For a detailed description of the Covenant and of the opinions of the Neighborhood Councils, see Comune di Bologna: *La Convenzione per il Risanamento dei Cinque Comparti PEEP/Centro Storico* (The Covenant for the Renovation of the Five *Comparti* of PEEP for the Historic Center), Bologna 1975.

20. Ufficio Tecnico Erariale (UTE).

21. Just to recall a few of them, I will mention the other cities of the Emilia-Romagna region, like Ferrara, Modena, and Cesena. A most notable example is the historic renovation plan for the urban center of Brescia, directed by architects L. Benevolo and G. Lombardi.

14 Planning for the Protection of Monuments and Buildings in Denmark

Ove Nissen

A Few Basic Facts

To other countries, Denmark and Holland may show some similar features which may lead to hasty conclusions as to the topography of the countries.

They are both rather small, situated in the temperate coastal zone in Northwestern Europe, and known for their efficient agriculture. These similarities may count heavily when you look at the international image of the two countries. But there are other features far more important, not least in a historical context. And there the differences are far more eyecatching than the similarities.

Even if both countries are small, the area of Denmark is about 30 percent larger than that of Holland. But the Danish population amounts only to 5 million as against 14 million for Holland, resulting in a population density of about 110 per square kilometer as against 380. The proportions have probably been the same throughout history. And the consequences are easily seen in the topography of the countries today.

Denmark has for more than 1,000 years been a united and relatively centralized kingdom with a strong landed gentry, and for 175 years (1670–1849) it was an absolute monarchy which was—although enlightened—probably more centralized than absolutist France.

The Netherlands, on the other hand, have throughout history had a number of centers, and even a number of more or less independent provinces or cities. The bourgeoisie was a powerful formation in Holland at a time when the number of city dwellers in Denmark was still insignificant. And trade and industry became a basis of society in Holland when a coin was something that a Dane hardly ever saw in his entire life.

The Protection of Monuments and Buildings in Denmark

The Preservation of Buildings Act
The first Danish Preservation of Buildings Act dates back to 1918. It is traditional in its setup. It foresees the scheduling of individual buildings for preservation in two classes, A

and B. Class A preservation includes the totality of a building, while class B preservation covers the exterior only. The reason for the passing of the Act at the time was a generally felt fear that a prospering trade and industry might in its eagerness to display its economic power in building threaten even the most precious gems in the nation's architectural heritage.

The Preservation of Buildings Act became, together with the Conservation of Nature Act of 1817, the first instrument to prevent unwanted development in town and country planning, where up to then only the law of the jungle applied. But weak instruments they were.

The Preservation of Buildings Act has undergone few substantial changes since 1918. But it has been supplemented through other legislation. It is still our most important act when it comes to protecting individual secular buildings of outstanding importance. Today around 3,000 buildings are preserved in respect of the Act, of which well over 500 are in Class A.

The Historic Buildings Council
The Historic Buildings Council—a collegial body with its own technical secretariat chaired by the State Antiquarian—supervises the buildings and suggests new buildings for preservation to the Minister for the Environment.

All work on preserved buildings beyond ordinary maintenance work must be reported to and approved by the Council, which may grant subsidies toward the costs.

Should an owner fail to comply with the decision of the Council, or should he apply for the demolition of the building, the minister may order its compulsory public purchase. Thus, the owner has the possibility of "blackmailing" the public into purchasing a preserved building, which he does not wish to maintain. This possibility, which has in fact only seldom been used, is likely to disappear with the reform of the Preservation of Buildings Act.

The funds available to the Historic Buildings Council for subsidies are very limited: less than $500,000 in the 1975 budget. It should be noted, though, that only private owners are subsidized. Publicly owned buildings are under the supervision of the council, but restoration costs are paid by the authority responsible.

For secular buildings of historic value owned by the state (not least the royal castles) the amount invested in maintenance and restoration can be estimated at about $3 million per year.

The amount paid by the municipalities toward maintenance of their property of historic value is probably about 50 percent of the state figure. A number of municipalities are further subsidizing private owners of historic buildings; the City of Copenhagen, for example, with about $250,000 in 1975, not counting subsidies toward the costs of rehabilitating slum clearance, and the City of Elsinore—one of the Danish Pilot Projects—with an annual $1 million toward the realization of a rehabilitating slum clearance of the entire medieval city.

Ecclesiastical Architecture
The vast majority of ecclesiastical buildings belong to the Lutheran State Church. Unlike the situation in such countries as Great Britain, however, the freedom of the church to make changes in its buildings of architectural value is very limited, as they underlie a strict supervision by the Historic Churches' Board—a body of the National Museum. The Ministry of Ecclesiastical Affairs set aside each year an amount for restoration works on historic buildings belonging to the state church—in 1975 $2 million.

The problem of abandoned church buildings has hitherto not presented itself to a degree that is known, for instance, in Amsterdam. In the one case known in central Copenhagen, the state proper has taken over responsibility for the building and its maintenance.

Planning and Building Legislation
The Preservation of Buildings Act considers the monument, but in isolation. The necessity of protecting coherent architectural milieus has been "discovered" only recently.

The Town Planning Act includes provisions allowing municipalities to freeze a status quo in an urban environment in the form of a town planning bylaw when this is indicated for historical or architectural reasons, while the Building Act gives the municipality the right to include in its building bylaws provisions allowing the building authorities to make building permits conditional on the fulfillment of provisions necessary to maintain or enhance the environmental qualities of a building's surroundings. Conditions for the permit may relate not only to the building proper, but even to its fencing, signs, etc.

The weaknesses of the planning and building legislation at present are, in relation to historical environments, two-fold: the application of the provisions is not constant or mandatory, and they do not prevent the demolition of the building.

At first the municipalities were not very eager to apply the new provisions, but the tide now seems to have turned. The pile of applications with the Historic Buildings Council for technical assistance in preparing inventories with a view to introducing protective planning or building bylaws is growing rapidly, and a bill for a new Municipal Planning Act, now pending before Parliament, will narrow considerably the possibility for an owner of a historic building covered by such bylaws to force a demolition or a public purchase.

The Slum Cearance Act

Only a few years ago slum clearance meant demolition. Only in recent years has it been realized that total clearance may mean giving up essential environmental values and waste of resources and even of money. In 1969 a new Danish Slum Clearance Act introduced the possibility of rehabilitating slum clearances when this was indicated for architectural and first of all for economic reasons.[1]

The costs for the carrying out of slum clearance programs are equally shared between municipality and state, and they are measured as follows: the Housing Commission estimates the average rent paid per year and unit in modern public housing in the area. The owner then receives the difference between the capitalized value of the yearly amortization of his investment and the rent revenue as estimated by the Housing Commission, a rent which he is then obviously forced to keep.

When the Historic Buildings Council is of the opinion that a rehabilitating slum clearance is indicated for architectural reasons, the share of the costs born by the state may be raised and in fact usually is to 75 percent as against a municipal share of 25 percent. This is obviously intended to inspire the municipalities to apply a rehabilitating slum clearance wherever it is indicated.

The 1975 budget foresees state subsidies towards slum clearance costs of $15 million. An estimated third will be spent on rehabilitating programs indicated for architectural reasons, but this share is expected to go up.

What Do We Spend?

When adding up the figures quoted we come to a sum of under $10 million as the total contribution of the Danish Government in 1975. Not a very impressive figure. But it is a net figure. It does not include technical staff, administration, etc. It must furthermore be seen in proportion to the smaller population and smaller quantity of historic buildings in Denmark.

It is to be expected that more will be spent than appears in the budget. The rising unemployment has caused the government to consider investing more money in projects which demand proportionally more manpower per krone invested. Projects to improve the urban and rural environment are high up on the list.

Private Initiative

Lobbies and pressure groups—these are terms which are probably rather negatively loaded as they are usually related to the more obscure and even corrupt aspects of life in modern societies.

Yet, conservation lobbies and pressure groups have been indispensable tools in the building up of a proper policy and legislation and a forceful administration in the field of landscapes, monuments, and sites. The Conservation of Nature Act and Preservation of Buildings Act of 1917 and 1918 were inspired and even to a large extent drafted by the Danish Union for the Conservation of Nature and the Society for the Preservation of Old Buildings. They were certainly forming lobbies and acting as pressure groups. And without their work the problems would hardly have been debated in Parliament until very much later.

Of more recent date is the Association of Danish Preservation Societies, an umbrella association of around sixty-five private organizations all over the country, with a revolving fund attached: The Fund for the Preservation of the Cultural Heritage. We are especially anxious to see the effects of the work of the foundation in the longer run. Because even if the citizens interested in monuments and sites have been organized as long as society has been aware of the preservation problem, and even longer, the economic investments necessary actually to solve the problems have been undertaken until very recently nearly exclusively by public authorities. A private revolving fund would certainly serve as an inspiration not least to local authorities with a view to intensifying their efforts in preserving the Danish architectural and cultural heritage as an integrated part in a harmonious environment.

Elsinore, A Pilot Project

Elsinore (Danish: Helsingor) is a town and municipality of 55,000 inhabitants in North Zealand, forty kilometers north of Copenhagen. It is probably best known for its castle, Kronborg, built by Dutch architects in the late sixteenth century, which is also the setting of Shakespeare's drama *Hamlet*. It has a well-preserved historic center: about 350 houses around two beautiful churches. It is also the gateway to the Scandinavian peninsula with beyond doubt the busiest ferry harbor in the world. And it is finally more and more becoming a part of the Copenhagen region with all the infrastructural implications of such a status. The main reason for selecting Elsinore is the decision of the Municipal Council in 1972 to relieve the pressure on the center by way of creating a second modern center south of the town, and to let 80 percent of the houses in the old center undergo rehabilitating slum clearance. This decision was taken after a public debate and public hearings which may well serve as guidelines for the practising of public participation in

planning, and the rehabilitating slum clearance is now well under way. The town contains great monuments to illustrate the complexity of problems involved in preservation operations and it is not least situated in a regional context suited for the illustration of the integration of the preservation of monuments and sites into an overall planning framework.

Note

1. The Danish word for slum clearance, *sanering,* actually means "to make a building fit or sound for human habitation."

Elsinore: A Plan for Rehabilitation of a Medium-sized Danish City

Bent Rud

Map of old houses in Elsinore. From *Old Houses in Elsinore,* National Museum, Copenhagen, Denmark, 1973.

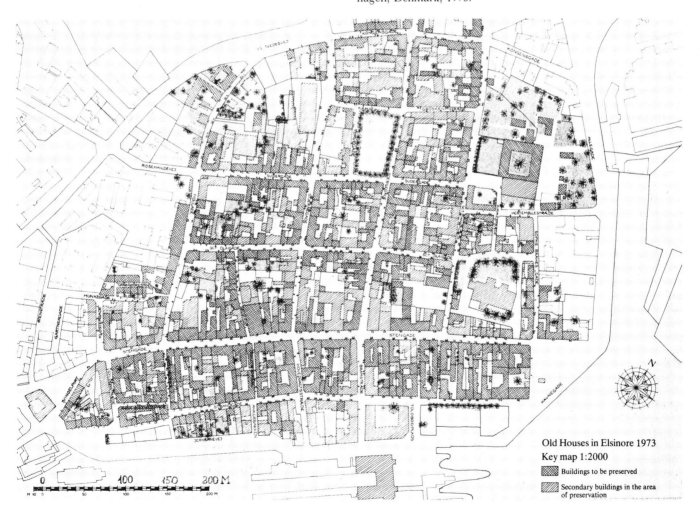

Old Houses in Elsinore 1973
Key map 1:2000

Buildings to be preserved

Secondary buildings in the area of preservation

Rehabilitation of a whole
residential street, "Lappen."
Photo from the City of Elsinore.

Reconstruction of an old house.
Photo from the City of Elsinore.

Rehabilitation of a large building in the main shopping center. Photo from the City of Elsinore.

Redesign of facades and signs.
Photo from the City of Elsinore.

"Gentlemen, you are welcome to Elsinore" (*Hamlet*, Act 2, Scene 2). I guess that your knowledge of Elsinore is limited to the fact that Shakespeare let his Tragedy of Hamlet, prince of Denmark, take place at Elsinore and at Kronborg Castle.

We do not know if Shakespeare had seen the town with his own eyes, but he might have been there. A company of English actors had played for the Danish king, Frederik II, when he lived at Kronborg and Shakespeare might have been among them as an actor.

I will not blame you if I am right, because Elsinore is an average Danish town or city (there is a cathedral now). Apart from Hamlet and Kronborg as tourist attractions there has not been much spoken of the city. But in these years European attention has been attracted to this little point in Scandinavia because of its present problems and its present ways of solving them.

But first a little historical background.

In early medieval times the economic center of the Baltic area was situated around the great herring markets near Skanoer in the southern part of Scania, now Swedish, at that time Danish. the Danish king had considerable income from the market duty, to which he was entitled in return for maintaining the "market peace."

When the herring went north, the markets decreased in importance and the king lost his revenues. As compensation he established the Sound Toll, a duty which all foreign ships had to pay. In return the king kept the sea free from pirates.

The Sound Toll was collected when the ships passed the northern entrance of the Sound, where King Erik in 1426 founded Elsinore and built the castle of Krogen. Monasteries and churches were also built. In the years after 1574 King Frederik II and his son Christian IV erected Kronborg Castle on the site of the former Krogen. The Sound Toll was abolished in 1857, and for the rest of the century the economic decline of the town prevented the citizens from maintaining their houses. Among the best were ones that had been built in the eighteenth and in the first part of the nineteenth century.

Today the city is in prosperous development due to its position as a gateway to the other Scandinavian countires, its short distance from the capital (45 kilometers), and its role as a shopping center for both Danish and Swedish customers.

The combination of the economic decline during half a century with consequent neglect in maintaining the houses, an enormous increase of the population, and a growing claim of area for shops has created a critical situation, which the municipality council now has decided to solve.

The main effort is large-scale slum clearance, which is developing just now. Every municipality with more than 25,000 inhabitants must, according to the Danish Slum Clearance Act, produce surveys and plans for clearance. Demand, method, and time schedule must be stated.

For more than 100 years we have had laws which gave the authorities the option of dismantling dwellings which were regarded as being injurious to health. In the year 1939 we got the first Slum Clearance Act. It was revised in 1959, 1969, and 1973. In its latest version the act says that in order to obtain an improvement of housing conditions cities should aim at "removing or improving antiquated or unsanitary dwellings, promoting a renovation of antiquated parts of town, helping families without dwellings find a convenient relocation, and producing the necessary administrative and economic basis for increasing slum clearance activity."

For several years pulling down and rebuilding was the normal interpretation of the term *slum clearance*. But today the idea of a conserving slum clearance is regarded as a quite usual thing.

For a city like Elsinore with such a rich architectural heritage the question of preservation immediately came up in connection with the problems of slum clearance. Prognoses concerning the future size of the city were made, and it was anticipated that the municipality would have 125,000 inhabitants by the year 2000. In order not to spoil the urban and natural qualities within the municipality, it was decided to limit the growth of the population to 70,000.

At the same time it was discovered that even with a stop in growth, there would be a demand for about 50,000 square meters of shopping area in the old city center. Such an extension would overburden the streets and buildings. So if the city center was to be preserved the great extension had to take place outside the center. This item was agreed to by the city council.

Before these important decisions were made, the population had been given much detailed information and was involved in the discussion through the press, through publications from the city council, and public meetings. A publication containing information about the concept of slum clearance, explaining the historical background of the present situation, was given free of charge to citizens through a distribution of 2,500 copies. Next it was decided by the municipal council to carry out a 20-year program of conservational slum clearance.

As a guide to the planning of the clearance, which comprised demolition of some and alterations of other buildings, the National Museum published a register of houses worthy of preservation. Slum clearance is a matter which influences people deeply in daily life. Therefore it was important also to know the attitude of the citizens toward the clearance plans.

For that purpose a sociological survey was made—perhaps the only one of its kind in Europe (see the next chapter). The survey was commissioned by the Municipality of Elsinore.

16 Slum Clearance and Preservation in Elsinore: People and Opinions

Nils Mortensen and
Ole Staer Anderson

A. The Objectives and Methods of the Study

Many people in Elsinore—not least those responsible for slum clearance planning—have an impression that the town center of Elsinore has not only a historical worth, but has also a particular atmosphere. It would therefore be very regrettable if slum clearance led to a disappearance of this atmosphere. Ideally, this sociological study should indicate what "atmosphere" in Elsinore consists of and how it can be preserved. A problem of this kind is, though, not easily explored in a sociological study. The problems needed, therefore, to be specified in such a way that it was possible to illustrate them within the framework of a smaller questionnaire study.

We decided to illustrate two main problems:

1. The residents' attitude to housing and neighborhood, their social contacts, and reactions to different types of housing environments.

2. A group of conditions actualized by restoration: residents' wishes regarding improvements of their dwellings, desires with regard to a residential area; their actual utilization of the existing back yards often found in connection with dwellings in the center of town, and their wishes with regard to the future shape, size, and uses of these yards; residents' general attitude toward a scheme of conservational slum clearance and, finally, residents' preferences with regard to where they would live, should they be required to leave as a result of the restoration, and to what degree they could afford to pay a higher rent in the completed, restored flats.

The method of the study consisted of sending a short questionnaire to a sample of residents in Elsinore. We were primarily interested in obtaining information from residents in the center of Elsinore, since it is they who will be affected by slum clearance schemes, but to have a comparison group, a sample from various blocks of flats outside the center was included.

The questionnaires were sent out in March 1973, and there were 136 replies from the town center and 154 from the control sample.

This return rate, about 75 percent, is a very satisfactory result. We found from the social description of the samples that there were relatively more elderly people and more from the highest status group in the town center sample than in the control sample. Even though there is a minority in the center of town who have lived there for 25 years or more, the sample as a whole does not consist of more "old Elsinorians" than the control sample. In spite of the fact that the block flats are newer in origin, there is no great difference between the average length of residence of people living in them and among the people living in the center. The former mention also, to a greater degree than residents in the center, that they have members of the family living nearby.

B. The Importance of Environmental Quality in the Older Elsinore

There is a marked difference between the residents in the town center and those in the block flats on the periphery, regarding attitudes toward the dwelling and evaluation of the neighborhood. These differences cannot be explained by differences in the social composition—for instance, by the fact that there are relatively more elderly and high status residents in the town center. People from the center apparently feel happier about their dwellings than those in the block flats, in that 54 percent against 36 percent reply that they are very often "really fond of" their flats and that only 36 percent in the center against 48 percent in the other sample state that they have plans to move. This result is all the more noteworthy in that flats in the center are, generally, of poorer quality than those in the control sample; flats in the center more often lack the "essentials"—22 percent haven't even a toilet in the flat. The residents in the center, though, also have more complaints about their dwellings than the control sample. The study, however, suggests that these "material" shortages are more than adequately compensated for by some "non-material" qualities, which are absent in the newer block flats. It must be the whole environmental milieu in the older Elsinore and the atmosphere

there which leads so many in the center to feel fond of their flats and to be reluctant to move. Another contributing factor is undoubtedly the low rents in the center—almost one-half of residents pay less than $35 per month for their flats.

The results indicate, also, different patterns of social contact between the two main samples. That problem deserves a closer study than has been possible here, but it appears that there are more forms for *informal* contacts in the center. One enters more easily into casual conversation with others, and feels less reserved with regard to making surprise visits to friends and acquaintances. Residents in the block flats score higher, though, regarding the number of families with whom they are on greeting terms.

Residents were presented with a number of questions where they were requested to evaluate their neighborhoods. There is a striking difference in the evaluations from the two areas in respect of which aspects in the housing environment one especially thinks of when considering atmosphere. People from the center believe, to a much greater degree, that there are a special tone and beautiful houses in *their* quarter—the old town—than could be found in the newer block flats. If, though, one compares the different answers to the questions on evaluation of the neighborhood, then the differences aren't so great. The explanation must be that the otherwise good milieu in the center is somewhat ruined by noise and disorder.

The results mentioned above begin to demonstrate a numerical confirmation that the older houses and narrow streets contain some qualities which modern buildings cannot provide. The results on satisfaction with dwelling, evaluation of the neighborhood, and social contacts are confirmed and supplemented by the results obtained from presenting residents with some pictures of different housing environments. Modern architecture with straight lines does not appeal to respondents in the present study.

The replies to other questions indicate that the preferred type of housing should not be too high—houses under 3 floors are evaluated highest, and they should have a varied and individual stamp. The newer constructions, which seem to be drawn with an oversized ruler, appear to be without personality and lacking in imagination, if not exactly cold, because of their "effective" appearance, while the older, low buildings lead people to set a cross against "humanly warm," "exciting," and "relaxed." These problems are hardly likely to be in line with what is practically relevant, yet they have a practical importance on a more general level. Indirectly, they support the idea that a reconstruction of Elsinore, which as far as possible would retain its old form—excepting the noise and disturbance—must be the best solution. The results indicate too that ideas about the qualities embedded in the old houses, narrow streets and intimate architectural details are not loose impressions, but rather identifiable factors in the environment, which influence the satisfaction of residents to such a degree that they compensate for the facilities lacking in their flats.

C. Deficiencies in Dwellings and Preferences in Reshaping the Neighborhood

To say that environmental factors can compensate for the lack of facilities is far from saying that residents in the center of town do not desire improvements in their flats. Up to a half of the residents here would like their flats to be modern, 37 percent would like less draft, and likewise, 37 percent would like the flats to be larger. But interestingly, the desire to *own one's flat* is given higher priority than the desire for a warmer and lighter residence. The primary wish of those in the control sample is for larger flats, and flats which are their own. The most pronounced wish in all the material is to own one's flat, and for it to be larger. The only group who do not emphasize these points are the elderly, while the younger express particularly the desire for a larger flat. In reply to the question of what should be close to the residence, everyone wanted the most important stores and "green areas" to be nearby. There was general agreement (with the exception of the elderly) that there should be a playground close by. There were also some who attached great value to living close to public transport—that applies especially to the elderly, and to the control sample. The opposite applies with regard to "a little place where one can buy a cup of coffee or a beer." This is primarily appreciated by young people and those from the center of town.

That which is least desired is to live close to streets with heavy traffic, and a large group are also reluctant to live near a public house. Opinions, then, seem to be quite sharply divided on the questions of "a little place" and "public houses." One ought to take into consideration here, that there are possibly different interpretations attached to "a little place" and "public house"—perhaps "harmless-cozy" and "violent-noisy," respectively. Aversion to public houses is—apart from among elderly people and those in the control sample—greatest among people from the lowest status groups.

It has been advanced that the smaller workshops and other firms situated in some of the back yards within the town center could be a positive element in the milieu. The results do not indicate that the residents themselves share this viewpoint. Workshops and the like rank relatively high on a list of things one *doesn't* desire close to one's residence.

We have mentioned mostly the environment and atmosphere in the older Elsinore. There are, though, other things which an influential group in the town set a high value on preserving, namely trade, which attracts many customers from outside town—not least from Sweden. One could imagine that there was here a dilemma: how, in the same part of town, can one create a good residential environment and an attractive trading atmosphere? The results indicate, though, that this is no dilemma. Residents in the center would like to have the most general shops and stores close to where they live. Moreover, they have nothing against "large stores which attract many people." Only 7 percent of residents in the center indicate the large stores as being something they would be most reluctant to live close to. It is presumably the noise from cars and buses they would be rid of; only a small minority seem to have anything against the pulsating hustle and bustle of pedestrians on the streets. We feel ourselves tempted to assert that the lively trading activity is itself a part of that atmosphere in Elsinore which, in turn, contributes to the high "satisfaction with residence" among those living in the center.

D. Arrangement of the Back Yards

The adaptation of back yards has been one of the big discussion points in the slum clearance plans, and we have in this study sought information about their present use, and desires with regard to how they might be arranged. The problem, though, is that there exist so many varying types of yards in the center of the town, such that in a study of this kind one can illustrate only the "back yard question" on very broad lines. Those residents with yards are far from using them as outside rooms; on the contrary. They are used as a place for bicycles, cars, and prams to stand in, a place to dry clothes, and so on. Asked why they don't use their back yards more, most people checked off the following replies: the yard is too dirty, too dull, and badly arranged. A clear difference can be detected, though, between those yards which people of the higher status group and those which the lower status groups have at their disposal. The lower status groups mention "not enough sun" as the most important reason for not using the yards more than they do.

With regard to replies to the question about how the back yard should be arranged, the most frequent wish is that it should be some type of garden. Seventy-nine percent would prefer that solution. The next most frequent wish is that there be a playground (41 percent). Despite the fact that around 40 percent of residents in the center have cars, only 5 percent would like the yards converted to parking lots.

If one takes these results as guidelines in the planning of reconstruction, it should be remembered that preferences are to some degree dependent upon factors like social status, age, and size of household. There are, for example, at present few families in the center with children—but it is not sure that this will be the case for those people who come to live in the flats after their restoration. That will depend, among other things, upon the size of the flats and the possibilities for economic subsidies.

E. Attitude Toward Conservational Slum Clearance

We have tried to take our bearings with regard to the residents' opinions about planned preservation in Elsinore. It is evident that residents, especially in the center of town, are positively disposed toward the preservation of the older part of town. In the center of town there is almost unanimity that "it is high time that some of the older houses were smartened up," and wide agreement that "the old houses in Elsinore are something really worthwhile to preserve." Replies to other questions indicate, though, that many believe that in some places there are "too many houses packed together in the center of Elsinore, and there should be a thinning out, especially in the back yards." On the other hand, residents tend to disagree with the sharper statement that "many of the old hovels should be pulled down to give place for modern houses." These attitudes can be taken as an indication that the large majority of residents can in principle accept the objectives embodied in the present reconstruction plans: a preservation of Elsinore's old houses, but demolition of those slums which have no historic value, together with an extensive clearing of the back yards. That does not mean that the municipality, when it presents plans for a particular block of flats to the residents and owners, will be met with nothing but sympathy and applause. One thing is to attach oneself in principle to an idea about reconstruction; another is to be faced with a concrete project, where one is required to offer one's own money. It is probably these problems which have emerged when, in questions about restoration, we have included economic considerations, for it is here that the positive attitudes yield somewhat. There are rather more who declare themselves in agreement than in disagreement with the statement: "The old houses should be retained if they can be repaired without costing too much." And those who agree and disagree balance each other with the statement: "If it becomes too expensive to live in the houses afterward, then I don't want any restoration where I live."

Up to now we have demonstrated an almost ideal confirmation of the planners' impressions, and an almost overwhelming support of the plans. Residents are most content with the older Elsinore environment, which they feel has a special atmosphere, and wish to retain the often tumultuous business and trade life in the center; they believe that the back yards should be arranged as a kind of outside living area and are almost more opposed to parking lots than "milieu-minded" planners.

But now, where we include the economic aspects, the picture begins—if not to change to the reverse—at least to reveal the hitches in carrying through the reconstruction. The key points are economy and the fate of residents in the town center while it is under reconstruction. It is here—in the concrete consequences for the individual citizen—that the most important practical problems will be centered, rather than in the detailed resolution of problems such as the placing of parking areas and arrangements for back yards, and it is undoubtedly here that the municipal authorities will meet with resistance, and that a negative attitude toward reconstruction will arise.

F. Rehousing and Economy

If one asks residents in the center of town whether they have plans to move, only 35 percent will reply "yes." If one asks where they would move, if they *had* to do so, 69 percent say that they will remain living "nearby" or another place in the center of Elsinore.

One can thus detect a widespread unwillingness to move, and a general desire to remain in the center of town in the event that moving became necessary. The younger age groups are, though, rather more willing to move and are more inclined to believe they would seek outside the center of town. Very few—12 percent—both from the center of town and from the control sample—would seek elsewhere than Elsinore.

If, in the accomplishment of reconstruction, the wishes of the residents are to be met, then our results imply that it is necessary to assure those residents who can't remain living where they are, *real* possibilities for other accommodation *in* the center of town. Even though some residents will not be affected, others will be required to move, either because their houses, with no historical value or a lack of necessary facilities, will be demolished, or because temporary housing is necessary during the work of reconstruction.

The question of real possibilities to remain is to a large degree an economic one. If residents are allocated flats in the renovated houses—which is possible at the stage where work begins on the second block—will they be capable of paying the higher rents which, in respect of the legally ensured subsidies, are required? Some 70 percent of residents in the town pay at present according to our information a rent of less than $60 per month, but the standards of the flats are at the same time rather low. According to the results from our study, residents in the center *could* pay about $90 for a "fully modernized flat in the vicinity," i.e., an average of about $45 more than at present. This is an average amount—there are some who could pay more, and some who can afford less. We do not believe, though, that the problems will *quantitatively* be so enormous. There are, in spite of everything, many who can remain where they are duing the restorations, and not all houses are being renovated to a degree that the expenses will be as great as new building. There should thus be reasonable chances that the majority of present residents could remain living in the town center through the present system of accommodation subsidies. But unless the municipality can in certain cases offer special subsidies, there are likely to be some groups of residents whose economic resources are too inadequate for them to accept a newly renovated flat.

G. Suggestions

Finally, we will try to step a little outside our roles as sociologists and put forward some suggestions. In the analyses we have tried to keep our own opinions in the background, but we will now forward some recommendations which we believe the results lead to. We hereby hope to indicate some otherwise unnoticed possibilities with the proposed reconstruction in Elsinore—and perhaps other places—and will in this way try to contribute to thorough discussion of reconstruction.

From the observation that 35 percent of residents in the center of town who wish to remain also have the desire to own their flat, here is perhaps an unnoticed financing possibility. The municipal authorities could buy the houses, and after they are renovated sell them to those residents who wish to buy. This way would possibly also avoid resistance to reconstruction, which is rooted in the unwillingness among present owners to pay the expenses involved in reconstruction. The resources for the municipality will thus derive from the later sale, while the money saved on that account could perhaps be used for a special subsidy fund for those residents who are badly placed with regard to paying the higher rents in the newly restored flats.

There are many problems involved in such a proposal, and there a number of legal and local political barriers. One of the most important problems in a too extensive use of flat ownership is the risk of speculation, wherein those groups who have the most modest economic means, who should especially be secured a place in the center of town, become neglected. But there are some alternatives or supplements to the solution of flat ownership; one could, for example, aim at cooperatively owned or municipally owned flats.

From our results, it is possible only to present broad generalizations of the desires of residents with regard to the arrangement of back yards, and there is much ground to cover before the general desire for "a form of garden arrangement" and "playgrounds" can be converted to the detailed resolution for the yard attached to a particular block of flats. The best method to obtain that development of a yard which meets the needs of residents as far as possible is, in our opinion, to involve residents in the decision-making process. The municipal authorities should consider delaying the preparation of detailed plans, pulling down, etc., until the future residents are installed. The details for a particular block could then be undertaken by a committee of residents, aided by municipal technicians and architects. One could, then, renovate according to "the principle of the unfinished solution."

We cannot by questioning residents more thoroughly than in the present study come to a better solution, since there—in varying degrees according to the blocks—will occur a change of residents in connection with the restoration work. Even the most careful solution of the yard arrangements, made by a third party (the municipality)

with support from various experts—architects, sociologists, historians, and psychologists—would, in our opinion, be unable to compete with a solution that the residents themselves in cooperation could produce. A "package" solution served to residents would from the start be unable to create that basis for cooperation and neighborliness, which a more independent solution by residents could. We do not feel ourselves competent to delve seriously into the local political problems and the accompanying conflicts of interest between tenants, owners, and business people.

Our suggestions, however, cannot avoid implications which touch on these different interests, so we have—somewhat reluctantly—involved ourselves in the political discussions in Elsinore. There exist conflicts of interests between the house owners, who perhaps do not themselves live in the blocks, and tenants, who can surely put forward their ideas, but where the implementation of suggestions are dependent upon the owners' disposition. There is therefore a need to aim at solutions which, as far as possible, will avoid these conflict issues.

Many residents would like to own their flats, and we have therefore suggested that the possibilities for this be made more open. We will at the same time link this with the previous suggestion. To obtain a more uniform conflict-free composition of residents in the blocks one could propose that the flats in the future obtain the status partly of owned flats, but (since an extensive application of this solution would injure the chances for the economically weak to remain in the center of town) also, and perhaps primarily, of cooperatively owned or municipally owned flats. However, as mentioned, we are cautious in coming into a debate on ownership. We have, though, felt induced to it, because our recommendation on resident or block committees would otherwise be like a wisp of smoke in the air.

17

The Jordaan and Haarlem Neighborhoods in Amsterdam: Planning for the Future of a Historic Neighborhood

Hans F. D. Davidson

Plan of Amsterdam, 1793. The Jordaan district lies on the right-hand side (west). From *Le Guide d'Amsterdam,* chez J. Covens et Fils. Photo by Hertziana.

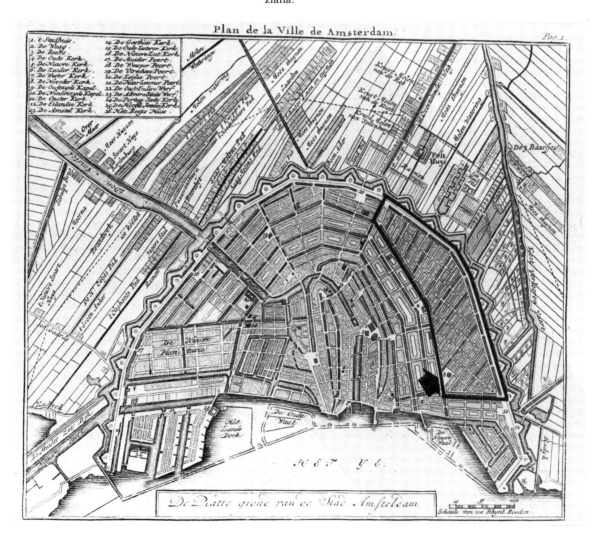

Aerial view of the northern part of the quarter. Courtesy of Department of Public Works, Municipality of Amsterdam, City Planning Section.

Schematic model of the second rehabilitation plan showing cleaned-out courtyards and occasional infill buildings. Courtesy of Department of Public Works, Municipality of Amsterdam, City Planning Section.

Street life in old Jordaan. Photo courtesy of Bureau Monumentenzorg, Amsterdam, Artica Press.

Street life in present-day Jordaan. Photo courtesy of Bureau Monumentenzorg, Amsterdam, Artica Press.

A clothing shop for the pioneers

A tourist shop

A poster announcing a folk-loristic performance, enshrining the dances of the lost working class

The curtainless windows of the newcomers, decorated with plants and other objects

A schoolyard for the children of the new families

A dilapidated section of the
Jordaan

An older inhabitant gazes out
of her window. Note the formal
lace curtains and the closed
appearance.

A traditional shop selling
tasseled and ornamental lamps
for the older families

Older inhabitants gossip in
front of a pioneering slogan,
"Workers of the world unite."
Photo courtesy of *Jordaan krant*,
the community newsheet.

All the facades of the Jordaan are being measured and drawn. Courtesy of Bureau Monumentenzorg, Amsterdam.

Restored courtyard in the Jordaan. The district, of 95 hectares, has over 800 listed buildings dating from the first half of the seventeenth century. Between 1953 and 1973, 330 buildings have been restored including a number of characteristic small courtyards. From reprint of "Report on Heritage Year," *The Architects' Journal* (Britain), February 25, 1976, p. 385.

New subsidized housing by
Aldo van Eyck and associate

Introduction

Amsterdam celebrated in 1975 its seven hundredth anniversary, but seeing the bad condition of large parts of the prewar city there was little reason to celebrate.

The nineteenth-century neighborhoods are relatively in the worst condition. But the situation in the inner city is also alarming.

The inner city has a great historic value, with its famous half-circle-formed canal plan and its over 7,000 registered monuments; with its 900 hectares, one of the largest historic inner cities of Europe.

It is precisely this large size and its valuable total urban structure that restricts the possibilities of planning for the future. Distances are too far to walk. Accessibility is a condition of life for a city, but traffic measures nearly always break into the historic structure.

The Jordaan Neighborhood

The Jordaan neighborhood is situated on the west side of the Amsterdam inner city.

This area came within the ramparts during the expansion of the city in 1612.

In contrast with the famous three-canal sector, the Jordaan was built up without any plan. The farmland was traversed by walks and ditches, along which people simply started to build. Walks became streets and ditches became canals. The ground was owned by some important men. It is clear that the same land speculation practices in evidence today were employed in those days as well. In contrast with the three-canal sector, speculative enterprise in the Jordaan resulted in small blocks and premises.

The houses were built mainly for servants of the rich merchants living along canals, for sailors, and for the large number of immigrants who came to Amsterdam.

The population statistics of the area are rather spectacular. We know that during the middle of the nineteenth century there were 54,000 people.

During the industrial revolution this number increased rapidly, to a maximum of 83,000 in 1890.

After that, the number of inhabitants of the Jordaan decreased because more space became available outside the inner city, in the so called nineteenth-century extensions.

At present there are more than 20,000 people in this area of seventy hectares. A little more than half of the existing floor space is used for dwellings: there are 126 dwellings per hectare, which is a rather high density. The population in 1975 consisted of a 50:50 mix of original working-class inhabitants, many of whom are elderly, and middle-income inhabitants, newcomers, artists, students.

The other half of the floor space is occupied mainly by small industries which became established in the Jordaan when large numbers of inhabitants moved from the area. Both large population at the end of the nineteenth century and the establishing of small industries thereafter have left their marks on the neighborhood. The courtyards were filled in with sheds. The businesses did not care much about the inhabitants. A conflict situation came into existence.

In the small houses, mostly economically weak businesses were attracted by the low cost of the buildings. When a business grew, it was forced to move away because of a lack of space for expansion within the area. Only a small number managed to stay in the newly built buildings, which are much too big for the scale of the area.

The intensive use of the area is expressed by a tremendous deterioration through lack of maintenance. Nearly half of the buildings are dilapidated.

Planning Process

In the twenties the housing department already had plans to improve parts of the area, but until very recently it has not been possible to get a plan accepted by all the different groups. In 1969 a plan that provided traffic corridors, parking garages, open space, and space for low-cost housing programs was turned down, mainly because it would have left little of the historic character of the neighborhood. The new attitude to planning of a new generation of planners and a newly elected city administration made it possible, after fifty years of planning, to establish a legal zoning plan for the Jordaan neighborhood.

What are the purposes of this plan?

As mentioned before there are still 20,000 people in the Jordaan.

With this population, it has the largest concentration of housing in the inner city and the city administration wants to keep it that way. We want to keep it possible for people to live in the inner city. To stimulate housing in this area a lot of improvements are necessary.

Not only the houses should be improved but, above all, the urban services and the facilities.

This plan reflects the present trend toward preserving old values, a feature found in plans for other cities. The old pattern of streets and canals will be kept. There will be no improvements for traffic and parking. The streets are too narrow, and large parking garages will not fit into the small scale of the area, a nearly insoluble problem for which we must find solutions.

In the future it will be tackled when we institute a system of parking regulations designed to prohibit cars not belonging in the area.

The necessary (green) open space will be created by cleaning the courtyards of sheds. Only in some places will we be able (under the plan regulation) to make small squares or other open spaces by demolishing some buildings.

While the number of inhabitants decreased, the number and quality of facilities also decreased, especially social and cultural facilities. It is of major importance, at the start of the renewal process, to keep up the facilities and bring them gradually to a higher standard, in order to attract those groups of inhabitants which are leaving the area and the city now. We have the intention of making the neighborhood suitable for families with children. The diversity of dwellings should be attuned to that purpose.

The average size now is 2.2 rooms per dwelling (in Amsterdam as a whole, 3.3). The zoning plan dictates a diversity of dwellings: 50 percent 3-room, 25 percent larger, and 25 percent 2-room apartments.

Larger dwellings require more space, but space is already in short supply. Increasing the floor space for housing and keeping the number of dwellings on the same standard means that floor space used by businesses will decrease. From the point of view of urban planning, it is necessary to replace some businesses, especially those which suffer from and those which cause congestion of traffic.

There are many shops in the neighborhood, possibly more than necessary.

They serve a larger area, thereby fulfilling a real city function, considering, for example, the large number of boutiques of different kinds. The shops are concentrated (and will be, according to the plan) along the narrow north-south streets which are important for pedestrian and bicycle traffic within the neighborhood. We are striving to make these streets free of motor traffic.

Description of the Plan

For purposes of formulating a zoning plan, we have divided the area into three parts; the North Jordaan, the South Jordaan, and the Marnixstraat. The North Jordaan takes up about five-eighths of the area. Here are relatively more dwellings than in the other parts; it is a shade better preserved than the other two, and there are relatively more monuments. The urban structure of a small scale fits better here for dwellings than for other functions. It is clear that the zoning for this part is housing.

The South Jordaan is about one-eighth of the area. Here are more businesses (60 percent), which have affected the scale of the neighborhood negatively. The zoning plan dictates, in addition to dwellings, businesses and offices because it is situated close to the business center of the city. It is hard to make traffic improvements in this area, so industrial businesses cannot be permitted.

The Marnixstraat is a long, narrow area, one-fourth of the whole neighborhood and of no historical value. Most of the buildings are in very bad repair, and there are some big public facilities located in the Marnixstraat, like the main police station, the drama school, and some institutions for elderly people. In a time of shortage of dwellings even the dilapidated houses of no historical value will remain as they are.

The plan is not yet in final form. Some blocks in the plan are grouped together. The frontage lines around these block-groups may not be changed, so the main urban structure of the neighborhood is fixed.

Inside the block groups small changes of frontage lines are allowed. On the map are indications for the specification of the block groups, including maximum and minimum space to build up, and permitted uses.

In the plan further guidelines are given on specifications.

Implementation

Initiatives from the city toward implementation will be limited. The city owns little land and only a few houses for elderly people.

Having adopted the zoning plan it is now possible, after many years of uncertainty, to examine a building proposal for conformance with provisions in the zoning plan.

Private initiatives can be the start of the implementation of plans for a block. As the block groups are relatively small, it is easier to detail the plans with the participation of those who are interested: inhabitants, workers, and owners. As long as block plans are not implemented everything can remain as it is. Another important advantage of having a zoning plan is that there is a basis for land acquisition by the city. One of the main problems of the preservation process is that the land is cut into small lots, all owned by different people, most of them not able to maintain their property.

The central authorities created facilities to appoint private project leaders in order to coordinate preservation activities. The city authorities set up project groups for several neighborhoods to streamline the process of urban renewal. These project groups are staffed by city officials from all departments involved in urban renewal.

The largest problem is the question of how to finance the whole process, especially when the aim is to maintain low rents of preserved dwellings at a level suitable for low-income groups living there now. Without subsidization by the central government, such a goal is not attainable.

Costs are high not only because the area is close to the center, but also because building costs have greatly increased. Relocating businesses will increase costs as well. The city is responsible for acquisition and vacancy.

After that, sites are leased to housing corporations if the site is large, or to private builders who initiate construction of new dwellings. Building on open sites between existing premises is 3 percent more expensive than normal house preservation. Even more expensive is preservation or reconstruction of monuments. A quarter of the total number of buildings in the area are monuments. The costs of these are three to four times as high as normal new construction. Recent subsidy programs, both from the Ministry of Cultural Affairs and from the Ministry of Housing and Planning, cover up to 68 percent of the building costs.

Unfortunately this is still not adequate for public housing.

The Haarlemmerbuurt (Haarlem Neighborhood): Planning with People

The Haarlemmerbuurt is a long, thin area at the northwest side of the inner city of Amsterdam. It has a population of lower- and middle-class people.

It was built between the end of the seventeeth century and the nineteenth century on both sides of the old connection road to the city of Haarlem that leads over a dike. Small businesses and shops were established along this road. The street that came into existence is still an important shopping center for a larger area, although it is declining in importance.

In the south, the area is bordered by the Brouwersgracht, a canal with large historic warehouses; in the north, by a railway viaduct.

At one place you can go underneath the viaduct and arrive on the "western isles," a picturesque area near the harbor.

In the sixties a number of blocks were demolished for a highway from the center of the city to the west. These blocks consisted of old nineteenth-century dwellings and small businesses. The open space that came into existence this way was hardly used for many years, because the points of view about the size of the road changed several times, and there were no decisions made.

One can imagine what a negative influence this kind of indecision has had on life in a neighborhood. Because of the demolition the number of inhabitants decreased enormously, and times became hard for the shops.

During the period of preparing for highway construction, there was some contact between people from the neighborhood and city officials. These talks were especially meant to reduce the inconvenience during the building process as much as possible. The neighborhood became really active when rumors arose that a number of buildings, consisting of a big church and some schools, were in danger of falling into the hands of speculators.

The alderman for public works and city planning was requested to visit the neighborhood.

There a large meeting was held in the already mentioned church and the population succeeded in obtaining a declaration from the administration that a plan for the neighborhood would be prepared. For the city administration this is a legal way to refuse building permits, in order to prevent undesirable development.

The consultations between citizens and officials increased, with the goal of formulating a list of principles on the future development of the neighborhood.

During a process (one evening a week), which lasted nine months, a group of citizens and a number of planning officials met together. The officials explained which items were important to formulate as a starting point. Discussions were held and the officials wrote proposals for a report. These proposals were discussed and where necessary changed until everybody agreed. Once, when officials and inhabitants could not come to an agreement on a point, they decided both points of view would be mentioned in the report.

Halfway and at the end of the process, all inhabitants were invited to general hearings to talk about the draft report, which was sent to every address in the neighborhood. After the second hearing the director of the planning department sent the report of principles for commentary to all departments involved in urban renewal. Finally the report, the minutes of both hearings, and all the commentaries were sent to the city administration.

It is now up to the administration to formulate its policy in its own report, based on the papers it received. It will offer its report to the city council for establishing the policy for the zoning plan.

Addendum

The following is an extract from a 1970 report on Urban Renewal in Amsterdam by the Planning Department which fills out the context of the neighborhood case studies.

The present urban condition of Amsterdam is that both the old part of the City and the nineteenth century area are decaying and that there is urgent need for basic renewal. While many Amsterdammers are living with the worsening conditions, they see only demolition, vacant sites, and no new dwellings. Therefore, the emphasis of urban renewal in Amsterdam must be on housing (slum clearance, new construction, housing rehabilitation, and relocation) and on the improvements of the residential environment (public transport, social-cultural facilities, play areas, parking, and other traffic measures).

The basic principle of urban renewal must be a focusing of attention on those people most affected by urban renewal and who, coincidentally, are usually those least economically self-sufficient. Three consequences of this policy are that first, the supply of housing constructed after World War II must be made available to lower-income groups. Second, the pre-War housing supply must be improved to meet present housing standards. Third, the recent new construction in Amsterdam and the surrounding region must contribute to the solution of lower income group housing problems.

It appears that in the nineteenth-century area, 30 percent of heads of households have an income of less than $2,700 annually. The average annual income is not more than $3,300. Assuming that a reasonable rent-to-income proportion is 17 percent of the gross family income, this results in a monthly rent of $45 at the $3,300 income level. Only a small number of nineteenth-century area residents are able to pay a monthly rent of $70 which would reflect an annual income of $4,700. Furthermore, such rent levels do not cover the

costs of new construction or even the costs of dwelling rehabilitation. Consequently, the housing policy for Amsterdam
must be based on a willingness to share the financial
burden. This also means that relocating low income people
requires access to the portion of the Amsterdam housing
supply which has previously been unavailable to low-
income people.

Such a financial policy will require large public expenditures. As an indication of magnitude, a new dwelling in
the Bijlmermeer, in 1971, receives a subsidy from the National Government of approximately $70 per month (not
including personal rent subsidy). In spite of this subsidy,
the rent, including the cost of parking, for the newest dwellings is approximately $150. Thus to lower the rent to $70,
the Government subsidy would have to be doubled. For new
construction in the built-up portion of the City, the Government subsidy would have to be even higher to achieve
comparable rent levels. Therefore, it is anticipated that the
proposed financial policy will require that 80 to 90 percent
of the total project costs must be underwritten through
annual but gradually reduced subsidies, or through a lump
sum payment from public funds.

Amsterdam alone cannot solve its problems associated
with urban renewal. Substantial support is needed from the
National Government, amounting to millions of dollars for
many years. Only with such assistance will Amsterdam be
able to extricate itself from the present crisis of decay. The
measures necessary for urban renewal include a multiyear
financial and legal plan to be underwritten and executed by
both the Amsterdam and National Governments. Since it is
unlikely that such measures will be available soon, and
since Amsterdam cannot further delay a response to press-
ing conditions, the City must immediately prepare a policy
for the short term that will be later compatible with the
policy to be prepared for the long term.

There is concern that policy intended to improve the living environment in the inner City and the nineteenth century area is in conflict with policy intended to maximize the
development opportunities for the economic vitality of
the City. Such concern does not appear justified when
measured against the effects of a housing shortage and bad
living conditions which erode the economic vitality of a
healthy society. In fact, these two policies are complementary since it will become increasingly necessary to solve
the housing shortage problem in order to strengthen the
economic functioning of Amsterdam. The central feature of
a solution must be the rapid increase in the housing supply
of standard, inexpensive dwellings for Amsterdammers, in

both the City and the region. To improve the environment
in Amsterdam, more development land is required, a
commodity no longer available in the City. It must be
recognized, however, that if the creation of urban settlements outside Amsterdam is not to endanger the existence
of the City, emphasis must also be placed in the quality of
life in the nineteenth century and older areas. This is the
task of urban renewal, for which both the general public
and the Government of Amsterdam must exert themselves
for many years.

Considerations for the Urban Renewal Program during the Next Few Years

In the 1969 report on urban renewal (*Stadsvernieuwing: De
Voorbereiding*), an attempt was made to outline the extent of
urban renewal necessary and to suggest a number of alternative approaches. In that report it was pointed out that
urban renewal cannot solely consist of total demolition
and reconstruction but instead of differentiated group of
renewal measures would be necessary to retain the livability of the City. Since that first Report, further insight
into the social, financial, and legal aspects of the renewal
process has been acquired, making it now possible to state
with certainty that reconstruction will play only a modest
role in the total range of renewal measures in the near
future. Furthermore, it is expected that in the long run during which larger scale reconstruction will occur, the process
of demolition and rebuilding of a given neighborhood will
be a process of many years, so as to maintain the existing
character of the neighborhood. This renewal approach,
therefore, is based on a desire to overlap preservation and
renewal. In general attention will be focused during the
next few years on improving the existing areas rather than
their complete reconstruction. Only in those places where
demolition and reconstruction can no longer be avoided will
these actions occur.

In preparing a short-term program, three factors play an
important role:
—the local conditions in each area of the City;
—the physical and economic feasibility of carrying out
improvement measures in a given area;
—the necessity for making the short-term improvement
measures compatible with the long-term renewal goals.

In assessing the urgency of deteriorated conditions in
a neighborhood, consideration is given to the degree of
deterioration; the quality of dwellings (size, availability of

kitchen and toilet, etc.); and, the quality of the surrounding environment (street capacity and condition, interior court-yard conditions, parking, etc.). The opportunities for carry-ing out reconstruction and rehabilitation in the short run are limited by the availability of land, financial resources, and the quality and quantity of alternative residential and business relocation space. For conservation and minor dwelling improvements, the spatial and architectural limitations are the major considerations.

An additional consideration to be made in carrying out renewal measures is the functional changes which are occurring. The population of Amsterdam has declined sharply in the last twelve years, from 872,500 in 1959 to 820,400 on January 1, 1971. In more recent years the annual decline has been about 10,000. This decline occurs mainly as a result of the thinning out of older parts of the City. The population characteristics are changing in these areas to an inadequate mixture of family types. Those in age groups 35 to 55 and 0 to 15 (the families with children) are leaving, as are those with medium and high incomes. Those who stay tend to be the elderly; single people; small, newly formed families; and, those with low incomes. This out-migration is eroding the functioning of the City. Further complicating the situation is that, in the older areas especially, the consequences of social and economic changes are absorbed only with difficulty. Constantly changing social needs and insights have led to great changes in living standards. These are expressed in an increasing spatial need per inhabitant, as for example demands for higher quality in dwellings with respect to floor area, space divi-sion, plumbing; higher standards for small businesses, industry and traffic; increasing needs for recreation (parks, swimming pools, clubs and meeting rooms, etc.); improve-ment of educational facilities; increasing standards in social services. The older areas of the City in particular lack proper facilities. The dwellings are old, the service levels are low, and accessibility within neighborhoods declines daily.

The consideration and tendencies identified above suggest the following priorities for an urban renewal program:
—Conservation, rehabilitation and renewal of the housing stock and residential neighborhoods;
—The functioning of the City as a whole (e.g., improve-ments in public transportation);
—Improvement of service levels (recreation, education, health, etc.).

These priorities must be translated into short- and long-term programs.

Editor's Postscript

A visit to the Jordaan in the summer of 1978 amplified Hans Davidson's paper. The tourist guide to the city tells nostalgically of the rich history of the Jordaan as a working-class quarter "when the women of the Jordaan used to dance around the street organ, their flannel skirts flying, while the men in their red neckerchiefs, their corduroy trousers, and their velveteen slippers, sauntered along to their favorite pubs, when their poverty was made bearable by the solidarity that existed between the Jordaaners who then, as now, all called each other 'uncle' and 'aunt'."

But this is not what one sees today. The dominant and visible culture is that of the young pioneers, who people the streets, ride their motorbikes, and strip away the tradi-tional lace curtains from their windows to reveal masses of indoor plants, creepers, and book-lined walls. One couple lives in a storefront with the whole living room as a stage-set display. Many sit out at the sidewalk bars. The city has placed concrete planters along some of the narrow streets, and brick cross-walks to slow traffic. It is not until one penetrates deeper into the back streets and northern part of the quarter that one really discovers the old inhabitants. Behind lace curtains, tasseled pink lamps, and pots of flowers, they are nearly invisible. In the darkness of a summer evening a few of the women still talk from window to window, or silently watch this street life. The few bars in this part are obscured by heavy curtains. The clack of billiard balls and the sounds of conventional music are the only clues to their presence. Traditional food, radio, lamp shops with standard advertising signs still remain, unlike the chic boutiques to be found in the racier sections of the quarter.

It seems that the working class have withdrawn from the streets. Contrary to conventional wisdom, it is they who seek privacy, while the young pioneers are gregarious, using the street as a social arena. It is the latter who are active in fighting the planners who wish to change the quarter, and it is they who penetrate and infiltrate with eager curiosity, just as in Raban's Islington, the farthest strongholds of the old working class. It is said that the working class tolerate their presence. Only the old working class are left now, for the young who wish to bring up families depart for the suburbs.

What is also striking, in talks with a conservation planner, is that neither the young pioneers nor the old working class particularly desire large family apartments. Yet this is what the planners are proposing in the interests of achieving a "balanced" community. Why? This is the surviving ideology of the planning profession. This is what they know how to do.

Two groups of planners now operate in the quarter. Those striving for balance are looking for sites on which to build new housing. They plan to clean out the back yards and enlarge sites, but these will be where the private rehabilitation of the young pioneers has not taken place. And here such a policy may threaten the networks of activities that still survive in the working-class sections. The second group of planners are from the monuments conservation section of the city administration. Since one-quarter of the buildings (800) are designated as monuments, the conservation planners, who have the task of preserving these buildings, are often in conflict with the first group of planners, and they too have met some public opposition, having been accused of raising rents through restoration. In a study of rental changes they claim, however, that in 75 percent of the restorations which are partial, rents and residents remain the same after restoration. In the other 25 percent which are nearly total restorations, rents go up and the population does change.

Besides the official planning agencies, private nonprofit rehabilitation and social service organizations now exist. But whether these efforts to improve the physical quality of the Jordaan will succeed in retaining the present mix of population remains a question.

18 Conflict and Participation in a Renewal Process in Stockholm: Birka

Thomas Miller and Boel Ahlgren

Birka: aerial view. From
Omradesplan for Birkastan.

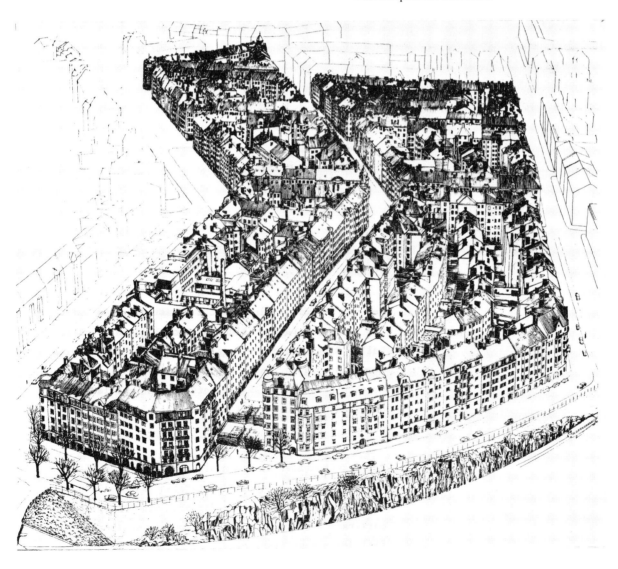

Birka: rehabilitation proposals
for courtyards. From
Omradesplan for Birkastan.

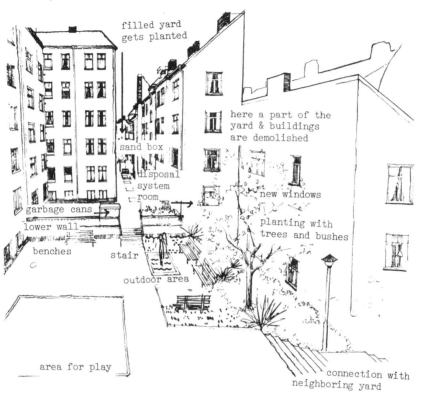

filled yard
gets planted

here a part of the
yard & buildings
are demolished

sand box

disposal
system
room

new windows

garbage cans

planting with
trees and bushes

lower wall

benches   stair

outdoor area

area for play

connection with
neighboring yard

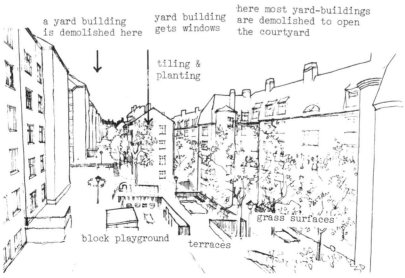

a yard building
is demolished here

yard building
gets windows

here most yard-buildings
are demolished to open
the courtyard

tiling &
planting

block playground   terraces

grass surfaces

The Birka area in the Stockholm inner city is in the process of being renewed. In the autumn of 1974, the Planning Board presented a Neighborhood Renewal Plan for Birka. The plan was to be the subject of extensive consultations with residents and landlords in the area.

Consultations of this type and magnitude are a new element in Swedish town planning. This paper attempts to evaluate the consultations in the context of the interaction of the various interests involved in the planning process.

1. Development Trends in Stockholm

The Greater Stockholm Region has 1.5 million inhabitants. It grew rapidly during the period of swift economic growth and structural change of the fifties and sixties. The effective demand for housing was enormous because of migration to the region and the increased purchasing power of the working class and the middle class. The government's housing policies were aimed at building as many dwellings as possible at this time. Mortgage funds were channeled toward large-scale housing projects.

With investment interest concentrated on mass production of new housing, inner-city neighborhoods were left to deteriorate. Other factors contributing to this deterioration were

1. "Building rights" plans which required demolition of existing buildings
2. Rent control (since 1942)
3. Construction bans in central business district (CBD) fringe areas
4. Lack of subsidized mortgage financing for renovation.

Landlords were neither legally nor economically forced to maintain their properties. In these times of acute housing shortage, virtually all dwellings could be let out with or without repairs, and real estate prices were not affected adversely by lack of maintenance.

In 1970—to the wonder and dismay of the planners—the region's population stopped increasing. Migration to the region is now plus or minus zero, and newly built multi-family residential areas in the suburbs have huge vacancy rates. The number of housing starts in the Stockholm region is less than half of what it was five or six years ago. The town of Stockholm itself has about 670,000 inhabitants, having diminished from a high of 800,000 in 1960.

There are very few vacant flats within Stockholm proper. The shrinking population is the result of rapidly rising dwelling space standards, an aging population, and the takeover of residential units by commercial uses. The inner city, where four-fifths of all dwellings have two rooms or less shows this tendency most clearly. Population figures are down from a peak of 450,000 in 1950 to 240,000 today and still falling.

This negative population trend and the fact that 25 to 30 percent of the inner-city population are over 67 years of age are catastrophic for the municipal finances. The problem for the town of Stockholm was to turn the tide of fleeing taxpayers and to respond to the increasing pressure from investors who now focused their attention on the renewal market in the inner-city.

2. Birka, a Residential Neighborhood in the Stockholm Inner City

Birka is a residential neighborhood in the Stockholm inner city with 6,000 inhabitants. It lies less than a mile from the center of the town with underground, suburban railway, and bus connections to all points in the metropolitan area. It is, however, surrounded on all sides by heavily traveled roads and railroad tracks. Access to open space and recreational areas is, therefore, not good.

The neighborhood comprises nine blocks. It has a uniform character because virtually all of the buildings were erected during a short span of years shortly after the turn of the century. The buildings are five- to six-story blocks with small back courts and rather large back houses. Many of the buildings were designed in Art Nouveau style by the same architectural firm. The facades are plastered and in some cases richly ornamented.

The buildings fronting on the street have a uniform height of 19.5 meters (five to six stories), which was stipulated as maximum in the Building Code of 1874. The buildings facing on the court vary in height from four to five stories, and the courtyards are often cramped and dark.

Over 60 percent of the 140 properties are owned by private landlords or developers, a third are cooperatively owned and seven are owned by the municipality. The technical standard and standard of maintenance of many of the 4,600 dwellings is low. About 40 percent lack central heating and three-fourths lack bathing facilities. The flats are small: only one in five is larger than two rooms.

The population in Birka has diminished steadily over the years. In 1920 about 18,000 people lived here. At that time the one- and two-room flats were inhabited by working-class families with several children and often with boarders. In the few large apartments, upper-middle-class families lived with their servants.

Today only a third as many people inhabit the Birka area. There is a predominance of elderly people and young adults. Sixty percent of the residents live alone, and there are few children. Overcrowding is certainly not a problem here today. The predominantly working-class population of the old Birka has become more mixed. The most numerous group in the neighborhood today is the middle class. Approximately 28 percent of the population are professionals, 52 percent white collar workers, and 28 percent blue collar workers. But incomes are not high. There are a large number of pensioners (22 percent) and students (11 percent) in the area. Over one-third have incomes under $5,000, over a third from $5,000 to $10,000, and under a third have incomes over $10,000. There is no cohesive foreign ethnic group in the area, but the percentage of immigrants is slightly higher than the average for the inner city. They are often concentrated in the least modern, most run-down buildings.

About 1,250 people are employed in the area—25 percent in manufacturing (a small food-processing plant, small workshops), 25 percent in retail trade (retail and other specialty shops), and the rest in office work, municipal service, and warehousing, etc.

A recent study done by the municipality showed that nine of ten residents of Birka are quite satisfied with their neighborhood. About one-third of the residents are, however, dissatisfied with their dwellings. Those who are dissatisfied complain about low standards or that the flats are too small. Even though the residents of Birka are on the whole positive towards their neighborhood, many complain of the lack of adequate open space, parks and playgrounds. For certain sections of the neighborhood, traffic disturbance is a problem.

Attitudes toward Birka and similar high-density inner-city areas have changed radically over the years. Criticism was leveled at the area even while it was still under construction, and Birka was the last neighborhood in Stockholm to be built with so few restraints on the developers.

Influenced by functionalist dogmas, planners and architects of the thirties were unanimous in condemning Birka and similar inner-city neighborhoods. As late as the early sixties it was thought to be self-evident that Birka should be razed and replaced by new housing. During the late thirties and early forties, plans were adopted for each block in Birka, specifying the height, bulk, and placement of buildings.

Building permits cannot be granted for the renovation of buildings which do not conform to the adopted plans. The plans had the effect, therefore, of stopping the modernization which had been taking place during the twenties and thirties. Many of the buildings were allowed to fall into disrepair. A fortunate result of this neglect is that the area has retained its character.

3. The Planning Situation Today

Why have the municipality and private developers suddenly become so interested in Birka? During the fifties and sixties, private developers had no difficulty in finding profitable new construction to invest in. Even if they had wanted to move into the renewal field, it would have been difficult. Residential mortgaging was concentrated on new, large-scale construction. It was difficult to find funding for renewal projects, and existing plans often ruled out renovation of the old buildings.

The fall-off in new construction has radically changed that situation. The new Housing Renewal Law provides funding and even incentives for renewal, and the Municipality has made necessary changes in the existing plans to allow renovation (see Appendix on legislation).

In 1970 the Board of Real Estate and the Planning Board started work on a new Housing Renewal Program which stipulated stepping up the pace of renewal and providing aid and incentives to landlords and developers for renovation.

A high rate of renewal activity means that the municipal authorities would be swamped with applications from property owners for building permits, for arranging government loans and for other aid. The authorities were in need of uniform policy statements for the various areas against which the individual applications could be tried. For this reason, the program called for the preparation of neighborhood renewal plans and "building plans" for each block to guide renewal activities.

In the late sixties, just before the housing construction market hit bottom, several private developers began to show an interest in Birka. Sixty percent of the approximately 100 privately owned properties in Birka changed hands after 1970. Many of them were sold two or three times, and around 70 percent bought by developers.

Studies of the Birka area were begun in 1972 and in 1974 the Department of Real Estate asked the Planning Department to prepare a neighborhood renewal plan for Birka. Such a plan has no direct legal implications, but it is used by the municipality as a basis for decisions on granting building permits and making building plans.

The Birka area became a pilot project for comprehensive renewal where not only the individual buildings, but also the traffic environment, open spaces, and municipal services would be improved. The reason for choosing Birka was the large concentration of substandard housing and the fact that developers were buying up one property after the other. The municipality did not want to lose the initiative.

4. Conflicts

The conflicts of interest which exist in all planning situations are often quite pronounced in the case of large-scale renewal. The buildings, the neighborhood, the social structure exist and are a part of peoples' lives. The questions involved are not abstract or hard to grasp, as in many other planning situations. They concern how much rent people will have to pay, whether or not someone's home will be demolished, etc.

The major source of conflict in the renewal of the Birka area is the clash between the desires of the local residents, market forces, and institutional policies. The local residents' goals are to remain in the neighborhood, maintain low rental levels, and have a say in the management of their own dwellings.

The developers' objective interest in a high rate of return on investments manifests itself in a desire to maximize the extent of renovation. They are encouraged in this by national housing and rental legislation and by municipal renewal policies.

The role of the municipality is ambiguous. Their avowed purpose is to direct renewal activity, but they are dependent on the private landlords and developers for effectuating renewal. The municipal goals for renewal are in some respects contradictory. On the one hand they say that residents should be able to remain in their accustomed environments, but on the other hand they want to change the population makeup of renewal areas. (The aging population should be made more "balanced" demographically in order that the tax base be increased and better use be made of existing facilities in the area.)

The municipality's desire to change the characteristics of the population is manifested in the Renewal Guidelines, which call for the merging of small flats to make larger ones. It is stipulated that after renovation a building should have 25 percent small units (one or two rooms), 50 percent medium-sized units (three rooms), and 25 percent large units (four rooms or more). This norm has long been used in the planning of new suburban areas in Stockholm, but it has not yet been applied extensively in renewal areas. At present about 80 percent of the dwelling units in Birka are one- or two-room flats. If the "25–50–25" guidelines are applied, many of these will disappear with renewal, and according to a survey, only 3 to 4 percent could afford to remain in the larger, more expensive renovated units.

5. The Planning Consultations

In the autumn of 1974, the City of Stockholm invited the Birka residents, the landlords, the Tenants' Association and other local groups to participate in discussions about the proposed Neighborhood Renewal Plan. This kind of consultation is something new in Swedish planning.

It is the result of increasing public pressure in matters of planning and the environment, and also a realistic assessment by the municipal authorities of the need for negotiations with the parties in a planning situation. Where ownership is extremely diversified, as in the Birka area, some kind of planning consultations are inevitable in order to avoid costly and time-consuming appeals.

The Neighborhood Renewal Plan can be seen as a policy statement concerning building renovation and renewal of the total environment. It is used as a basis for discussions with the parties involved in the renewal process and for preparing building plans for the individual blocks. The plan deals with the buildings, the courtyards, the traffic system and parking facilities, and the distribution of public services in the area.

The major proposals of the plan are

1. That certain buildings be demolished primarily to improve the courtyards by allowing more sunlight to penetrate and giving space for common play areas
2. That all the courtyards in a block be merged so that each building would have direct access to common areas within the block
3. That a large number of trees be planted
4. That certain streets be closed in order to avoid through traffic in the area.

The Planning Consultations were not supposed to deal with questions related to the renovation of individual buildings. These questions were instead to be the subject of negotiations between the Board of Real Estate and the property owners in question. The purpose of the planning

consultations was said to be "to get a clearer picture of the desires and priorities of those concerned about the renewal of the Birka area, to give the parties concerned the opportunity to take part in the planning of their neighborhood."

The Consultations were to be organized around block committees in each of the nine blocks where the landlords and representatives for the tenants could discuss questions of principal nature as well as concrete matters such as improvement of the courtyards, etc.

Each block committee was to elect four representatives to a coordinating committee where the Landlords' Association, the Tenants' Association, local chapters of the political parties, and other associations would be represented. Planning Department staff were to take part in the discussions in the coordinating committee.

The Planning Board rented a shopfront in Birka where the plan could be exhibited and meetings could be held. Planning Board staff were to be stationed in the shopfront to answer questions about renewal.

To inaugurate the Planning Consultations and inform about the Neighborhood Renewal Plan, the Planning Board held a public meeting in a rented hall in Birka. About 400 people were expected and 1,300 showed up (approximately 25 percent of the adults in the area).

6. Results of the Consultations

The first stage of the Planning Consultations took place during the spring of 1975, and the results have been compiled. An impressive amount of activity has taken place. More than 300 residents took part actively in the Consultations and related activities, and many more were involved sporadically.

Each of the nine block committees met about six times and had divided themselves up into a number of subcommittees to discuss housing renovation, courtyard improvement, traffic, and the social and economic consequences of renewal. All of the block committees have produced written reports.

The Consultations led to many spontaneous initiatives being taken by area residents. A group of activists began publishing a local newssheet, "Birkabladet," with information to tenants and discussion about the tenants' demands. After the Consultations had taken place, a public meeting was arranged where the block committees presented their reports and the principal issues were discussed. The committees have circulated a petition with their demands in regard to renewal activity in Birka.

The Planning Consultations evolved into a broad-based attack against the "25–50–25" guidelines and against the efforts by developers and the municipality to carry through a more extensive renovation than the tenants need or want. The central demands which were put forward by the Birka residents were

1. Every tenant shall be guaranteed the right to move back to his own building (or at least to the neighborhood).
2. Rental levels shall be kept within reasonable limits.
3. Tenant influence over planning and renewal must be guaranteed.

Together with other neighborhood groups, the Birka residents staged a demonstration in front of Town Hall the evening the Town Council debated the "25–50–25" renewal guidelines.

When the Consultations ended officially in June 1975, most of the participants felt a strong need to continue their work. They had concentrated on principal issues of renewal, and it was now time to focus attention on concrete discussions about renovation on a building-to-building basis. Several of the block committees wanted more time to penetrate the problems of courtyard improvement and traffic separation and to work out their own plans. The committees have, therefore, demanded that the Consultations continue during the autumn of 1975.

To meet the need for an organization through which the Birka residents could take common action in planning and renewal matters, a new coordinating committee was created by the residents with representatives from each block. This group organizes and coordinates the continuing efforts by the residents to influence the renewal process.

7. Evaluation

One criterion for judging the relative success of the Consultations could be the degree of participation, a second the amount of information which changes hands, and a third the number of conflicts which are solved or avoided. The evaluation may differ depending on whether it is done from the viewpoint of the municipality, the residents, or the landlords.

The questions which we felt must be answered in order to evaluate the results of the Consultations are

Did the Consultations go according to plans or were there major deviations?

Why did so many residents participate actively? Were participants representative of resident opinion?

What consequences did the Consultations have for the three major groups of actors in the renewal process: the residents, the landlords, the municipality? Were their relative positions strengthened or weakened?

Did the Consultations go according to plans or were there major deviations?

It was thought that the coordinating committee, with its more official character, would be the center of interest. Instead interest was focussed on work in the block committees, and the functions of the coordinating committee were restricted to summing up the proposals and demands presented in the block committees.

The work in the block committees proceeded quite differently from the way it was envisioned by the Planning Board. It turned out that the landlords did not take active part in the Consultations. This is probably due to the fact that most of them are only marginally affected by the Neighborhood Renewal Plan. As property owners, moreover, their interests are to a large extent satisfied in existing legislation, and they have established channels of communication with the municipal authorities.

The failure of the landlords to take part in the Consultations meant that they could not function as fora for discussions between two groups with conflicting interests. Instead they became organizations for forwarding the demands of the residents. A strong, unified, and aggressive resident opinion developed.

Another major deviation concerned the issues around which the discussions centered. The "25–50–25" renewal guidelines and the question of the extent of renewal quickly became the two most crucial issues for Birka residents. The treatment of these issues will determine whether or not the present residents can remain in the area. It is therefore understandable that the tenants' main interest was directed toward these matters and not—as the Planning Board had hoped—toward the question of improving the outdoor environment.

This does not mean, however, that the Planning Board did not get answers to the questions they posed. All of the block committees have discussed the Neighborhood Renewal Plan in detail and have documented their viewpoints in written reports. Even though emphasis was placed on more principal issues of renewal, the original purpose of the Consultations was achieved.

Why did so many residents participate actively? Were participants representative of resident opinion?

First of all, the Consultations concerned matters which were immediate, which affected all residents directly, and which everyone could have a viewpoint on. A second reason is the relatively high percentage of young adults in the area who have enough time, interest, and energy to get involved. Of equal importance perhaps is the fact that many of the older residents gave active encouragement. Many of them had lived in the area for so many years that moving would be a catastrophe.

The local chapter of the Tenants' Association played an important role in activating residents. They felt that the presentation of the Neighborhood Renewal Plan could function as a catalyst for organizing area tenants. They appointed a liaison for each block whose duty it was to organize meetings in every building and to ensure that every building elect representatives to take part in the Consulta-

tions. They succeeded in recruiting representatives for most of the buildings and convinced skeptical tenants to participate actively in the proceedings. About 100 buildings with 70 percent of the neighborhood residents were represented in the Consultations.

The makeup of the block committees was typical of the area's population. About half of the participants were in their twenties or early thirties while the other half were over sixty. There was a strong unanimity of opinion around the central issues in most of the committees.

Most of the buildings were represented, but there was a tendency for buildings where some kind of change was imminent to be overrepresented.

What consequences did the Consultations have for major groups of actors in the renewal process?

The questions the residents ask in the face of renewal are: Will I be forced to move? Can I afford the new rent? Can I get needed improvements done? The Consultations were not designed to provide answers to these questions. They have, however, benefited the residents in several other ways, and have helped create the conditions necessary for greater tenant influence over renewal at a later stage.

The Consultations have played the role of catalyst, and have initiated a considerable amount of activity among area residents. Birka residents have gained insight into how the municipal government functions and where to apply pressure. An extensive discussion about the goals and means of renewal has gotten underway.

A direct consequence of the Consultations is that the residents have organized themselves. In many of the buildings, building committees have been formed which have already proved their worth in rental negotiations with landlords. An extensive social process is also taking place in Birka, a process which may have far-reaching social and political implications. The many meetings often fill a social function and have led to new personal friendships and a greater sense of community.

The Planning Consultations have weakened the landlords' position in the sense that their tenants are now better informed about their rights and how to fight for them. A united tenant opinion may also, in certain cases, be used by the municipality to justify a proposal which a landlord opposes. (In other cases, however, the landlords will be able to cite tenant opinion against municipal demands that a wing of a building be demolished, that certain flats be merged, etc.)

What were the consequences of the Consultations for the Municipality? One could surmise that the municipal authorities, as initiators of the Consultations, would be most greatly benefited by them. The existence of major policy discrepancies between various levels and branches of the municipal government can, however, explain the fact that although the Consultations were initiated by the municipal authorities, the results were in some ways disadvantageous for them.

The Consultations seem to have led, for example, to a considerable amount of resident hostility being leveled—rightfully or not—at the municipal authorities. Residents were embittered not so much by the Neighborhood Renewal Plan itself, as by the renewal guidelines which became known to them through the Plan. The public debate about the guidelines was generated to a great extent by the Consultations. The debate contributed to a recent defeat in the Town Council of a proposal to apply the guidelines in another part of town.

A positive result of the Consultations for the Municipality is the amount of concrete information they have received about conditions in the area and about the residents' needs and desires. The Planning Board has expressed interest in the detailed proposals for block renewal and courtyard improvement which have been presented by several of the block committees. Planners and municipal officials have been forced to take the residents' demands for a say in the planning process more seriously.

Appendix

1. Legislation Relevant to Conservation and Renewal

Proclamation Concerning Public Buildings 1920 with later amendments; buildings belonging to the State can be declared as landmarks (330 listed buildings and groups of buildings as of 1974).

Historic Building Act (1960) Buildings not belonging to the State can be declared historic buildings by Office of National Antiquities. A preservation order stating how the owner shall care for the building is issued. Listing *may* entitle the owner to economic compensation if the present use is improved or made more expensive. (260 listed buildings as of 1974.)

The Building and Planning Law (1947) and Statutes (1959) Conservation areas can be delineated. Within these, "zone" plans can be adopted with detailed provisions as to size, placement, color, material, design of roofs and windows, etc., of new and renovated structures.

Building permits are required for all new construction, substantial alterations, changes in appearance, and demolition of structures. The city architect can require that "the exterior of a building be given such a form and color as are required by the townscape or the landscape. . . ."

Construction bans pending plan approval can be applied for by the municipal Department of Building and Planning.

Demolition bans can be issued by the municipality, for example, in order to preserve historically or culturally noteworthy buildings or for renovation.

2. Financing

National government low-interest financing is available both for new construction and for renovation. The amount that can be borrowed for renovation is equivalent to the construction costs for the same amount of space in new construction.

Where excess costs are due to cultural values in the building, the "mortgage ceiling" can be raised.

For buildings of historical interest, a new form of financing is available—"supplementary loans" which are interest and amortization free for a limited period. This is a form of subsidy for keeping rentals at an acceptable level. The city's own Conservation Authority (City Museum) has done a detailed inspection of the entire area and described and classified every building. The city itself has assumed a certain amount of responsibility for the conservation at least of the facades of a number of buildings.

At present, an additional subsidy is available for renovation of multifamily housing. Up to 20 percent of the renovation costs or maximum $1,500 per dwelling unit can be given to the builder.

3. Rental Legislation

The rent control law of 1942 had held rents in the inner city areas at a low level, but resulted in under-the-table purchase of rent-controlled apartments, poor maintenance, and extremely low housing densities. Rent control has gradually been replaced by the new rental law which bases rental levels on a "use-value" system where non-profit municipal housing is taken as the norm. Rentals must not exceed rents paid in comparable units in nonprofit housing.

Another point of interest in the rental legislation is the strong right of tenancy. The lease is renewed automatically and the tenant cannot be evicted against his will except for failure to pay rent or damage to the property. Change of ownership or the demolition of the building are not valid reasons for eviction or revoking a lease. In case of demolition or renovation the landlord is responsible for finding an apartment comparable to the present one. The tenant has the right to move back into a renovated apartment.

19 Recent Amenity Measures in British Urban Planning

David L. Smith

Bolton: general improvement area, where streets have been closed for pedestrian and play use

Introduction

1. Amenity has been described as a key concept in British urban planning. It is widely used but poorly defined; it is normally associated with aesthetic factors but sometimes refers to the provision of essential facilities.

2. Two recent housing and planning measures are much concerned with the idea of amenity: general improvement areas (GIAs) and conservation areas (CAs).

Under section 28 of the 1969 Housing Act, District Councils and London boroughs have the power to declare "general improvement areas" in areas of predominantly residential property. These are areas in which, in the absence of plans for redevelopment or other major changes, there is a potential for the improvement of the houses themselves and their surroundings. Official advice suggests that the houses in such an area shall have the prospect of thirty years' life after rehabilitation. A report proposing the declaration of a general improvement area may be prepared and submitted to the appropriate authority by any "suitably qualified" person or persons, whether or not they are officers of the authority. Government approval is not required at any stages of the declaration process, though the Secretary of State must be informed of the authority's decision.

Authorities are encouraged to carry out environmental works for which an expenditure of £200 per dwelling is allowed—50 percent of which is repayable by a grant from central government. These works consist of such things as tree planting, providing play spaces, grassed or paved areas, parking spaces, and garages and may also extend to, for example, repairing and renewing fences. Local authorities may use compulsory purchase to acquire land for these purposes! Also advocated are the renewal or replacing of street lighting, the repair of road surfaces, the exclusion of through traffic, and the conversion of a highway into a footpath.

Under section 31 of the Act, the local authority must inform the residents and owners of property in a GIA about the action they intend to take and they must also publish, from time to time, information about assistance available for area and house improvement.

GIAs are designated by local authorities under the Housing Act 1969 for the rehabilitation of older housing areas. Government Grant Aid is provided for house improvement and environmental works. Around 1,500 GIAs have been declared.

Planning authorities have been required, since the introduction of the Civic Amenities Act, 1967, to determine which parts of their area are "areas of special architectural or historic interest" and to designate them as "conservation areas" in order "to preserve or enhance" their "character or appearance" (section 277, Town and Country Planning Act, 1971). Under the Local Government Act, 1972, it has become a duty of the district authorities, but country councils may also designate conservation areas. Designation, which follows a similar procedure to that described for GIAs, carries with it very few specific obligations and no automatic grant aid, but the historic buildings legislation (Historic Buildings Act, 1953, Local Authorities Historic Buildings Act, 1962) and other planning powers are expected to be used to achieve improvement. Under section 10 of the Town and Country Planning (Amendment) Act, 1972, the Secretary of State may make grants or loans to conservation areas of outstanding interest. The authorities have a statutory obligation to advertise proposed development in conservation areas and, under the 1972 act, they may seek from the Secretary of State the power to control the demolition of any buildings in a conservation area. The government's memorandum on conservation areas, issued with the MOHLG Circular 53/67, Civic Amenities Act, 1967, Parts I and II, suggests that the appropriate improvement measures include the reduction of traffic, the selection of well-designed street furniture, the removal of unwanted direction signs, unsightly advertisements, and miscellaneous clutter, the planting of trees, and the promotion of collective "face-lifts" of the kind pioneered by the Civic Trust.

CAs are also designated by local authorities for the protection of areas of special architectural or historic interest.

Government Grant Aid is provided only for buildings and areas of outstanding national importance. Over 3,000 conservation areas have been designated since the passing of the Civic Amenities Act 1967.

General Improvement Areas

3. The need for GIAs was seen in terms of the following objectives:

Physical: to improve the housing stock.

Political: to replace the drive for more new houses.

Social: as an alternative to redevelopment which destroys communities.

Economic: to be cheaper than wholesale replacement of houses.

4. As this work was developed in a housing context the main professional contributions came from public health experts and housing managers together with some interest from architects and planners in relation to the environmental improvements.

5. The administrative responsibility for GIAs remained firmly with the local authorities with an occasional initiative to be taken by a residents' group. Local authorities were occasionally held back by spending limits and the need for Government approval for compulsory purchase of properties.

6. Progress in designating areas was slow, and was only marginally speeded up in some areas by improved grant levels in 1971 (See Table 1). The designation of general improvement areas failed to increase markedly the number of houses improved, partly because environmental improvements were not quickly undertaken and also because these were not necessarily regarded as an incentive for private investment.

7. The impact of GIAs was much affected by economic and geographical factors: in London the demand for improvable housing led to speculative development and the displacement of tenants (gentrification). In less prosperous regions where the demand for housing was less, there was insufficient incentive for owners to contribute to house

Table 1. The Geographical Distribution of General Improvement Areas (August 1969–August 1973)

Region	No. of GIAs Declared, 31 January 1972	% Share	No. of GIAs Declared, 31 August 1973	% Share
Northern	44	15	130	18
Yorks and Humberside	32	11	95	13
Northwest	43	13	129	16
East Midlands	24	9	60	9
West Midlands	26	9	50	7
East Anglia	8	3	12	2
Southeast	56	20	104	15
Southwest	20	7	31	4
Wales	29	10	93	13
	282		704	

Note: The increased share of GIAs declared between January 1972 and August 1973 in the Northern, Yorks and Humberside, Northwest and Wales regions reflects the special grants for intermediate and development areas introduced by the Housing Act 1971.

Table 2. The Geographical Distribution of Conservation Areas (August 1967–August 1973)

Region	No. of Conservation Areas Designated 31 August 1973	% Share England and Wales only
Northern	111	5
Yorks and Humberside	137	6
Northwest	113	5
East Midlands	198	9
West Midlands	231	10
East Anglia	117	5
Southeast	1013	44
Southwest	266	12
Wales	126	5
Total: England and Wales	2312	
Scotland	210	
Total: England, Scotland, and Wales	2522	

improvement when a better environment could be more readily obtained by a short move to a modern suburban house.

8. The measure therefore has not been generally successful, and the amenity aspects of environmental improvement have been little used and often ineffective. There have been some unexpected side effects of the improvement legislation especially in London.

Conservation Areas

9. The Civic Amenities Act, which provided for conservation areas, represented a logical extension of the provisions for protecting individual historic buildings and paralleled developments in Europe (especially France). The Act was politically uncontentious and warmly welcomed by interest groups.

10. The ideology supporting CAs was very much that of the architectural historian wishing to conserve good townscapes of national and local interest. Wider arguments about the conflicts between conservation and growth were seldom raised.

11. CAs, like GIAs depended upon local authority initiative but voluntary preservation groups played a major part in proposing areas for designation. Central government had some difficulty in setting rules for the selection of areas and had subsequently to define areas of outstanding interest for the purposes of state grant.

12. The measure was popular with local authorities and normally with residents. Table 2 shows the distribution of conservation areas with an especially effective coverage in the wealthy southeast. Ninety-three percent of those towns selected by the Council for British Archaeology had been designated as conservation areas by the end of 1973 in this region but only just over 50 percent in Wales and Scotland.

13. The success of CAs was again affected by differences in economic pressure in different parts of the country: gentrification again occurred in London and in some villages but insufficient demand for property has undermined conservation schemes in some other places.

14. CAs have been generally more successful and acceptable than GIAs but only in the narrow terms of preserving fine buildings and their environment.

Comparisons and Conclusions

15. One of these measures was cautiously used as an element of government housing policy and has already been changed to take account of difficulties encountered, especially in London; the other formed part of a developing movement for conservation, was enthusiastically taken up, and has subsequently been much reinforced.

16. These measures illustrate three aspects of amenity, those concerned with
a. public health
b. general environmental improvement (civic beauty)
c. architectural conservation.
GIAs illustrate (a) and (b), CAs illustrate (b) and (c).

17. These measures also illustrate aspects of planning: the need for coordination—better illustrated by the GIAs based on the fundamental need of improved housing; the adoption of a sensitive process approach—evident in the long term perspectives of conservation and in the vigilance of local groups; and the role of participation—broader and more significant in the case of GIAs and restricted to specialized interests in the case of CAs.

18. Three general lessons emerge about the role of professional and political values in such measures and particularly the scope for the imposition of firm standards, the dangers of disruptive social effects and the significance of underlying economic factors and lastly a need for a general planning approach based on coordination, monitoring, and participation.

Case Study: The Bolton General Improvement Area

Bolton is an old industrial town of some 250,000 people in the north of England. An area of 300 nineteenth-century terrace houses were declared part of a GIA under the 1969 Housing Act. With 50 percent grant aid from the Central Government for house improvement and environmental works ($\pounds$200, or $400 per dwelling) the program was administered by the local authority. Several dwellings now have indoor bathrooms, and exteriors are newly painted. The scheme has converted streets into pedestrian areas (see photo) which are play spaces for children, leaving the cars to be parked in near alleys.

The area is inhabited entirely by working- and lower-class people with an above average proportion of pensioners. The area adjoins industry on one side and a new housing development on the other side.

This was not an area under pressure for change, as has been much more common in London districts such as Barnsbury, or Pimlico. The effectiveness of the program was mainly dependent on incoming younger households.

An extract from a Bolton Housing Committee report of March 1973 describes the results of a questionnaire.

The Social Aspects of Improvement

Method The social aspects of general area improvement in Bolton presented here were assessed by means of a questionnaire which was circulated in specific streets in Brooklyn Street and Viking Street GIAs where area improvements have been completed or nearly completed, so that residents were able to express comprehensive opinions on the schemes.

General Results Fundamentally, the questionnaire responses illustrated the success of the general area improvements, 84 percent of the respondents noting the positive impact of the works. Furthermore, 60 percent of the respondents considered an owner/occupied or rented dwelling in their GIA as preferable to other forms of residence within their varied financial capabilities, namely a more modern rented or owner/occupied dwelling or a more modern Corporation house or flat. Indeed, only 10 percent stated an overall preference for the Corporation dwellings, which are perhaps the most direct alternatives.

Age of Residents It was noted in the Introduction that the population structures of Viking street and Brooklyn Street GIAs exhibited marked imbalances with twice the average number of residents in the over 50s age groups. However, the declaration of these areas as GIAs and their

upgrading into attractive but cheaper alternatives to more modern residential areas has resulted in the attraction of younger age groups to the area. Whereas, overall, the incidence of households whose heads are in the 18–30 year age group is only 4.2 percent in these two areas, over the last three years, no less than 26.7 percent of the incoming households' heads belonged to this age group.

Residents' Views on Amenities What is evident from the questionnaire is that the functioning of the area is more important to the respondents than the appearance. Pedestrianization, irrespective of its abuse by children on cycles, was considered of paramount importance by the under-40 age group, while the over 40s generally thought that the street lighting improvements were of greatest significance. The planting on the other hand seemed of least importance to all age groups perhaps because it has caused problems in excess of its visual usefulness in the form of a nuisance from playing children. Indeed, many of the respondents consider that a playground would be an important addition to the improvements of their areas, perhaps because of this. Also, a high proportion of older respondents expressed a primary interest in the provision of a telephone kiosk, a feature which would similarly raise the functional amenity of these areas.

Complaints and Comments The major complaint which has arisen in connection with the area improvements is the length of time taken to complete them, a matter which has been an unfortunate product of the experimental nature of these pilot general improvement schemes. Apart from this, other complaints were concerned with the design of the improvements. For example, the nuisance created by dogs and playing children, particularly where the planted areas were not walled, and the congestion of the back street one-way system by parked vehicles. However, not all the comments were adversely critical. In particular, a number of respondents observed that pensioners needed further financial help with improvements or suggested that the Corporation should purchase pensioners homes and improve them. Yet, as 85 percent of the household heads within these two

GIAs who have not applied for grants belong to the over-50 age group, 53 percent being pensioners, it is evident that older residents generally and not simply pensioners require assistance in this respect. This assistance could immediately be provided by giving additional publicity to the facilities for loans which the Housing Committee resolved in February 1970 to provide for this expenditure on house improvements.

Addendum: Conservation Areas and General Improvement Areas, 1978

Conservation areas and general improvement areas are still regarded as important policy instruments for the improvement and protection of historic areas and the improvement of areas of older housing. While the rate at which new districts have been identified for improvement has been considerably reduced since the enabling legislation was first introduced, the tasks of building restoration and rehabilitation and environmental enhancement continue apace, assisted by new financial provisions.

About 4,000 conservation areas have been designated in England, Scotland and Wales since 1967. Over 450 of these have been recognized by the Department of the Environment as "outstanding" for the purposes of grant aid for environmental works from a fund currently amounting to around £2 million per annum.

The Town and Country (Amenities) Act 1974, originally introduced, as in the case of the Civic Amenities Act 1967, as a Private Member's Bill, has increased local authorities' powers in relation to conservation areas and has obliged them to prepare and announce plans for their enhancement.

The Housing Act 1974 increased the rate of grant for the improvement of dwellings within general improvement areas and introduced "housing action areas" to deal with districts consisting of a particularly-high proportion of rented accommodation. These new powers increase the protection for tenants during the improvement process and incorporate assistance for the carrying out of repairs. Although the rate of grant for building rehabilitation is higher than in general improvement areas (75 percent as opposed to 60 percent) the level of environmental grant is lower.

By the end of 1977 nearly 1,200 general improvement areas had been declared (since 1969) and 272 housing action areas (since the beginning of 1975). The rate of general improvement area declarations has dropped from over 150 per annum prior to 1974 to a rate which is now comparable to that of housing action area declarations at just below 100 declarations per annum.

A recent report of a comprehensive study of general improvement areas undertaken by the Department of the Environment concludes:

Since the passing of the 1969 Act area improvement through the medium of GIAs has become accepted by local authorities as a significant and useful means of improving the quality and condition of the nation's housing stock. Not all GIAs have been successful so far and it seems that the critical elements in a successful GIA lie in the initial selection of the area and in securing the commitment of both the local authority and the local residents to the programme of improvement which declaration implies. (Improvement Research Note 3/77 "General Improvement Areas 1969–1976," Department of the Environment, London, March 1978).

20 Inner London: Policies for Dispersal and Balance

Graeme Shankland, Peter Willmott, and David Jordan

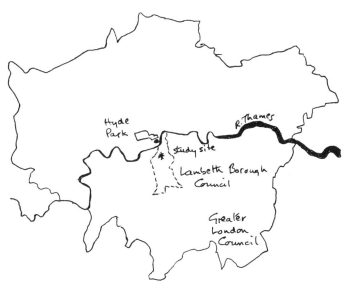

The study area, Lambeth and Greater London

Housing types in Stockwell showing the complicated mix of public and private housing in London's inner city resulting from pre- and postwar housing programs. From a map by Shankland Cox Partnership.

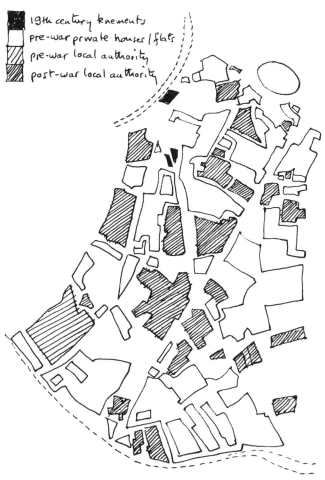

19th century tenements
pre-war private houses / flats
pre-war local authority
post-war local authority

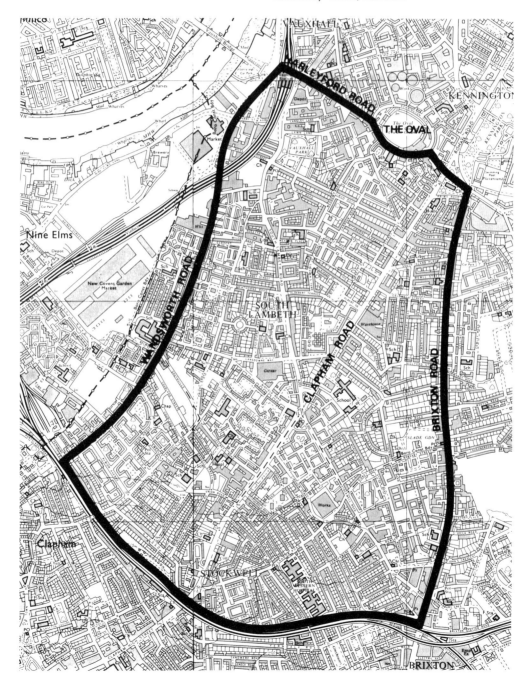

Development proposals of 1973
for the study area. Map by
Shankland Cox Partnership.
Courtesy Her Majesty's
Stationery Office, London.

Aerial view of Stockwell from a
high-rise building showing pre-
war local authority housing

Aerial view of the Landsdowne
Square "oasis." Photo by Mark
Lintell.

Aerial view of postwar public housing (foreground), old terrace housing (middle ground), and prewar public housing (background)

An old row of terraced houses

A partly rehabilitated row of
terraced houses with a public
housing high-rise block at the
end of the street

Rehabilitation of a street with barely discernible infill housing. From *Linton Grove: Knight's Hill*. Report by Shankland Cox Partnership with Edward Hollamby, Director of Development, Lambeth, June 1976.

Small structural steelwork and textile industry buildings in a Stockwell residential area

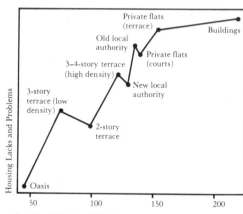

Density and dissatisfaction. Surveys of residents in different housing types found a clear correlation between "child density" and dissatisfaction. The scale of developments measured by the numbers of dwellings seen from a number of points is also correlated with dissatisfaction.

Reprinted from *Lambeth Inner Area Study* (Inner Area Studies, Department of the Environment; London: Her Majesty's Stationery Office, 1977), by permission of Her Britannic Majesty's Stationery Office.

Introduction

1. This paper summarizes the conclusions of three and a half years' work in Lambeth. Our study there, like those in Liverpool and Birmingham, included two elements, research into the characteristics of inner city areas and their residents and a series of action projects intended to try out small-scale innovations that might ease their problems. Our various research studies and action projects have been separately reported in a series published by the Department of the Environment. Fourteen reports have appeared so far and others are in the press, as is the book which brings all the material together and draws the main policy recommendations from the study as a whole.

2. The first task was to choose an area within Lambeth. We sought an area sufficiently "typical" to allow us to propose policies of wider relevance. This meant it had to contain a fair concentration of inner city problems—poor housing, unemployment, vandalism—and a reasonable mixture of the housing types, social classes and ethnic groups of Inner London. We selected the area shown in the map. It had a population of about 50,000. In common with many of those residents, we call the district Stockwell.

3. We had to break the work down in separate subjects, such as jobs and housing, while recognizing that these were inter-related. This summary is organized into different sections with policy proposals under the various headings, but we try to show some of the inter-connections and we believe that, taken in combination, the proposals offer a coherent and sensible strategy for Inner London.

4. Though some of our policy suggestions match those from the companion studies in Liverpool and Birmingham, others do not. In particular, for example, we argue that there are parts of Inner London, unlike Inner Liverpool and to some extent Inner Birmingham, where the population pressures are still so strong that further dispersal is needed.

We have not the space here to list our proposals, or the evidence underlying them, in detail; we have tried at least to indicate the objectives and the general approach. The specific proposals are set out in provisional form in an earlier report[1] and in final form in the forthcoming book.[2]

The People and Their Views

5. At the outset we undertook a household survey covering about 1,000 households and the 2,000-odd people in them aged 16 and over. This was to collect factual information and also seek out people's own views and aspirations to help identify the problems of the area and what might be done about them. We canvassed local opinion in other ways, maintaining contact throughout the study with local community groups such as neighborhood councils, tenants' associations and residents' organizations.

6. Like the rest of Inner London, Stockwell contained a relatively large and growing proportion of one- and two-person households. At the same time it contained rather more children than Inner London or Greater London generally. A fifth of the population were "coloured"; this proportion, though lower than in nearby Brixton, was higher than in most parts of Inner London. There was a rather smaller minority of immigrants from southern European countries such as Italy and Greece.

7. The study area contained proportionately more low-skill people than the rest of Inner London or Greater London. The main recent changes locally have been a larger-than-average increase among professional and managerial people and a decline among skilled manual workers, with the proportion of semi-skilled and unskilled workers remaining stable over a period in which it has fallen in the country as a whole. In this sense, therefore, Stockwell has been becoming "bi-polarised," with less people in the "middle" of the class spectrum and more at the "top" and "bottom."

8. The strongest impression from the people in Stockwell, in contrast with those interviewed in a national survey, was their concern about what was happening locally. There were two kinds of complaint: about the physical environ-

ment and about other residents. The environmental complaints focussed upon the poor quality of much of the older housing, the unattractive appearance of the area, the need for more parks and open spaces (especially for children's play), the need for the streets and housing estates to be kept cleaner and, on council estates in particular, criticisms of poor maintenance and management. The complaints about other people were directed against "outsiders," on grounds of colour or because they were "rough" or "problem families." There was also criticism of the behaviour of children and young people, and fear of vandalism and crime.

9. Most of these complaints could be traced to one of two main causes. The first was the relatively large concentrations of people, especially children, in some council estates and some streets of older houses. This helped to generate characteristic inner city pressures: more litter, more vandalism, more conflict over children's play, more stress generally between families.

10. The second main cause was the constant shifting of families in recent decades, exacerbated by council redevelopment schemes and the decline in privately-rented housing. Few people had friends or relatives nearby. Many were therefore more inclined to be critical of neighbors or their children. There had been an erosion of community spirit and a weakening of the informal controls which can help contain vandalism.

Poverty

11. A particular question that the study tried to answer was whether, as is commonly believed, the population of inner areas like Stockwell contains a large proportion of people in poverty or with social problems.

12. Rather more families in the study area than in the rest of the country were below the "poverty line" (the supplementary benefit level plus 20 per cent). This was partly because the district contained more single-parent families than elsewhere and partly because three times as many ordinary families with children in Stockwell were in poverty. Many wives worked and this was usually enough to

lift their family above the poverty line. Wages were low and housing costs high. In Stockwell, as elsewhere, the overwhelming majority of the poor were old people and families with children.

13. "Problem families," those whose problems are compounded by psychological difficulties or anti-social behaviour, are probably more common in such areas than elsewhere. But they are still rare; in Stockwell they amounted to less than one family in 40.

14. There was not a strong association between income poverty and poor housing. This was mainly because of the intervention of the local authorities. Nearly half of Stockwell's households were council tenants. In Small Heath, Birmingham, where the proportion of council property was much lower, the link between income poverty and poor housing had not been broken.

15. Low income and poor housing are the main forms of deprivation, whether in combination or separately. Hence any serious attack on the problems of the inner city needs both to increase incomes and improve housing. We therefore gave particular attention to easing the pressures in housing, to increasing employment—the most effective form of income support—and to the need for a more effective income maintenance scheme. The first two of these are major themes of the rest of this paper.

Attack on Poverty: Local and National

16. Something can be done to relieve poverty by local measures. We propose a special programme to direct additional resources to selected parts of inner city areas, for small-scale physical improvements and for more intensive welfare support where there are concentrations of deprived people. Some method must be devised to identify the areas most in need and channel resources to them.

17. Such measures would go some way to easing the special inner city dimensions of poverty. But the problem is a national one and requires nation-wide policies. A new comprehensive national scheme for income maintenance is needed, ensuring in particular higher pensions for old people and higher children's benefits. Such a scheme should

redistribute income to those who are poor, by a method which is automatic (avoiding low take-up) and preserves the incentive to work. We recognize that such a scheme cannot be introduced in the immediate future, and that there are technical difficulties, but we argue that the opportunity should be seized now to prepare what would constitute a "post-Beveridge" scheme for the 1980s.

Jobs

18. Job opportunities and the ability of residents to earn are fundamental. As well as directly affecting people's living standards, they have a major influence on the resources available to support local shops, other facilities and council services. Stockwell residents face serious job problems: high unemployment, low earnings and many young mothers working to supplement inadequate incomes. Difficulties are greater for men than for women; for manual workers, particularly the less skilled, than for other workers; for black than for white workers; for school-leavers and young adults than for people at other stages in life.

19. In the local labour market, which includes Central London where half Stockwell's residents work, job opportunities and the skills of people needing work have increasingly become out of balance. On the one hand there are people out of work or earning very little; on the other hand certain kinds of skilled jobs cannot be filled.

20. This mis-match has several causes. First, manufacturing and other industry has declined rapidly in Inner London over the last decade or so, much more than in the rest of the country. Secondly, there has been a national shift from less skilled manual work towards professional, technical and administrative jobs, and this process is further advanced in London than elsewhere. The change obviously has serious implications for areas like Stockwell with a predominantly manual labour force lacking skills or educational qualifications. Such inner areas also suffer disproportionately when the national economy is in recession.

21. The low-skill people, who are the most vulnerable, have not been able to change occupations to meet the changing structure partly because of the lack of suitable training schemes. Many school-leavers are not equipped to enter the growing non-manual sector, even to acquire manual skills, because of low standards of basic education. Nor have low-skill workers been able to move from Inner London to places outside where job opportunities are better for them.

22. We propose three main lines of employment policy. The first is to slow down or check the decline of manufacturing industry in Inner London, and to create new job opportunities where possible. The second is to increase the skills and educational levels of the population. The third is to help less-skilled and lower-income people to move out of Inner London.

23. Under the first heading, central and local government can help. Industrial Development Certificates (IDCs) act symbolically as a deterrent to investment and should be removed from Inner London. We also propose some relaxation on Office Development Permits (ODPs) in suitable areas. To cherish existing firms, local authorities should relax planning controls over industry and commerce, for instance allowing some "non-conforming" industrial users to remain, stopping large-scale clearance in areas containing small businesses, allowing for expansion where possible and relaxing traffic and parking controls. To encourage the birth of new firms, local authorities should set aside land for small industrial estates, providing workshops in advance.

24. The construction industry could play an important part in creating immediate local job opportunities with career prospects, if a continuous programme of housing and environmental improvement were guaranteed. Many local people have relevant skills and experience which are being under-used. Construction could also employ a sizeable number of the local unemployed, both in skilled jobs and in those for which training could be given.

25. On vocational training, despite recent government initiatives, the resources available in Britain are still far below the levels in most European countries. Skill Centres are few and far between, the nearest to Lambeth being in Croydon and Poplar apart from a small annexe in Sydenham. In such centres as exist there are not enough courses

or places. Little is provided for young people who have missed out on apprenticeships. Rates of pay or allowances for trainees are often too low to attract applicants. A major expansion of training opportunities is therefore needed, with higher trainee allowances. The government should also support financially the training schemes of individual firms.

26. More emphasis needs to be given in schools to basic academic skills and to vocational preparation. If children thought that their education would lead to better jobs, they would take it more seriously.

27. It must be recognized that what can be done to arrest the decline of jobs in Inner London is limited, and that even a sizeable expansion in training will not in itself overcome the mis-match of jobs and skills. There must therefore be far more effective measures to help the less skilled and less affluent to move, if they so wish, to Outer London and further out in the London Region where there are more jobs for them. This would make it easier for those with skills in demand in Inner London to find housing there.

Housing Stress and the "Housing Trap"

28. Although some of those moving out would be replaced by newcomers, the main gain would be a reduction of pressure on inner city housing. Symptoms of this pressure are relatively high house prices, high densities, widespread multi-occupation, long council waiting lists, squatting and homelessness.

29. Of course some people are already able to move out of Inner London, and have been doing so in their thousands since the turn of the century. Densities have fallen. But the benefits have not been evenly shared. As the Milner Holland Committee showed in 1965[3] and as we confirmed in Stockwell, lower-density areas have had most of the gain from out-migration and higher-density areas have stayed much as they were. Meanwhile those moving have predominantly been the better-off non-manual and skilled manual workers. Our survey showed that something between a quarter and a third of households, mostly those with children, would move if they could. But the less skilled and less affluent among them, the very people who now most need to move for new jobs, have little chance of doing so.

30. These families are thus caught in what we call the "housing trap." The choices available to them are owner-occupied houses, which they cannot buy, and public housing, to which they are denied access. Few can go to Outer London boroughs because the authorities there have discouraged public housing for Inner Londoners and, lacking the skills in greatest demand, they have been largely excluded from the new and expanding towns.

31. Thus at present the low-skill workers of Inner London are trapped behind an almost impenetrable cordon. Yet to help them move would meet their own wishes, reduce the mis-match in employment, arrest the social bi-polarisation of the inner cities and, by easing the pressures, make it possible to improve things for those who remain. We do not believe that further dispersal will impoverish London: a less congested London should be cheaper to run.

Balanced Dispersal

32. We therefore propose a set of policies for "balanced dispersal" out of Inner London. The objective is to help more low-income families who want to move out to do so. Since they cannot afford to buy, they need rented public housing.

33. As most potential migrants do not want to move far, the bulk of this housing should, as far as possible, be in Outer London or in areas immediately beyond. Access to Outer London housing will depend on a "co-ordinated allocation system" such as had been proposed by the Greater London Council and the London Boroughs Association; the objective should be to give Londoners in all boroughs equal access to public housing, so as to help migration from Inner to Outer boroughs. To increase the housing for rent available in Outer London to inner city residents, private houses should be purchased by local authorities.

34. Further out, we propose the construction of rented housing, close to existing settlements in selected parts of the Green Belt and, further out still, in the proposed "growth areas" of the South East, near to towns like Reading and Crawley. On a wider scale, we propose a National Mobility Pool, made up of a proportion of council house vacancies from all local authorities. This would help long-distance migrants in general and, by improving labour mobility, contribute to economic recovery.

35. The government has recently altered the allocation arrangements for new towns to include Londoners in housing need who are looking for jobs. This is welcome, but it is as yet not clear how far Inner Londoners will benefit. Since many new town houses go to Outer Londoners and since some of these are council tenants, a further move, in advance of the co-ordinated allocation system, would be to arrange that say 50 per cent of the Outer London council housing thus vacated is automatically made available to Inner Londoners.

36. Because of the social costs of forced movements within Inner London, we would seek to encourage population stability inside the inner city. Thus we are making two suggestions which may seem contradictory: that people should be encouraged to move if they want to move and stay if they want to stay. This apparent contradiction is not a real one. People differ in what they want. Some seek new homes, usually houses with gardens, in new districts, usually at lower densities than those in Inner London. Others prefer inner city life. We justify the two-pronged policy, apart from its contribution to the two major problems of community breakdown and concentrations of high child density, because it will give people more choice over their lives.

Housing and Planning Policies

37. Housing and planning policies inside Inner London are discussed under four main headings: rehabilitation and redevelopment, tenure and management, housing design and the future role of town planning.

38. There is no justification for further large-scale redevelopment in Inner London. The "housing gain" this sought to achieve has proved illusory; such gain is better sought further out.

39. There is, however, a danger that the current shift to rehabilitation could go too far. In many urban areas, a proportion of the housing stock will not be worth retaining, so that some new building will be necessary. Decisions about this should be made on a house to house basis. The resulting schemes will often combine rehabilitation with some redevelopment.

40. Putting more emphasis on rehabilitation should permit greater sensitivity to community ties. But if rehabilitation involved wholesale displacement it could be socially as disruptive as redevelopment. The management of rehabilitation should encourage continuity of residence in a neighborhood for people who want it, for example by renovating properties without families having to move.

41. We assume that the private rented sector will continue to decline in the inner city as elsewhere. A programme of social ownership should replace it, using different forms of agency and sponsorship, thus encouraging a more flexible provision and allocation of housing. To improve the housing remaining in private tenure, "fair" rents will in time need to rise, matched by controls to ensure that improvements are carried out. For similar reasons, public sector rents should also rise. To avoid hardship among poorer tenants, public and private, assistance with rents needs to be maintained at adequate levels and more efficiently distributed.

42. The quality of housing management on council estates needs to be improved. To this end caretakers, who need to be resident, should receive better housing and increased status. The scope of tenants' participation in housing should be established by a series of experiments involving various degrees of delegation and responsibility.

43. One objective of management, and of council allocation procedures in particular, should again be to allow continuity of residence in a locality over a person's lifetime and from one generation to the next. At the same time, child densities should be reduced by encouraging families to

move from estates where they are over-concentrated. This will be made easier by the reduction in pressure following population dispersal. Flats in such estates—mainly inter-war buildings and newer point blocks—are in any case often unattractive to families. If they were helped to move, more of these flats could be made accessible to young people setting up home in Inner London. The GLC and several boroughs have started to move in these directions.

44. New housing designs should recognize people's dislike of large-scale monolithic schemes. Cost yardstick arrangements and regulations inhibiting variety should be amended. Existing estates should be enlivened, for example by putting in shops and nurseries, by giving private gardens to ground-floor tenants, or even by pulling down some old blocks to let in light and air.

45. In view of the crucial link between satisfaction and density, housing design and layout should avoid high density. For any level of density there is a strong link between the level of investment and the costs of management. Since investment in housing is likely to continue to be low in future, new schemes should be designed more simply so as to reduce the demands on management.

46. The design and layout of housing should take account of the "defensible space" concept, particularly in terms of access ways, grouped garages and open public areas. New buildings and layouts should encourage the use and management of ground areas by the people who live there. The space immediately outside the dwelling should be private. The space beyond this should be semi-private and capable of being supervised from small groups of dwellings. More remote spaces such as children's playgrounds and football pitches need formal supervision. All spaces should be well-lit, overseen and appear to belong to somebody. Deck access seldom meets these conditions and should therefore be avoided. So, for the same reason, should underground open-access car parking.

47. There is not likely to be much housing redevelopment in areas like Stockwell, and housing is the major land use. Nor is there much scope for major physical restructur-

ing through new roads, open spaces or other large projects. This suggests that town planning needs to shift its emphasis towards encouraging and managing the kinds of small-scale change likely to be most relevant, the detailed planning of small sites and of such local environmental schemes. In other words, there needs to be a new and more sensitive style of working geared to the management of small-scale urban change.

The Delivery of Welfare

48. Local services need to be organized in ways that will help residents more effectively. The boundaries of different services are in general not aligned with each other; this leads to poor co-ordination between services and to confusion among potential users. Workers in the various services have difficulties of liaison with their colleagues in other agencies. Many residents do not know where to go for help; finding out often costs them time, expense and unnecessary journeys; and when they get there the complexity of the system often prevents it working properly.

49. The boundaries of different local services should be matched, under the external pressure of a Location and Boundaries Committee. This would be a Standing Committee of the local authority (for example, Lambeth) but arrangements would be made for other public services to be represented.

50. Workers from different services should be brought together locally in a multi-service team, meeting regularly, promoting liaison and improving the comprehensive management and delivery services. Such a multiservice team could come together in a community service center, where most services would be concentrated.

51. In addition, information—as distinct from services—needs to be made available at the most local level, for instance through what we, in an action project, have called "local information posts." In this project local residents, after a period of training, were employed part-time in their own homes by the local Citizens Advice Bureau. This experiment, which may be discontinued, has not in our view been adequately tried out. Such services, providing new

forms of access from below, can facilitate the flow of information in the reverse direction, feeding back consumers' views about what is needed.

A Programme for Inner London

52. Our proposals complement each other. The main links in the chain of reasoning, to sum up, are:

i. As well as measures to strengthen Inner London's employment base and improve training programmes, an essential part of policy must be to help low-skill people to move where the jobs are increasingly found.

ii. Since many such people want to move out of Inner London, anyway, a scheme for balanced dispersal will have no shortage of applicants. It will arrest the social "bi-polarisation" of Inner London.

iii. Balanced dispersal will make it possible to reduce densities among those who stay behind, and generally to improve housing conditions and the local environment.

iv. A parallel policy of encouraging population stability among those who remain, helped by the abandonment of wholesale clearance and its substitution by more selective small-scale rehabilitation and development, will contribute to better relationships between residents and more effective informal control of vandalism and petty crime.

v. More sensitive housing management, resident caretakers supported by better maintenance and cleaning services, fuller involvement by tenants, and housing designed to a more human scale will all help to improve the quality of inner city life.

vi. A new government programme, giving extra help to inner areas where deprived people are concentrated, will ensure that more resources are available locally. Improved access from below, boundary co-ordination and the creation of multi-service teams will lead to a more effective delivery of services and a more efficient use of resources. In time, the introduction of a comprehensive national income maintenance scheme will relieve poverty inside and outside the inner city.

53. Some of our specific proposals have already been accepted or are under discussion. This is not surprising: there has been a continuing debate over the last three years or so in which we have participated. Some London Boroughs, including Lambeth and Wandsworth, are already taking a more flexible line over planning decisions affecting industry. Some housing authorities are trying to reduce child densities and starting to widen access to their older stock. The Department of the Environment has somewhat relaxed the rules governing access to new towns. However, these constitute only the first steps towards a comprehensive programme for the inner city.

54. Most of our proposals have, moreover, not yet been accepted. The scarcity of resources will delay some of them. But an early start can and should be made on others.

55. The first thing is to end unnecessary restrictive interventions by central and local government. Action on these could have immediate effect. Examples are the removal of IDCs in Inner London, the relaxation of ODP's and the complementary relaxation of planning controls in Inner London over industry and commerce.

56. The second set of measures are those which are particularly urgent. This includes expanding job-training facilities in or near Inner London, and giving travelling and other help to improve access to training elsewhere. A steady programme of inner city renewal and improvement should play a large part in retraining and job creation in the construction industry in Inner London.

57. There should be an immediate start on the purchase of existing homes outside Inner London, together with more generous assistance with removal expenses, as the first stage in the programme of balanced dispersal. The necessary legislation should be passed and the arrangements made for a London coordinated allocation system. This should be the first step towards a National Mobility Pool of council housing, to help not only Inner London but other job seekers needed for industrial recovery.

58. Inside the inner city selected schemes of local improvements should be mounted in areas where physical and social conditions are bad, and where a rapid change can be effected.

59. Finally, further lessons for policy would be learned and some relief given to inner city areas, elsewhere as well as in London, by launching further action projects in the field. These projects should be designed to have an immediate effect in deprived areas and should include some which test new forms of local authority initiative involving several departments.

60. Action along these lines could produce results within months, bringing recognizable improvements in the daily lives of the most disadvantaged residents of Inner London. This would, of course, be only the first stage in carrying through the fuller set of proposals which, over a longer period of time, would offer a means of bringing the society and economy of Inner London into a better balance.

Notes

This study was carried out under the auspices of the UK Department of the Environment through the Shankland Cox Partnership and the Institute of Community Studies.

1. Inner Area Study, Lambeth, *London's Inner Area: Problems and Possibilities* (IAS/LA/11, DOE, 1976).

2. Graeme Shankland, Peter Willmott, and David Jordan, *Inner London: Policies for Dispersal and Balance*, Report of an Inner Area Study in Lambeth, HMSO, 1977 (ISBN 0-1-751141-2, £6.00 and postage).

3. *Report of the Committee on Housing in Greater London*, HMSO, Cmnd. 2605.

Charles McKean

Community Action, a radical magazine which acts as a newsheet for action groups throughout Britain, devotes issues to problems such as community protest tactics, petitioning and squatting, and provides critical analyses of the latest government programs. It is typed on cheap paper with "tough" graphics. Cover of *Community Action*, no. 11, November–December 1973.

Two examples of cartoons from
Community Action

The Japanese water garden in Covent Garden (designed by Keith Cheng) is an object lesson in how to design a tiny space into a much loved park. The garden has now been replaced by development. From Charles McKean, *Fight Blight* (London: Kaye & Ward, 1977, p. 75). Photo by Jim Monahan.

The splendid Camden Lock scheme in London, where canal-side buildings have been taken over by craft shops and studios, restaurants, a market, and similar activities. It is now firmly part of the tourist circuit. It is also under threat of imminent redevelopment. From McKean, *Fight Blight*, p. 142.

The Kentish Town Fun Art
Farm. The community work-
shop is in the center, and cows
and goats are kept in the sheds
on the left. From McKean,
Fight Blight, p. 45. Photo by
Alex Levac.

The backs of Black Road houses before improvements.

The backs of Black Road after improvements. From McKean, *Fight Blight*, pp. 106, 107. Photos by Rod Hackney.

Cover of the *BEE* (*Bulletin of Environmental Education*), which has been a primary instigator of town trails, urban studies centers, and other ways of teaching children and others about their cities. This drawing, from a Dutch poster by Jan van der Pol, combines the ideas of a garden city with those of urban conservation. Courtesy *The Bulletin of Environmental Education* and Jan van der Pol.

BULLETIN OF ENVIRONMENTAL EDUCATION

BEE

TOWN & COUNTRY PLANNING ASSOCIATION

Doves

Glass panels set into south-facing attic roofs to make greenhouses On the north side you keep your seed- boxes

The Greening Of The Cities

Mulching - no weedkiller inter-cropping - no monoculture

Compost bin, turning all kitchen refuse into organic fertiliser

Public transport

stinging nettles for soup

white bike

potatoes in a barrel

BEE 55   **25 PENCE**   **NOVEMBER 1975**

Reprinted from *Fight Blight* (London: Kaye and Ward Ltd., 1977)

Action Groups

The terms Action Group, Local Community Group, Community and Amenity Society are all in current use in Great Britain and it is necessary to investigate precisely what they mean if powers of supplementing or replacing Council work are to be devolved.

Most action or community groups have been formed in response to some direct threat, usually that of redevelopment, and as long as the threat persists participation tends to remain high. Problems arise when such groups try to translate local enthusiasm for *preventing* something happening, into *proposing* something new or into taking on some permanent duties. As a rule, action groups are not organised for continuing administration.

Different again are the civic and amenity societies (the title seems to be interchangeable) which are generally conservationist in attitude, although some share the beleaguered attitude of the action groups (the only difference between them being the quality of the respective areas the groups were formed to protect). However, many of the thousand-odd such societies registered with the Civic Trust *do* have the facility for on-going administration and some have set up building trusts and similar ventures. Tenants' associations, ratepayers associations, Chambers of Commerce and the like organizations are what their titles imply, and usually display the narrowness of interest one might expect. There can be some surprising exceptions.

The proliferation of such groups makes local Councils chary of public participation, since they claim that it is not possible to know which really speaks for the community. For example, there are two local bodies, both of which claim to speak for the local community in Covent Garden—the officially supported, widely based Forum on the one hand, and the active, successful and pushing Covent Garden Community Association on the other. Predictably they do not always see eye to eye. Councillors maintain that such groups only represent the active vociferous minority, leaving the silent majority completely indifferent; perhaps they should look to their *own* elections in this case, where, very frequently, voting figures are unlikely to represent the majority of the total electorate, and in London only 29 per cent of the electorate! In reality, councillors are concerned at the erosion of their power and prestige, and are therefore hardly likely to welcome any change. In view of which it is not surprising that Edinburgh District Council, for example, recently voted against the establishment of community councils.

The reason why local participation is restricted to a handful is firstly that the power of doing anything has been removed from local levels to distant Castles of Despair which are impossible to influence and dangerous to lobby unless you want to join the black-list; secondly this remoteness of power has led to a gap between the act (voting for a councillor) and the physical result (a new housing development in 15 years). This gap between power and its consequence will have to be closed if people are going to participate; conversely, if local people were aware that a parish council or other local organization were going to take over lettings for a local housing estate (as is the case in Russia) they would participate soon enough. The experience of co-operatives indicates that where power is manifest the participation rate may rise to 75 or 80 per cent.

Common Interest

Many action groups and pressure groups believe that they have totally different aims to other action groups, and some take on an overtly political stance. For example, the magazine *Community Action* (a valuable source of help and information) appears to take a Marxist approach while *Undercurrents* is anarchist, and the Civic Trust newsletter is regarded by some—particularly on the left—as conservative.

A great deal of common interest is obfuscated by political irrelevance, and this common interest is that the members of all societies are volunteers, and that they are passionately interested in improving local conditions. A recent editorial in *Community Action* (no. 13) said, "If community action is to have any meaning at all then it must be based on people sharing their experiences with others who are fighting the same issues." The magazine was referring to specific issues such as housing conditions and slum clearance programmes, but *effectively the fundamental issue which those groups are fighting is the same one as all groups are fighting—namely the problem of remoteness and the lack of power to influence the local environment* (environment in its widest sense). Some groups are extremely unwilling to share their experiences for the benefit of others, and in certain cases this verges on paranoia. In 1975, the RIBA "London Exhibition," which was being held in the Covent Garden Flower Market, invited the local community association to explain how the association had achieved its aims, converted its warehouse, dug its garden, planted its trees. The association refused to participate. Many of those interviewed in the process of compiling this chapter were emphatic that they and *only they* could have done what they did. What was the use, therefore, of telling other people about it? A notable exception to this were the Friends of the Earth, who appeared willing both to inform and learn from others.

It is a sad fact that action groups tend to attract into them a certain type of person who is *competitive* in nature, frequently with the attitude, "My community is better than yours," or "Our festival is more successful than yours;" and needless competition between local groups and personalities leads to yet more squandering of that valuable asset—volunteer enthusiasm—and yet greater weakness in the face of those distant remote Councils. If community and action groups could only concentrate on what they had in common rather than upon the organizational or ideological differences, very much more would be achieved.

Local Organizations

There is an essential functional difference between an action group and a permanent organization, and this might be best explained by an analogy taken from recent events at the Ffestinniog Railway, which is a voluntary effort to rebuild a railway line through the hard hills of North Wales. Until recently the work was carried on entirely by volunteers who spent weekends in a labour camp—the equivalent of an action group. Now that a successful conclusion can be perceived in the distance, the authorities are prepared to back the scheme and have provided money for full-time staff; instead of the staff helping volunteers, volunteers now help full-time staff. Many volunteers have been put off by this change, and have retired from the project. In other words, the Ffestinniog project has now a permanent life of its own. It has ceased to be an action group and has become an organization. There is a similarity between this development and the relationship between the Waterways Recovery Group (volunteers) and the British Waterways Board (officials). Action groups certainly require money and help, but for certain types of activities—only rarely do they require permanent staff.

The Soho Society

The rise of the Soho Society to its present position as the local community organization for trades, shops and residents of Soho is a very good example of what can be achieved. Until five years ago, the life of Soho had been draining away under the combined attack of office development, official neglect of its residential environment by the Local Council, and the general attitude that Soho was the sin centre of London. Indeed at the inaugural meeting of the Society, many of those present felt that it was too late to reverse this trend. The morale of the Soho Community was very low: rubbish was collected at 2 A.M., waking up local residents; most of the local facilities such as schools and laundrettes had closed; clubs and strip joints were creating a great deal of noise and unpleasantness throughout the night; there were several major areas of Soho coming up for development; and the Council itself had demolished streets for no specific purpose. The general attitude was that no *nice* person would really like to live in Soho, and that sooner or later all the residential accommodation would be redeveloped, with alternative dwellings being provided elsewhere for those who were displaced. The first stage in the restoration of morale was the winning of some redevelopment battles—particularly that over the John Snow site in Lexington Street, and the saving of a row of early eighteenth-century houses in Broadwick Street. The Society was also able to keep far closer tabs on the development of the area, in such matters as illegal changes of use from flats to offices, or the moonlight flit of a strip joint from one basement to another, than the Council. Soon clubs and strip joints were surprised to find that they were reported for noise at night. In fact, Soho Society was founded just in time to revive the normal but decayed community mechanisms, and has established a newspaper *Soho Clarion*, a dancing team and a football club. But there are still threats: the Council is keen to demolish the ancient blocks of Victorian flats, although they are not prepared to provide new housing in Soho themselves.

Like many local societies, the Soho Society is not without its extroverts, and the day after Lord Goodman made his famous speech calling for angry young men with fire in their bellies who would help solve the housing crisis, Stephen Fry rang him to suggest that he should provide money for a Soho housing association. He got it. Coincidentally seven other people within the society had set up a co-ownership housing association (for which funds were unfortunately not available—and the City Council was obstructive about providing land). The two propositions merged into the Soho Housing Association which is now registered with the Housing Corporation. Dickon and Charlotte Robinson, who were among the orginators of the Housing Association, point out that the value of their own local association is the power that it gives to local groups to provide housing for local people. The prospect of a large, distant, housing association taking over local endeavour is almost as inimical to them as letting the Council take it on themselves, since the small scale sensitive "feel" of the operation is lost. The obstruction encountered from the Council was based on the attitude that Soho Housing Association was a "bunch of amateurs;" the "amateurs" won, and the first scheme, consisting of 27 flats in Great Pulteney Street and Bridle Lane, has been granted planning permis-

sion; while another development of 30 more flats in Marshall Street has been submitted. Further schemes are being prepared for Royalty Mansions (Meard Street) and the St. James's residences. If these schemes are successful, before very long the Soho Society will be the main housing authority in the Soho area. Another conservation society—the Camberwell Society—has just taken steps in the same direction, by reviving a local, dormant housing association to promote house building and conversions in that district.

Co-operatives

A different form of initiative can be seen in co-operatives, which can be of several types: (a) a tenant co-operative managing a Council estate; (b) a co-operative managing the rehabilitation of a housing action area, most of the houses of which have been purchased by local authority (as in the Birnam Road area of Islington; (c) a co-operative which owns the building and the land itself, borrowing the money against the mortgage; and (d) a co-operative which sets up as a joint non-profit-making venture in business. An interesting tenant management co-operative is that recently set up by the Greater London Council GLC in the St. Katherine Estate, Wapping, East London. The Housing Rents and Subsidies Act "enables a local authority to reach an agreement with a co-operative for the exercise by the latter at a particular estate of virtually all the local authority's housing powers without forfeiting government subsidy." In the case in question, some 167 pre–1945 dwellings are involved, on an estate which was mostly empty awaiting modernization which had to be dropped as a result of cuts. The Stephen and Matilda Tenants Association negotiated the establishment of this co-operative with the GLC, and will become responsible for the management and maintenance of the estate. The remaining tenants were given the choice to stay in the buildings and help with the co-operative or leave, and those tenants who had already left were given the choice to return. The co-operative will operate general management, the lettings, the collection of rent and rates, caretaking and day-to-day maintenance, while the landlord—the GLC—will remain owner, and contractor for specified works. The GLC will pay, to the co-operative, monthly, an amount which in total will be equivalent to the pooled cost of management and maintenance per dwelling for an estate of that type," and it will be this money that the co-op will use to their own ends. A similar co-operative venture is proposed for the Juniper House, Kender Estate, Deptford, and for other estates. The Government's attitude towards co-operatives such as this is as follows:

Co-operatives should not be seen simply as a means of relinquishing responsibility for problem estates or for functions which are proving troublesome.

Purists may argue that the management co-op achieves little. They would be wrong. Tenants living in squalor have a chance to reverse these conditions as well as having the opportunity to decide things for themselves. How different this is from, say, the Council's attitude to tenants on the North Peckham Estate, London, where tenants are being *allowed* to choose the colour of their own front doors (*Building Design*, 19 November 1976).

Fairhazel is a co-operative which owns a group of mansion blocks and houses in North West London, dating from about 1890, which they have bought with a mortgage from Camden Council. The mortgage also provides funds to do the repairs and rehabilitation which have become necessary through lack of maintenance, and Fairhazel is expected to bring the buildings up to a standard which will be sound for at least another 30 years. Of course, as everybody now realizes, buildings such as these have an indefinite life as long as they are well maintained and meet the needs of the inhabitants. Being a co-operative, the inhabitants have a greater say in what is to be done than is normal, and the architects for the scheme have to have an office on site to advise, particularly in the evenings when tenants arrive home from work. It must be novel for the architects to have over 117 clients in a single development.

The finances are tortuous. The Government provided £605,000 to Camden Council, which was lent to Fairhazel against a mortgage to purchase the freeholds. It might be questioned whether the capital purchase price was not too high for blocks of decaying mansion flats, or indeed whether the conversion cost which has been estimated at about £10,000 per flat is not excessive. These costs can be afforded since the Government is underwriting the difference between the rent income (or mortgage repayment) and the cost of the mortgage—which would come to almost 80 per cent of the total cost. Thus the scheme has a similar subsidy arrangement to that of Council housing, and can in no way be thought of as paying for itself. A more interesting exercise might have been to have tailored the amount of conversion exactly to what could be afforded: in other words *minimum change commensurate with reasonable living conditions*. Further and more elaborate changes could have been made when the individual tenant's income permitted, or when the co-operative collectively had managed to find some finance. There are still three advantages to this co-operative over the normal procedures of demolition and redevelopment: firstly, the great length of development time during which the land and buildings are empty is avoided and this accommodation will always be in use; secondly, the very fact of being members of a co-operative is stimulating participation and community spirit by the tenants—a feature not frequently remarked in new Council schemes; and lastly, even at a cost of £15,000 per flat, the scheme is probably cheaper than the Council cost of a new redevelopment.

The Black Road Scheme, Macclesfield

A completely different type of action was taken by local residents in the Black road area of Macclesfield, whose houses, dating mostly from 1813 to 1817, had been zoned for clearance in 1968 but, as the result of lack of finance to implement the demolition, were still standing in 1972. By the time the clearance programme was resumed, a local residents' committee had been set up with its own architect resident, Rod Hackney, and a builder, Tom Lawton, who surveyed the 32 properties and put up the case that a General Improvement Area should be declared (under the terms of the 1969 Housing Act) rather than demolition.

They lobbied the local Council, and the Department of the Environment left the decision up to the local Council on the grounds that although the Department had doubts that the buildings were worth it, local conditions should prevail. Rod Hackney makes the significant comment,

The residents all along avoided any personal criticism of local government officers and elected representatives . . . their insistence on avoiding criticising individuals within the local authority had a great bearing on the outcome of the first fight to save their homes, and subsequently the successful management of the general improvement area. (Royal Society of Health Conference on Housing Improvements.)

Finally, the Council approved a General Improvement Area on the grounds that the residents thought their homes were still viable, and were prepared to invest in them; and that the new legislation (namely, the Housing Act 1969) had altered the situation on which the 1968 clearance order had been made. Council voted £250 per house for environmental works, provided temporary rented accommodation for those people whose houses were being improved, and were prepared to award maximum improvement grants where appropriate.

The Black Road Area Residents Association planned the building operations so that many of their own residents participated in the actual construction tasks. They supervised the works during progress. They co-ordinated all activities relating to the work on site. They arranged financial help for the scheme and established temporary housing for themselves while individual house improvement work commenced. Transport and removal facilities were arranged to and from temporary housing. . . . As there were no roads within the scheme the residents built a temporary road for the contractors so that they could gain access to the site, and for storing materials. This, of course, saved a considerable amount of money. Before the road could be built, all the residents had to dedicate over to the group part of their private land thus allowing the roadworks a route through what were previously their gardens. (This route has now been converted into an open area with paving, playspaces, seating, trees, flowers and shrubs). The sharing of land had other advantages. It allowed extensions to be built on former neighboring land where difficulties arose in

the planning of extensions. It did away with the old "rights of way" and especially the "rights of light."

The Local Authority needed convincing quickly that the Group had indeed put their money where their mouths were, and the residents needed something to show in a short space of time what they could achieve in actual construction terms. So, while the overall scheme was being planned, Rod Hackney converted his own house at 222 Black Road as a show house. The bricklayer in the group, Tom Lawton, took upon himself the role of main contractor, one of the electricians did the rewiring, other residents helped in the demolition of chimney breasts, knocking down walls, carting away rubbish . . . and they also helped in redecoration works. After three months, the show house was complete. The Council were impressed with the first conversion.

Building prices had soared since the scheme was first thought of, and to keep pace with these inflationary trends and not to overspend on the amount of mortgages being offered, the residents have had occasionally to do more of the house improvement work themselves. For example, if the house costs increase by £50, then the resident for the house concerned offers his labour to the contractor for a couple of days resulting in the appropriate saving . . . most of the residents worked on the building site in the evenings and weekends.

No single house is the same as any other. The completed improved houses all reflect the wishes and requirements of the residents. . . . The windows and doors are all different; there are many types of staircase . . . the kitchen layouts are all different . . . some residents had shower cubicles, others a bath . . . many wanted fireplace features.

The Local Authority, on their part, have acted responsibly in their interpretation of the building regulations for older buildings. Rigid, inflexible standards have not been asked for. . . . The results have satisfied everybody. This was not a simple task of upgrading older houses to the 12 point standard as laid down in the 1969 Housing Act, but rather a detailed exercise in accommodating the wishes of the individual residents, and at the same time producing new homes for them to live in and of which they could be proud, and call the result their own. (Black Road Area Residents Association, writing in *Community Action* magazine, June–July 1974.)

This scheme was subsequently given an award for good design in housing (GIA Category) by the Department of the Environment. These buildings are not large, not spacious, and are very close together; yet the combined efforts of the tenants, coupled with the fact that they did not wish to leave their houses, however cramped, have produced an environment for which the tenants and occupants are themselves responsible, and that is the ultimate aim. Rod Hackney's conclusions from this scheme are as follows:

a. The rectangular site chosen for the pilot scheme proved ideal in its internal arrangement of spaces for a successful environmental improvement scheme. It showed that without any works to the surrounding roadways a successful environmental scheme could concentrate on simply tidying up the "backs," the areas between terraces, and making the house improvement and environmental improvements compatible with each other.

b. By concentrating on a small compact area and making sure that all the houses were improved the Group were able to ensure that their houses, being within self-contained boundaries, would not prejudice future plans for immediately surrounding areas.

c. The Group decided at the outset to establish a successful precedent. Once this had been achieved they then expected the future to take a similar course as long as the financial incentives were still available for house and area improvement.

d. Rather than sit back on their laurels once they had saved their homes, they simply transferred the energy displayed in their campaign to the practical implementation of the house and area improvement scheme.

e. Lastly, they embarked on a campaign to save their homes knowing that there were right in what they wanted. They were willing to sacrifice personal gain to see the joint effort succeed. In many respects they took most of the people they dealt with by surprise. The Group's single minded aim to get on with the job of improving their homes and the energy they displayed in achieving this aim, guided by their basic common-sense attitude, were the hallmarks of their achievements. (Taken from the transactions of the Royal Society of Health's Conference on Housing Improvements.)

Although there have been no further schemes similar to Black Road as yet, it is possible that the approach will grow in popularity and there are indications that Prospect Road

GIA in Cambridge, the Heckford Park GIA in Poole, Dorset, and a few others may develop along similar lines. In London there have been a number of public enquiries into slum clearance (part 3 of the Housing Act, 1957) which have subsequently been won by the residents who then organized a co-operative rehabilitation of their houses. Chris Whittaker is a professional involved with such cases, one of which was an enquiry into a group of houses—including 18 owner-occupied houses—close to central London. The inspector confirmed the compulsory purchase order (against the wishes of the residents) but the Secretary of State dissented on the grounds that the houses were "improvable for a number of years." Whittaker is now involved in helping the residents to establish a co-operative housing association, through which improvements to the houses will be effected. It may well be that this approach will put a far smaller charge on public funds if a redevelopment scheme had been implemented.

Advice in Glasgow

There is a major psychological difference between a group identifying its own problems and trying to solve them (as in Macclesfield or Covent Garden) and a body of outsiders coming in to give advice. The latter is particularly necessary where local people are so bludgeoned by Councils that they do not believe that there is any alternative open to them but to accept Council proposals. In Glasgow, for instance, the official attitude towards tenement buildings has been that they constitute an out-of-date form of housing and should be demolished—no matter what the tenants or owners might think. A recent song puts this well:

They're pullin' doon the tenement next tae oors,
Tae send us oot tae Green Belt, trees an' floors;
But we dinnae want tae go,
And we've surely telt them so,
Oh they're pullin' down the tenement next tae oors . . .

ASSIST is a research unit of Strathclyde University which was founded in 1972 following a thesis by Raymond Young (in 1969) on voluntary tenement improvement, and the practical experience he had gained from moving to Govan in 1970. Govan was one of Glasgow's notorious Comprehensive Development Areas, and one of the centres of the near-defunct ship-building industry. Glasgow Corporation was eventually persuaded to declare part of it a Treatment Area, and no less than its Lord Provost opened the Assist shop. A study of 200 houses revealed that a high percentage of owners and tenants wished to remain in the area despite the grim environment caused by twenty-five years' decay and neglect. The architecture shop soon found that local residents did not distinguish between the types of advice required, and the "shop" had to have other professionals available to give advice on matters ranging from rent rebates, where to find a plumber, to the break-up of marriages. Soon it developed in to a mini local authority (in the best sense of this term) in that on certain days of the week officials from the corporation visit the shop where they can meet enquirers and give help. Thus, apart from the valuable work in pioneering tenement rehabilitation and public participation, ASSIST has pioneered a method by which the skills of the Council can be made available at a very local level, avoiding all the inhibiting factors usually associated with "going up to the Council." Significantly, in Glasgow of all places, the tenant or occupier is now choosing himself whether to stay in a tenement and have it improved, or to move to accommodation elsewhere. The concept of tenant freedom of choice is a bitter pill for a dictatorial corporation to swallow, and it is to be hoped that is has not merely lodged in the corporation's throat.

Conclusion

Action, community, conservation and pressure groups are likely to remain so, and fulfil a valuable function. However, on-going supervision of a local area is best undertaken by a parish council in consultation with them and the district Councils should be prepared to devolve to parish councils power and money for parish councils to look after themselves. It is ironic that parish councils have power, but generally speaking, exist only in rural or small town areas. There is a far greater and more urgent need for their city cousins, the community councils, few of which (as far as I know) yet exist. These should have similar powers to parish councils, such as that of raising property taxes. It is a great pity that their establishment depends upon the voting of the councillors of existing districts (who have an innate bias against supporting such organizations). Finally, the policy of co-operation between all sectors of the community should be fostered and encouraged since it will provide resources where none at present exist, and will restore self-respect to people, particularly in blighted areas.

22

Towards New Perceptions of the Environment: Using the Town Trail

Brian Goodey

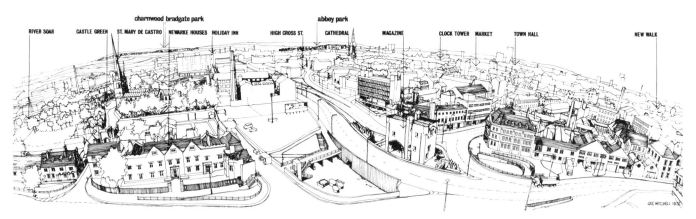

charnwood bradgate park   abbey park

RIVER SOAR   CASTLE GREEN   ST. MARY DE CASTRO   NEWARKE HOUSES   HOLIDAY INN   HIGH CROSS ST.   CATHEDRAL   MAGAZINE   CLOCK TOWER   MARKET   TOWN HALL   NEW WALK

GEE MITCHELL 1972

Extract of a map of the Leicester Town Trail, 1972. From *Bulletin of Environmental Education (BEE)* (London: Town and Country Planning Association, 1972).

Dylan Thomas Uplands Trail, Swansea. Courtesy of Swansea City Council Planning Department.

```
SWANSEA
P: DYLAN THOMASUPLANDS TRAIL, 1976

This trail, amply illustrated with Dylan's own
words, takes the town tracker round the area where
Dylan Thomas was born and lived for the first 20
years of his life - the Uplands in Swansea.  It is
one   of the earliest residential areas to be dev-
        eloped as a result of industrial and comm-
            ercial growth in the 19th century. Res-
              earched by 11 year old girls from
                 Oakleigh House School.  Illus.
                with lovely old           photos
                  like this
                    one.
```

GWYDN TERRACE, UPLANDS, SWANSEA

A children's model, 21 feet long, of Hythe Street, made by 80 pupils of 10 and 11 years at Hythe Primary School. From reprint of "Report on Heritage Year," *The Architects' Journal*, February 25, 1976, p. 375.

Advertisement from *The Daily Mirror* announcing a children's competition for Wide Awake Trails in their own towns. From *BEE*, no. 69, January 1977.

"My Journey to School," a project done by a twelve-year-old in an urban studies course sponsored by the Front Door project.

My journey to school

"My journey to school" — a project by 12 year olds in an urban studies course.

Every morning I leave my house at 8.20. to go to school. It was built when my mum was a little girl. All the houses in the street are all the same, except the people have painted them different colours.

I catch the bus on the corner next to the garage. There is no litter bin at the bus stop so there are always tickets and ice cream papers lying around. On the way, we pass the estate where my friend lives. His flat is on the fifth floor and he says the lifts are always out of order always on the ground walls are scribbled on and some of the floor, all the broken. windows are The next big building is the hospital. They finished building it last year. Some of the houses in the High Street are quite old, but have been made into modern shops, with large windows. At night it looks good with all the windows lit up.

PETROL

The church on the corner is over a hundred years old, and has stained glass windows.

My friend comes to school on the tube, but I prefer to travel by bus as you can see more.

ABC   HABITAT

Our school is very modern. It is made of concrete, glass and looks and and steel a greenhouse. feels like

There are playgrounds, football pitches and a few trees.

Examples of drawings from the Front Door project set up by London's education authority, planning and architecture department, and the Royal College of Art. Schoolchildren (aged 16–19) in Pimlico go out and draw buildings and places, which are then discussed with professionals and others as a source of mutual education. The remarkable detail of the children's drawings provoked the editor of *The Architectural Review*, Lance Wright, to write: "The moral of these drawings for architects is that 'incident' is worth every penny. Looking at it the other way round, is it not possible that the blankness of today's buildings arises because we suspect that nobody is looking? Why should we cater for a roving and inquiring eye if it is not the habit of the eyes to rove and inquire? Some of the unsatisfactoriness of buildings must be due to this gap in our education. After all, if people were not taught to read, literature would quickly perish. On the other hand, if—thanks to Front Door—good, hard, serious seeing were to become part of everyone's mental habit the effect on building design would be startling. How quickly we pull ourselves together when we know that somebody's looking. More power to Front Door: may it open quickly." Front Door was steered by Kenneth Baynes and Eileen Adams. From *BEE*, no. 70, February 1977.

Reprinted from *The Bulletin of Environmental Education,* London, July 1975.

In this chapter I want to cover four main aspects of town trail production and use. As a preliminary I shall define and suggest the utility of trails, but I want to concentrate on the things to consider when preparing trails for local use, the process of development and evaluation, and the townscape elements which might be included. In conclusion I will illustrate trail-making from two Birmingham examples. This chapter does not attempt a survey of the field as one has already been published elsewhere,[1] neither does it attempt to list the two hundred odd trails which are now available as this task has been taken in hand by the British Tourist Authority who will be publishing such a list in the near future.[2] What I hope to do is to point out the relative simplicity of the town trailing idea, its low cost to the local authority and its potentially high yield in terms of formal and informal education and leisure.

1. Background to Town Trails

a. *What are they?* Both urban trails and walks may be regarded as planned and self-guided routes through urban areas which may be walked by anybody who is interested, and which are indicated either by markers in the townscape, or (more commonly) by published route leaflets or brochures. Such a definition excludes the majority of guidebooks which, although detailing local attractions and including maps, seldom link the two elements in a programmed manner. Both walks and trails reveal urban place to the observer, encourage perception rather than mere recognition of environments, add value to place through use, and provide a framework for visitor management in town or city.

There are however, some distinctions between walk and trail. The *walk* tends to itemize structures, provide historic and architectural background, and invite aesthetic appreciation and enjoyment of what has been preserved or conserved. The *trail,* a more recent development in the tradition of nature trails, has the added dimension of demanding from the user a response in terms of the quality of environments observed. It follows that the walk and the trail may differ considerably in terms of the route chosen, the audience considered, the range of matters covered, and the social purpose for which the activity is intended. As a generalisation, the walk guide will allow the casual visitor or interested resident to use a well-illustrated guide to view the conserved and attractive areas of a town. The trail will allow teacher and student to explore typical *and* exceptional areas of a town as a basis to further classwork and possible community action. Such use is not, however, exclusive and both the Leicester and Newcastle Town Trails, though developed in the educational context, have achieved wide public use.[3]

Both walks and trails can trace their origins back to the nineteenth century perambulation, walks which citizens took to get to know their towns better. Guides have been produced throughout the twentieth century, and with the fairly recent growth of interest in conservation issues, amenity societies have taken on board the responsibility for local guides which have often been in a walk or trail format. The development of trails for educational purposes, like the development of urban studies centers, may be seen as the urban parallel to developed rural interpretation techniques—the nature trail and field studies centers. The first English nature trail (imported from the USA) was established in 1961 and there are now over five hundred, which, it will be remembered, are used both for environmental interpretation *and* visitor management.

Although walks and trails are now better developed in Britain than anywhere overseas, the Boston Freedom Trail and the Vienna city walk both pre-date the first British examples.[4]

The first British amenity society walk seems to have been that for Faversham, produced in 1865 and supported by local authority funds.[5] The first town trails, both produced in 1972 by staff of teacher training colleges, were the Leicester Town Trail, which was created by a geography department, and the Architectural Trail in Dudley, part of a local history project.[6]

Since 1972 there has been a rapid development of general and specialist local walks and trails. I would estimate that there are now about two hundred available in 1975, although this number is likely to increase rapidly, encouraged by European Architectural Heritage Year, the British Tourist Authority and the Council for Urban Studies Centres. Until very recently, development has been on an ad hoc basis but BTA is about to publish a list of trails and their sources for tourist use and will act, informally, as a clearing house for new trails, offering support through the national and regional tourist boards.

Of the two hundred or so trails available, we can identify four main sources; (a) commercial publishers, (b) public bodies, (c) local voluntary groups, and (d) educational institutions.

Commercial publications focus on our major cities, especially London, and offer well-produced but basic guides. Some experiments have been attempted with tape cassette guides (in London and York) and there is evidence of increasing commercial interest in the idea. Local authority walks and trails are increasing rapidly in number, especially from new Leisure/Amenity departments and from Planning departments with an interest in local conservation. But by far the largest number of trails have come from local amenity groups and ad hoc groups of educationalists or schools. In both situations, the making of the trail has proved as big an attraction as the final product, allowing local historians, photographers, etc. to indulge their hobbies to profitable ends, and students and teachers to undertake research or project work with a useful and visible outcome. Trails especially offer both the learning experience of designing and producing route and brochure, and the experience of observing and analysing the environment en route. Thus the trail brochure preparation has served as a student project at primary, secondary and professional education levels, as well as a voluntary service project for university students and, frequently, as a project for teachers attending a local teachers' center for "in-service" training, or for students at a College of Education.[7]

But in this great flurry of trail-making activity there is a need to stop and ask what we need trails for. Are they such an obvious benefit to the community, what do they involve in terms of investment, and how are they used?

b. *Why we need them.* The most important reason for advocating the development and use of trails is to reassert the individual relationship between the individual and the environment. So much has been said about cities and urban life in recent years that to suggest each individual has perceptions of place worth developing and articulating often appears foolish in the face of complex technological and management problems which have become synonymous with "the city." Given increasingly sophisticated public and educational information techniques, of which the universality of aerial images of place is but one simple example, we have all tended to remove ourselves from place. We ride rather than walk, and by riding in car, bus, train or plane, our images of place are blurred and we are only able to abstract the most obvious features, usually the biggest or best publicised. The Midland Bank advertisement of a few years ago which collapsed all the major tourist buildings of Europe into one street scene was only acknowledging a situation in which we tend to use a visual shorthand, a mere recognition, rather than a perception of individual places. The confusion between media, and especially television, as art and as replication of reality, has led to a tendency to distance ourselves from the reality of places and events and even the camera viewfinder can act as a baffle between our experience and the reality beyond the lens. To this we must add the tendency of the media to discuss the urban condition in universal terms, denying the importance of place and presenting an acceptable—yet totally unacceptable—list of urban problems. Our images of place become generalisations, better represented by fiction than by fact.

This tendency to consume places, both through the media and through tourism and recreation, is likely to be reversed by recent events. Because we are not likely to stray so far from home, because media budgets are likely to be trimmed, because government funding will not allow a continuation of recreational extravaganzas, we are all going to be forced to consider the value of our immediate surroundings. Walks and trails offer a method of engaging the user with local place, by pointing out in an informal way the density of information and values available. Using video equipment to draw the trail user into unlikely situations can involve a large investment but marking a trail or linking up existing building plaques can be cheap and effective. Graphics in the evniorment, like those developed by Gordon Cullen for the redevelopment of Coventry town center, represent a long term investment in place, but as much can be achieved through the well-designed but cheaply produced brochure.

Considering the local authority context specifically, the value of walks and trails must be seen in two major areas. First of all in the context of formal education, where a prod from the local inspectorate or teachers' center, followed by a low-cost high-yield course of the type which I will discuss later, can yield several local trails which can be used interchangeably as local schools get to know each others' territory. These trails may also provide the appropriate basis for other, more formal routes to be developed by the authority. Usually the city or town center offers the most obvious target, with a random array of preserved and interesting buildings which can be linked to local museums and points of interest by a general trail. But enthusiasm, often hidden behind leisure-time hobbies, may be harnessed within local authority departments and the quiet planning assistant may well prove able to unite a personal interest in railways with office facilities in producing a trail which surprises even the most informed resident.

What most effective local trails require is the enthusiasm of local information sources, combined with the technical skill of educators, planners, draftsmen and librarians working informally together. A sophisticated local trail, printed and widely circulated, can still be produced at about 30p a copy, but this is the upper end of the scale and many effective school trails which are available to the public have been as cheap as the price of duplicating paper will allow.

And what is the outcome of the trail-making activity? Such phrases as "local pride" come easily to mind, and practical experience suggests that students and members of the public who begin to invest attention in a place become more concerned for its condition. The presence of visitors, attracted to a trail, can also give the resident pride in his surroundings, and the problem student turned informed local guide is not an idle dream. By guiding the process of trail making and by informing through trail literature, the local authority may be able to draw the local population into a closer relationship with environmental decisions and trails produced by local groups can often highlight street ephemera which the broad sweep of planned redevelopment can so easily remove.

Trails, then, are an interpretative tool appropriate to our times. Their success will, however, depend on local initiative and careful planning.

2. Points to Consider in Developing and Evaluating Trails

In this section of the chapter I want to suggest a few of the key points to be considered in developing a trail. The first decision to be made is, of course, the purpose of the trail. The trail will, it is hoped, have a clear purpose relating to a particular user group, or possibly to various user groups:

User Groups
i. Supervised school parties in various age groups
ii. Unsupervised groups or individuals of school age
iii. Students in general tertiary education
iv. Special student interest groups, e.g. architecture, history, engineering
v. Teacher training or refresher groups
vi. Local general interest organizations/individuals
vii. Local subject interest groups/individuals, e.g. amenity, architecture, history, art, photography
viii. Visiting English-speaking groups/individuals from other parts of the UK, the Commonwealth
ix. Visiting non-English-speaking groups/individuals
x. Special user groups:—the elderly, the disabled (in mobility, sight, hearing)

Resident Groups

i. Residents in properties on the trail route

ii. Commercial users en route—consider access, clients, nature of work undertaken, etc.

iii. Authorities (public or private) responsible for properties, land or access on route.

Whatever the group, or groups involved, the production process would seem to involve a standard series of considerations which we can outline under these headings: Pre-planning, Choice of Route, On the Trail, The Brochure, Trail Launching and Management.

Pre-planning

i. Is the proposed trail part of a programme of local recreation planning, tourist management, environmental education? If so, where does it fit in? If not, then should it be part of such a programme?

ii. Does the proposed trail duplicate existing facilities or information? Are similar trails being prepared locally for this or other local routes? Should there be a coordinated local programme?

Choice of Route

iii. Is the proposed distance realistic? Are there alternative sections for long and short walks? Does the route return to the starting point; if not, what transport facilities are available?

iv. How does the route relate to mobility? What slopes and steps are involved; are there alternative paths; are there resting points for the tired?

v. What are the safety precautions? Obviously traffic can be a major hazard, but so too are precarious viewpoints, accessways, water bodies and disused buildings. Safety must also be considered in relation to the existing, and expected, increase in pedestrian flow.

vi. Are there appropriate vantage points? Sketching, photography and group discussion en route are elements of enjoyment in a trail; are open spaces available for these?

vii. Is legal access available to buildings and locations discussed en route? If not, can permission or opening be obtained?

viii. Is the route flexible enough to allow individual meanderings from the set path?

ix. Does the route offer shelter such as churches, museums, open houses, shops, both to avoid inclement weather and to provide interior–exterior contrasts?

x. Are the required range of public facilities available? These must include toilets, food and drink, access to public transport and parking, sources of information, camera film, etc.

On the Trail

xi. Is it possible to mark the trail in the townscape? If so, how much information is on wayside markers and how does this relate to the guidebook material?

xii. Is the route general or specific? Does the trail provide a general introduction to the route, or does it emphasize one series of specific elements?

xiii. Is variety in the environment revealed? Are contrasting visual, sonic and small environments suggested; is the head jerked skywards and to the floor as well as in the more normal "straight ahead" position?

xiv. If the trail is to be subject specific, ensure that the best available expertise is used in design; the enthusiastic user will soon spot an amateur production.

xv. Is there an opportunity to evaluate environmental quality en route? Can the trail be used as an educational experience, relating to existing problems as well as to past life?

The Brochure

xvi. Is the published brochure an effective tool for use en route? Is it brief, stimulating, legible, and easy to handle when walking?

xvii. Is the brochure accurate? Does the map check with the route, do both check with current traffic and planning conditions? Are historical details correct? Are ownership and access details correct?

xviii. Is the brochure ahead of its time? The brochure should predict a year ahead in terms of possible environmental change. The local planning department should be asked to check details here.

xix. Do illustrations in the brochure highlight or add to

the experience en route? There is little reason to include elements which the user can observe.

Trail Launching and Management

xx. Have plans been made for a pilot test of the trail and brochure? The proposed route should be tested in detail by sample user groups, often including schools, local amenity groups and the disabled.

xxi. When the trail has been tested, are there appropriate opportunities for launching the trail in relation to a local historical event or festival, or as part of a planning participation exercise?

xxii. Has a publicity programme been developed to launch the trail—local press, radio and TV? Inform local bodies which may be interested—local authority departments including planning, education, social services and recreation; local amenity and civic organizations; librarians and museum staff; clergy; school staff, local colleges and teachers' centers. Also inform those national organizations which might assist promotion; copies of the trail to the following will ensure widespread coverage: British Tourist Authority; Civic Trust; Library, Royal Institute of British Architects; Education Unit, Town & Country Planning Association.

xxiii. Has an information programme been developed? Local suppliers, including tourist centers, churches, hotels, bookshops, cafes and pubs, should be briefed and supplied. Statutory service buildings are seldom open when the majority of users will want the brochure.

xxiv. Are follow up information sources available on the route, does the brochure indicate other local sources of information?

xv. Is there a process for evaluation of the trail? User needs should be monitored, changes en route reflected and management needs responded to.

3. Trail Content

Moving to the content of the trail, the key determinants will, of course, be the features of the area to be covered and the user group for which the brochure is intended. It is, however, important to remember that the environment always offers us more than we readily take and that as a result we tend towards stereotyped searches for set pieces. Already in trail-making this has led to concentration on a rather narrow band of environmental elements and I want briefly to suggest how the ambit of any trail making activity can be extended.

Essentially the information in a trail consists of descriptions of landscape (and more especially "townscape") elements. These are largely, though not entirely, of the built-form variety. Take, for example, the list under "C":

Cafe	Cinema
Canal	Clock
Car park	Common land
Change of level	Conservation area
Chapel	Cottage
Chimney	Courtyard
Church	Cross.
Churchyard	

(And there are probably many more, appearing in most urban settings, which I have omitted). Now add to such a list, a series of descriptors, providing detail on specific features or sites. I'm going to read the whole list to stress the possible breadth, a breadth from which "age," "architectural style" and "decoration" are too often taken as the only useful headings:

Access	Enclosure
Adaptability	Feeling
Age	Form
Architectural style	Geometry
Change	Grouping
Colour	Height
Condition	Historical associations
Decline	Improvement
Decoration	Intimacy
Degree of modification	Juxtaposition
Design	Light and shade
Distance	Literary associations
Documentation	Materials

Mystery	Size
Notoriety	Structure
Place	Territoriality
Quality	Texture
Relationships	Three-dimensionality
Smell	Tidiness
Sound	Value
Safety	Views
Scale	Visibility.

Whether these elements and descriptors are given to the trail user, or whether they are covered or hinted at in questions or on-trail activity, there is a very wide range to choose from. While teachers are likely, as I shall illustrate later, to use quite a range of these ideas, there is a danger that the amenity or conservation trail will perpetuate the tradition of informed yet limited architectural comment.

By assembling a collection of existing trails prior to developing your own local series, hints as to what to include may quickly be gathered. At this juncture I can only suggest a few themes which deserve attention in whatever area is concerned.

While people are the most important element in the townscape they do not stand still and are therefore rather difficult to build into a trail. But there are always places where people meet or rest, where both the tradition and the current patterns of human behaviour can be described and examined. Housing is another universal urban theme, and here history, building science and social conditions can all be explored. Why was a particular design selected for a particular site, and how does the physical arrangement of property affect behaviour? Material from local authority files could well be included to provide the decision-making background to landscape features. More important in relation to housing, how have residents structured their surroundings and revealed themselves to the public?

Commercial premises, of whatever age, may be interesting from the architectural point of view, but they also represent service location and the use of buildings for marketing purposes. How have styles of marketing changed and how do different facilities in the same town compare both visually and functionally? Again, local authority departments will have available both the rationale and the design details of changes, providing background to the contrast between historical shopping streets and new pedestrian areas.

While these considerations may be seen as fitting within the tradition of history, geography or environmental studies curricula, there is, of course, a very strong design element in the townscape, not only at the macroscale, but in street and building furniture. The humble cafe window may reveal several periods of graphic design and it is surprising how much design history can be derived from the local shopping center. This is especially true of the twilight areas of our cities where old commercial buildings remain in use, and where industrial archaeology may just be in the townscape rather than being neatly surrounded by a museum boundary. Pavement surfaces may still reveal horse cobbles and tram-lines, while walls retain gas brackets and evidence of the past that would have been cleared in the more "attractive" areas of the city.

Lettering and writing in the townscape provide a vital source of information for the local historian and English teacher. Fast departing are the Victorian office blinds but walls above the natural eye-line can still reveal much concerning pre-television street life where the walls were often the medium for all. The type and design of commercial signs or doorplates can still tell of the multi-functional use of older factories or houses.

To these permitted elements we can add those of the informal city where fly posting on certain disused sites very quickly becomes a tradition and where youth or immigrant cultures look for their information. There are Birmingham walls where one goes to find out about West Indian soul or Irish show band performances, just as there are informal rock concert announcements in every European city from Paris to Hull. There is the informal city as expressed in individual house decoration, especially evident in immigrant inner city areas, and there is the informal city of personal statements, of spray-on graffiti on public or private walls, a territorial statement or news item.

The first step with all these features is to stimulate, through the arrangement of the trail route, and the text of the document, the seeing eye and the array of other senses. Seeing should encourage a search for explanations, and may stimulate action. Action will tend to circulate around the issues of conservation — interpreted broadly—and of environmental quality and several planning authorities have already seen the trail as an integral preliminary to participation in the local planning process. The trail is used to marry the planners' perceptions of the area with those of the various resident groups.

In conclusion I want to draw on the practical experiences of trail-making with which I have been associated in Birmingham; this to emphasize the activity rather than the academic survey. Two recent events illustrate very different examples of the trail in action.

4. Brum Trails

Soon after the establishment of the Council for Urban Studies Centres in London, a local committee—now known as the Birmingham Urban Studies Centres Committee—was established in the second city. It has now been functioning for a year and has 25 members drawn from educational interest groups, environmental and architectural societies and community organizations. Representatives of the local authority libraries, education and Chief Executive's staff also attend. Like other local groups, we have found the establishment of an Urban Studies Centre to be a very tough proposition given the current economic climate, and given a legacy of trail-making by several of the Committee members, we have emphasized this area of work. Recently we published our first "Brum Trail" for public distribution; earlier duplicated trails having been limited to educational use.[8] Brum Trail 1 is a major capital investment, involving about £1,000 for a print run of 4000. The trail described is intended for the tourist and casual visitor and features the city centre. The brochure, which retails at 30p (probably the maximum price possible for this type of document) is intentionally "glossy" and was designed as

part of contracted project work by students of the Department of Visual Communication at Birmingham Polytechnic. The text was prepared by a geography teacher, an education department inspector and a social worker. The trail is being sold by the City Information Department and from initial reactions it seems as though it will be used widely by industrialists receiving overseas visitors.

The production of a glossy general introduction to the city follows the pattern adopted by several amenity societies elsewhere who, like us, hope to establish a role in the city. Due for production in a cheaper, offset litho format later this year is a trail around the Birmingham Outer Circle bus route, a 2 hour journey which passes through many of the suburban villages now engulfed by the city. This route was the subject of a bus company guide in the 1920s and we hope that the trail will encourage local exploration by school groups and by the general public. For later publication we have planned a canalside trail and, in association with Shelter, a housing trail for a Birmingham inner urban area. In addition we may be able to circulate more widely trails or walks prepared by other groups in the city.

5. Educational Trails in an Urban Environment Course

Of more immediate relevance to educational needs in Birmingham was a course held during three days of March (1975), involving twenty-seven teachers from a cross section of Birmingham schools. The course was held at the Educational Development Centre in Birmingham and had the advantage of media and reprographic resources at that Centre. Organized by the City Education Department it involved instruction and practical work in trail preparation and because it was obviously successful, and might therefore be copied with profit elsewhere, I want to go into some detail on the planning and product of this course.

Financial resources involved were limited, possibly involving £100 in terms of equipment, fees, etc., but the course organizer developed a strict programme involving a number of people with specific skills to offer. In the first morning there was discussion of types of trails, education potential of trails, route selection, the trail document and the environmental elements which might be included. A local geography teacher who had made considerable use of trails outlined his programme, and the education officer of the Central Library Local History section outlined the facilities which his department had available. Most teachers then paired off and, in the afternoon, made a preliminary walk on their selected trail. The following day was devoted entirely to field and library research in the chosen area and on the final morning participants drafted sketch maps and outline details of their trails. The final afternoon was devoted to reports on the routes and strategies chosen. Overall it was clear that the brief encounter had allowed teachers to exchange ideas on trail-making and fieldwork, but more important, it had allowed each of them to reveal intimate knowledge of local areas. Of the fourteen trails outlined few generalizations can be made—most involved a part information/part questionnaire format, a map and a route averaging two miles. There is no better way for me to illustrate the potential of trails than to outline briefly the trails developed by these teachers, who offered them with such introductions as:

"I want to involve the children completely, using all their senses."

"The last few days have been a eye-opener for me, I had no idea what went on behind those factory walls. . . . I was handed brochures and found that the furniture they made was used in our school."

". . . and when we get back to school a mass of things we can follow up with; the trail can be walked several times."

". . . this is a 'get to look at the area' trail; I can't say 'get to know' it as they already live in it, but get to *look* at it."

". . . the idea of the thing is to get them to look at things which they know already . . . and to bring other things to class . . . it's an opening up point."

I want to close, therefore, by offering very brief notes on the fourteen trails developed, emphasizing the approach taken and the elements discussed. This in the hope that some of these ideas will strike a responsive note in your local area:

a) Largely industrial trail around school area with emphasis on all the senses; points to smell, see and feel. Perhaps into what goes on behind factory walls.

b) Section of Birmingham city center with an emphasis on change from canal basins and wharves to civic buildings and entertainment. Involves conservation area and canal-side features.

c) Historical trail through suburban shopping center, once a village street, illustrating evidence of village past and modern land use. Uses gravestone evidence, taped discussion with elderly resident and upper floor of a factory for aerial view.

d) Outline route through inner city and suburban area to link sites for intensive study of housing and of natural environment (canal feeder reservoir).

e) Suburban Housing trail for ROSLA students. Trail mapped but commentary on tape, focusing on public housing types by period, inviting comment on design, effect on residents and land use.

f) Inner Urban Area trail for junior school. Almost entirely question format through small, redeveloping area, supplemented by historical maps.

g) Infants' School in Inner Urban Area. An inspired trail covering a very small area. Children have simple map excerpt round wrist and paper direction arrow on finger. Two main themes, one a search for local worthy whose statue is near end of trail, the other a search for lines (lines for traffic control, building lines, etc.).

h) "Village" area and suburban Edwardian housing trail involving two successive walks round mile long route. The first walk emphasizes evidence as to history (including access through pet shop to original smithy furnace, local epidemic tombstones, etc.). Second walk done with two historical maps to allow charting of local change.

i) Suburban area viewed against physiographic theme. Trail follows a ridge from which flow streams into a river valley which forms the return loop of the trail. Emphasis of landform, evidence of agriculture and milling plus expansion of public and private housing. Sophisticated trail for high ability students.

j) Tree trail in suburban area. Intended for secondary school children, largely immigrant, requiring remedial English. Remedial work through trail and botanical preparation: fieldwork involves suburban tree identification and condition reporting.

k) Development of Sutton Coldfield trail, emphasizing historical change and present condition. Includes reference to energy use by commercial buildings—heat and lighting waste.

l) Road Safety Trail on major city road, trail prepared by Road Safety Officer involving very small section of major road. Discussed how traffic patterns evolve, effect of traffic on pedestrians and how safety measures are used. Historical material on changes in traffic management and ordered observation of traffic and pedestrian response. Intended for use by a number of city schools.

m) Suburban trail linking points for intensive study, including housing, recreation land and shopping behavior.

n) Riverside trail between two bridges. One side of the river trail emphasizing natural environment and river development, the other involving land use (waste tip, drains, disused sewage works).

These brief notes hardly do justice to the work done in 48 hours but what emerges quite clearly is the very wide range of possibilities which personal interests, school location, age range and class ability and the teachers' skills lead to. In fact, the range of trails outlined here is wider than that achieved by the over 200 "published" trails. The plan in Birmingham is to complete these trails and to reproduce them for local use. A stencil-bank will be maintained and in the next few months teachers involved will meet again for a day's evaluation of three or four of the completed trails.[9]

Although my rather intensive association with trails and trail-making had led to a degree of scepticism with regard to the attractive, yet rather hollow, parades past historical gems, the trail format as used by these teachers illustrates the potential of this low-cost educational technique which relies for success on the infinite variety available in the immediate built and natural environments, and on the special subject called "local knowledge" in which nearly every child is able to shine.

Notes

1. Brian Goodey, *Urban Walks and Town Trails: Origins, Principles and Sources,* Research Memo 40, Centre for Urban and Regional Studies, University of Birmingham. This is available from the Publications Officer, CURS, Selly Wick House, Selly Wick Road, Birmingham 29, price £1.50. In addition there is *Learning from Trails,* Schools Council Project Environment Series, Longmans, 1975, £1.90 but this has very little reference to the urban trails discussed in the present paper.

2. The list of trails is now available from Publications Department, British Tourist Authority, 64 St. James Street, London SW1. Price 30p.

3. See K. Wheeler and B. Waites, Leicester Town Trail in *Bulletin of Environmental Education* (Special edition), Nos. 16/17, Aug.–Sept. 1972, and S. Brown and A. French: Newcastle Quayside Trail in *Bulletin of Environmental Education,* No. 33, January 1974.

4. . . . *Freedom Trail . . . Boston,* Freedom Trail Foundation, Inc. A number of new trails were prepared by the Office of the Boston Bicentennial for use in 1975–6. The *Vienna Walk* was established in 1956.

5. Faversham Society, *A Walk around the Town and Port of Faversham, Kent.* Faversham Society with Swale District Council, 4th edition, 1974.

6. M. Carpenter, *An Architectural Trail in Dudley* (Handbook and Workbook volume), Urban History Project, Dudley, Dudley Teachers' Centre, 1972.

7. As examples, a trail developed and "published" by primary school students is available for Bristol (from The Head, St. Nicholas' Junior School, Lawford's Gate, Bristol 5). For a secondary school trail see the Beverley Town Trail, currently in production by the Environmental Society, Beverley High School, Beverley, Humberside. Students of the Department of Landscape Architecture, Glos. College of Art and Design, Pittville, Cheltenham produced an urban trail with student and teacher booklets in 1973.

8. *Brum Trails 1* is published by the Birmingham Urban Studies Centres Committee and is available, price 38p (post free) from The Adviser for Environmental Studies, Education Department, Margaret Street, Birmingham 3.

9. Details of the course and of the eventual availability of the various Birmingham trails thus produced are available from the address given in note 8.

23

European Charter of the Architectural Heritage

Adopted by the Committee of Ministers of the Council of Europe on September 26, 1975

The Committee of Ministers,

Considering that the aim of the Council of Europe is to achieve a greater unity between its members for the purpose of safeguarding and realizing the ideals and principles which are their common heritage;

Considering that the member states of the Council of Europe which have adhered to the European Cultural Convention on 19 December 1954 committed themselves, under Article 1 of that convention, to take appropriate measures to safeguard and to encourage the development of their national contributions to the common cultural heritage of Europe;

Recognizing that the architectural heritage, an irreplaceable expression of the wealth and diversity of European culture, is shared by all peoples and that all the European States must show real solidarity in preserving that heritage;

Considering that the future of the architectural heritage depends largely upon its integration into the context of people's lives and upon the weight given to it in regional and town planning and development schemes;

Having regard to the Recommendation of the European Conference of Ministers responsible for the preservation and rehabilitation of the cultural heritage of monuments and sites held in Brussels in 1969, and to Recommendation 589 (1970) of the Consultative Assembly of the Council of Europe, calling for a charter relating to the architectural heritage;

Asserts its determination to promote a common European policy and concerted action to protect the architectural heritage, based on the principles of integrated conservation;

Recommends that the governments of member states should take the necessary legislative, administrative, financial and educational steps to implement a policy of integrated conservation for the architectural heritage, and to arouse public interest in such a policy, taking into account the results of the European Architectural Heritage Year campaign organized in 1975 under the auspices of the Council of Europe;

Adopt and proclaim the principles of the following charter, drawn up by the Council of Europe Committee on Monuments and Sites:

1. The European architectural heritage consists not only of our most important monuments: it also includes the groups of lesser buildings in our old towns and characteristic villages in their natural or man-made settings.

For many years, only major monuments were protected and restored and then without reference to their surroundings. More recently it was realized that, if the surroundings are impaired, even those monuments can lose much of their character.

Today, it is recognized that entire groups of buildings, even if they do not include any example of outstanding merit, may have an atmosphere that gives them the quality of works of art, welding different periods and styles into a harmonious whole. Such groups should also be preserved.

The architectural heritage is an expression of history and helps us to understand the relevance of the past to contemporary life.

2. The past as embodied in the architectural heritage provides the sort of environment indispensable for a balanced and complete life.

In the face of a rapidly changing civilization, in which brilliant successes are accompanied by grave perils, people today have an instinctive feeling for the value of this heritage.

This heritage should be passed on to future generations in its authentic state and in all its variety as an essential part of the memory of the human race. Otherwise, part of man's awareness of his own continuity will be destroyed.

3. The architectural heritage is a capital of irreplaceable spiritual, cultural, social and economic value.

Each generation places a different interpretation on the past and derives new inspiration from it. This capital has

been built up over the centuries: the destruction of any part of it leaves us poorer, since nothing new that we create, however fine, will make good the loss.

Our society now has to husband its resources. Far from being a luxury, this heritage is an economic asset which can be used to save community resources.

4. The structure of historic centres and sites is conducive to a harmonious social balance

By offering the right conditions for the development of a wide range of activities, our old towns and villages favored social integration. They can once again lend themselves to a social mix.

5. The architectural heritage has an important part to play in education.

The architectural heritage provides a wealth of material for explaining and comparing forms and styles and their applications. Today when visual appreciation and first hand experience play a decisive role in education, it is essential to keep alive the evidence of different periods and their achievements.

The survival of this evidence will be assured only if the need to protect it is understood by the greatest number, particularly by the younger generation who will be its future guardians.

6. This heritage is in danger.

It is threatened by ignorance, obsolescence, deterioration of every kind and neglect. Urban planning can be destructive when authorities yield too readily to economic pressures and to the demands of motor traffic. Misapplied contemporary technology and ill-considered restoration may be disastrous to old structures. Above all, land and property speculation feeds upon all errors and omissions and brings to nought the most carefully laid plans.

7. Integrated conservation averts these dangers.

Integrated conservation is achieved by the application of sensitive restoration techniques and the correct choice of appropriate functions. In the course of history the hearts of towns and sometimes villages have been left to deteriorate and have turned into areas of substandard housing. Their restoration must be undertaken in a spirit of social justice and should not cause the departure of the poorer inhabitants. Because of this, conservation must be one of the first considerations in all urban and regional planning.

It should be noted that integrated conservation does not rule out the introduction of modern architecture into areas containing old buildings provided that the existing context, proportions, forms, sizes and scale are fully respected and traditional materials are used.

8. Integrated conservation depends on legal, administrative, financial and technical support.

Legal

Integrated conservation should make full use of all existing laws and regulations that can contribute to the protection and preservation of the architectural heritage. Where such laws and regulations are insufficient for the purpose they should be supplemented by appropriate legal instruments at national, regional and local levels.

Administrative

In order to carry out a policy of integrated conservation, properly staffed administrative services should be established.

Financial

Where necessary the maintenance and restoration of the architectural heritage and individual parts thereof should be encouraged by suitable forms of financial aid and incentives, including tax measures.

It is essential that the financial resources made available by public authorities for the restoration of historic centers should be at least equal to those allocated for new construction.

Technical

There are today too few architects, technicians of all kinds, specialized firms and skilled craftsmen to respond to all the needs of restoration.

It is necessary to develop training facilities and increase prospects of employment for the relevant managerial, technical and manual skills. The buildings industry should be urged to adapt itself to these needs. Traditional crafts should be fostered rather than allowed to die out.

9. Integrated conservation cannot succeed without the co-operation of all.

Although the architectural heritage belongs to everyone, each of its parts is nevertheless at the mercy of any individual.

The public should be properly informed because citizens are entitled to participate in decisions affecting their environment.

Each generation has only a life interest in this heritage and is responsible for passing it on to future generations.

10. The European architectural heritage is the common property of our continent.

Conservation problems are not peculiar to any one country. They are common to the whole of Europe and should be dealt with in a co-ordinated manner. It lies with the Council of Europe to ensure that member states pursue coherent policies in a spirit of solidarity.

Contributors

Paolo Ceccarelli, born in 1934, is Professor of Urban Planning at the School of Architecture, University of Milan. In 1963–1965 he was associated with the Joint Center for Urban Studies of Harvard and M.I.T. as a Harkness Fellow. Since then he has taught and done research work in several European and African countries. His major areas of interest include political aspects of planning, urban social-movements, and current trends of change and reorganization in local government. Under a Wolfson Fellowship he is presently carrying on a comparative study of the urban fiscal crisis in Great Britain and Italy.

J. P. Barendsen is Head of the Department of Public Works and City Development, Utrecht. He has a background in public administration and constitutional law and is a lecturer in the Institute of Public Administration, Utrecht.

Adam Fergusson is a freelance journalist who has been writing on environmental, economic, and political subjects in Britain for more than twenty years. His first articles exposing the fate of Bath appeared in *The Times* (London) in 1970. Born in Scotland in 1932, he now lives in London. He read history at Cambridge University and is the author of two novels (*Roman Go Home*, 1969; *The Lost Embassy*, 1972) and one economic study of the Weimar inflation (*When Money Dies*, 1975).

Turgut Cansever is an architect and art historian who is Director of the Greater Istanbul Master Plan Office.

Nicole Brasseur, formerly a social worker in the North Quarter of Brussels, has become an administrator in the Agglomeration Council, which brings together the nineteen municipalities of Brussels.

Francis Strauven, born in 1942, is an architect and architectural historian. He has carried out research into the history of modern architecture in Belgium; and organized the exhibitions "La Construction en Belgique, 1945–70," and "Victor Horta." He is also administrator of Les Archives de l'Architecture Moderne, and a member of the Editorial Board of the Dutch Review *Wonen-TA/BK*, and teaches theory and history of architecture at Hasselt and at the Technical University of Eindhoven. He has written articles on Brussels Art Nouveau, the Arts and Crafts Movement, De Koninck, and Kroll.

René Schoonbrodt, born in Limbourg, Belgium, in 1935 is lecturer in Sociology at the Architecture School of La Cambre in Brussels and Director of the Department of Housing and Regional Planning at the Walloon Regional Development Society in Namur. Member of many Official Consulting Committees, he is the Chairman of the Atelier de Recherche at d'Action Urbaine (ARAU) and the Chairman of Inter-Environment Brussels, which groups the different local working committees in Brussels. He has worked twelve years as consultant in a trade union in Belgium.

François d'Arcy has been Professor of Political Science at the University of Grenoble (France) since 1970. He is Director of the Centre de Recherche sur l'Administration Economique et l'Aménagement du Territoire (CERAT) and author of *Structures Administratives et Urbanization*, Paris, Berger-Levrault, 1968. He has directed several collective research projects on urban policy funded by French governmental agencies and has taught at Yale University, at the University of Montreal, and at the Universite de Québec à Montréal.

Lisa Ronchi, architect and planner, was born in Venice, and practices in Rome. She has designed houses, schools, hotels, resort areas, and low-cost housing developments. For many years she headed the editorial staff of the magazine *L'Architettura* and has been coordinator, with Bruno Zevi, of the Seminars for American Architects on the Fulbright-Hays Fellowships Program.

Jonathan Raban has been a professional writer since 1969 and is a Fellow of the Royal Society of Literature. Previously he was a lecturer in English Literature at University College of Wales Aberystwyth and at University of East Anglia, Norwich, and was a Visiting Lecturer at Smith College in Massachusetts in 1972. He is the author of several books of literary criticism (including *The Society of the Poem*, 1971), of *Soft City* (1974), and of several plays for

radio, television, and stage. He has been a reviewer and journalist for several periodicals including the *Sunday Times* (London), *New Statesman*, and *Encounter* and is currently working on a book provisionally titled *The Arabian Looking Glass*, on (particularly urban) life in modern Arab countries.

Dionysis A. Zivas is Professor of Architectural Design at the National Technical University in Athens, Greece. He has carried out research studies on Greek vernacular architecture, the relations between present-day life and the monuments of the past, and the disappearance or abandonment of historic Greek settlements and centers. He has designed several modern buildings (hotels, factories, and others) and has won awards in seven architectural competitions. He is also a consultant in regional planning and development studies. His publications include *The Architecture of Zante, Zante Architectural Miscellanies*, "The Private House in the Ionian Islands," and *Educational Facilities and the Community*, a report for UNESCO. He is director of the work team that is developing proposals for Plaka under the auspices of the Ministry of Public Works.

Tomislav Marasovic is scientific consultant at the Town Planning Institute of Dalmatia; Assistant Professor at the Architectural Faculty in Zagreb; Lecturer at the Specialized School for the Protection of Monuments in Rome; Codirector of post-graduate studies on the protection of the historic heritage at the University of Split; Editor-in-Chief of *Urbs*; and member of the National Committee of ICOMOS for Yugoslavia. He has published a number of studies and articles on the history of architecture, mostly on Diocletian's Palace and pre-Romanesque architecture, and on the protection of monuments.

Francesco Bandarin was born in Venice in 1950. He works as a consultant for the Metropolitan Plan for Venice and is research associate at the University of Venice. He received his Laurea in Architecture at the Istituto Universitario di Architettura di Venezia and his master's in City and Regional Planning at the University of California, Berkeley. He is author of several articles on the issues of historic renovation and planning reform in Italy.

Ove Nissen, born in 1943, is a lawyer and Head of the International Affairs Section of the National Academy for the Protection of Nature, Monuments and Sites of the Danish Ministry of the Environment. He was Secretary to the Danish National Committee for European Architectural Year (1975) and Chairman of the Preparatory Committee for the European Architectural Heritage Exhibition, *A Future for Our Past* (Amsterdam, 1975). He is member of the Committee for Regional Planning and the Architectural Heritage of the Council of Europe.

Bent Rud, born in 1919, is an architect and Chief Antiquarian of the National Agency for the Protection of Nature, Monuments and Sites of the Danish Ministry of the Environment. He is Secretary to the Historic Buildings Council of Denmark and a member of the Committee for Regional Planning and the Architectural Heritage of the Council of Europe and of the Danish ICOMOS National Committee.

Nils Mortensen and **Ole Staer Anderson** are Danish sociologists who carried out the home surveys in Elsinore.

Hans F. D. Davidson is an architect-planner, Head of the Central District City Planning Section, in the Department of Public Works of the Municipality of Amsterdam.

Thomas Miller has an MS in urban planning from Columbia University and is a researcher in the Department of Urban and Regional Planning at the Royal Institute of Technology, Stockholm. He has published numerous articles and research reports on public participation in planning, including *Citizen Participation in Planning; Evaluation of the Traffic Consultations in Stockholm, 1973–74*, Stockholm, 1977 (Swedish), and *Can Ordinary People Influence Planning? Evaluation of Planning Consultations in Hedemora*, Stockholm, 1978 (Swedish).

Boel Ahlgren is an architect in the Department of Housing, Stockholm, and member of the Stockholm Municipal Council (councillor).

David L. Smith, MA, MCP, graduated from Oxford in 1963 and Liverpool in 1965. After working at the Greater London Council, he spent several years at the Civic Trust, where he became a specialist in urban conservation. In 1970, he joined the Centre for Environmental Studies in London, where he wrote *Amenity and Urban Planning*. He later joined the Urban Deprivation Unit at the British Home Office.

Graeme Shankland, educated at Cambridge University and the Architectural Association, is senior partner in the Shankland Cox Partnership, an interprofessional group of planners, architects, land economists, and transportation consultants, which is one of Britain's leading planning firms. He was Senior Architect Planner for Hook New Town and has been planning consultant to Liverpool, Bolton, and several British counties, to the Port of London Authority, the Roskill Commission, and the Welsh Office. His overseas work has included commissions for the Overseas Development Administration (Kingston Waterfront Renewal, Jamaica), the French Government, the Yugoslav Government (South Adriatic Tourism and Conservation Plan), and the United Nations (conservation studies). He has also been the author of numerous articles on planning in Britain.

Peter Willmott, a sociologist, is director of the Centre for Environmental Studies and has been coauthor with Michael Young of *Family and Kinship in East London, Family and Class in a London Suburb*, and *The Symmetrical Family*. He is also the author of *The Evolution of a Community* and *Adolescent Boys in East London*. He is a part-time Professor at the School of Environmental Studies, University College, London, and has been Visiting Professor at the University of Parks.

David Jordan, born in 1942, is a sociologist/planner with experience in Britain and Africa and was project director of the Lambeth Inner Area Study.

Charles McKean has been Administrator with the Royal Institute of British Architects, London, for almost ten years, and has done different jobs within the Institute, including Secretary of the London Environment Group and Secretary of the Eastern Region of the RIBA. His previous publications include *Battle of Styles, Guide to Modern Buildings in London, 1965–75, Living Over the Shop,* and *Funding the Future.*

He was a member of the winning team in the River Clyde Ideas Competition. He has done some part-time lecturing and is preparing further architectural guides. He is Secretary of the RIBA's Community Architecture Working Group.

Brian Goodey is Senior Lecturer in the Joint Centre for Urban Design and in the Department of Town Planning, Oxford Polytechnic. He trained in geography at Nottingham University and Indiana University and taught and directed research at the University of North Dakota, and Birmingham (U.K.). He has a continuing interest in environmental perception and interpretation. His publications include *Perception of the Environment* (1970), *Images of Place* (1974), and *Interpreting the Conserved Environment* (1977).

Index

Page references in italics refer to illustrations.